Imperialism and Revolution in South Asia

Imperialism and Revolution in South Asia

Edited by Kathleen Gough
and Hari P. Sharma

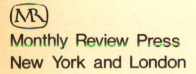

Monthly Review Press
New York and London

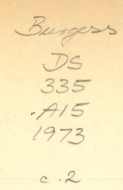

Library of Congress Cataloging in Publication Data
Aberle, Kathleen Gough, 1925–   comp.
    Imperialism and revolution in South Asia.
    Includes bibliographical references.
    Contents: Historical background and the impact of imperialism and capi-
talism: Gough, K. Imperialism and revolutionary potential in South Asia.
Bagchi, A. K. Foreign capital and economic development in India: a schematic view. [etc.]
    1. South Asia—Politics and government. 2. South Asia—Economic condi-
tions. I. Sharma, Hari P., joint comp. II. Title.
DS335.A15 1973   320.9′54′05   72-92029   ISBN 0-85345-273-3

First Printing

Manufactured in the United States of America

Contents

Preface   vii

Part I
Historical Background and the Impact
of Imperialism and Capitalism

1. Imperialism and Revolutionary Potential in South Asia
   by Kathleen Gough   3

2. Foreign Capital and Economic Development
   in India: A Schematic View
   by Amiya Kumar Bagchi   43

3. The Green Revolution in India: Prelude to a Red One?
   by Hari P. Sharma   77

4. Some Trends in India's Economic Development
   by Paresh Chattopadhyay   103

5. Neocolonial Alliances and the Crisis of Pakistan
   by Hassan N. Gardezi   130

6. The State in Postcolonial Societies:
   Pakistan and Bangladesh
   by Hamza Alavi   145

7. Structure and Contradiction in Pakistan
   by Feroz Ahmed   174

Part II
The Roots of Struggle in the Villages

1. Peasant Classes in Pakistan
   by Saghir Ahmad   203

v

2. Harijans in Thanjavur
by Kathleen Gough   222

3. Thanjavur: Rumblings of Class Struggle in Tamil Nadu
by Mythily Shivaraman   246

Part III
The Rise of Revolutionary Movements

1. The Songs and Revolution of Bharathi
by David Ludden   267

2. Peasants and Revolution
by Hamza Alavi   291

3. The Communist Movement in India
by Mohan Ram   338

4. The Red Sun Is Rising:
Revolutionary Struggle in India
by Inquilab Zindabad   359

5. Revolutionary Movements in Ceylon
by Jayasumana Obeysekara   368

Part IV
Bangladesh and the South Asian Crisis

1. The Social Background of Bangladesh
by Ramkrishna Mukherjee   399

2. The Structural Matrix of the Struggle in Bangladesh
by Feroz Ahmed   419

3. Explosion in South Asia
by Tariq Ali   449

Notes on the Contributors   467

Preface

American social science research on South Asia is remarkably lacking in studies dealing with the dynamics of imperialism as well as with the revolutionary movements that have arisen to destroy this system. This book is a modest attempt toward meeting that lack. It is intended for general readers in Western countries and for students in the early stages of South Asian studies.

The book was planned and the essays solicited by Saghir Ahmad, Kathleen Gough, and Hari Sharma in response to a request by the editors of the *Bulletin of Concerned Asian Scholars* for a collection of South Asian studies. We are especially grateful to Jim Peck, Mark Selden, and Perry Link of the Committee of Concerned Asian Scholars and to Susan Lowes of Monthly Review Press for their advice and generous editorial help. We also warmly thank the contributors to the volume, who corresponded with us over long distances and periods of time. Many of the authors rewrote their essays in light of the momentous events of 1971, while themselves under heavy pressure of scholarly or revolutionary work.

The contributors to this volume come from diverse fields and political tendencies. They include academic researchers, journalists, and revolutionary partisans. Among them are representatives or supporters of several different Marxist parties, in addition to writers unaffiliated with any organized political group. Therefore the essays contain different theories and conclusions on such important questions as the nature of the state and of the class relations in South Asian countries, as well as the character of these countries' relations with the advanced capitalist powers, with the Soviet bloc, and with China. Such differences of theory are linked with differences over strategy and tactics for revolution. The authors are, however, united both in approaching social problems from within the Marxist tradition and in their commitment to revolutionary social change. We thought it desirable to include a variety of viewpoints because the revolutionary movements of South Asia are themselves at present diverse and fragmented, and also because we believe that the success of the South Asian revolution will require unity in struggle on the part of most of those now to be found in the various revolutionary groups as well as on the part of vast millions of their fellow countrymen.

The first part of the volume concentrates on historical background and on the processes of imperialism and capitalism and their impact on South Asian societies before and after the attainment of political independence in the late 1940s. The second part concerns the daily lives and changing class relations of villagers in two South Asian regions—West Punjab in Pakistan and Tamil Nadu in India—and their potential for revolutionary struggle. The third section deals with the genesis, strategy, and tactics of revolutionary movements in India and Ceylon. Finally, the essays in the fourth section focus on the massive repression and subsequent resistance struggle in East Bengal in 1971, the structural matrix of these events, and the implications of the Indo-Pakistan war and the creation of Bangladesh for South Asia's revolutionary future.

Our beloved comrade and colleague, Saghir Ahmad, died accidentally in July 1971 while this book was in progress. We dedicate it to the cause that united us.

Kathleen Gough
Hari P. Sharma

Part I

Historical Background and the Impact of Imperialism and Capitalism

1. Imperialism and Revolutionary Potential in South Asia

Kathleen Gough

When India, Pakistan, and Ceylon gained home rule more than two decades ago, their leaders set forth certain goals for their futures. These included control of their own political and economic destinies, increased productivity and improvements in livelihood, education, and health, mixed private and state-planned economies, some cooperative institutions of production and distribution, and movement toward socioeconomic equality. Land reform and industrial development were central to these goals. All three nations were to be Western-style party democracies with progressively broadening franchise in elections at national, provincial, and local levels.

By the late 1960s it was clear that these programs had failed or were failing. The three South Asian nations had more, not less, foreign investment and foreign control of their economies than in the 1940s. All were heavily indebted to the United States, the Soviet Union, and various Eastern and Western European powers. Some development had occurred in both agriculture and industry. Despite rapidly growing populations, there had been modest increases in gross national products and per capita incomes. The social character of wealth and its maldistribution were, however, such that a number of observers had concluded that the living conditions of a substantial proportion of the people had deteriorated since independence. In spite of land reforms and trade union struggles, incomes were more unequal and both urban and rural classes more polarized than in the 1940s. In most regions there were higher proportions of landless laborers, casual workers, and unemployed than ever before. It was estimated that, in 1961, 38 percent of India's rural population and 54 percent of its urban population received fewer than the daily 2,250

Earlier versions of this article appeared in the *Bulletin of Concerned Asian Scholars*, Winter 1972, pp. 77–97, and in *Monthly Review*, March 1972, pp. 25–45.

food calories per capita that nutritionists regard as essential for continuing health under Indian conditions. The picture was unchanged in 1967–1968 except for an increased gap between the richest and the poorest in spending for consumption.[1] The per capita calorie intake was even lower in Pakistan and (despite a much higher per capita income) only slightly better in Ceylon.[2] At least five million Indian children died each year from lack of food.[3]

Effects of Imperialism

The root causes of these failures have been explained in a number of recent analyses of imperialism and of the economies of Third World countries,[4] although there are of course important variations among the South Asian nations.

After they gained political independence in the late 1940s, India, Pakistan, and Ceylon tried to pursue paths of capitalist development, despite the emergence of a state sector in their economies and despite governmental rhetoric about "socialistic patterns." They did so with economies that were severely distorted and impoverished by over a century and a half of colonialism and in which there were already large enclaves of foreign ownership.[5] The choice of the capitalist path, and the fact that the governments were themselves drawn from the various indigenous classes of property owners, precluded effective planning of national resources for the welfare of the majority.

In all three countries the capitalist classes proved unable to solve their economic problems in the postwar period of monopoly capitalism and technological, financial, and trade dominance by the industrial nations. Because of increasingly disadvantageous terms of trade, foreign exchange crises occurred and forced the South Asian governments to rely on loans from the industrial nations.[6] The acceptance of "aid" in turn led to increased foreign ownership, especially of newly developing industries. The United States has led overwhelmingly in the penetration of India's and Pakistan's economies through government loans in the past two decades, although British private investment is still greater, in toto, than is American; other nations— especially the U.S.S.R., West Germany, Japan, France, Italy, and Canada—are subsidiary creditors.[7] In Ceylon, British and other sterling area firms continue to own the most private property, but West

Germany has contributed the largest loans, with the United Kingdom, the United States, and Japan as close competitors.[8] India and Pakistan came to rely heavily on foreign aid during the 1950s, especially after a foreign exchange crisis in 1957 and 1958; this also brought a change toward greater foreign investment in industry. In those same two years Ceylon also experienced a deterioration in its balance of payments, and in 1961 became heavily dependent on foreign aid. The country has had a series of foreign exchange crises since 1966 as a result of drastic falls in the export prices of tea and rubber, coupled with increases in the prices of imported rice, machinery, and machine-made goods.[9]

The harmful effects of foreign aid and investment are illustrated by Ahmed and Chattopadhyay in this book.[10] Both cause a growing proportion of the receiving country's surplus wealth to be siphoned off to the donor countries as private profits or as interest. As this process continues, more and more of the dependent country's foreign exchange earnings are used to service the foreign debt rather than to import needed capital equipment or consumer goods.[11] When the dependent country approaches bankruptcy, it has to rely on short-term emergency loans rather than on long-term development loans. Emergency loans, as from the International Monetary Fund, require, however, that the dependent country undergo austerity measures that involve severe cutbacks in welfare programs. Because of its foreign exchange crisis, for example, the supposedly left-leaning government of Ceylon, newly elected in 1970, had to resort to emergency borrowing from the International Monetary Fund and was therefore prevented from carrying through even modest programs for welfare and new employment. This formed the background for the growth of mass unrest in 1971.[12] The Ceylon government's resort to sudden, external military spending to put down revolt increased its indebtedness, so that most of its programs for hospitals, education, and cheap transport were aborted.[13] Even apart from such emergency situations, the withholding of aid has several times been used to force the South Asian governments into economic and political policies they would not otherwise espouse.[14]

Foreign aid and foreign investment produce a distorted structure of production which is harmful to the receiving nation. Although industrial development occurs, it is restricted and its content is influenced by the capital owners' need for profit in both donor and recipient countries. Since it is tied by foreign aid, the receiving country has to buy capital equipment from the donor country that is often expensive and unsuited to its needs. Many factories are merely assembly plants; many cater to luxury wants rather than to social welfare. The acceptance of aid means that the dependent country pays high prices for foreign technical experts and knowledge while alarming numbers of its own educated citizens remain unemployed or abroad.[15] Counterpart funds deriving from the repayment of loans in the currency of the dependent country are used by the creditor nation to finance foreign enterprises, set up educational and research institutions, publish books, and disseminate propaganda, all of which support reactionary groups and policies and amount to cultural, political, and economic imperialism.[16]

Until the mid-1960s, the heavy importation of food grains through sales, loans, and grants by the United States and other governments to all three South Asian nations staved off the need for serious land reform and kept agricultural production and relations semistagnant. When food surpluses from North America declined in 1965, United States advisers recommended the new technology of the "green revolution," involving improved seeds, fertilizers, and tractors supplied by the industrial nations. Although unevenly distributed, these measures did increase output.[17] They have, however, as Sharma and others point out in this volume, increased landless labor and unemployment while widening the gaps among rural incomes, and therefore have stimulated agrarian unrest.[18]

Growing dependence on imperialism enhances the growth of monopoly among indigenous capitalists, whose largest corporations become increasingly linked with those of the advanced capitalist nations through collaborative agreements. The concentration of capital ownership is accompanied by increased income gaps between large and small property owners, between higher and lower grades of salaried workers, and between all of these and most manual laborers. It is also accompanied by an increase in urban unemployment. Class polarization, in the towns and in the countryside, shows up in statistical studies of changes in consumer expenditures. In their study of Indian poverty, Dandekar and Rath conclude that, between 1961–62 and 1967–68, per capita consumer expenditures among the bottom 5 percent of villagers declined slightly while those of the rest of the bottom 20 percent virtually stagnated. Among town dwellers, partly as a result of the migration of rural unemployed to the cities, consumer expenditures declined among the bottom 40 percent. By contrast, both in the towns and in the countryside, living conditions improved considerably among the top 30 percent of the people, with the increase in consumer expenditures being sharper the closer one came to the top of the income scale.[19]

Increasing amounts of military "aid" have had the most harmful effects on South Asia's people. India spends a third of its federal budget on military supplies. About one-third of Pakistan's foreign loans have been for military spending. Ceylon's military budget was modest until recently, but suddenly shot up in the spring of 1971 when the government imported large quantities of weapons.[20]

In South Asia as a whole, the emphasis on military aid has resulted from a number of factors: (1) The Soviet Union and the United States have competed for control of the region, with each selling military supplies to both India and Pakistan. (2) China, faced with confrontation by both the Soviet Union and the United States via India, has maintained a diplomatic alliance with, and supplied economic and military aid to, Pakistan. (3) Specific interstate rivalries and border wars have occurred between Pakistan and India and between India and China. These international conflicts have been used by the governments of both India and Pakistan to deflect popular anger away from hardship and repression in their own countries and toward external enemies, as in the recent war. (4) The U.S.A., the U.S.S.R., and lesser powers have aggressively competed for South Asian markets for their military products. (5) In 1971 the Pakistani and Ceylonese governments purchased large quantities of additional weapons to put down internal revolts.

In addition to impoverishing the people, military aid adversely affects the class structure and quality of life even when it is not used directly for massacres. Within the ruling elite, such aid increasingly makes the military the dominant partner vis-à-vis the bureaucracy and the bourgeoisie. As Feroz Ahmed points out (p. 421), Pakistan's industrial bourgeoisie was initially so small and politically so weak that it proved unable to organize political parties effectively. Backed by the United States, a dictatorship operating through the bureaucracy and the military came to power in 1958, with a resulting loss of democratic freedoms. In India and Ceylon political parties, led by rival groups among the landlords and the bourgeoisie, have persisted up to the present. In both countries, however, economic failures and social unrest have been met by increasing curtailment of democratic processes and growing resort to administrative fiat and, recently, to military terror. Overall, in all three countries foreign aid has fostered the growth of a reactionary neocolonial elite of capitalist junior partners, bureaucrats, and military men, who link the subordinate peoples of their own countries with the governments and corporations of the imperialist nations.

Soviet foreign aid, especially important in India, was at first expected by many to help build a strong public sector and to combat the effects of private foreign investment. In fact, however, as Ram indicates, Soviet aid has provided an infrastructure for the development of monopoly capitalism and has exacerbated the harmful effects of Western aid. Since 1965 the Soviet Union has exported very large quantities of weapons to India. More recently, it has begun to invest in privately owned Indian factories which use Soviet raw materials to manufacture goods with cheap Indian labor; the goods are re-exported to the Soviet Union or to Third World countries that are industrially less advanced than India. Like Western aid, Soviet aid seems generally to have been used to control certain Indian industries, to provide profits on the sale of capital goods to India, to use Indian labor cheaply, to make India a base for capturing its internal markets or those in other, less developed countries, and to enhance political control through combined economic and military loans.[21]

Imperialist interference enhances disparities in development among regional and ethnic groups as well as between economic classes. The disparity between West Pakistan and East Bengal is now the best documented, for recent events have highlighted the colonial status and nationalist aspirations of Bangladesh. There are, however, similar regional and ethnic disparities within West Pakistan, where Punjabi ruling and propertied groups dominate the economies of Sind, Baluchistan, and the North West Frontier Province.[22] In India, the past decade has seen the development of a similar industrial dominance in northern and western India, especially in Gujarat, Bombay, and Maharashtra, where the largest monopoly corporations developed historically. By contrast, West Bengal's engineering and textile industries, once highly developed, have stagnated. In general the eastern Indian states of West Bengal, Bihar, Orissa, and

Assam, like Kerala in the south, have come to resemble subcolonies which provide raw materials for export and for the industrially more favored Indian states.[23] Much of the industrial capital of West Bengal is also owned by groups in western India.

Regional and ethnic disparities in employment and wealth create competitive struggles among the educated classes in different linguistic areas, castes, and religions. Western social scientists usually concentrate their analyses on these forms of competition, seeing in them the perpetuation of "traditional" birth-status groups. Today's competition among the educated classes of regional and ethnic groups for jobs in the bureaucracy and the military, and for budgetary allocations, educational institutions, industrial licenses, and political power through the ballot box, is not, however, traditional; rather, it is a feature of state capitalism and of the unequal relations that have developed within each nation.

Beneath these ethnic struggles among bourgeois and petty-bourgeois classes, more significant class struggles on the part of vast numbers of propertyless people are latent or have already burst forth. The educated middle class leaders of bourgeois regional parties skate on thin ice in their efforts to escape internal colonial domination while at the same time holding their own propertyless classes in subjection. If, however, the highly educated classes of any given region are continuously barred from access to what they regard as their legitimate share of power and wealth, it is possible that they may join the poor in struggles for the socialist transformation of their own regions.

Revolutionary Weaknesses

Despite the sharpening of class struggle, India, Pakistan, and Ceylon lack strong and unified revolutionary socialist movements. Although they have recently waged heroic struggles, the revolutionary groups in India and Ceylon are still fragmented. In East Bengal in 1971, an invading army forced a national liberation struggle upon the people, but one for which its Marxist groups were unprepared in advance. Several reasons suggest themselves for the present weakness of the Left forces and for their failure to bring about a revolution in previous decades.

First, the Marxist parties in these countries emerged four to five decades ago under the influence of the Russian Revolution. Given the failure of their earlier militant efforts, the older leaders in these parties have lost the *élan* necessary to cope with a new revolutionary situation, and their theories and methods are outmoded. In the case of the pro-Moscow Communist parties, there have also been ideological changes since the mid-1950s, so that these parties now eschew revolutionary struggle.

Second, in spite of the long history of the Marxist parties, I suggest that objective conditions in the subcontinent were not conducive to large-scale revolutionary struggle until four or five years ago. It is true that South Asia has suffered the most abysmal poverty, marked periodically by devastating famines, ever since the British began to wreck and plunder its economy in the late eighteenth century. Since that time sporadic revolts by former rulers or by peasants, tribespeople, religious groups, or guerrilla movements have been quite common and the spirit of rebellion has never died. Significant Communist-led peasant revolutionary struggles did, moreover, take place shortly before and after independence, notably in East Bengal after the famine of World War II and in Telengana during the uncertainties of the change of power. There was also a revolt in the Indian navy, and Communist-led uprisings occurred in Madras, Kerala, and other states. These were, however, localized actions confined largely to particular tribal or low caste groups or to a narrow range of peasant classes.

In my view, the main reason why nationwide revolutionary struggle has not occurred in this century is that, unlike China or Southeast Asia, the Indian subcontinent was not subjected to competition between colonial powers or to invasion by a new colonial power before or during World War II. Its economic and political structures therefore remained more stable. Having consolidated their rule over the whole subcontinent in the latter part of the nineteenth century, the British were able, despite uprisings, to maintain strong political and military control. After World War II, when they could no longer sustain that control, they transferred political power to the indigenous bureaucratic and bourgeois classes without external interference. The partition of India and Pakistan did, of course, give rise to the deaths of up to a million people in Hindu-Muslim conflicts; but that slaughter, and the religio-national hysteria attending it, distracted attention and deflected energy from class struggle.

The transfer of power to native rulers in the late 1940s raised hopes of new democratic freedoms, civil liberties, economic development, and social welfare. To some extent these hopes were sustained through two decades of modest industrial and agricultural expansion and through the spread of capitalist relations, which gave rise to social mobility. In this connection it is noteworthy that even during the 1960s, when incomes polarized and the condition of those at the bottom of the class structure deteriorated, that of at least 60 percent of both the urban and rural populations of India improved slightly, although very unevenly with respect to class and income level. This may partly explain why, despite growing rebellion in certain regions and classes, the bulk of India's people still seem willing to stay on the parliamentary road.

Having failed to achieve revolutions in earlier decades, the Communist Party of India (CPI) and both the Communist Party and the Trotskyist Lanka Sama Samaja Party (LSSP) in Ceylon became involved in parliamentary politics soon after independence. Their leaders are now inured to electoral maneuvering, to the detriment of revolutionary work. Yet large numbers of peasants and workers still owe allegiance to these parties, which did conduct militant struggles in the 1930s and late 1940s and at various times have made small gains on behalf of their followers through trade union activities. Clinging to the parliamentary path, the leadership of these parties currently puts a brake on revolutionary organization.

The policies of the socialist states have by no means consistently fostered revolutionary development. During World War II the Soviet Union discouraged the Communist parties of South Asia from any course approaching revolution; since 1951 it has played the same role through Cold War and peaceful coexistence policies. For the past few years the Soviet Union has provided massive military aid to the anticommunist government of India and, to a lesser extent, to that of Pakistan; it also gave large-scale aid to the Ceylon government during the purge of revolutionaries in March–April 1971. In July 1971 the Soviet Union signed a treaty of friendship with the Indian government, and by its sponsorship of the Indian invasion of East Bengal in December 1971 helped Indian bourgeois power to expand in the subcontinent and to set up a military apparatus capable of crushing Marxist revolutionary movements both in eastern India and in Bangladesh. In this effort the Soviet Union and the Indian government received support from the leadership of the pro-Moscow Communist parties of India and East Pakistan (CPI and CPEP) and from the independent parliamentary Communist Party of India-Marxist (CPI-M).[24]

China's policy, although in theory favorable to revolution, seems fully explicable only in terms of China's perception of its own immediate national interests. For while China has called for revolutionary struggle in India, Burma, and Indonesia since 1967, it has discouraged such struggle in Pakistan since 1962 because of China's diplomatic alliance—first with Ayub Khan and later with Yahya Khan.[25] In the spring of 1971 the Chinese government approved and even materially aided the massacres of revolutionaries and common people in both Pakistan and Ceylon.[26] During the liberation war in East Bengal in March–November 1971, the Democratic Republic of Vietnam appeared, in fact, to be the only socialist nation to come out in open moral support of the indigenous freedom fighters of Bangladesh.[27]

Finally, there have no doubt been subjective errors on the part of the various South Asian revolutionary groups. Mohan Ram refers to some of them in his article in this volume and in his books.[28] In particular, two errors seem central: historically, an overreliance on the theories and policies of foreign parties, whether Soviet, British, Chinese, or others; and, in the past five years, the failure of the main Marxist parties to leave the parliamentary path and assume responsibility for channeling revolt among the youth and the poor.

Class Structure

A central problem in estimating revolutionary potential is the nature of the class structure. It is necessary to ask: What are the main classes? Which class dominates the state apparatus? What is the nature of the relations between classes? Which classes can be expected to support the revolution? Who are the main class enemies, internal and external?

These are complex questions to which no completely satisfactory answers seem available. First, it is noteworthy that in India the Communist movement has received strongest electoral support in states which have the poorest food supply and the highest proportions of landless laborers, and in which both these conditions have been exacerbated in the past twenty years: Kerala, Tamil Nadu, Andhra Pradesh, and West Bengal, where between 45 and 89 percent of the people are estimated to lack the food *calories* (let alone the food content) necessary for adequate subsistence and where between 34 and 37 percent of the agricultural population were landless or near-landless laborers in 1963–64. By contrast, the right-wing Jan Sangh and Swatantra parties are strongest in Rajasthan, Madhya Pradesh, Gujarat, Uttar Pradesh, and Punjab—states where much lower percentages (between 13 and 26) of the people are estimated to receive inadequate food calories and where the percentage of landless or near-landless laborers is as low as 12–23 percent of the agricultural work force.[29] It is not argued that absolute poverty or landlessness directly "cause" support for communism, but it is suggested that revolutionary ideology will be stronger and more widely accepted in states where the largest proportions of the people have suffered relative deprivation in food supply, living standards, and landholding over a period of years. Where smaller proportions have suffered deprivation, right-wing parties may gain support from people of middle rank who are afraid of losing their security or being attacked by the poor.

Again, it is not argued that revolutionary movements will necessarily *start* among the poorest peasants and landless laborers. In fact, at least some of India's armed revolutionary movements in recent decades have tended to *arise* in one of the types of circumstances specified by Eric Wolf as having high revolutionary potential, namely, that in which an ethnically distinct (in this case, tribal) peasant people, especially one living in a defensible mountain area, has been robbed of part of its land through entry into the market economy and the modern state, but retains a certain independence and tactical mobility on its own terrain.[30] This has been the case among the tribal people in the hill regions of Bengal, Telengana, and Kerala, where revolutionary upsurges took place in the 1940s and late 1960s, as well as in the case of the nationalist wars of the hill tribes of Assam. Other categories of people among whom armed revolt has more recently occurred are the educated but unemployed or underprivileged youth (Ceylon and India) and the slum populations of cities, especially Calcutta. Nevertheless, it is argued that once an armed revolutionary movement has gained strength, it has large potential support in areas with masses of poor peasants and landless laborers, and that regions experiencing an increase in the proportions of these classes are ones in which revolutionary ideologies are most apt to take hold.[31]

In spite of differences among them, all the present Communist parties or revolutionary Communist committees of South Asia, except the revolutionary Fourth International party (the Lanka Sama Samaja Party-Revolutionary, or LSSP-R) and the Janata Vimukthi Peramuna (JVP—People's Liberation Front) of Ceylon,[32] see the economies of their countries as divided into two sectors. One, the larger sector, is seen as still "feudal" or "semifeudal" by virtue of its mainly pre-industrial technology, low level of capital investment in agriculture, and dependent and exploitive relationships. The other and smaller, although growing, sector—the capitalist sector—involves modern industrial production, including mechanized farming, through wage workers. Alternatively, some Marxist writers regard all production through wage work, whether mechanized or paleotechnical, as capitalist, and all or most tenant farming as feudal or semifeudal.

It seems to me, however, that this Marxist "dual economy" thesis is scarcely more satisfactory than a bourgeois dual economy approach has proven to be. Rather, whether as tenants or wage workers, South Asian peasants and workers seem, in recent decades, to have been drawn almost universally into the world economy of capitalist imperialism and to have become involved in production and distribution relations that are, at the least, transitional to capitalism. Thus, although some "feudal" or precapitalist *features* may still survive in some production relations in a few areas, such as special levies on produce by landlords, debt labor, unpaid labor service, or the combining of landlords' economic powers with unofficial judicial powers, the economy cannot be divided into capitalist and precapitalist *sectors* of relationships, since all are interrelated and are involved in the world capitalist system.[33] The South Asian peasants and workers have, however, been drawn into the capitalist world specifically as objects of imperialism, that is, as super-exploited people who provide surplus product not only directly to landlords, moneylenders, merchants, industrialists, financiers, and other local figures, or to their own governments, but also indirectly to corporations and governments of the imperialist nations, in what André Gunder Frank has aptly called "the contribution of the poor to the welfare of the rich." The expansion of capitalist relations for the South Asian peasant and worker has meant not a substantial increase in prosperity, as has happened among the more fortunate farming and working classes of the industrial nations and as Indian Communist analysts seem to expect it to mean, but increasing polarization of class relations and incomes and greater immiserization for large numbers of peasants.

In my view, landlords, rich peasants, middle peasants, poor peasants, and landless laborers have existed in both precapitalist and capitalist South Asia, but their proportions and relations of production have undergone a series of complex changes in the colonial and neocolonial periods. Studies of these changes are needed for the different regions, of a kind carried out by Wertheim for Indonesia and by Wolf for Russia, China, Vietnam, Mexico, Algeria, and Cuba.[34] In general, precapitalist relations were characterized by a relatively self-sufficient village economy, hereditary tenancies of varying kinds and hereditary rights in land or its produce for the different classes of peasants, legal bondage in serfdom for poor peasants, and (where they existed) slavery for landless laborers. In these precapitalist relations, economic surplus was extracted from the producer by noneconomic (i.e., legal and political) means. Colonial and neocolonial (or "underdeveloped") capitalist relations have involved varying degrees of absorption into the commodity economy of world capitalism. Along with this has come loss of self-sufficiency of the village or other local region; the marketing of increasing amounts of agricultural produce; the disappearance of legally hereditary tenancies and of tenants' and laborers' hereditary rights in land or its produce; the private ownership of land (i.e., bourgeois property relations); acute competition for and intensive marketing of land, a kind of marketing of labor through contractual, competitive, and often short-term tenancies; and polarization of the class structure, involving a reduction in the proportion of middle peasants and an increase in those of poor peasants and of "free" but impoverished and insecurely employed landless laborers. As Shivaraman, Saghir Ahmad, and Sharma point out in this volume, both land reform and the introduction of modern techniques of agriculture have accelerated the growth of landless wage labor during the past two decades.

The difference between the "dual economy" and the "single, international economy" approaches has implications for the nature of the state and for revolutionary strategy. All the Communist groups of South Asia, except the JVP of Ceylon and the tiny Fourth International groups, postulate a "two-stage" revolution, although they differ over the precise character of the stages, over which classes will bring the two stages to completion, and, above all, over how the stages are to be realized. The first stage involves getting rid of imperialism and feudalism through one or another combination of workers, peasants, petty bourgeoisie, and nonmonopoly bourgeoisie. It culminates in the establishment of an independent economy and society led either jointly by the national bourgeoisie and the workers (the "national democracy" of the CPI) or dominated by the workers and peasants, with the national bourgeoisie as either stable or vacillating allies (the "people's democracy" of the CPI-M and the various Maoist groups). The second stage involves a socialist revolution in which, presumably, private ownership of the means of production will be abolished and the bourgeoisie as a class will cease to exist.

These analyses all seem imperfect, partly because there is no dual economy and partly because the separation into two revolutionary stages is unnecessary and mechanical. As Alavi has pointed out, under conditions of neocolonialism, the imperialists and the native landed classes are not allies against a nascent national industrial bourgeoisie, as they are, to some extent, in classical colonial societies.[35] The time for an independent capitalist, or even a "noncapitalist" (but nonsocialist), stage is past—that bus has been missed—since multinational corporations, chiefly (though not exclusively) emanating from the U.S.A., dominate the capitalist world's economy by virtue of their technological and financial superiority. In the post-independence period these corporations, and the imperial governments that represent them, have penetrated the economies of each South Asian country to such an extent that they are fast reducing its industrial, merchant, and financial bourgeoisie, its landlords, its bureaucracy, and its military to the status of segments of a single neocolonized bourgeoisie. In spite of the complex rivalries between these segments and between the various imperial powers to whom they appeal for support, and in spite of certain limited and relative autonomy in relation to each other and to the imperialists, their leading groups are forced to band together with the imperialist bourgeoisie against the revolutionary forces of peasants and workers of their own countries. The main enemies of the revolution in these countries are therefore the governments and bourgeoisies of the imperial nations, while the immediate enemies are all the large domestic property owners (merchant, landed, financial, or industrial). The more the domestic property owners' interests are threatened, the stronger become their ties to the military and civil bureaucracies, which are recruited mainly from their midst.

This does not mean that the revolutionary forces must necessarily "fight the whole lot at once." Although they have proved able to organize localized class struggles by tribal people, low caste people, poor peasants, landless laborers, and urban poor against their immediate oppressors, the South Asian revolutionary leaderships may not be able to mobilize the people en masse over large areas until the military has assumed political power in all three countries and until alien intervention has provided external enemies. Such "external enemies" may come initially from linguistic groups located around the metropolises within each nation and be deployed against outlying groups of different ethnic origin in the more exploited hinterlands, as happened with West Pakistan's invasion of East Bengal. The rapidity with which the major industrial powers rushed military aid to Ceylon in the recent crisis suggests, however, that "external enemies" will eventually be supplied from outside each nation by one or another of the superpowers or their satellites. (Already, indeed, the counterinsurgency operation in Ceylon has featured Russian technicians and Gurkha soldiers from India.) After such invasions, patriotic people from all sections of the indigenous propertied classes are likely to cross over to the side of the poor peasants, the landless laborers, the revolutionary youth, and the working class, as happened in China and Indochina.

Rebel and Revolutionary Movements

Despite the nonrevolutionary approaches of the established Marxist parties, spontaneous revolts and planned revolutionary movements did arise in the subcontinent during the late 1960s, against the background of increasing deprivation and class polarization. In 1968 a popular outburst of students, workers, and peasants swept both wings of Pakistan for five months and forced the resignation of President Ayub Khan. While no new organs of power representing the mass of propertyless people were forthcoming from this whirlwind, it did compel the promise of elections with universal franchise for the first time in the history of Pakistan. The far Left, under the populist umbrella of the pro-Peking faction of the National Awami Party, was weak in Pakistan because of its support for China's alliance with the Pakistani dictatorship. After the rebellion, however, three revolutionary groups emerged in favor of East Bengali armed struggle against the West Pakistani dictatorship and for an independent, socialist East Bengal: the Maoist East Bengal Communist Party (Allaudin-Matin group), active in the Rajshahi, Chittagong, Pabna, Jessore, and Kushtia districts; the truncated National Awami Party led by Maulana Bhashani (known as the Bhashani-NAP to distinguish it from the pro-Moscow or Wali-NAP); and the Maoist Coordinating Committee of Communist Revolutionaries centered in Dacca, the capital city. A third Maoist group, the East Pakistan Communist Party (Marxist-Leninist), or CPEP-ML, led by Muhammad Toaha and Abdul Huq, received recognition from China. This group, like its opposite number in India, favored armed struggle against landlords and bureaucrats but opposed any nationalist struggle that might divide Pakistan.

In India, armed revolutionary struggle became publicized in May 1967 with a peasant revolt in Naxalbari district of West Bengal. The revolt was led by local Communist cadres who subsequently broke away or were expelled from the Communist Party of India-Marxist (the CPI-M), which was then prominent in the state government of West Bengal. Although the Naxalbari effort was crushed within a few months, by mid-1969 groups of revolutionary Communists, dubbed Naxalites, were organized in at least eight of India's seventeen states. Armed struggle which predated the Naxalbari revolt was continuing in the hill district of Srikakulam in Andhra Pradesh, and sporadic guerrilla actions were occurring in other states. Some, although not all, of the Naxalite groups had combined in April 1969 to form the Communist Party of India (Marxist-Leninist), or CPI-ML. The party had an avowedly Maoist program and received approval from the government of China. Although it was difficult to judge the significance of the several Maoist tendencies from North America, it seemed likely that a revolutionary communism which would draw heavily on Chinese theory and experience had come to India to stay.

Even in those parts of India where there were no obvious symptoms of revolutionary class struggle, things had changed drastically.

The Congress Party, which had brought the country to political independence in 1947 and had governed it virtually single-handedly, lost heavily in the 1967 elections. Its majority in the Central Assembly was decreased and it lost control of eight of India's seventeen state governments. There was a general sense of growing political polarization accompanied by growing prominence of both far-right and far-left parties. The former, represented by the Hindu communalist Jan Sangh and the "free enterprise" Swatantra Party, led the governments in Orissa and Delhi. The latter, led numerically by the CPI-M and supported by the pro-Moscow Communist Party (CPI) and other groups, won in Kerala and Bengal. Since independence, the Communist movement had been strong among sections of the Indian workers and peasants in the heavily populated coastal regions of Bengal, Andhra Pradesh, Tamil Nadu, and Kerala—states with unusually high proportions of landless laborers and rural and urban unemployed. It was also strong in certain tribal hill regions of Bengal, Andhra Pradesh, and Kerala.

The political party picture as represented in election results did not, moreover, fully reflect the growth of class struggle in India. One sign of this growth was the fact that whereas, in the early 1960s, village elections had tended to be fought between factions led by opposed groups of landlords, by the middle-to-late 1960s in many parts of the country they were being fought under a variety of party banners, essentially between landed and land-poor classes.[36]

Both of the Communist parliamentary parties (CPI and CPI-M) condemned the "adventurism" of the Naxalites and were instrumental in their repression in West Bengal. By 1970, however, both parties were being pushed by the impatience of the landless and the working classes into leading strikes, land seizures, and other militant actions. In many parts of India one read constantly of *gheraos*— the spontaneous encirclement by workers or peasants of people in authority (cabinet ministers, landlords, and plantation or factory managers)—to compel them to fulfill some immediate demand.

In Ceylon the main revolutionary group was the Janata Vimukthi Peramuna (People's Liberation Front). Organized clandestinely in 1966, the JVP leans toward a Maoist interpretation of Asian society in its belief that the peasants form the main revolutionary force under the leadership of the urban workers. It regards the society of Ceylon, however, as fully capitalist rather than semifeudal and semicapitalist, and believes that Ceylon's ruling class constitutes a neo-colonized bourgeoisie that is beholden to the imperialist powers. The Ceylon peasants are, in the JVP view, seen as mainly belonging to the category of rural proletarians. Students and other educated youth are also seen as an important revolutionary force.

The JVP emerged publicly to support "progressive" candidates during the May 1971 elections. A number of its leaders were, however, arrested on trumped-up charges by the pre-election United National Party government. After the elections these leaders were not released; instead, the JVP came under increasing repression by the new United Front government in late 1970 and early 1971. During this period spokesmen for the JVP began to receive some support from, and to appear on platforms with, leaders of the revolutionary Trotskyist party of Bala Tampoe (the Lanka Sama Samaja Party-Revolutionary, or LSSP-R), with a following among rubber workers and in the Ceylon Mercantile Union, and of the Young Socialist Front, a newly formed trade union among the Tamil tea workers. In this manner the JVP, hitherto supported mainly by Sinhalese village peasants, developed closer relations with revolutionary groups representing the two other main sectors of Ceylon's propertyless classes: the urban proletariat and the plantation workers of Indian origin.

Except among Tamils of Jaffna in northern Ceylon and among Roman Catholics, the Front gained wide support from peasants, plantation workers, and educated youth, especially of the lower-ranking Sinhalese fishing and service castes. It procured large quantities of weapons, some of which were stored in universities. London newspapers reported that they were destined to be used in an insurrection in which guerrillas would simultaneously occupy police, army, radio, electric, and telecommunications stations.[37] Whatever the JVP's time perspectives may have been, however, the government of Ceylon struck first.

Repression

In 1970 and 1971, cataclysmic events, with some similarities, occurred in all three countries of the subcontinent. The three nations held general elections. Parties were elected with large majorities which seemed to many to reflect progressive, albeit gradualist, tendencies rather than far-right or far-left "extremism." In Ceylon a United Front of Mrs. Bandaranaike's Sri Lanka Freedom Party

(SLFP), the Trotskyist Lanka Sama Samaja Party (LSSP), and the pro-Moscow Communist Party swept the polls in May 1970, defeating the supposedly more conservative United National Party. In Pakistan, various splinter groups of the Muslim League and other right-wing parties were completely defeated in December 1970—in West Pakistan by the social democratic Pakistan People's Party; in East Pakistan by the Awami League with its six-point program of autonomy for East Bengal. The latter represented chiefly Bengali middle class aspirations for employment for the educated and for escape from the colonial exploitation to which East Pakistan had been increasingly subjected by the West Pakistani ruling elite. In India in March 1971, Mrs. Indira Gandhi's New Congress Party won a landslide victory based on the slogan "Remove Poverty and the Privy Purses of Maharajas" (i.e., the state-paid incomes of former princes). In most areas the New Congress Party trounced the more conservative coalition of the Opposition Congress, Jan Sangh, and Swatantra parties.

In all three countries, however, some revolutionary groups boycotted the elections. These included, in Pakistan, the CPEP-ML, the Bhashani-NAP, the East Bengal Communist Party, and the Coordinating Committee of Communist Revolutionaries; in India, the CPI-ML and various other Maoist groups; and in Ceylon, the LSSP-R. They boycotted the elections either because of objections to the constitutional framework or because of their conviction that parliamentarism was played out and only revolutionary struggle could change the common people's lot. Those parliamentary parties which were theoretically dedicated to revolutionary change so moderated their policies or so entangled themselves in electoral arrangements with bourgeois parties that they offered no clear programmatic alternatives.[38] As a result, the largest mass of votes went to the seemingly more progressive of the established parties.

Within months of the elections, the governments of Pakistan and Ceylon carried out preemptive slaughter of those dissident groups which threatened their own power. In Pakistan Yahya Khan rejected the election results, with their verdict of national dominance by the Awami League and provincial autonomy for East Bengal. Backed by continuing U.S. military aid, West Pakistani forces invaded East Bengal (which contained a majority, or 77 million, of Pakistan's total population of 120-odd million), massacred large numbers variously estimated at 600,000 to 3 million people, and drove almost 10 million refugees into neighboring West Bengal in India. Five thousand refugees died of cholera, and many more thousands, both in West and East Bengal, of famine. In West Pakistan, amid an economic crisis and labor unrest produced by the war, the government carried out mass arrests of trade unionists, students, political leaders, striking workers, intellectuals, and newspaper editors in every province. Numerous leaders and members of the Kisan-Mazdoor (Peasant-Worker) Party in the North West Frontier Province, of the pro-Moscow National Awami Party, and of the People's Party were arrested. A total of about 800 arrests without trial was reported on September 15, 1971, and there were public floggings of an unknown number of dissenters.[39]

In Ceylon, the Bandaranaike government suddenly declared a national emergency on March 15, 1971. On slight provocation, or apparently even on trumped-up charges, the government carried out a massacre of youths suspected of membership in or sympathy with the People's Liberation Front. Estimates of the numbers killed vary between 1,500 and 10,000;[40] about 16,000 were jailed. A year later, at least 14,000 remained in jail without trial and in danger of massacre, according to a February 1972 report by Jayasumana Obeysekara written since his article in this volume.[41] During April 1971 the three-party revolutionary front fought back vigorously. Its guerrillas, estimated at 30,000–80,000, confronted the initial Ceylon government forces of about 18,000.[42] Western reporters stated that the insurrectionists almost succeeded in overthrowing the government on the night of April 5. This may, however, have been an exaggeration designed to justify the government's massive resort to external military aid and the killing of young people, some of whom were captured and then executed without trial. The goal of the government forces was evidently to uproot the front's infrastructure before it could spread further. "We have learned too many lessons from Vietnam and Malaysia. We must destroy them completely," Lieutenant Colonel Cyril Ranatunga, a Sandhurst graduate, is reported to have said. A senior officer told reporters, "Once we are convinced prisoners are insurgents, we take them to the cemetery and dispose of them." [43] In the course of this counterinsurgency operation the Ceylon government received military aid from Britain, the United States, the U.S.S.R., the United Arab Republic, India, Pakistan, Yugoslavia, and Malaysia,[44] and a $30 million interest-free loan from China. The North Korean embassy was accused by the government of helping the insurgents and was expelled, but no evidence was produced against members of the embassy staff. Youthful revolutionaries—independent, Trotskyist, and Maoist—thus found themselves fighting a bourgeois government which included Communists and Trotskyists in its cabinet and was aided by the U.S.A., the U.S.S.R., and China. Each of these three powers took the position that the rebels were, as a letter from Chou En-lai to Mrs. Bandaranaike put it, "a handful of persons" trying to create "a chaotic situation," aided by "foreign spies." [45]

Repression in India was less dramatic and more localized, but nonetheless real. Mohan Ram describes in this book the Indian government's deployment of troops against tribal peasants in Andhra Pradesh on March 1, 1971. West Bengal was heavily occupied by the Indian army in advance of the March elections and has remained so since. In several states, especially in eastern India, thousands of Naxalites or alleged Naxalite supporters, and considerable numbers of the CPI-M, were arrested under emergency measures in 1971. Many hundreds, perhaps thousands, were shot in jails or in the streets.[46] While in Pakistan, therefore, the nation itself was shattered as a legitimate moral entity by the acts of its own government, in India and Ceylon parliamentary process and the rule of law were made a mockery. This impression was reinforced by the government's increasing tendency to suspend state legislatures on the pretext of breakdown of law and order, as it did in Punjab, Bihar, and West Bengal.

The Separation of Bangladesh

In East Bengal two centers of resistance to the West Pakistani invasion and military dictatorship became prominent during the liberation struggle of March–November 1971. One of them was bourgeois nationalist and was coordinated by nonrevolutionary leaders. It consisted of the Awami League and its allies, the pro-Moscow Communist Party, the Wali-NAP, and the Bangladesh National Congress representing East Bengali Hindus. As titular head of the more radical and anti-imperialist Bhashani-NAP, the aged peasant leader Maulana Bhashani held one of the eight seats in the coordinating committee set up to advise the Awami League Provisional Government. Bhashani was, however, under observation in India and was separated from his party members in East Bengal. The provisional government had its headquarters in West Bengal, where the surviving Awami League leaders fled in March 1971. It armed and trained East Bengali partisans in India with the help of the Indian government, and in early November was reported to have set up an administrative base at Dinajpur in northeastern Bangladesh inside a liberated zone.

The other center of resistance was the revolutionary National Liberation Struggle Coordination Committee, formed in April 1971 and composed of the Bhashani-NAP, the Coordinating Committee of Communist Revolutionaries, the East Bengal Communist Party, and several student, peasant, and worker unions. On June 1 the Committee called for a united military struggle, along with the Awami League and all other resistance groups, to establish a "democratic social system, anti-imperialist, antifeudal, and antimonopoly capital in character." Their program included the setting up of village administrative committees, the stoppage of taxes to the West Pakistani government, the ending of usury and of the hoarding of food grains, the punishment of quislings, the reduction of the landlords' exploitation of peasants and landless laborers, the development of small, self-sufficient economic regions, and the training of guerrilla squads for sabotage and hit-and-run attacks on the West Pakistani forces.[47] Resistance forces under these two fronts were estimated at 50,000–100,000 guerrillas in mid-October 1971, in addition to some 10,000–15,000 regular troops of the East Bengal regiment and the East Pakistan Rifles. They were fighting a West Pakistani force of about 80,000 and claimed to have killed 20,000 West Pakistani military men.

A third, independent group was the pro-Peking East Pakistan Communist Party (Marxist-Leninist). This party continued to carry on "antifeudal" attacks against landlords and police, especially in Noakhali district. In spite of China's official support for the West Pakistani dictatorship, some sources reported that the CPEP-ML was receiving weapons from China; others, however, denied this. The CPEP-ML attempted to lead struggles on two fronts, against the West Pakistani invaders and against soldiers of the Awami League who entered Bangladesh after training in India.[48]

While the National Liberation Coordination Committee called for unity with the Awami League in the military struggle, the latter rejected such unity. Unofficial reports from Calcutta in September 1971 stated that Awami League leaders were trying to weed out the more radical youth from their training programs and feared the takeover of the movement by socialist revolutionary forces. It was obvious, moreover, that the Indira Gandhi government could not look favorably on the supplying of weapons to East Bengali guerrillas similar in character to, and having ties with, the Naxalite groups in India. In October 1971 a new force—the Mujib Bahini, composed mainly of students loyal to Sheikh Mujibur Rahman, the leader of the Awami League who was imprisoned in West Pakistan—began to be sent in from Calcutta to counter the growing influence of leftist forces in Bangladesh. The East Bengal Labor Movement (part of the National Liberation Struggle Committee) reported armed encounters with the Mujib Bahini in its newspaper of October 1971.[49] Meanwhile, ordinary Mukti Bahini (liberation army) commanders, supposedly under Awami League leadership but emanating from Bangladesh, were reported to be more radical and more concerned about the welfare of the common people than were the Awami League administrators.[50]

Early in November 1971 the resistance forces in East Bengal won significant victories over the West Pakistani army. By November 6 they were estimated to control a quarter of the territory and to be capable of moving freely throughout the province.[51] Guerrilla fighters, as distinct from the conventionally trained forces of the Awami League sent from India, appeared to be gaining control in at least four districts. In Noakhali district, the CPEP-ML was reported to be in command and to be fighting Awami League forces entering from India even more fiercely than the Bengalis were fighting the West Pakistani troops.[52] In general it seemed clear that the Bangladesh liberation movement was becoming radicalized. Such developments threatened not only the West Pakistani government but that of India, which could not afford to see a socialist liberation struggle fully unleashed in East Bengal, let alone in some wider area involving large parts of eastern India.

The Indian government's dilemma was further sharpened as the parliamentary CPI-M raised a formal demand for the "right of self-determination for nationalities in India" while drawing parallels between West Bengal's semicolonial status in relation to western and northern India and that of East Bengal in relation to West Pakistan. With more than two hundred industrial units closed, and with spiraling unemployment and prices, the CPI-M slogan, "Don't forget, Indira and Yahya are the same," had a disturbing cogency. There also seems little doubt that the continuing influx of refugees from East Bengal imposed serious economic and social problems and the threat of civil strife in West Bengal.

Border clashes were meanwhile intensifying between Indian and West Pakistani forces in East Bengal. By November 8, Indian forces had crossed twice into Bangladesh in response to West Pakistani shelling of Indian border towns. By November 3, ten Soviet planes with spare parts had already reached India, and on November 11 U.S. military intelligence claimed that three Soviet merchant ships had left the U.S.S.R. the previous week with 5,000 tons of military equipment bound for India.[53]

In the week beginning November 21, there was a large-scale invasion of East Bengal from India. The Indian government continued until December 3 to claim that most of the invaders were Mukti Bahini. Both foreign observers and the West Pakistani military asserted, however, that hundreds of thousands of regular Indian troops with Soviet equipment were fighting in East Bengal before the end of November. Pakistan declared war and bombed Indian cities on December 4, charging that India had invaded West Pakistan. In a sharp two-week war, the Indian forces then "liberated" the whole of East Bengal, placed it under an Awami League government, subdued the West Pakistani forces, and declared an independent Bangladesh. Yahya Khan resigned on December 17. Zulfikar Ali Bhutto, the new president of West Pakistan, leads the Pakistan People's Party which emerged dominant in West Pakistan's elections of last December; he has also been a prominent emissary to China. Bhutto released Sheikh Mujibur Rahman, who returned as Prime Minister of Bangladesh. The government of India sent back the East Bengali refugees, many of them to villages previously laid waste and depopulated by West Pakistani forces. Between December 1971 and March 1972, India, Burma, France, and several other nations, including nine out of thirty-one Commonwealth countries, recognized Bangladesh as an independent state.

Although it appeared, understandably, to be welcomed by a large proportion of East Bengalis, the Indian invasion did not effect liberation of the Bangla nation. While claiming that the East Bengal situation was an internal problem that could be negotiated only between the West Pakistani government and the Awami League, the Indian government contravened an overwhelming United Nations vote for a cease-fire, invaded foreign territory, and imposed a satellite government. The war temporarily emasculated the genuine national liberation struggle of the East Bengalis, while asserting the class interests of the Indian bourgeoisie and the petty-bourgeois Awami League and furthering Soviet penetration of South Asia and confrontation with China.

The Indian government's claim of humanitarian concern for the refugees was to be doubted. Although the refugees' plight was undoubtedly appalling, the Aid India consortium provided $950 million just before India invaded East Bengal—the Indian estimate of the refugees' minimum maintenance costs until March 1972. The war itself created thousands of new refugees. It was doubtful whether the refugees who had fled to India—chiefly Hindu and mainly landless—could be resettled peacefully by being forced back to their former villages without adequate provision for their safety and livelihood.

The invasion of East Bengal and the chauvinism engendered by it in India appear to have been used as a cover by the Indian government for a massive assault on the Left in West Bengal and other parts of India. Its state assembly suspended, West Bengal had already been governed for several months by direct federal rule under military occupation. Increasing massacres of alleged Naxalite revolutionaries and of their friends and families were carried out in the second half of 1971, some in broad daylight, by police or by gangs of hoodlums armed by the Congress Party—hardly a good omen for the "democratic, socialist" future projected for Bangladesh. During the first week of the invasion it was reported that half of India's paramilitary Central Reserve Police arrived in West Bengal and that some 10,000 leftists were arrested.[54] The new wave of arrests seemed to have involved a deliberate assault not only on alleged Naxalites but especially on the parliamentary CPI-M, the strongest contender in the state elections scheduled for March.[55] On November 26 a massacre of leftist political prisoners was reported to have occurred in Alipore jail, with from six to fifty prisoners beaten to death with clubs and an estimated 237 seriously wounded.[56] Subsequent reports described comparable atrocities, and plans were said to be under way to transport thousands of pretrial political prisoners to special detention camps. In all, the "liberation" of Bangladesh appeared to have camouflaged shattering blows to independent (as distinct from pro-Moscow) Marxists, as well as to Maoist groups and their supporters in West and East Bengal.

Among the great powers, the Soviet Union obviously gained in influence and control of South Asia from these events. The trend was not new, for the Soviet Union had supplied about two-thirds of the foreign military aid to India in recent years. During the Bangladesh war, however, the Soviet Union clearly emerged as the champion of Indian expansionism.

Although the United States appeared to have been outmaneuvered by the Russians and by India and to be virtually paralyzed during the invasion, it probably lost little in terms of concrete interests in South Asia. As Eqbal Ahmad has emphasized, the United States also bore a heavy responsibility for the Indo-Pakistan war as well as for the West Pakistani genocide that preceded it, for it had supplied about 85 percent of Pakistan's military aid and 30 percent of India's in recent years.[57] The American design of staving off revolution in the region was, moreover, too closely linked with that of the Soviet Union for irreparable conflict between the two to develop. The elaborate courtesy displayed between the generals of India and Pakistan during the military surrender in Dacca, and the Indian officers' concern to protect their Pakistani colleagues from Bengali mob vengeance, were paralleled by the U.S. advance tip-off to the Russians that it was bringing the Seventh Fleet into the Indian Ocean in case the Indian action went out of control.[58] Meanwhile the United States mollified the West Pakistani government by its show of moral indignation against India, while retaining intact the U.S. investments in both countries and its Middle Eastern alliances involving Pakistan. Despite shifts in influence (and in financial and military responsibility for maintaining capitalism in South Asia), the United States and the Soviet Union remain deeply entrenched in imperialist control in both India and Pakistan. Whether under the immediate tutelage of India or of West Pakistan, Bangladesh, with an Awami League government, seems likely to resume its status as a subcolony with a double imperialist alignment.

Of the major powers, China appears to be the main loser in terms of national self-interest, for it has lost Pakistan as a united, friendly buffer state and, as a result of the war, lies more open to Soviet or Indian assault via a satellized East Bengal. Throughout the conflict China appeared more concerned with the integrity of Pakistan than with the character of the contending forces, a fact that seemed to have made the Chinese government either myopic or indifferent to the fascism of the Pakistani junta and to the Bengalis' genuine claim to national liberation. After a promise of aid to Pakistan in March 1971, however, the government of China appeared to have acted with reserve. While publicly maintaining that the Pakistani conflict should be settled internally rather than by international aggression, the Chinese withdrew aid to Yahya Khan in later phases of the conflict and urged him to make a viable political settlement in East Bengal.[59] China also sought friendly relations with India and negotiations between India and Pakistan up to the time of the invasion. It seemed likely that while trying to maintain friendly relations with Bhutto's government in West Pakistan and perhaps in future recognizing the Bangladesh government, while also giving aid to any genuine liberation movement that might reemerge in East Bengal, the Chinese would concentrate on their own defenses against possible probes by India or the Soviet Union.

In West Pakistan President Bhutto's government tried to regain popular confidence by dismissing major military and political leaders, restoring a measure of civil freedom, and undertaking economic reforms. At the same time Bhutto reassured the West that he had no intention of nationalizing foreign concerns. The difficulty of such measures is that if they go far enough to benefit the people, they alienate the native and imperial bourgeoisies, the military, or the bureaucracy (or all four) and thus invite the government's overthrow. If, however (as in Ceylon in 1971), they do not go far enough, they may fail to stave off revolt, which by March 1972 appeared to be already pending in parts of West Pakistan.[60] In addition, without a popularly accepted, planned reorganization of production, palliative reforms are costly and Pakistan can afford costly concessions even less than Ceylon a year ago. The civil and intellectual climate of Pakistan may improve for some months but its long-range problems cannot be solved without struggle.

Although the cool calculation with which its government picked off East Bengal inspired awe in India, the invasion only temporarily solved some problems and deepened others.[61] The Indian government did not in fact secure the national liberation of the ethnically and linguistically distinct East Bengalis; rather, it consolidated its own highly centralized power over eastern India while indirectly bringing East Bengal under Indian hegemony as well. (Already in January 1972 a Bengali friend reported that Indian bureaucrats from West Bengal and Orissa were arriving to help the Awami League set up its government.) Through its support for the Awami League and the dismemberment of Pakistan, however, the Indian government legitimized and raised hopes for a genuine national independence movement—hopes equally dear to the Kashmiris, the Nagas, and the Mizos in India, as well as to the West Bengalis themselves. It will be harder for the Indian government to crush the aspirations for self-government of these nationalities now that it has, however hypocritically, asserted the right of East Bengal to secede from Pakistan.

Most immediately, the Indian invasion undermined the frontier between East and West Bengal and thereby ideologically and concretely linked the struggles of the Bengali peoples. During 1971 the CPI-ML and the CPEP-ML aided each other's assaults on landlords and police in the two wings of Bengal. By extending Indian military occupation throughout this vast ethnic region of some 120 million people, the Indian government has invited the realization of its own worst nightmare: the liberation of a Red Bengal. If the Indian government withdraws its troops soon, the Awami League government (which did not dare to enter Dacca until Indian troops had secured it for them) will be ill-equipped to resist the demands of its own people. If India maintains its occupation of East Bengal, it can do so safely only with Sikh or Hindu forces from other than Bengali regions of India. East Bengalis can be expected to grow disaffected and may unite with their western brethren to oppose Indian control.

Despite Soviet and Indian plans for the economic reconstruction of Bangladesh, the sorry plight of India, with its unemployed, half-starving millions, makes it unlikely that these plans will fare better in East than in West Bengal. In Bangladesh, moreover, the problems that bedevil all South Asia have been grievously compounded by genocide, flood, famine, international war, and the destruction of communications and productive plants by both invaders and indigenous fighters. When their hopes of national freedom are not met, the people's anger will mount.

India's invasion of Bangladesh has changed the balance of forces among the imperialist and native bourgeoisies in South Asia, further shattering its obsolescent social system, but it cannot free the common people or assuage their economic and social woes. Only through self-mobilization in a long struggle for socialism under their own revolutionary leadership can South Asia's people gain control of their destiny.

Prospects

After a year of repression, the revolutionary groups of South Asia appear to be undergoing reassessment and regroupment. Widespread, coordinated guerrilla struggles seem to be temporarily halted in India. Since early 1970 the CPI-ML appears to have lost some of its organized support among peasants and to have become an urban terrorist movement concentrating on the assassination of police, landlords, moneylenders, businessmen, and political enemies in the CPI-M in Calcutta and smaller towns.[62] In the summer of 1971 the party split into two groups led, respectively, by CPI-ML Chairman Charu Mazumdar and by Ashim Chatterjee, leader of the West Bengal-Orissa-Bihar regional committee. The nature of the split was not entirely clear to outsiders, but some reports stated that while Mazumdar supported the East Pakistan Communist Party's armed struggle against both the West Pakistani invaders and the Awami League soldiers, Chatterjee favored nonresistance to the West Pakistani troops on the grounds that Yahya Khan's government played an anti-imperialist role by virtue of its alliance with China.[63] Other reports stated that the Chatterjee faction opposed the Mazumdar tactic of small group assassinations of individual "class enemies" and favored a return to mass struggles to distribute land and crops and to fight police and paramilitary personnel in the countryside. In June 1971, moreover, Mazumdar himself directed the CPI-ML cadres to spread out again from Calcutta into the countryside. Beginning in April 1971, CPI-ML cadres had been seizing hundreds of rifles from police and private citizens throughout West Bengal, presumably in anticipation of larger struggles than those they had previously carried out with primitive weapons. On October 7, 1971, after a year of silence about the CPI-ML, the Chinese news agency Hsinhua approvingly cited its gun-seizing campaign, attacks on police, and land and crop distribution, but ignored its urban terrorism, thereby reasserting some support for the party while perhaps encouraging it to reunite and work in the villages.[64] If this occurred, the CPI-ML and the Andhra Pradesh Revolutionary Communist Committee—the most significant Maoist formation outside the CPI-ML—might be able to effect a rapprochement. At present, however (March 1972), the APRCC is also temporarily stalled, having undergone massive repression and with most of its leaders imprisoned.

In Ceylon, large-scale revolutionary struggle has been temporarily crushed by the arrests and assassinations of cadres and their supporters. Gun-seizing, sabotage, and occasional assassinations were reported to be continuing in North Central Ceylon in September 1971.[65]

In Bangladesh the invading Indian and Awami League troops met armed resistance in December 1971—both from the CPEP-ML in Noakhali district and from sections of the National Liberation Struggle Coordination Committee, especially in Pabna district. Mukti Bahini troops, who had been fighting the West Pakistani military prior to the Indian invasion, were required to hand in their arms to the Mujib government after the separation of Bangladesh, but large numbers secretly retained their weapons. In February 1972 some of these guerrillas were reported to be entering the national army or the militia of Bangladesh in the hope of eventually installing a military government more responsive to the popular will than that of Sheikh Mujib. Shortly after the creation of Bangladesh, Maulana Bhashani, leader of the radical NAP, pledged support to Mujib's government and to the parliamentary process, as did the Comilla district leadership of the East Bengal Communist Party.[66] By early March 1972, however, Bhashani had raised a public outcry against famine and soaring prices and called for a mass demonstration in Dacca. At that date, therefore, it appeared possible that the revolutionary groups of Bangladesh might reunite against the Mujib government under the umbrella of the Bhashani-NAP, which retained the strongest following among the peasantry.

Certain interesting features characterize all the socialist revolutionary groups in South Asia. A large proportion of their leaders and cadres are young and highly educated. They have to struggle against the parliamentary policies and even the physical attacks of the established Marxist parties, whether pro-Moscow, independent Communist, or Trotskyist. At the same time it is essential that the revolutionary forces should be—and it is likely that they will be—augmented soon by young cadres from these older parties, many of whom are disillusioned with parliamentary politics and are increasingly subject to a degree of repression from the ruling class that cannot be adequately met through nonrevolutionary forms of defense.

The revolutionary groups are opposed by the Soviet Union. Some of them, even when Maoist in orientation, have had to struggle without the support of China, and some have been actively opposed by China.

Flexibility, a break with past South Asian Marxist groups, new alignments which crosscut some of these groups and some ancient enmities within the Marxist fold, and independence of external socialist mentors seem to be required of the South Asian revolutionaries in the immediate future, as do efforts toward unity with each other. During the resistance struggle in Bangladesh in the spring of 1971, a militant of the National Awami Party put the matter crisply to a reporter: "We don't worry whether China openly supports us or not, whether Russia tries to mediate, or America tries to replace Yahya Khan. We have to wage our own battle, and we are sure to win." [67]

March 14, 1972

Notes

1. Dandekar and Rath, "Poverty in India," *Economic and Political Weekly* (Bombay), January 2, 1971, p. 38.
2. For comparisons of calorie intake and general nutrition in India, Pakistan, and Ceylon, see Gunnar Myrdal, *Asian Drama* (Pantheon, New York, 1968), Vol. I, pp. 538–551. For contrasts between the rising per capita income of Pakistan in 1958–1968 and the fall in living standards of peasants and workers, see Tariq Ali, *Pakistan: Military Rule or People's Power?* (Jonathon Cape, London, 1970), p. 153, and Richard Nations, "The Economic Structure of Pakistan: Class and Colony," *New Left Review*, No. 68, July–August 1971. In Ceylon, although per capita income has been rising, the real wages of at least some sections of workers declined during the 1960s. Taking the average wage of workers in the tea

and rubber industries as 100 in 1939, the index number of real wages rose in most years to reach 177 in 1956, but then fell gradually, remaining at 170 from 1964 to 1967. Taking the average wage index of most of the Colombo working class as 100 in 1939, the real wage index rose in most years to reach 254 in 1960, but then fell to 233 in 1965 and 1966, rising again, however, to 241 in 1967 (*Ceylon Year Book*, 1970, pp. 215–216).

3. *Newsweek*, June 17, 1963, reporting on the World Food Congress held in Washington, D.C., under the auspices of the United Nations. Quoted by Felix Greene, *The Enemy* (Random House, New York, 1970), p. 150.

4. See especially Harry Magdoff, *The Age of Imperialism* (Monthly Review Press, New York, 1969), and Robert I. Rhodes, ed., *Imperialism and Underdevelopment: A Reader* (Monthly Review Press, New York, 1970).

5. Chiefly in export crop plantations, coal mines, metallurgical works, jute factories, import and export firms, banking, and distributive networks selling imported consumer goods. To the profits of these must be added the "Home Charges" drawn from Indian revenues for British services, the interest on loans made to the Indian government for building railroads and telegraph systems, and the income from British shipping and trading firms, from which Indians were excluded. The total annual capital flow from undivided India to Britain in 1939 is estimated at about 200 million pounds sterling. See Michael Barratt Brown, *After Imperialism* (Heinemann, London, 1963), pp. 174–175; Sofia Melman, *Foreign Monopoly Capital in the Indian Economy* (People's Publishing House, New Delhi, 1963), p. 42. For some effects of foreign investment in Ceylon during British rule, see Fred Halliday, "The Ceylonese Insurrection," *New Left Review*, No. 69, 1971, p. 59.

6. For the loss of purchasing power experienced by Third World countries in general due to decline in the terms of trade between 1961 and 1966, see Magdoff, op. cit., p. 158.

7. Michael Kidron points out that official figures for foreign investment are lower than estimates of foreign-controlled assets. Kidron quotes an estimate for 1961 for India of about Rs. 14,000 million (about U.S. $2 billion at 1971 rates of exchange) for total foreign-controlled assets. This was slightly more than two-fifths of the total in the organized or large-scale private sector, or one-quarter of the modern sector as a whole (Michael Kidron, *Foreign Investment in India* [Oxford University Press, 1965], p. 186). Taking into account the distribution of foreign capital in big industry, mining, plantations, banking and big business, and its use to control large amounts of Indian capital, Bettelheim concludes: "Foreign capital can . . . be said to share the control of the Indian economy with domestic capital on what is very nearly a fifty-fifty basis" (Charles

Bettelheim, *India Independent* [Monthly Review Press, New York, 1968], p. 59). In 1961, 77 percent of the foreign private capital invested in India was British, but the proportion is declining. British capital accounted for 28 percent of the value of new foreign capital issues sanctioned between April 1956 and December 1964; U.S. capital for 32 percent; West German for 8 percent; and French for 6 percent. Kidron estimates that between 1948 and 1961 private foreign investment in India more than doubled; in that period foreign investors took out of the general currency reserve nearly three times as much as they contributed directly (Kidron, op. cit., p. 310). Total capital imports into Pakistan increased by 100 percent between 1955 and 1965, and were expected to increase by another 100 percent between 1965 and 1970 (Tariq Ali, op. cit., p. 225). The increase in American private investment in both India and Pakistan in recent years is an adjunct of the U.S. predominance in foreign loans to both countries. At the end of India's Third Five-Year Plan (1965), out of a total of Rs. 58,700 million of foreign aid, the International Bank for Reconstruction and Development had provided Rs. 42,000 million and the International Development Association had provided Rs. 2,800 million, both largely controlled by the United States. The United States itself had provided Rs. 12,800 million, excluding PL 480 loans; the U.S.S.R., Rs. 4,800 million; the U.K., Rs. 3,300 million; West Germany, Rs. 4,500 million; and Japan Rs. 1,400 million. Italy and Czechoslovakia had each provided more than Rs. 600 million. There has since been a spectacular increase in aid from the U.S.S.R., Rs. 6,000 million of supplementary aid having been granted in 1965 alone (Bettelheim, op. cit., p. 289). U.S. aid has not declined, however: by September 1969 India had received a total of Rs. 84,060 million from the United States, the IBRD, and the IDA—70.6 percent of the total world aid distributed from these sources between 1951 and 1969 (R. P. Mullick, "Indo-U.S. Rapport: Two Faces," *Frontier* (Calcutta), February 26, 1972). In Pakistan, out of a total of about Rs. 28,000 million of foreign aid up to 1969, the International Bank for Reconstruction and Development and the International Development Association between them provided Rs. 4,519 million; the U.S.A., Rs. 12,683 million; West Germany, Rs. 1,974 million; the U.K., Rs. 1,755 million; Canada, Rs. 1,652 million; and Japan, Rs. 1,433 million. The U.S.S.R., China, France, and Yugoslavia each provided more than Rs. 500 million.

8. In 1966 and 1967, Ceylon received Rs. 42.3 million in project loans and Rs. 193.9 million in commodity loans (a total of Rs. 236.2 million). Of this total, the U.K. provided Rs. 56.5 million; Canada, Rs. 13.2 million; the U.S.A., Rs. 32.4 million; West Germany, Rs. 70.6 million; Japan, Rs. 31.3 million, and India, Rs. 10.1 million (*Ceylon Year Book*, 1970, p.

196). Ceylon paid out Rs. 109 million in 1969 as foreign investment income and Rs. 142 million (about U.S. $10 million) in 1970 (Central Bank of Ceylon, *Annual Report*, 1970, p. 195).

9. In 1947 Ceylon earned $170 million by exporting 287 million pounds of tea; but in 1970 total earnings were only $188 million, with the export volume at 459 pounds. Thus between 1947 and 1970 the export volume of tea increased by 60 percent but the export value increased by only 10 percent. In the same period rubber export volume increased by 95 percent; rubber export value, by 85 percent. In 1966 Ceylon's external resource gap of Rs. 541 million was the highest in the period 1952–1966. Thereafter, the external resource gap rose to Rs. 649 million in 1968 and Rs. 1,235 million in 1969. In 1970 the resource gap was Rs. 1,124 million (Central Bank of Ceylon, *Annual Report*, 1970, pp. 11–20; see also Fred Halliday, op. cit., p. 70).

10. See also Hamza Alavi and Amir Khusro, "Pakistan: the Burden of U.S. Aid," in Robert I. Rhodes, op. cit., pp. 62–78, and Hamza Alavi, "Imperialism, Old and New," *The Socialist Register 1964* (Monthly Review Press, New York, 1964), pp. 104–126.

11. By 1965, India owed its total prospective export earnings for the next six to seven years to repay foreign debts already incurred. By 1966, 26.9 percent of the value of India's exports and 15.7 percent of the value of Pakistan's exports was used to cover foreign debt *service* and profits on foreign investment (Magdoff, op. cit., p. 155). By 1969 the percentage had risen to 30 percent in the case of Pakistan (Embassy of Pakistan, *Pakistan's Five Year Plan, 1965–70*, Report Series, December 1969, p. 1). By 1970 more than 50 percent of Ceylon's new total receipts from foreign aid were required to cover her foreign debt service (Central Bank of Ceylon, *Annual Report*, 1970, p. 196).

12. See Cheryl Payer, "The IMF and the Third World," *Monthly Review*, September 1971, pp. 47–48; *Daily Telegraph* (London), "Ceylon Revolt Caused by Broken Promises," April 12, 1971.

13. B. H. S. Jayawardene, "Post Mortem," *Far Eastern Economic Review*, July 10, 1971, and "Weighing the Pearl," ibid., July 17, 1971.

14. The United States, for example, threatened to cut off food aid to India and Pakistan during their border war of 1965; the same threat was made to India in 1966 in order to force her to permit Standard Oil of Indiana to market fertilizers in India at its own rather than at government-controlled prices. In June 1962 Ceylon nationalized 63 gas stations owned by Esso Standard Eastern, Inc. and Caltex Ceylon, Ltd. U.S. aid was broken off in February 1963 and was not restarted until the United National Party government came in in July 1965 and agreed to compensate the firms at acceptable rates (Magdoff, op. cit., p. 128).

15. Ceylon's total registered unemployed citizens numbered 150,000 out of a population of 11.0 million in 1965. They numbered 500,000 in early 1970, and 700,000 in late 1970, out of a population of 12.3 million. In 1965 Ceylon had 10,723 university students; in 1967, 14,512. Educated unemployed youth have increased disproportionately to the unemployed in the population as a whole (*Ceylon Year Books*, 1965–1970, passim; Fred Halliday, op. cit., p. 74). The *Daily Telegraph* reported on April 20, 1971, that 14,000 unemployed graduates were estimated to have joined the cause of the People's Liberation Front.

It is estimated that over 100,000 persons with scientific, engineering, or medical qualifications are unemployed in India, while 30,000 more are abroad ("Magnitude of Brain Drain from India," *Technical Manpower*, Division for Scientific and Technical Personnel, CSIR, Vol. XIII, No. 2, February 1971, as quoted by Kamalesh Ray, "Unemployment and the Brain Drain," *Economic and Political Weekly*, September 25, 1971, p. 2059).

16. See A. Sinha, *U.S. Threat to India's Sovereignty* (Book Club, Calcutta), for a detailed account.

17. See Hari P. Sharma's article in this volume for the recent increase in India's food production, and Richard Nations (op. cit.) for that in West Pakistan. Ceylon's United National Party government decided in 1965 to put 46 percent of its internal budget into growing food due to the ruinous cost of importing rice caused by the price rise on account of the war in Vietnam. Ceylon's paddy (unhusked rice) production rose from 36.3 million bushels in 1965 to 76.8 million bushels in 1970. Even so, with rapidly decreasing imports and a growing population, Ceylon's people consumed slightly less rice per capita in 1970 than in 1965 (Central Bank of Ceylon, *Annual Report*, 1970, Table 3, Appendix).

18. For an excellent treatment see Francine R. Frankel, *India's Green Revolution: Economic Gains and Political Costs* (Oxford University Press, Bombay, 1971); and Thomas B. Wiens, "Seeds of Revolution," *Bulletin of Concerned Asian Scholars*, April–July 1970, pp. 104–108. A. K. Gopalan, an M.P. and peasant organizer of the Communist Party of India-Marxist, recently charged that 25 percent of agricultural laborers had been thrown out of work in areas where the green revolution had been introduced (*Times of India*, October 20, 1971, p. 5).

19. Dandekar and Rath, op. cit., p. 38.

20. As a result, Ceylon's budget deficit is now over Rs. 930 million, the highest since independence (*Far Eastern Economic Review*, August 28, 1971, pp. 15–16).

21. See Mohan Ram, *Maoism in India* (Vikas Publications, Delhi, 1971), pp. 175–178.

As of early 1972, the Soviet Union controlled 80 percent of India's electricity-generating equipment industries, 80 percent of oil extraction, 34 percent of refineries, 80 percent of heavy engineering industries, 30 percent of iron and steel industries, 60 percent of electrical equipment industries, and 25 percent of power industries. With respect to India's export trade, the U.S.S.R. controlled 57 percent of India's export of wool, 75 percent of woolen garments, 53 percent of cotton, 75 percent of jute, and 51 percent of skins (Tarun Roy, "Fresh Pastures," *Frontier*, February 26, 1972).

22. Hamza Alavi, "Bangladesh and the Crisis of Pakistan," *The Socialist Register 1971* (Merlin Press, London, 1971).

23. Sumanta Banerjee, "Cracks in the Government Structure," *Economic and Political Weekly*, January 2, 1971, p. 14.

24. The CPI-M arose from a split in the old CPI in 1964. See Mohan Ram, *Indian Communism: Split Within a Split* (Vikas Publications, Delhi, 1969), and his article in this volume.

25. See Tariq Ali, op. cit., pp. 138–148, for China's relations with the government and the revolutionary groups of Pakistan.

26. On April 13 the *Pakistan Times* published a letter from Chou En-lai to Yahya Khan which congratulated him on having done "a lot of useful work" to uphold the unification of Pakistan, some two weeks after the West Pakistani invasion and large-scale massacres in East Bengal. Noting that "the unity of the people of East and West Pakistan [is] the basic guarantee of Pakistan to attain prosperity and strength," the letter went on: "Here it is most important to differentiate the broad masses of people from a handful of persons who want to sabotage the unification of Pakistan." The letter warned against the expansionism of India and the efforts of India, the Soviet Union, and the U.S.A. to exploit Pakistan's internal problems (*Pakistan Times*, April 13, 1971, reprinted in *New Left Review*, No. 68, July–August 1971, p. 46). The Chinese also announced an interest-free loan of $100 million to Pakistan (*Financial Times*, May 14 and June 17, 1971) and $30 million to Ceylon (*Ceylon Daily News*, May 27, 1971). At a later date the Chinese government appears to have privately withdrawn its support and material aid to Yahya Khan in view of the large-scale massacres of revolutionaries and common people in East Bengal and the size of the refugee exodus, but it continued to support the Pakistan government publicly throughout the events of 1971. While the Chinese fear of Indian and Soviet intervention proved fully justified, the government of China must in my view be blamed from the point of view of socialist internationalism as well as humanitarianism for failing to analyze the colonial exploitation of East Bengal, discouraging the revolutionary movements in Pakistan from

arming the people and carrying out militant struggles after the uprising of 1968, and giving material aid and public support to a fascist government while it engaged in genocide—and while China was meanwhile proclaiming that "what is happening in Pakistan at present is purely an internal affair" (*Pakistan Times*, op. cit.).

27. The Consul General of the Democratic Republic of Vietnam reportedly extended the support of the DRV to the "Bangla People in their struggle for freedom against the occupation forces of West Pakistan" (*Times of India*, October 20, 1971, p. 6).

28. *Indian Communism: Split Within a Split*, 1969, and *Maoism in India*, 1971, both by Vikas Publications, Delhi.

29. Dandekar and Rath, op. cit., pp. 29–30; *India Votes*, ed. by R. Chandidas, Ward Moorhouse, Leon Clark, and Richard Fontera (Humanities Press, New York, 1968), pp. 256–265.

30. Eric Wolf, *Peasant Wars of the Twentieth Century* (Harper and Row, New York, 1968), p. 293.

31. In Naxalbari, moreover, poor peasants and landless laborers are reported to have actually led the struggle once it had been called for by the peasant convention. See Kanu Sanyal, "Report on the Peasant Movement in the Terai Region," *Liberation* (monthly journal of the Communist Party of India-Marxist Leninist, or CPI-ML), Calcutta, November 1968. For Hamza Alavi's view that it is crucially important to involve the middle peasants in revolutionary struggle, especially in the early stages, see "Peasants and Revolution," reprinted in this volume. For my own view that the middle peasant is dying out as a significant category in India in many regions, see Kathleen Gough, "Peasant Resistance and Revolt in South India," *Pacific Affairs*, Winter 1968–69, pp. 526–544, and "The Indian Revolutionary Potential," *Monthly Review*, February 1969, pp. 23–36.

32. "Neo-colonialism prevails in the country today. According to existing social relations there is a capitalist system here. Ceylon is a capitalist society designed to fulfil the class needs of the foreign imperialists and their allies. There is no feudalism in our country today. Only a few remains of the old feudal system are to be found . . ." ("The Peasantry Is the Main Force of the Ceylon Revolution," *Vimukthi*, organ of the Janata Vimukthi Peramuna, or JVP, No. 4, September 30, 1970, quoted by Fred Halliday, "The Ceylonese Insurrection," *New Left Review*, No. 69, September–October 1971, p. 77).

33. For further statements of this position see Kathleen Gough, "Peasant Resistance and Revolt in South India," op. cit., and S. A. Shah and Kathleen Gough, "Class and Agrarian Change: Some Comments on Peasant Resistance and Revolution in India," *Pacific Affairs*, Fall 1969,

pp. 360–368. See also Sulekh Chandra Gupta, "Some Aspects of Indian Agriculture as Revealed in Recent Studies," and A. R. Desai, "Sociological Analysis of India," in *Rural Sociology in India* (Popular Prakashan, Bombay, 1969), for supporting data and arguments.

34. W. F. Wertheim, *Indonesian Society in Transition* (W. Van Hoeve, Ltd., The Hague, 1959); Eric Wolf, op. cit. A. R. Desai, ed., *Rural Sociology in India*, op. cit., is a pioneering work in that direction.

35. Hamza Alavi, "Imperialism, Old and New," *The Socialist Register 1966* (Monthly Review Press, New York, 1966).

36. Hari P. Sharma, "Changes in Local Level Politics in India," paper presented at the Third Annual Conference of Punjab Studies, University of Pennsylvania, Philadelphia, Pa., May 6–8, 1971; Kathleen Gough, "Communist Rural Councillors in Kerala," *Journal of Asian and African Studies*, July and October 1968, Vol. 3, No. 3–4, pp. 181–202.

37. See "Terror Raid Warning to Colombo," *Daily Telegraph*, April 13, 1971. For further information on the Ceylon repression and uprising, see Fred Halliday, op. cit.; "Armed Uprising in Ceylon" (anon.), *Monthly Review*, January 1972; and Jayasumana Obeysekara's article in this volume. Part of my information on Ceylon was provided by Professor Michael Egan, Department of Anthropology, University of British Columbia, who spent some months there shortly after the uprising.

38. These parties included, in Pakistan, the pro-Moscow National Awami Party (Wali faction); in India, the pro-Moscow CPI and the independent CPI-M; and in Ceylon, the pro-Moscow Communist Party and the Trotskyist Lanka Sama Samaja Party, which actually entered a United Front with the Sri Lanka Freedom Party of Mrs. Bandaranaike.

39. See *Pakistan Forum*, June–July 1971, p. 1, and *Bangladesh*, Toronto, September 15, 1971.

40. The official government figure for those killed is 1,500 but that is generally admitted to be too low. For higher figures and for accounts of the repression and the uprising that followed it, see "Revolution Replaces Rhetoric," *Economic and Political Weekly*, May 22, 1971; "Shambles of Bandaranaike Socialism," ibid., July 17, 1971; "Ceylon and East Bengal," *Frontier*, May 15, 1971; "Ceylon: A Decisive Year," ibid., July 14, 1971; and *Far Eastern Economic Review*, September 11, 1971, pp. 16–17.

41. The report runs in part as follows: "There are 14,000 prisoners held in neo-concentration camps under inhuman conditions. On a number of occasions the army has shot into the camps, causing deaths. The conditions inside these camps are intolerable and nobody, not even a government deputy, is allowed to visit them. We have collected evidence from a number of people fortunate enough to be released after 9 or 10 months inside these camps; we also have information smuggled out of prisons.

At the slightest provocation the detainees are baton-charged or shot at. Food is bad, diseases spread quickly due to overcrowding. They are tortured for information and 'difficult' cases are either bumped off or kept in solitary confinement; they are allowed to leave their cells only once a day and that too only for an hour. The government does not know what to do with them. They cannot bring them to trial because they have no real evidence against them. There is a move afoot to change the law of evidence in order to make it possible for the prosecution to permit the use of confessions even when obtained by force."

42. *Daily Telegraph*, April 19, 1971.
43. *The Times*, London, April 19, 1971, p. 1.
44. *Daily Telegraph*, April 13–18, 1971, passim.
45. *Ceylon Daily News*, May 27, 1971; reprinted in *New Left Review*, September–October 1971, p. 91. Although it opposed the JVP and the revolt, the pro-Peking Communist Party of Ceylon came under suspicion and its leader, N. Sanmugathasan, and many of its cadres were arrested.
46. See "Now the CPM's Turn," *Frontier*, May 8, 1971; "CPM on Jail Killings," ibid., June 5, 1971; "What Goes on in Jails," ibid., July 17, 1971; "Dialogue with Naxalites," ibid., August 14, 1971; "Shades of Indonesia," ibid., August 21, 1971; "The Hunting Hounds," ibid., August 28, 1971; "Cossipore-Baranagar," ibid., September 18, 1971; Mohan Ram, "Little Law, Less Order," *Far Eastern Economic Review*, July 10, 1971.
47. *The Red Mole* (London), September 15, 1971.
48. See "Dawn of a New Era in East Pakistan," May 1971, and Charu Mazumdar's statement, "Pakistan and the Role of the Communist Party," June 29, 1971, in *Liberation* (Calcutta), April–June 1971; reprinted in *Chingari*, P.O. Box 32, Station F, Toronto, July–October 1971.
49. Shapan Ghaani: "Bangladesh: Leftist Vignettes in Half a Revolution," *Far Eastern Economic Review*, March 4, 1972, p. 20.
50. Derek Ingram, "A Land Where Hope Dies," *The Province*, Vancouver, B.C., November 4, 1971.
51. *New York Times*, November 6, 1971.
52. *Far Eastern Economic Review*, November 20, 1971, p. 19.
53. *New York Times*, November 12, 1971.
54. Fred Bridgland reporting from Calcutta, *Vancouver Sun*, Vancouver, B.C., November 27, 1971.
55. "West Bengal: Liquidation of the Left," *Economic and Political Weekly*, December 4, 1971.
56. *Le Monde*, November 30, 1971, and *Frontier*, December 4, 1971.
57. Eqbal Ahmad, "Military Victory Will Not Eliminate Refugee Problem," *American Report*, December 24, 1971, p. 5.
58. *Far Eastern Economic Review*, January 1, 1972, pp. 8–9.
59. T. J. S. George, "Peking's Pre-War Message to Pakistan," *Far Eastern*

Economic Review, February 5, 1972. At a meeting with some 75 Pakistanis at the United Nations on December 17, 1971, Mr. Z. A. Bhutto was asked why the expected Chinese help to Pakistan did not materialize in the course of the Bangladesh conflict; he replied: "Such expectations were unrealistic. I was about to begin a vacation in Rome after a meeting with President Sadat of Egypt when I was summoned to Pakistan and asked to go with a military delegation to China. The Chinese told me frankly and clearly that they were extremely concerned over the liquidation of leftists in East Pakistan by the right-wing Razakars, armed by the government. The Chinese also explained their uneasiness over the failure of Pakistan to reciprocate the Chinese support of Pakistan; e.g., Pakistan's silence over the U.S. invasion of Cambodia and Laos. China is not our *susral* (home of the in-laws) that we can expect anything, anytime, of them without giving anything in return" (*Pakistan Forum*, January 1972, p. 7).

60. Tariq Ali, "After the Defeat: A Bleak Future," *Intercontinental Press*, March 13, 1972, pp. 274–275.
61. For an analysis of some of these problems, see Aijaz Ahmad, "Bangladesh: India's Dilemma," *Pakistan Forum*, November 1971, pp. 11–15; see also Feroz Ahmed, "A Reactionary War," ibid.; and Tariq Ali, "The Indian Subcontinent: A Bourgeois War Could Only Accelerate the Process of Disintegration," *The Red Mole*, November 29, 1971, p. 2.
62. "Urban Guerrillas in Calcutta," *Economic and Political Weekly*, July 10, 1971, pp. 1379–1382.
63. The latter position is combated by Mazumdar in his article "Pakistan and the Role of the Communist Party," op. cit. For discussions of the demoralizing impact of China's Bengal policy on Indian Maoists in 1971, see Mohan Ram, "Polycentric Maoism," *Economic and Political Weekly*, June 26, 1971, pp. 1277–2378, and Sumanta Banerjee, "Maoists: Doing Without China?", ibid., July 3, 1971, pp. 1321–1322.
64. Mohan Ram, "Peking and Indian Marxists," *Economic and Political Weekly*, October 30, 1971, p. 2234.
65. *Far Eastern Economic Review*, September 4, 1971, pp. 16–17.
66. Shapan Ghaani, "Bangladesh: Leftist Vignettes in Half a Revolution," op. cit.
67. *Times of India*, May 8, 1971.

2. Foreign Capital and Economic Development in India: A Schematic View

Amiya Kumar Bagchi

In this paper I shall try to describe certain modes of dominance by foreign capital to which India has been subjected. For this purpose I have dealt with more than two centuries of Indian economic history, often in a very hurried fashion. While such a brief view has obvious limitations, it brings home the fact that the relations between Britain and India vary tremendously as far as the modus operandi of colonial exploitation is concerned. Only the fact of economic domination of India by Britain remains constant from 1757 to at least 1914. In the literature on capitalist imperialism the effects of imperial domination have been neglected as compared with the motives of imperial expansion. It is the intention of this paper partly to remedy this defect. In the last section of the paper I shall submit that although political dominance of India by Britain ceased in 1947, India remained firmly within the sphere of influence of the advanced capitalist countries, and that this relation of dependence of Indian capitalism on advanced capitalist countries and, for certain limited purposes, on the countries of the Soviet bloc imposes limitations on India's economic development. However, this statement should not be taken to mean that this external constraint is the only hindrance to Indian economic growth; on the contrary, the distribution of incomes and economic power and, more broadly, the relations of production make this dependence on more advanced countries inevitable, given that the avoidance of absolute stasis is desirable even from the point of view of the ruling classes in India.

This paper covers, except for the last part, the same period as R.

This paper was read at the Seminar on Historical Models in the Study of Tradition and Change held at the Indian Institute of Advanced Study, Simla, in October 1969. It was first published in *Frontier* (Calcutta), September 25, 1971. It was revised in mid-1970; hence there are no references to later developments.

P. Dutt's *India Today*.[1] However, it stresses certain aspects of the colonial relationship which Dutt either overlooked or underplayed. First, domination of India by Britain is considered not simply as an aspect of the development and expansion of British capitalism but as a crucial feature of the domination of the whole world economy by the advanced capitalist countries of Western Europe and North America. As the position of Britain among the advanced capitalist nations changed—from that of a challenger against Dutch supremacy to that of the undisputed leader of Western European capitalism and then to that of a country which has lost its preeminence to the U.S.A. and several other advanced capitalist countries—so did the function that India performed as the servitor economy for the advanced capitalist countries. Secondly, in contrast to Dutt, I do not want to imply that the gain to Britain from the exploitation of India was equivalent in any meaningful sense to the loss to India. In fact, the system of plunder of India practiced by Britain almost certainly involved a "deadweight loss": much of the destruction of livelihood of ordinary Indians was totally pointless from the point of view of the gain accruing to the destroyers. I would not want to maintain, with Dutt, that "the spoliation of India was the hidden source of accumulation which played an all-important role in helping to make possible the Industrial Revolution in England."[2] While the exploitation of India provided Britain with an important source for accumulation of capital, other sources—e.g., the slave trade, trade with North America, the displacement of artisans and small peasants during the industrial and agricultural revolutions—were probably much more important; in any case, the causes of the Industrial Revolution are to be found in the evolution of British—and, more generally, of European—society rather than in the exploitation of colonies as such.

Finally, in contrast to Dutt, I emphasize the distortion of the earlier economic structure rather than its destruction, caused by British rule. In emphasizing the destructive role of capitalist imperialism, Marxist writing has tended to overestimate the progressive role of alien capitalist penetration. A naive faith in the progressive role of capitalism is shared by essentially conservative thinkers like Schumpeter (cf. his characterization of the function of capitalism as "creative destruction").[3] In my view, British imperialism created in India a structure of society which made its evolution into a modern capitalist economy well-nigh impossible. The frustration of social evolution did not stem simply, or even primarily, from the brutal exploitation of ordinary people; it was due much more to the noncompetitive structures fashioned by British rule, and to the precapitalist formations shored up by the peculiar action of capitalist imperialism on the Indian economy. All these qualifications notwithstanding, it will be obvious from the sequel that the very posing of the problems raised in this paper has been made possible by the challenge to modern social science thrown out by Marx and his followers.

Britain succeeded Holland as the leading capitalist country of the world about the middle of the seventeenth century: the financial center of Western Europe moved from Amsterdam to London, and much of the trade of the Western world came to be carried in British rather than in Dutch ships.[4] Britain went on to become the first industrializing country of the world, and from 1815 to 1914 was the military, political, and economic leader of Western Europe and thus of the whole world.

India came under British political domination at the time Britain began to forge ahead of other countries in manufacturing and trade, and throughout the history of the "new" British empire and of British economic leadership of the world India had a "special relationship" with Britain: in L. H. Jenks' words, "It is India which has made the empire."[5]

The functions that India served in the British imperial scheme were intimately related to—in fact, were the direct or indirect cause of—the changes that India underwent during British rule. The first, and at the same time the most enduring, function was to provide a part of the surplus in the form of products or raw materials to be used in Britain for consumption or production, or for bullion, finished products, or raw materials to be traded for the products of other countries to be appropriated by Britain. During the major part of the rule by the East India Company the mode of appropriation of this surplus was plunder in one form or another.[6] The plunder took the form of (a) exaction of tributes in bullion or treasure or in the form of commodities; (b) purchase of products at lower-than-world market and Indian free market prices; and (c) use of the resources of conquered territories for further conquest in India. Some exploitation through "legitimate" trade and the development of commercial products such as indigo, opium, and sugar also took place. But the raising of these products by European planters very often involved extra-market coercion. In any case, during this phase the mechanism of exploitation remained primitive and the quantitative importance of exploitation through development or "free trade" was small compared with the later phases. The most striking results of such primitive exploitation are well known: famine, extensive depopulation, and reversion to more primitive modes of existence, including the destruction of urban centers.[7]

The second important function which India performed was to provide markets for British manufactures. The finding of a market for Britain's most important staple in the nineteenth century—cotton piecegoods—was accomplished in several stages. At first the British home market was barred against Indian cotton goods by means of prohibitive tariffs and regulatory measures typified by the sumptuary laws.[8] But Britain continued to serve as the major *entrepôt* for Indian cotton goods for Western Europe and the Western hemisphere. Meanwhile the conquest of India by the East India Company led gradually to a fall in the marketed output of Indian piecegoods because of (a) the discriminatory prices paid by the East India Company to Indian weavers; (b) the virtual cessation of purchasing by Indian rulers; and (c) internal tariff duties imposed against Indian goods. It should be noticed that Indian-woven cotton cloth remained competitive with British machine-made cloth well into the first two or three decades of the nineteenth century and that Indian hand-loom production had received a major setback through purely political and administrative measures adopted by the British government even before power-looms had ousted hand-looms in Britain (during the 1830s).[9]

These policies of state patronage were used by the British rulers to expand the market for British goods in India, just as they had been used earlier (in the seventeenth and eighteenth centuries) to bring Britain to the forefront of West European capitalism.[10] "Laissez faire" succeeded mercantilism as the ruling doctrine in Britain only when its rulers had achieved unchallenged predominance in the economic field. Even then this doctrine remained strictly selective in its application to India or to other colonies, as is shown by even a cursory examination of the policies actually pursued by the British government in India in the nineteenth century.[11] The use of state power by capitalist classes is the rule rather than the exception, and it was by denying that use to the Indian capitalists that Britain retained her economic hegemony in India for such a long time, as we shall presently see.

Before we move on to the next phase of the colonial story, we should note that, strictly speaking, the East India Company had not used any drastically new measures to thwart the hand-loom industry. Weavers were often paid lower-than-market rates by powerful patrons even in pre-British times; internal customs duties were levied throughout India in the seventeenth century. What the British rulers and traders did was to use these discriminatory practices with a deadly efficiency, unknown in pre-British India, and for goals that would have appeared extremely strange to Mughal or Maratha ruling groups.

Then, too, Britain was learning from India while at the same time slowly strangling the foreign trade in Indian piecegoods. The British trade in woolens had become practically stagnant by the middle of the eighteenth century, and in any case it would be futile to try to sell woolen textiles to the West Indies colonies or to West African slave suppliers. As a result, the expanding trade in cotton goods which was built up in conscious competition with the external trade in Indian piecegoods, following many of the technical devices adopted by Indian weavers and dyers, filled major gaps in the British trading network. But the pupil very soon surpassed the master: the motives or the organization for the technical innovations, and their fruition in fast-expanding foreign trade, were largely outside the purview of Indian society as it was then organized.

I believe that this problem of how a superior economic and social system interacts with a less advanced one should be studied far more intensively in future. The tendency has too often been to postulate a unilateral influence emanating from a superior system to the inferior one, and then to simplify the mode of that interaction even further by assuming that all the complexities of the less advanced system are somehow removed and the latter simply becomes a less developed image of the superior system. One of the most poignant lessons of colonialism is that the weaknesses of colonial societies can be ruthlessly exploited and preserved by the imperial country for its own advantage, and that colonial societies cannot become mirror images of the metropolitan societies so long as the colonial relationship persists.

The second phase of colonial relations between India and Britain lasted approximately from 1830 to 1914. For the purposes of our discussion we shall single out three main features characterizing this period: (1) the exploitation of India through public works; (2) the maintenance of a formal policy of free trade in India; and (3) the use of Indian export surpluses for the financing of transfers of capital and men from the European countries to the new colonies of the U.S.A., Australia, New Zealand, Canada, and South Africa.

Karl Marx wrote in 1853:

> There have been in Asia, generally, from immemorial times, but three departments of Government: that of Finance, or the plunder of the interior; that of War, or the plunder of the exterior; and finally, the department of Public Works. . . . Now, the British in East India accepted from their predecessors the department of finance and of war, but they have neglected entirely that of public works.[12]

The East India Company had started to remedy this defect by repairing old canals and digging new ones before 1853; but public works began in earnest with the building of railways with government guarantees after Lord James Ramsay Dalhousie, the Governor-General of India, had submitted the case for railway construction for military purposes. The story of railway development in India is well known. There is a certain ambivalence in the economic historians' assessment of the British record in India in this respect. It is admitted that many railways were unprofitable for a very long time and that almost until the very end of the nineteenth century India's government incurred a net financial loss on account of state railways. It is also admitted that because of the government policy of pampering British investors in Indian railways, there was an unduly large outflow of dividends and guaranteed interest payments.

Was all this financial loss, including loss of foreign exchange, perhaps overcompensated by social gain? After all, Indian external trade did expand at a rapid rate, and there did take place an increase in the output of many commercial crops. Against these gains, we should set the definite deterioration in the distribution of income among Indians and as between Indians and Europeans; the tendency toward an increase in the economic distance between the favored ports and the interior regions; the incalculable damage done to natural drainage systems and the creation of malarious swamps leading to extensive depopulation and enervation of vast masses of people; and the wastage of the capital resources that could have been used to develop alternative means of transport such as good roads or navigable canals that would be more immediately useful to a larger number of Indians. Above all, the capital resources could have been used to develop industry. As it was, the development of railways in India was not called forth by any prior economic growth in the country. It did not lead to the generation of new incomes from unemployed resources since a large part of the total expenditure was remitted abroad.[13] Finally, in most industrializing countries, probably the most notable impact of railway development lay in the development of capital goods industries and technological innovation in engineering: locomotive factories in England have, for example, been called "universities of mechanical engineering." [14] All these dynamic external effects of railway development were thwarted by British policy.[15]

By contrast with the development of railways, the development of irrigation works has met with almost unqualified approval from Indian nationalists and British officials alike. However, while the effect of canals in expanding the exportable surplus of food grains and commercial crops has been noticed, their effect in making the poorer strata of society ever more destitute and even more dependent on moneylenders, landlords, and the government has been overlooked. The forthcoming book by Elizabeth Whitcombe will fill a large gap by providing a detailed analysis of the impact of irrigation works on the North West Provinces and Oudh between 1860 and 1900.[16] The introduction of canals and of payment for irrigation facilities in money, and the continual enhancement of rents (assessed in money) in expectation of higher average yields, led to a shift of emphasis to the "better" food grains such as paddy and wheat and to commercial crops such as sugarcane, indigo, or cotton—and away from the millets which were the staple diet of the poorer sections of the people. In many areas the construction of canals without adequate drainage facilities led to extensive waterlogging and salinity, ultimately converting millions of acres of land into arid desert. The cultivator had no protection against such external diseconomies of canals. Even where waterlogging was not a menace, the easy availability of canal water in good years destroyed the careful husbandry of the small cultivator who very often used seasonally constructed *kutcha*[17] wells. In the years when there was an unexpected failure of rains and the canals could not supply water for the *kharif* [18] crops, there was total disaster—particularly in respect of staple food grains, since the best land was usually preempted for cultivation of indigo or sugarcane. The introduction of canals, combined with the intrusion of external demand, made extensive cultivation by large landowners profitable and, correspondingly, their exploitation of the landless strata of the small peasants more intense.

If there had been a large-scale development of industry, an increase in agricultural production would have supported such development and Indian cultivators would not have been so vulnerable to business cycles in advanced capitalist countries. The small cultivators or landless laborers could have been absorbed in industry and, with continued economic growth, could have escaped the tyranny of rural slums. But such a development would have been contrary to the basic interests of the ruling classes of Britain, and the maintenance of formal free trade or, rather, "one-way free trade" (in R. P. Dutt's words) provided the best guarantee against such a development.

The century from 1815 to 1914 has been characterized as the era of Pax Britannica and the era of the gold standard. In spite of large-scale failure of the Latin American countries to honor the loans granted them by private British investors at the time of liberation, in spite of the Crimean War, and the wars at the close of the nineteenth century to parcel out the Ottoman Empire and to partition Africa, there was remarkable stability in the international payments mechanism. This stability was maintained to a very large extent by "Britain's ability to maintain a deficit on her visible trade with one half of the world which she balanced by a surplus with the other half." [19] Britain's capability to generate surpluses was matched by her willingness to lend vast sums of capital to the new colonies, including the U.S.A., which for a long time had a balance-of-payments deficit with Britain. For this process to proceed smoothly, however, it was necessary that the countries linked to Britain through trade and investment should usually maintain an equilibrium in their balance of payments. In particular, Britain's deficits with other countries should be balanced by the surplus of some empire country (or countries) with the latter. This function was performed by India's export surplus with other countries, which was in turn matched by her deficit with Britain. In the first part of the century it was Indian opium sales to China which enabled Britain to square her accounts with the Heavenly Kingdom; later, Britain's cloth sales to China increased and Indian opium sales became more important for balancing the budget of the government of India than for balancing the imperial accounts. In the latter part of the nineteenth century, however, Indian exports to the U.S.A., to South American countries, and to Europe became crucial for financing British deficits with the U.S.A. and Europe.[20]

These trade relations were consonant with the international investment pattern that had developed in the nineteenth century, primarily centered on Britain. Britain built up foreign assets worth about £4,000 million by 1914,[21] with most of this investment concentrated in the U.S.A., Canada, Australia, New Zealand, and South Africa; India and nonwhite colonial countries generally received small fractions of this capital.[22] In fact, apart from the investment in railways and other public utilities of India, there had been very little net transfer of capital from Britain to India. Most of the net transfers of capital were made to countries to which white settlers migrated in substantial numbers. Thus the mechanism of international trade and investment in the nineteenth century was a powerful apparatus for mopping up the surpluses of today's undeveloped countries—particularly, India and China—in order to transport, feed, and equip the white settlers of the new colonies.[23]

But why did British capital migrate to the new colonies and not to India? The answer is twofold: racial affinity and prospects of industrialization. In the first place, India was already a densely populated country, and there was scant prospect of imposing a colony of white settlers permanently on the Indian population. In the second place, the U.S.A., and all the white colonies within the British empire, adopted all the measures of state patronage for the growth of industries—including a heavy dose of protection against British goods—which were denied to Indian industry in the name of free trade.[24]

The formal policy of free trade in India served to keep this external payments mechanism in trim. This policy helped to find markets for British manufactures: India became the largest market for Britain's exports of cotton goods, which in turn were the single most important item of British exports until almost the end of the nineteenth century. This was especially important because tariff barriers were coming up against the import of British manufactures into all the European and colonial countries ruled by white settlers. Furthermore, Britain had to keep alive a formal policy of free trade to prevent retaliation against exports of Indian goods in the hard currency areas, because, as we have noted, Indian export surpluses with such areas were vital for the smooth functioning of the imperial payments mechanism and of the gold standard. British administrators in India were fully aware of the importance of India in the imperial trading network. Thus D. T. Chadwick, of the Indian Civil Service (later Sir David Chadwick), wrote in 1917:

> . . . whilst India's purchases are mostly made inside the Empire, her sales are mostly outside the Empire. The importance, therefore, of foreign markets to India's trade is clear, and consequently the importance of these foreign markets to England's sales to India, because imports are paid for by exports.[25]

Such a policy of formal free trade and laissez faire did not prevent systematic discrimination in official policy in favor of British goods; nor did formal recognition of the equality of Indian subjects prevent the systematic practice of racial discrimination against Indians in respect of appointment to official positions or entry into profitable fields of enterprise—particularly in foreign trade, organized banking, and industry. These discriminatory policies, coupled with the lack of industrialization, thwarted the growth of entrepreneurial strata among the Indians—particularly in eastern, northern, and southern India—during the latter part of the nineteenth century.

It is against the background of this "special treatment" for India, when most of the West European countries and many of the new colonies were achieving industrialization, that the controversy of the "drain" acquires added significance.[26] There were disagreements between Indian nationalists such as Dadabhai Naoroji and Romesh Dutt, and British economists such as Sir Theodore Morison and J. M. Keynes, about the actual size of the drain.

By charging the loans made to the Indian government at the market rate of interest, and by capitalizing the assets owned by British citizens in India at the "normal" rate of interest and calculating their annual yields in perpetuity, the latter could show that the size of the "drain" was overestimated by the Indian nationalists. The

British economists, however, conveniently ignored the fact that the profits were made and assets were built up by British residents in India largely by deliberately excluding Indians from fields of foreign trade, organized banking, and such manufacturing industries as jute goods and engineering. In most of these fields, the needed skills could be relatively easily acquired and technical innovations were not rapid, so that the problem of keeping up with international competition was not overwhelming. Under such conditions the positions of privilege were maintained by British businessmen through the use of political means buttressed by an essentially racist ideology.

Hence it is legitimate to assume that but for such political barriers, Indians would have entered these fields easily and eliminated most of the profits made by the Europeans. In order to assess the loss to the Indian economy, we should estimate the (cumulative) difference, over time, between the actual output enjoyed by Indian citizens and the output they could have earned if India were allowed to pursue the same industrializing policies as Canada and Australia were pursuing and if the discrimination against Indians in government, business, and foreign trade could be ended. Obviously, such a difference would be far larger than the sum (over the same period) of the "drain" estimated by the usual methods.

During the period 1870–1914, among the modern industries in whose ownership the Indians had any important share, only the cotton mill industry grew, though rather slowly. Most of the growth occurred in the output of exportable agricultural commodities. In the absence of domestic industrialization, Indian producers of agricultural goods became extremely vulnerable to international business cycles: the so-called Great Depression of 1873–1896 had a very bad effect on the real incomes of Indian producers. With time, as the rate of growth of Indian national output remained low, the gap between potential output and actual output also grew.[27]

The fact that India failed to industrialize at the end of the nineteenth century had certain extremely important effects on the structure of the economy and society. I shall deal with what I consider to be the most damaging and most enduring result of this failure. With the growth of population, stagnation in industrial production, and the closure of the higher offices and more profitable occupations to upper class Indians, both the rich and the poor were made increasingly dependent on a single source of income: land. With the partial introduction of a market in land and the removal of many protective devices built into the traditional systems against the total separation of a cultivator from a permanent claim on the income of the land he tilled, a large number of people in rural areas found themselves unemployed for a large portion of the year. When private property in land had not been given precedence over all other social relations, the cultivator was guaranteed a minimum income either in absolute terms or as a fraction of total produce, in spite of underemployment or seasonal unemployment. (The *jajmani* system was one of many arrangements for such sharing of output.)

But with the introduction of money as the major medium of exchange and with the doctrine of saleability of all commodities including labor, this situation changed. Formally, there was pure competition among laborers and landlords: the landlords could get as many laborers as they wanted at the going wage. But in actual fact there was persistent disequilibrium in the labor market since a substantial fraction of the laborers (including people who owned very small plots of land) could not find employment throughout the year at the going wage. In this situation, obviously formal pure competition cannot persist: when a laborer finds that he cannot get a reasonable assurance of a job for most of the year at the market wage, he will opt out of the free market and bind himself to a landlord who will assure him the minimum customary income (which may be lower than the "subsistence wage") for the year or sometimes for his lifetime. Thus the ideally free market with pure competition degenerates into myriads of bargains between landlords and laborers or between moneylenders and indigent debtors, with the landlords and moneylenders holding the whip hand.

The British rulers, of course, derived some benefits from this situation: with the formal abolition of slavery, indentured laborers for Mauritius, Fiji, or Natal, or laborers for the tea plantations of Assam could be procured at wages that were lower than the going rate in the relatively prosperous agricultural areas of India, precisely because such laborers had been deprived of the security—however insubstantial in face of natural hazards or barbaric political systems—provided by the traditional social organization.

But the more permanent effect of this change—extensive underemployment among laborers and monopsonistic control of labor by rural landlords and moneylenders—is still with us today. The fact of the absence of real pure competition in rural labor markets has escaped many of our economists; hence production functions are being fitted and momentous policy conclusions drawn on the assumption that laborers are indeed free in rural India.[28] Competition among capitalists breeds the urge to improve production methods. The absence of competition in turn helps to keep a "slack" in the system, and capitalists can live like rentiers off the fat of the land. On the other side, since production methods do not change, except very slowly, it remains profitable to retain systems like crop-sharing and the employment of laborers as virtual serfs. Many European planters in Bihar found it profitable to turn into *zamindars* (big landlords who leased their lands to sharecropping tenants) when natural indigo failed in competition with artificial dyes. Again, Parry's of Madras, managing agents of the largest sugar mills in south India, found it more profitable to rent out land to peasants than to cultivate it themselves, using modern methods and large doses of fertilizers.[29]

When the upper classes were ousted from positions of profit and official power, they, too, were subjected to extensive unemployment and underemployment; the consequences are evident in absentee landlordism, the tremendous stress on security, the proliferation of public offices paying salaries, and the widespread practice of nepotism in business and administration. I am not implying that upper middle classes or professional classes in other countries have been free from such practices (see, for example, W. J. Reader's work on the "trade unionism" of the professional classes in England). But there is evidence that many older institutions—such as the Hindu joint family system—acquired a formal and legal rigidity under British rule which they did not have before. In most cases such rigidification was a defensive response; in some cases, as with the Chettiars, this was a measure to take advantage of the peculiar opportunities afforded under British rule.[30]

The second important effect of thwarted industrialization was the wastage of the investable surplus that was actually generated in the economy. Indian princes, landlords, and traders often bought gold and jewelry because there were no fields of industry in which their savings could be profitably invested. Of course gold and jewelry served other purposes as well, such as maintenance of status when real power had evaporated, conformity to traditional patterns of behavior, and so on. But we should not attribute conspicuous consumption or the hoarding of bullion only to rigidity in behavior patterns, particularly since we know that many wealthy Indian princes did invest heavily in industry when the opportunity for profitable investment in such a field presented itself.

In a situation in which nature was unpredictable and the government, the moneylender, and the landlord were going to exact their dues at predictable intervals, Indian peasants rightly bought bullion as the best hedge against uncertainty. Again, one can find supplementary motives for purchases of bullion, but the economic motive should be given its due importance. That Indians bought gold primarily as security against bad times was partly shown during the depression of the 1960s, when gold flowed out of India in vast quantities.

In the preceding analysis, I have not dealt directly with the influence of earlier, pre-British social organizations on later developments, nor have I discussed the deliberate administrative or political devices adopted by the British to keep precapitalist institutions alive. On the first score, I would merely plead ignorance. If the fact of creation of underemployment of formally free labor through colonial rule is granted, the deviation from the norm of pure competition in the labor market must follow. But the forms such deviations would take would depend both on the preexisting organization and on the precise legal provisions made by the colonial power.[31] On the second score, I would plead that the deliberate political and administrative decisions in preserving the precapitalist social structures have been overemphasized. It is often implied that without strenuous efforts to shore up precapitalist structures in India, they would have collapsed, and that the fact of colonial rule is no more relevant for a theory of stability of such structures than that the British had a misguided attitude of paternalism. Thus Barrington Moore, in a widely discussed book,[32] points out that India became a "landlords' paradise" under British rule, but he fails to bring in the influence of the economic aspects of colonial rule in preserving such a state of affairs: the implication is that the British had simply not been ruthless enough in destroying such structures. My contention is that, on the contrary, it is precisely because of the thwarting of industrialization in nineteenth-century India through colonial rule that absentee landlordism and all the tortuous features of the tyranny of the moneylender, trader, and landlord flourished there.

It should be pointed out—because the same phenomenon has continued to this day—that, within the imperial framework, India was exploited not only "in the long haul," through the thwarting of industrialization, but also through the more short-term mechanism of business cycles that originated in advanced capitalist countries. When the latter (particularly the British) suffered a crisis, the terms of international lending would be tightened, and the holding of stocks of primary commodities—mainly the produce of colonial countries—would become difficult. In general, for this reason alone, if for no other, in a recession the prices of raw materials would fall more than the prices of industrial products which formed the major part of Britain's exports. Hence the underdeveloped countries, including India, would suffer more than the industrialized countries through the instability of terms of trade of primary products.[33] Not only did such a mechanism operate over the usual eight- or nine-year cycles; it also operated over longer periods, as during the Great Depression (1873–1896). This period was also characterized by the virtual demonetization of silver bullion and coins—the main medium of exchange in India before the closing of the mints to the coinage of silver money. There is no sufficiently detailed and rigorous analysis of the movements of India's terms of trade during this period. But many indications point to the inference that the Great Depression helped the industrialized countries to acquire food and raw materials at lower prices and thereby increase the rate of transfer of real resources from the colonies to themselves, primarily at the cost of the nonwhite colonies of the Western countries.

The legal and administrative system which the British tried to introduce—making land as well as other assets fully saleable commodities under the principle of equity—was twisted by the twin stresses of the preexisting forms of use of power in society and the constriction of rural (and urban) society because of economic stagnation. In a more dynamic and more independent society, the laws would have been changed to suit the basic economic conditions; under actual Indian conditions, the British legal heritage remained to further impede the process of change until the present day.[34]

The third phase of India's relations with the advanced capitalist (and more recently, socialist) countries opened with World War I. In this phase its links with the erstwhile overlord of the capitalist world, the United Kingdom, were somewhat loosened, and India entered into a situation of multilateral dependence on the group of advanced capitalist countries. However, during the period 1914–1945, the pace of these changes in relationships was slow for three reasons: first, much of the interwar period was one of recession and instability for the capitalist world, so that the U.S.A., the new overlord, retreated into an isolationist position, at first politically and then economically as well. Second, as far as India and eastern and southern Asia were concerned, Britain was involved in a direct struggle for markets with Japan; hence, Britain seemed to be struggling not against the U.S.A. but against the "Asian power," Japan. As a result, the more important battle between the U.S.A. and the U.K. was often obscured. In the third place, during the depression of the thirties, the depression in the British economy seemed to offer an opportunity to Indian capitalists to acquire British-owned assets and gain economic independence. Therefore, in many respects the interwar period is best treated as a period of transition from the older types of relationships of unilateral dependence of India on Britain to the newer type of dependence on the advanced capitalist countries as a group, led by the U.S.A.

Even before World War I the U.S.A. had already emerged as the leading manufacturing nation; after the war, it also became the leading creditor nation. Britain lost a large fraction of its foreign investments as a result of the war, but hung on to all its political dependencies and managed to increase the size of its political empire. By means of a confidence trick in which the other capitalist countries acquiesced, British currency still remained the major international currency of exchange, although the dollar had come to be almost equally acceptable. This trick was played out during the crisis of September 1931, when Britain was forced to go off the gold standard and all the capitalist countries became involved in a series of devaluations and tried to use all the restrictions against imports of other countries that have ever been thought of, to the detriment of each other.[35] The foreign investments of the U.S.A. practically ceased after the onset of the depression of the thirties; as a result, in 1938 the accumulated foreign investments of the U.K. still exceeded those of the U.S.A.[36]

During the interwar period, the capitalist world was further shaken by the aftermath of the Bolshevik Revolution and the exit of Soviet Russia from a network of capitalist-imperial domination. As a result of these international developments and of internal political developments in India, India's position vis-à-vis Britain improved. It gained fiscal autonomy after World War I, and a policy of "discriminating protection" was adopted from 1924 on. Protective tariffs were used—albeit haltingly—to shelter some existing Indian industries against foreign competition. Tariff protection was not accompanied by other measures of state assistance on a significant scale; however, the "doldrums" of the 1920s were succeeded in 1929 by the worst depression the capitalist world has yet gone through. As a result, India's exports suffered badly and its terms of trade seriously deteriorated: in the 1930s, agricultural prices declined to a far greater extent than industrial prices. Hence, despite tariff protection for some Indian manufactures, the rate of industrial growth in India could not be high. But by the end of the 1930s India did achieve a fair degree of self-sufficiency in the manufacture of simple consumer goods and some producer goods, such as cotton cloth, sugar, matches, paper, cement, and steel.[37] Since the rate of growth of private and public demand was fairly low, India rarely suffered any balance-of-payments difficulties during the interwar period.

One of the consequences of the difficulties of the capitalist world during the interwar period was that India's value to British capital declined considerably. India could no longer supply the export surpluses to balance the imperial accounts with the rest of the world. India's place in this respect was taken by Malaya, whose tin and rubber now regularly helped Britain to square accounts with countries outside the sterling area.[38] The finances of the government of India were also frequently embarrassed during the 1920s: public investment—which before World War I generated demand for such products of British firms as railway locomotives, construction materials, and steel—rarely reached the prewar levels. In the early 1930s a large part of the British holdings of Indian government and railway securities was repatriated, thereby aggravating India's deficit on capital account but also reducing the expected future earnings of British investors from India.[39]

As far as British ownership of capital in existing private manufacturing, banking, and trading enterprises was concerned, there was probably little actual transfer of such ownership to Indians before the onset of World War II. But Indians began to invest on a much larger scale than the British in new enterprises and industries. As a result, their share in the industrial capital of the country increased. Indian capitalists also found the British government more responsive to their demands. (This responsiveness was directly stimulated by the growth of the freedom movement and by the need of the British to find allies among the wealthier classes in India.) Nevertheless the freedom of maneuver that the Indian capitalists achieved during this period proved to be transitory. Large international companies or cartels had already begun to dominate world capitalism, and India could not escape from their grip, particularly in fields in which advanced and rapidly changing technology had come to prevail. When India adopted protectionist policies, foreign companies found it profitable to set up branches and subsidiaries to defend their existing markets and to exploit the markets for domestic manufactures that were fostered behind the wall of protection. The Imperial Chemical Industries set up a manufacturing capacity in India at the end of the 1930s, and companies like General Motors set up assembly plants for cars. On the other side, Indian firms entering new fields of industry (such as the manufacture of textile machinery, or of railway locomotives, or their parts) sought the collaboration of foreign firms for plant design and process know-how, as well as the use of licenses and patents. Thus the stage of "dependent capitalism" was inaugurated in India in roughly the period from 1937 to 1946. From being a colony kept only to extract raw materials or sell primitive types of manufactured commodities, India graduated to become one of the outer satellites in the capitalist planetary system, with the United States as the central star.

It is often claimed that the world is going through a "second Industrial Revolution" and that newcomers are able to ride on the crest of a new wave of technical dynamism in the capitalist world. In reality, only the well-established capitalist nations, or small enclaves such as Hong Kong or Taiwan which act as supply depots for the American military establishment or as intermediaries in East-West trade, have been able to participate in this technical dynamism. Together with most of the capitalist countries of Asia, Africa, and Latin American, India continues to be in a position of unilateral economic subservience to the advanced capitalist countries. The racist ideology which underpinned and rationalized this subservience prior to World War II continues to perform its functions in excluding all the nonwhite nations except the Japanese (accorded an "honorary

Aryan" status by Hitler and an "honorary white" status by modern South Africa) from the white man's club of advanced capitalism.

The independence of India in 1947 did not mark a basic change in its relations with the advanced capitalist countries. It can be argued that the Indian National Congress led by Nehru *could have* taken a decisive step toward socialism in 1947; after all, this step was not taken. Indian capitalists emerged from World War II as a class with a far larger control over the existing means of production in the country. But they also emerged with a far lesser inhibition against collaboration with foreign firms; the entry of foreign capital was welcomed. Their class interests overcame their patriotic misgivings about domination by foreign capitalists, and no major conflict between the bigger Indian capitalists and foreign capitalists from advanced capitalist countries has surfaced until now.[40]

After a few years of dithering the government of India adopted a policy of encouraging private enterprise with all the means at its command. The main content of "planning" in India was increased government expenditure and manipulation of an apparatus of control, built up since the days of World War II, for guaranteeing domestic markets for Indian manufacturers (and Indian branches or subsidiaries of foreign firms). The government started its own manufacturing activities only in fields which were considered too risky by private enterprise, or which demanded larger volumes of capital than the private capitalists could mobilize. Private entrepreneurs—however much they might grumble or protest against "creeping socialism"—interpreted the government actions correctly and invested massively (by comparison with past standards), if not always in socially beneficial activities.

If these increased doses of private investment and government expenditure had been accompanied by a shaking of the foundations of precapitalist structures surviving in India, it is possible that India would have escaped the public humiliation of having to borrow to feed its millions and to carry on a rather unambitious development effort. But in the absence of a drastic increase in saving, in efficiency of operation, or in physical effort, India soon ran into serious balance-of-payments difficulties. The accumulated foreign exchange reserves were practically exhausted by 1959, and since then India has depended on loans from advanced capitalist and Soviet-bloc countries to meet persistent deficits in foreign trade accounts; many public declarations of intent notwithstanding, these deficits have tended to increase rather than diminish over time.[41]

The result of these deficits has been a steady erosion of India's bargaining strength vis-à-vis the debtor countries and international financial agencies; this has been reflected in unfavorable terms of lending and in direct or indirect pressure on India's economic policy exerted by creditor countries and international agencies. Over time, the proportion of grants to the total public foreign "aid" has declined, and the proportion of India's export earnings preempted for debt repayment and servicing obligations has increased. Furthermore, the utility of foreign loans to India has been diminished by various arrangements for tying aid to specific projects, to donor countries, and to technical or managerial assistance from donor countries. India's economic policy has been periodically checked by various International Monetary Fund and World Bank missions, and by other Wise Men from the West. Under pressure from the U.S. government and U.S.-controlled international agencies, the government of India has relaxed many controls on foreign investment. In June 1966 a reluctant government of India was more or less forced to devalue the rupee after American and World Bank "persuasion." [42] Such "pressures" or "persuasive" arguments have often been welcomed by top Indian capitalists who have profited by the leaders' insistence on allowing private enterprise to have fuller play.

Soviet-bloc assistance has played a countervailing role and has strengthened India's bargaining position vis-à-vis the advanced capitalist countries. The Soviet Union and its allies have provided assistance for the development of such key sectors as heavy engineering or machinery construction, for which Western assistance was either not available at all or available only on extremely unfavorable terms. The financial terms of Soviet assistance have been much better than those of Western aid, from India's point of view. The Soviet Union has also been willing to provide generous training facilities to Indians. Finally, through bilateral trade arrangements and through willingness to accept payment in rupees, East European countries have considerably lightened India's foreign exchange cost of repayment of foreign loans.

But Soviet assistance has been only a fraction—usually not more than a fifth—of the total foreign assistance extended to India. It has also not been available, and is not likely to be available, in one of the crucial areas where India's performance has been poor: food supply. Finally, in many fields of industry, the techniques available from the Soviet-bloc countries are obsolete compared with the techniques that can be imported from advanced capitalist countries; hence, if India is to develop sophisticated manufactures for export, she cannot rely solely on Soviet-bloc countries for the import of advanced technology.

India's increased dependence on foreign assistance for the supply of essential consumer and capital goods is connected intimately with her failure in domestic economic policy. While during the Second Five-Year Plan period there was an apparent redirection in the government's public investment strategy toward the development of heavy industries, this was not matched by any effective measures to increase the rate of savings of the economy. Nor did the government succeed in controlling total private consumer expenditure or its allocation between major types of consumer goods. Total demand in the economy and its division between major sectors were more dependent on private actions than on public intentions. The government succeeded neither in rousing the enthusiasm of ordinary people for growth and development nor in persuading the capitalists to save substantially larger shares of their increased income. Ordinary people remained illiterate, technologically backward, and without much motivation for a drive toward the betterment of their economic performance.[43]

A major reason for India's dependence on foreign aid has been her inability to raise agricultural production at such a rate that she becomes more or less self-sufficient in the production of agricultural commodities, including food grains. The sluggishness of Indian agricultural growth has been due not simply to the lack of new inputs or information, or to the lack of proper incentives to farmers, although these played an important part in the late 1950s and still continue to play a part—though a less important one. One basic difficulty has been that Indian farmers have not been acting within a purely competitive environment. The richer farmers, many of whom belong to old *zamindar* families or to prosperous professional or business families, have been able to act as monopsonists within the village and have been cushioned against the consequences of economic changes by this "monopolistic slack." The poorer farmers have been deprived of the resources on which they might have drawn in a more competitive environment, and the landless laborers have been practically without any defense against exploitation by the more substantial landowners. Furthermore, the feeble moves toward cooperation or communal effort have been thwarted by the power and greed of the richer groups, so that the abundant source of energy in underemployed rural labor has not been tapped. In this environment, the rapid enrichment of some of the more wealthy landowners through government subsidies and through the use of new varieties of seeds and technology, to the utter neglect of their social or ecological consequences, has caused widespread rural unrest and has arrested the spread of the admittedly patchy "green revolution." [44]

Suppose, however, that despite all these obstacles, the "green revolution" does lift Indian agriculture from stagnation, that a higher rate of saving and a higher degree of efficiency enable India to export more[45] and import less (in comparison with her national income); will India cease to be an outer satellite in the system of dependent capitalism? In order to answer this question we examine the role of large international corporations in India and the evolving relations between India and other underdeveloped countries of Africa and Asia.

In our study of the growing sectors of Indian manufacturing, we find that the participation of foreign firms in such sectors has grown rather than diminished over time. This is particularly true of machinery and machine tools, drugs, fertilizers, and petrochemical industries.

A survey of foreign collaboration agreements carried out by the Reserve Bank of India[46] yielded the information shown in Table 1. In the course of the same survey, data were collected regarding the payments of dividends, royalties, etc., solely to foreign companies by all companies (including public sector corporations, but excluding departmental undertakings and branches of foreign companies) with foreign collaboration agreements.[47] Figures on these payments are listed in Table 2.

It should be noted that although 1966–67 was a year of recession for Indian industry as a whole, the payments to foreign companies on dividends, etc., increased by a substantial margin that year. This is not just because of the usual jitteryness of foreign firms during acute recessions and balance-of-payments difficulties. Foreign firms have tended to be uniformly more profitable than Indian joint-stock

Table 1

Distribution of Companies with Technical Collaboration,
by Industry and Date of Incorporation

	Machinery and machine tools,		Chemicals and allied products,	
	1948–55	1956–64	1948–55	1956–64
Subsidiaries of foreign companies	1	14	5	11
Companies with minority foreign capital participation	3	37	12	31
Companies which have only technical collaboration arrangements with foreign companies	9	23	4	15

Table 2

Total Dividends, Royalties, Remittances and Other
Technical Collaboration
(Rs. millions)

1956–57	138	1962–63	382
1957–58	135	1963–64	362
1958–59	140	1964–65	449
1959–60	193	1965–66	447
1960–61	243	1966–67	626
1961–62	340		

companies in recent periods, and have improved their performance, particularly in industries like drugs and chemicals, during the recession period of 1966–1968.[48]

India has received a modest stream of private foreign capital from abroad in recent years, as is shown by the figures in Table 3.[49] The price of this foreign investment has been not only a high rate of profit (13–14 percent on an average) realized by branches or subsidiaries of foreign firms, but also a steady relaxation of controls over repatriation of capital, terms of foreign participation in Indian ven-

Table 3

*Long-term Foreign Business Investments from Abroad
into the Indian Private Sector*
(Rs. millions)

	Gross inflow	*Net inflow**
1963–64	1089	812
1964–65	1424	1056
1965–66	1122	671
1966–67	2404	1679
1967–68	1882	909

* The net inflow is almost certainly exaggerated by the overvaluation of foreign capital and undervaluation of the remittances from India. The 1966–67 figures are also affected by the devaluation of the Indian rupee.

tures, effective relaxation of controls over dividend rates and other types of payments, imposition of restrictions by foreign firms over exports from India, and so on. (Not only private but also state-owned enterprises have accepted such restrictions.) Sometimes, although there is a declared government policy against allowing foreign firms or big business houses in India to act in certain ways, actual decisions are taken in flat contradiction of such policies. This is best illustrated in the case of the decision of the government to license a fertilizer plant to be put up in Goa by the Birlas. In this instance the government has not only acted against the declared policy of not allowing the large industrial houses to further increase their controls over key industrial fields, but it has also allowed foreigners (U.S. Steel, International Finance Corporation, and some foreign banks) to acquire 65 percent of the equity holding of the company;[50] this last decision is against its declared policy of not allowing foreign capital to acquire the majority of the shares in joint ventures.

Further, the government has had to sanction foreign collaboration agreements, containing restrictive clauses, between private Indian companies and their foreign patrons. It has itself accepted restrictive clauses in the collaboration agreements between public sector enterprises and their foreign collaborators. Thus, in the survey of foreign collaboration agreements carried out by the Reserve Bank of India, it was found that out of 70 foreign collaboration agreements entered into by government companies, 38 had restrictive clauses, of which 35 were restrictions related to exports.[51] The government is now engaged in seeking foreign collaborators in a large number of public sector enterprises, particularly in the petrochemicals field.

If India remains primarily a private enterprise economy, with or without a substantial public sector, its gains or losses from international economic relations will be mainly dependent on the performance of Indian industrial corporations vis-à-vis foreign international corporations. If Indian corporations are to do well in the world trade in manufactures, they should be able to generate a high rate of technical progress either through research carried out in India or through an efficient exploitation of techniques developed in other countries. India's present social structure and its associated characteristics—a low rate of literacy, a hierarchical system of transmission of information, and a low degree of social mobility—are inimical to the generation of new techniques.

In order for Indian entrepreneurs to import new techniques from abroad (by buying up or leasing patents or obtaining licenses for the use of know-how) and exploit them courageously, the economy must grow quickly; and entrepreneurs should look to foreign markets whenever home demand tends to falter and try to keep the supply lines for these markets clear even in the face of mounting home demand for exportables, and they should save and invest at high rates so that they are not held back by frequent shortages of capacity.[52] Since all these desirable traits have been conspicuously missing in the performance of the Indian economy since independence, there is every reason to believe that Indian firms will remain as dependent as ever on foreign firms for their technology and for the development of their capital stock and their markets, particularly in the field of sophisticated manufactures. This dependence will, of course, be all the more abject if India also suffers from recurring balance-of-payments deficits.

The lines of escape from this labyrinth which suggest themselves all prove to be of little use. The first escape route is through the fraternal aid of Soviet-bloc countries. This help cannot in the long run put the Indian economy on a self-reliant path because it cannot correct the growth-arresting behavior of Indian society: neither literacy, nor diffusion of knowledge, nor the performance of the bureaucracy, nor the rate of saving and investment can be altered by Soviet-bloc assistance unless the Soviet authorities start out to engineer a social revolution in India. This last alternative is ruled out both by the unwillingness of the Soviet government to engage in such a dangerous game and by the improbability of its success were they foolhardy enough to try it. There is another weighty reason why Soviet assistance cannot rescue Indian capitalism from dominance by international finance capital, supported by international managerial and technocratic capital. The Soviet-bloc countries themselves have failed to evolve a set of socialist rules of international trade, and they find the restrictions imposed by bilateral trade agreements and other bureaucratic arrangements increasingly irksome.[53] In consonance with the dominance of managerial cadres in the guidance of these economies, their foreign economic relations are increasingly converging to the pattern set by Western capitalist nations. The Soviet Union provides the leadership in this process of "rationalization" of their international economic relations by bypassing bilateral arrangements in favor of various arbitrage operations, and by setting up international corporations (including banking and trading corporations) on its own or in cooperation with companies based in other advanced or backward capitalist countries.[54] The U.S.S.R. has now started to use all the instruments usually wielded by international corporations based in advanced capitalist countries to further its own economic interests in competition with the latter, and to the detriment of the economic independence of the backward capitalist countries it helps.[55] In this situation, the relation of Indian private firms (or public sector enterprises) with international corporations or departmental agencies based in Soviet-bloc countries will approximate more and more the pattern of relations between firms of less developed and more developed capitalist countries.

The second possible line of defense of Indian firms against domination by international corporations based in advanced capitalist countries is for Indian firms to operate in countries that are even less developed industrially than India or are too small to develop manufacturing facilities of every kind. This could be accompanied by an expansion of India's exports to these less advanced countries. In the recent past, India's exports to the less developed countries of Africa and Asia have expanded faster than its exports to other countries. Agreements have been entered into with countries like Iran and

Mauritius for joint ventures there. The Birlas are stated to have put up plants in several countries of Africa and Asia.[56]

Nevertheless, these developments have been very limited and do not promise to be either far-reaching or long-lasting. In the first place, these less developed countries are eager to develop facilities of manufacture in precisely the fields in which India presently enjoys an advantage. In order to be able to continue as foreign investors in these ventures, at least two conditions must be satisfied: India should be able to supply technology and managerial skill which are not noticeably inferior to what is available from more advanced countries. Secondly, India must have the capital to export in right quantities. India at the moment enjoys an export surplus with several of these less advanced or smaller countries. This would have been an advantage if the two above-mentioned conditions had been satisfied. But as things are developing, India's balance-of-payments deficit with more advanced countries is far larger than its balance-of-payments surplus with the less developed countries, and hence it cannot afford to convert its export surpluses with these less developed (or smaller) countries into foreign investments. Even if India were prepared to do so, the technology it would be able to provide would be unlikely to meet the requirements of its trade partners in all fields.

India's ability to pursue such schemes of foreign investment in Asian and African countries is further constricted by its weak bargaining strength in relation to its creditors, as well as by the reemergence of Japan as a dominant economic and political power in Asia. The World Bank has already frowned publicly on Indian joint ventures abroad,[57] and other foreign creditors are likely to be even less benign about India's foreign investment projects whenever they encroach on their preserves. Even if the American and West European powers were inclined to encourage India's sub-imperial ambitions in Asia as a measure of defense of the "free world" in the East, Japan has emerged effectively to crush all such ambitions. Japan's Gross National Product is now only second to that of the U.S.A. among the advanced capitalist countries; its national income is expanding at the fantastic rate of more than 10 percent per year, and its foreign trade is expanding even more rapidly. It has become either the largest or the second largest source of imports or destination of exports for Burma, Iran, Malaysia, the Philippines, Singapore, Thailand,

Taiwan, South Vietnam, South Korea, and Australia.[58] Japan enjoys an export surplus with many of these countries, but is prepared to help its debtors with massive increases of foreign "aid" through the Asian Development Bank, through private investment in those countries, and through bilateral government agreements; Japan is also now prepared to shoulder "political responsibility"[59] to match its economic power. The Asian Development Bank is specifically designed as a vehicle for the realization of Japan's aims of dominating the field of aid to the smaller Asian countries.[60] India is the second largest contributor to the funds of this bank, but has not been able to take a leading part in its affairs. Japan has already displaced India as one of the five countries with a right to nominate an executive director of the IMF, and India will now have to put its candidate to the electoral test just like the other ordinary members of the IMF.

If India's performance in the economic field continues to be as disappointing as it was in the 1960s, its ability to exploit smaller or less developed countries will be even further impaired. Countries like Malaysia, Thailand, Iran, or Taiwan, with faster rates of growth than India and with higher initial per capita incomes, will demand more and more sophisticated consumer goods (and producer goods) and will turn to countries like the U.S.A., Japan, Germany, or Italy, which are able to lead the capitalist world in the development of new commodities and techniques. Thus, if the present trends continue, India will lose further instead of doing better in these countries.

India can escape its fate of helotry to the advanced capitalist countries by effecting a thoroughgoing socialist revolution and shooting out of the capitalist orbit. Otherwise, the economic dominance of advanced capitalist countries, spearheaded by large international corporations, over India's economic life is likely to grow rather than decline. Large and small Indian business houses will be compelled to collaborate with these international corporations for access to advanced technology, modern management, and growing markets. These international corporations are "international" only as regards their field of operation; most of the giant international corporations are firmly controlled by their home boards, and the degree of centralization of management has increased rather than diminished in recent years.[61]

Paradoxically enough, a limited degree of success of the Indian economy in freeing itself from the burden of official foreign debt is

likely to lead to a greater degree of thralldom of modern Indian industry to international business houses. As the pressure on balance of
payments eases, there will be increasing pressure on the government,
both from domestic and foreign business houses, to lift the controls on
the inflow or outflow of funds into or from India, and the attractive-
ness of India as a field for investment by foreign firms will also increase. In the "natural" course of things, because of their superior
technology and superior management methods and, above all, because of vast financial superiority, international business corporations will acquire a larger and larger share of Indian industry. The
alternative to that development, within the present socio-political
system, is an economy saddled with bureaucratic controls at every
stage. The only thing that can be said in favor of such an economy is
perhaps that it will not be as efficient in oppressing the people as the
American ideal of a progressive, free enterprise economy could be.

Notes

1. R. Palme Dutt, *India Today* (Bombay, 1949).
2. Ibid., p. 108.
3. J. A. Schumpeter, *Capitalism, Socialism and Democracy* (London, 1966),
   Chapter VII.
4. See Charles H. Wilson, "The Economic Decline of the Netherlands," in
   E. M. Carus-Wilson (ed.), *Essays in Economic History*, I (London, 1963),
   pp. 254–269; Charles H. Wilson, *England's Apprenticeship, 1603–1763*
   (London, 1965).
5. L. H. Jenks, *The Migration of British Capital to 1875* (first published in
   1927; reprinted in London, 1963), p. 206.
6. Maurice Dobb, in Chapter 5 of his *Studies in the Development of Capitalism*
   (London, 1963), discusses the mercantilist policies that were pursued by
   capitalist countries during the period of primitive accumulation.
7. There are differences of opinion among economic historians about the
   importance of India as a source of capital for Britain during the period
   of the Industrial Revolution. But there is general agreement that profits
   of foreign "trade" with India and with other British colonies were one of
   the most significant sources of capital and that expanding trade in trop-
   ical produce was one of the major dynamic forces propelling economic
   growth. See, in this connection, P. Deane and W. A. Cole, *British Economic Growth 1688–1959* (second edition, Cambridge, 1967), Table 22; P.
   Deane, *The First Industrial Revolution* (Cambridge, 1965), Chapter 4; and
   E. Hobsbawn, *Industry and Empire* (London, 1968). It appears from Table

22 in Deane and Cole, op. cit., that throughout the period 1722–1723 to 1797–1798, Britain had a huge import surplus with East India—this is what one would expect when exploitation took the form of unreimbursed imports.

8. See P. J. Thomas, *Mercantilism and East India Trade* (London, 1926; reprinted in London, 1968), chapters III and V–VIII; also R. P. Dutt, *The Economic History of India Under Early British Rule* (London, 1906), Chapter XIV.

9. See, in this connection, J. G. Borpujari, *The British Impact on the Indian Cotton Textile Industry 1757–1865* (Ph.D. thesis submitted to the University of Cambridge, 1969).

10. Charles Wilson, op. cit., p. x.

11. Sabyasachi Bhattacharya, "Laissez Faire in India," *The Indian Economic and Social History Review*, January 1965.

12. Karl Marx, "The British Rule in India," written on June 10, 1853, published in the *New York Daily Tribune*, June 25, 1853, and reprinted in Karl Marx and Frederick Engels, *On Colonialism* (Foreign Languages Publishing House, Moscow), p. 33.

13. "More than one-third of the capital invested in Indian railways down to the early eighties was spent in England for railway iron and the cost of its importation to the East. The importation of coal from England and the building and operation of railways with staffs which were English from foremen up and who had to be paid according to English standards, diminished further the benefits which could accrue to Indians from railways" (Jenks, *The Migration of British Capital to 1875*, pp. 227–228).

14. S. B. Saul, "The Engineering Industry," in D. H. Aldcroft (ed.), *The Development of British Industry and Foreign Competition, 1885–1914* (London, 1968).

15. Jenks summarizes: "Again the remittance of capital for railways in India did not take the form of consumers goods. It did not follow upon a manifested rise in the standard of living. And it did not call to life in India a vigorous industry to provide structural materials" (Jenks, op. cit., p. 227).

16. E. M. Whitcombe, *Agrarian Conditions in North West Provinces and Oudh, 1860–1900* (Ph.D. thesis, London University, 1968).

17. Unfinished, roughly constructed; in the case of wells, lacking masonry work.

18. Summer crops, harvested in September.

19. Charles Wilson, "Economic Conditions," in F. H. Hinsley (ed.), *New Cambridge Modern History.* XI: *Material Progress and World-Wide Problems: 1870–1888* (Cambridge, 1967), p. 55.

20. S. B. Saul, *Studies in British Overseas Trade* (Liverpool University Press, 1960), chapters III and IV.

21. A. H. Imlah, *Economic Elements in the Pax Britannica* (Harvard University Press, Cambridge, Mass., 1958).

22. See Brinley Thomas, "The Historical Record of Capital Movements to 1913," and Matthew Simon, "The Pattern of New British Portfolio Investment 1865–1914," in J. H. Adler (ed.), *Capital Movements and Economic Development* (London, 1967), pp. 3–32 and 33–36, respectively.

23. See, in this connection, C. K. Hobson, *The Export of Capital* (London, 1914), pp. xiv–xv, and Brinley Thomas, "Migration and International Investment," in B. Thomas (ed.), *Economics of International Migration* (London, 1958), pp. 3–16.

24. See, for example, H. G. J. Aitkin, *The State and Economic Growth* (New York, 1959).

25. D. T. Chadwick, "The Trade of India with Russia, France and Italy," *Journal of the Royal Society of Arts*, December 28, 1917, p. 97.

26. For a summary of the controversy, see Bipan Chandra, *The Rise and Growth of Economic Nationalism in India* (New Delhi, 1966), Chapter XIII, "The Drain," pp. 636–708. For Keynes' view, see his review of Morison's *Economic Transition in India* (London, 1911) in *Economic Journal*, September 1911, pp. 426–431.

27. From the summary account given by Bipan Chandra it appears that Indian nationalists stressed the drain of investable capital through remittances of British citizens from India and official remittances for Home Charges, and talked about the compulsory sale of Indian exports so as to lead to fluctuations in terms of trade; but they did not question the whole framework of British economic policy leading to the thwarting of indigenous entrepreneurship, the spread of knowledge, and technical inventions of all kinds.

28. For an exception, see Daniel Thorner, "Employer-Labour Relations in Indian Agriculture," in Daniel and Alice Thorner, *Land and Labour in India* (Bombay, 1962).

29. See Indian Tariff Board, *Oral Evidence on the Sugar Industry*, Vol. IV (Delhi, 1938), p. 126.

30. Compare the description of how important Chettiar families changed from a system of individual ownership to one of joint-family ownership of property in Shoji Ito, "A Note on the 'Business Combine' in India," *The Developing Economies* (Tokyo), Vol. IV, No. 3, 1966.

31. Dr. Elizabeth Whitcombe, in the thesis cited earlier, has discussed many forms of such deviations both in the market for labor and in the market for land in the context of Uttar Pradesh in the nineteenth century.

32. Barrington Moore, Jr., *Social Origins of Dictatorship and Democracy* (London, 1967).

33. See R. Triffin, "The Myth and Realities of the So-called Gold Stand-

ard," in R. N. Cooper (ed.), *International Finance* (Penguin Books, Harmondsworth, Middlesex, 1969), pp. 38–61.

34. See E. M. Whitcombe, op. cit., chapters IV, V, and VI, for a thorough discussion of how the British legal system introduced its own distortions into the prevailing social conditions. Dr. Whitcombe stresses that the unimpeded working of the law of equity often came into conflict with the political desideratum of preserving the landowning classes from the consequences of their own extravagance, mismanagement of estates, and the working of the new laws relating to indebtedness. Very often the estates were sold under the laws of debt and then restored to the previous owners through the working of Courts of Wards and other protective devices set up by the British Administrators. For an extremely illuminating comparison of the interaction of legal and economic factors in Britain and Ireland (whose position in many respects resembled India's), see E. Halevy, *England in 1815* (London, 1960), pp. 205–255.

35. See League of Nations (Ragnar Nurkse and W. A. Brown, Jr.), *International Currency Experience (1944)*; also R. Triffin, "The Thrust of History in International Monetary Reform," *Foreign Affairs*, April 1969, pp. 477–492.

36. See William Woodruff, *The Impact of Western Man* (London, 1966), Chapter IV and tables IV/1–IV/4.

37. On the growth of private investment in India, see my book, *Private Investment in India, 1900–1939* (Cambridge University Press, 1972), Chapter 3.

38. See A. E. Kahn, *Great Britain in the World Economy* (New York, 1946), chapters XI–XV.

39. On foreign, mainly British, investments in India during the interwar period, see A. K. Banerjee, *India's Balance of Payments* (Bombay, 1963), chapters 5 and 6.

40. See Michael Kidron, *Foreign Investments in India* (London, 1965), chapters I and IV.

41. This situation has changed slightly in 1970–71, but the smaller deficit in the balance of payments may have been bought at the cost of a lower rate of industrial growth. I have examined the problems connected with inflows of foreign capital into India in greater detail in my paper, "Aid Models and Inflows of Foreign Aid," *Economic and Political Weekly*, Annual Number 1970 (Vol. V, Nos. 3, 4, and 5), pp. 223–234.

42. Kuldip Nayar, who was at the time Information Officer of the Prime Minister of India, documents this open secret in *Between the Lines* (Allied Publishers, Bombay and Calcutta, 1969), Chapter III. While Indian officials have alleged that there was an implicit promise that American aid would flow again if the rupee were devalued, American officials have denied this. Understandably, Indian politicians have not been keen to air their grievances in public.

43. The basic reasons for the failure of the Mahalanobis strategy in India have been analyzed in my paper, "Long-term Constraints on India's Industrial Growth 1951–68," in E. A. G. Robinson and M. Kidron (eds.), *Economic Development in South Asia* (London, 1970).

44. For discussion of the factors operating against the spread of the "green revolution" and its likely effects in terms of social and political disparities between rich and poor farmers, see *Report of the Agricultural Prices Commission on Price Policy for Kharif Cereals for the 1968–69 Season* (New Delhi, September 1968), pp. 3–5; Clifton R. Wharton, Jr., "The Green Revolution: Cornucopia or Pandora's Box?", *Foreign Affairs*, April 1969, pp. 464–476; and W. Ladejinsky: "Green Revolution in Bihar, the Kosi Area: A Field Trip," *Economic and Political Weekly*, Review of Agriculture, September 1969, pp. A147–A162.

45. As a result mainly of the industrial recession and partly of the export promotion measures taken after devaluation, Indian exports rose by 13.5 percent in 1968–69 over 1967–68 (the export earnings in 1967–68 in terms of foreign exchange were only marginally higher than the annual average recorded during the Third Five-Year Plan period). However, in 1969–70 the rate of growth of exports was very small, falling to 1.5 percent per annum or less. See Government of India, *Economic Survey 1969–70* (Delhi, 1970), pp. 46–51; *Economic Times*, March 18 and 20, 1970.

46. *Foreign Collaboration in Indian Industry: Survey Report* (Reserve Bank of India, Bombay, 1968).

47. Ibid., p. 9.

48. "Finances of Branches of Foreign Companies and Foreign-Controlled Rupee Companies, 1963–64," *Reserve Bank of India Bulletin*, July 1966, pp. 732–746; "Finances of Branches of Foreign Companies and Foreign-Controlled Rupee Companies, 1965–66," ibid., June 1968, pp. 737–753.

49. "India's International Investment Position in 1965–66 and 1966–67," *Reserve Bank of India Bulletin*, August 1969, pp. 1121–1161, Table 3 (p. 1131); "India's International Investment Position in 1967–68," ibid., March 1971, p. 358.

50. See *The Statesman* (Calcutta), January 2, 1970.

51. *Foreign Collaboration in Indian Industry*, p. 97.

52. Some of the factors governing the rates of growth of modern industrial economies and their export markets are brought out in N. Kaldor, *Causes of the Slow Rate of Economic Growth of the United Kingdom: An Inaugural Lecture* (Cambridge University Press, 1966), and in R. Vernon, "International Investment and International Trade in the Product Cycle," *Quarterly Journal of Economics*, May 1966, pp. 190–207.

53. Yugoslavia was the first East European country to walk out of rupee trade arrangements with India, insisting on payments in hard currency in future (*Economic Times*, March 7, 1970).

54. There have already been allegations that bilateral trade agreements have been used by Soviet-bloc countries to resell Indian products abroad, thus deposing Indian export prices.

55. See Marshall I. Goldman, "The East Reaches for Markets," *Foreign Affairs*, July 1969, pp. 721–734.

56. *Economic Times*, February 20, 1970.

57. Ibid., June 26 and 27, 1969.

58. See *U.N. Economic Survey of Asia and the Far East 1968* (Bangkok, 1969), "Asian Economic Statistics," Table 20.

59. See Kiichi Aichi (Japanese Minister for Foreign Affairs), "Japan's Legacy and Destiny of Change," *Foreign Affairs*, October 1969, pp. 21–38. See also *Economic Times*, April 17, 1969 ("Japan Offers to Double Aid to ECAFE Countries"), and March 29, 1970 ("Japan's Bid to Become Top Aid-Giver").

60. See the articles by T. Edwin on the Asian Development Bank in *Economic Times*, April 18 and April 20, 1969.

61. See Raymond Vernon, "Economic Sovereignty at Bay," *Foreign Affairs*, October 1969, pp. 110–112.

3. The Green Revolution in India: Prelude to a Red One?

Hari P. Sharma

So startling have been the achievements of the "green revolution" in recent years in India and other Asian countries that the 1970 Nobel Peace Prize was awarded to Dr. Norman E. Borlaug[1] for his "remarkable contribution to the enlargement of the world's food supply, particularly in underdeveloped nations." The implication is that food and peace go together, as Dr. Borlaug himself has remarked.[2] Yet peace is hardly the crop being harvested in the fields of India. Besides the increased amount of food produced by the green revolution, there is a growing amount and intensity of political polarization along class dimensions. The twin effects are mentioned by an American observer, Clifton R. Wharton, Jr., who calls the green revolution, on the one hand, a cornucopia which is "believed to have lifted the spectre of famine in the immediate future and to have postponed the prospect of Malthusian population disaster," and, on the other, a Pandora's box whose "very success will produce a number of new problems which are far more subtle and difficult than those faced during the development of new technology." [3]

Let us note first the achievements, and postpone the "problematic" aspects until later. To quote Dr. Borlaug, "Never before in the history of agriculture has a transplantation of high-yielding varieties coupled with an entirely new technology and strategy been achieved on such a massive scale, in so short a period of time, and with such great success." [4] In India the High-Yielding Varieties Program (HYVP) began in 1965 under the "new strategy in agriculture" of the Union (i.e., central government) Food and Agriculture Ministry.

This is a revised version of a paper originally presented at a conference on "Asia in the 1970s: Problems and Prospects," held November 12–13, 1971, at Carleton University, Ottawa. I am grateful to Kathleen Gough and Martha Gimenez for their many valuable comments on an earlier draft.

Limited experiments with the dwarf Mexican variety of wheat had already been conducted during the two previous years, and a model for the new strategy existed in fifteen districts distributed throughout India, where an Intensive Agricultural Development Program (IADP) had been started by the Ford Foundation in 1961. In 1965, 250 tons of seed of Mexican dwarf wheat varieties were imported. By the end of the decade the HYVP Program had been extended to large parts of India and included, in addition to wheat, the production of rice, maize, and several varieties of Indian millet. The results were visible in output figures: as against the pre-green revolution record crop of 12.3 million tons of wheat in 1964–65, production rose to 16.5, 18.7, and 20.0 million tons during the 1968, 1969, and 1970 harvests, respectively.[5] Although less spectacular, significant improvements have been recorded in such cereals as paddy and maize. Consequently, the total food grain production rose from 88.4 million tons in 1964–65 (a record year) to an estimated 106 million tons in 1970–71.[6] At this rate, India should be self-sufficient for food within a year or two.[7]

High-yielding varieties of seeds require increased amounts of chemical fertilizers and water and foster new agricultural operations. For example, the consumption of nitrogen increased from 538,000 metric tons in 1964–65 to 1.2 million metric tons in 1969–70. A total of 70,000 private tube wells was reported to have been sunk in 1969–70 alone. In 1968 unsold tractors accumulated at the two factories in production, but in 1970 prospective purchasers were required to make written application and wait one or two years for delivery. Five factories now produce some 18,000 tractors per year; 35,000 additional tractors were imported in 1969–70.[8] Consumption of pesticides increased from 10,304 tons in 1961–62 to 28,200 tons in 1968–69.[9]

Details from particular districts highlight the magnitude of the change. Thus a USAID-sponsored study of Ludhiana district in the Punjab records:

> Between the pre-package year of 1960–61 and 1968–69, the area under irrigation increased from 45 percent to 70 percent, mainly as the result of the rapid installation of tube wells. Again, between 1960–61 and 1967–68, consumption of fertilizers increased more than thirteen times, from 8 kilograms to 110 kilograms per cultivated acre. More

dramatic still, in the short period between 1965–66 and 1968–69, the acreage under the new Mexican dwarf varieties expanded from a minuscule 170 acres to an overwhelming 420,000 acres, or an area accounting for 90 percent of the total acreage under wheat. Finally, and the surest measure of success, yields per acre in Ludhiana increased from an average of 16.9 maunds [a maund equals approximately 82 lbs.] in 1960–61 to over 40 maunds in 1968–69, that is, by over 120 percent.[10]

Because of the above-average size of the landholdings and other favorable conditions in Ludhiana, it is an atypical district; yet the same USAID study in four other districts (in the states of Andhra Pradesh, Tamil Nadu, Kerala, and West Bengal) reported similar, if more modest, progress in agricultural productivity.[11]

For decades, using cultural variables to disguise their ideologies, apologists for imperialism have been describing the Indian peasantry (and the peasantry of other developing societies) by reference to such characteristics as ineptitude, passivity, lethargy, religiosity, traditionalism, lack of the Protestant ethic, etc. In a few short years, however, the peasants of India have transcended their "cultural milieu" to make a major breakthrough in productivity. Just as cultural factors cannot explain the present shifts in the economic behavior of the peasantry, it was—and to a certain extent still is—a mistake, if not an outright ideological camouflage, to attribute India's underdevelopment to the cultural traits of its people.

The question, however, remains: why did the breakthrough occur at the time it did? After all, the government in India had been systematically trying to affect agricultural productivity since 1952, when community development and agricultural extension programs were instituted. Thousands of government-employed village-level workers all over India were pleading with farmers, with little if any success, to adopt new and better seeds, fertilizers, improved implements, etc. Even increased irrigation facilities were reported to have been unused or underutilized. Numerous U.S. teams of experts, under one auspice or another, came and went; yet agriculture remained stagnant.[12] Why, then, the sudden spurt in the second half of the 1960s? To attribute this development to a sudden technological breakthrough, as is often done, is overly simplistic. Here it is not necessary to go into the well-known debate as to whether it is technology which drives economic forces, or the economic and social institutions (as expressed in the relations and forces of production and their mutual interaction) which necessitate and facilitate technological innovations. The simple fact is that the "new" technology supposedly underlying the present agricultural revolution in India is hardly new. Most of the new inputs, including the Mexican dwarf varieties of wheat, have been known for quite some time to Indian agricultural experts, who have also been trying to introduce them to Indian farmers. The green revolution in India has occurred not because of the *introduction* of new technology, but because of the *acceptance* of new technology by the farmers. And this acceptance owes little, if anything, to the numerous social scientists, Indian and American, who for two decades have been engaged in research on the so-called diffusion process, identifying crucial variables—cultural or otherwise—which affected the process. The answer lies rather in the institutional and structural shifts which Indian rural society has been undergoing in the past two decades and which have created the prerequisites for the Indian peasantry, or for at least a section of it, to stage the present breakthrough.

Before we attempt an examination of these shifts, however, let us turn to the other, "problematic" aspect of the green revolution. Later we shall see that what lies behind its success is exactly what is creating the so-called new problems.

While much-needed extra food is being produced by the green revolution, it is certainly not producing peace. About the time agricultural fields turned greener and harvested crops bulkier, social relations grew tenser. Peace and harmony were hardly ever the salient features of Indian village society, the many idealized and romanticized accounts notwithstanding; but what emerged in the late sixties was both qualitatively and quantitatively different. Unlike the traditional village-based conflicts between factions within the dominant landowning groups, which involved localized symbols of power and prestige, the new conflicts emerged along class lines. Not that class conflict has been unknown to the Indian peasantry; weaker, exploited sections in rural India have risen repeatedly against their oppressors. With some notable exceptions, however, these peasant uprisings have lacked cohesive leadership and class ideology.

A nationally cohesive political leadership is perhaps still lacking, yet the present rural unrest is unmistakably distinguished by its massive scale and militant overtones. The now well-known peasant uprising in Naxalbari in 1967 was a symptomatic outburst which set the tone and character of things to come. From one harvest to the next, from one part of the country to another, the unrest spread. It took various forms: Gandhian *satyagrahas* (acts of nonviolent civil disobedience), massive land-grab marches, forceful seizures of harvested crops, unionized demands for higher wages and, increasingly, the physical annihilation of landlords. The form varied, the content was the same; and in the process the line of demarcation became clearer. The other side—landlords, rich peasants, rentiers, paymasters—responded differently, depending upon their strength and organization. Sometimes they fled to the cities, to return only when their allies in the state apparatus (the police, the army) made it safe for them to do so. At other times they retaliated with force. In the village of Venmani in East Thanjavur, for example, they attacked the landless laborers' hamlet at midnight. Shooting into the air, they forced everybody out of his or her house, pushed as many as they could into a single hut, and set fire to it. Forty-four people—men, women, and children—were burnt alive while the jubilant landlords stood guard to prevent anyone from escaping.[13]

The Venmani incident was unusual only in terms of its brutality and the size of its toll.[14] Armed attacks by the landlords and moneylords have increased in frequency as the farm laborers have become increasingly organized and militant. Much of the initial impetus has come from West Bengal, Kerala, Andhra Pradesh, and Tamil Nadu, but such class confrontations are no longer confined to these traditional regions of Left influence or to the economically more depressed areas. They have gradually spread to practically every state in the country. Even in the Punjab, where the ratio of agricultural laborers to landowners is among the lowest, there has been a sharp increase in open hostility between upper-caste landowners and Harijan laborers. Many cases have been reported of attacks against Harijans by thugs hired by the landlords.[15] In some areas the landlords have not even needed to hire thugs; the local police force, all too willing and just as thorough, has done the job. Nor has the repressive role of the state been limited to the use of the police force. In the last few years thousands of military and paramilitary troops have been deployed to many parts of India to engage in "search and destroy" missions to maintain "law and order."

So pervasive has been the change in the political climate of rural India that only the most naive would ignore it. Violent confrontations have become so commonplace that the daily newspapers now report them in a most matter-of-fact and perfunctory fashion, often as small news items in obscure columns. Yet hardly a week goes by in which some such incident is not reported.

Perhaps it would be too much to say that rural India as a whole has reached a stage of polarized politics, but the trend is in that direction. Even the national organization of the Gandhian Sarvodaya Movement (an organization which has persistently espoused the "harmony and integration" ideal of rural India and, true to Gandhi's anti-class bias, has vigorously denied differences of class interests in the countryside) faced much internal turmoil when some of its veteran leaders, late in 1969, engaged in public heresy by acknowledging the inevitability of class conflict.[16]

Such, then, have been the political developments in a countryside which has been simultaneously experiencing revolutionized agriculture. The Union Home Minister, Y. B. Chavan, was expressing a genuine fear when he declared in late November 1969: "Unless the green revolution is based on social justice, I am afraid the green revolution may not remain green." [17]

Is it a mere coincidence that the two developments—an increase in agricultural productivity and an increase in class-oriented tensions—have occurred simultaneously? Obviously there is no simple causal relation between the two, precisely because both surfaced at about the same time. Yet the two are not unrelated: for one thing, the green revolution has definitely accentuated the circumstances that led to the politicization of the peasantry. But there is more to it. In order to fully grasp the significance of the two trends and the interrelation between them, one must study what has happened in India over the past two and a half decades, particularly with respect to agrarian relations.

Gross economic inequalities and strong feudal elements in social relations were two of the most pronounced ingredients of India's agrarian structure when it gained political independence in 1947. The underlying factor was, of course, the question of land: its ownership, its cultivation, and the distribution of its products. The land tenure systems of that date were extremely varied and intricate. In general, however, they were products of preexisting local conditions which the British had adapted to their own interests while conserving the feudal exploitation of the peasantry. Regardless of whether the area fell in former British India or in the native princely states,[18] and whether the prevailing tenurial system was of the *zamindari, ryotwari*, or *mahalwari* type,[19] at the time of independence a highly skewed landownership pattern, a substantial proportion of landless or near-landless peasants, and an extremely exploitive landlordism of a semifeudal kind were among the features which characterized the Indian agrarian system as a whole. Although regional variations were undoubtedly important, the following are some of the main highlights of the countrywide agrarian structure as it existed shortly after independence:

1. As much as 59 percent of the cultivators' holdings in 1951 were below 5 acres each, accounting for only 15.5 percent of the total area under cultivation. Taking 10 acres as the cutoff point—the generally agreed-upon minimum size for an "economic holding" by Indian standards—more than 78 percent of the holdings fell below this level, accounting for only 33 percent of the total land. On the other hand, holdings of over 25 acres constituted only 5.6 percent of the total holdings, while taking up 34.4 percent of the land.[20] These figures, significant as they are to show the inequalities in the system, relate only to cultivators' holdings (whether owned or leased) and do not reflect the pattern of ownership.

2. Only about 29 percent of the total agricultural population in 1951 were what could be called peasant proprietors. Between them they owned 40–45 percent of the agricultural land. This group included some rich peasants who, besides themselves engaging in cultivation, leased part of their land to tenant farmers.[21]

3. The remainder of the land—55–60 percent—was under the control of feudal landlords (variously known in different parts of the country as *zamindars, talukdars, malguzars, narwadars, jagirdars*, etc.), who made up fewer than 2 percent of the total agricultural population.[22] A part of this land was owned by various religious and charitable institutions, particularly in the south; but the priests who reigned over these institutions were no different from other feudal lords. Through the medium of a large stratum of feudal sub-proprietors and intermediate, noncultivating tenants, most of this land was cultivated by tenant farmers.

4. Approximately 42 percent of the agricultural population consisted of tenant farmers,[23] falling into two major categories: occupancy tenants and tenants-at-will. Occupancy tenants enjoyed legal protection in the form of fixed rents and permanent and heritable rights to the land they occupied. The rights of the tenants-at-will, on the other hand, were not even nominally defined by law. Often they were only subtenants of the occupancy tenants. In any case, they had no security of tenure and their rent was exorbitant, ranging between one-half and two-thirds of the crop they produced. In some places it was as high as 75–80 percent of the crop. Exact estimates of the extent of the two types of tenancy are not available, although it seems that tenancy-at-will was the far more prevalent pattern. For example, in the pre-partition Punjab, while occupancy tenants cultivated only 7.3 percent of the land, tenants-at-will cultivated about 48 percent.[24] In any case, the fact remains that tenancy cultivation, as a form of extreme feudal exploitation of the peasantry, was a prominent feature of Indian agriculture. In 1951 as much as 43.2 percent of the total land in cultivators' holdings was made up by the area taken on lease.[25] Furthermore, insecurity of tenure and exorbitant rents were not the only form of exploitation of tenants by landlords. *Begaar* (unpaid labor) on various kinds of construction, agricultural, or household works, and a multitude of special levies—in some places as many as fifty—were additional burdens imposed by the landlords upon their tenants. Any special expense which the landlord had to incur—on death, birth, or marriage, on buying a car or an elephant, on sending his son to be educated in England, on receiving important guests, on, in fact, anything—was passed on to the tenants in the form of levies. And there was no escape. Failure to meet these demands could result in severe beatings and tortures, in the sale of what little belongings the tenants had, or in outright eviction from their tenancy.[26]

5. At the very bottom of the agrarian structure were, of course, the laborers, constituting 28 percent of the total agricultural population. Most of them did not own any land, not even the small patches on which their meager dwellings stood. Their main, and in most cases only, source of living was physical labor on farms—whenever it was needed, which was in many areas limited essentially to the peak agricultural seasons, and for whatever payment (often in kind) the landlords were willing to make. In some parts of the country such la-

borers were even attached to their landlords in permanent bondage because of indebtedness inherited through generations. Not only did they live the most miserable life in terms of poverty,[27] but also, since most of them belonged to the group of exterior castes or Untouchables, they carried with them the most dehumanizing stigma. In many areas they were not permitted to approach, let alone to touch, those of higher caste.

In addition to the above features of the agrarian structure, there was the usurious exploitation of the moneylenders, usually local traders operating within the village or in nearby towns. Often the big landlords themselves were moneylenders or traders; at the very least, the two had very close ties.[28] In 1951–52, 75.7 percent of the total agricultural credit came from these local moneylenders, who were reported to be charging as much as 24 percent annual interest on loans.[29]

The scene was thus one of a pauperized peasantry, plundered by feudal landlords and moneylenders through rack-renting, illegal exactions, usury, and the application of brute force. According to one estimate, in 1950–51 land rent and moneylenders' interest amounted to Rs. 14 billion, which was about a third of the value of the country's total farm produce that year.[30] Under such circumstances, abject poverty, sporadic starvation, and periodic famines characterized rural India.

Another factor should be emphasized to place all this in proper perspective. Although since the mid-nineteenth century the Indian village had been increasingly drawn into the orbit of international capitalism and was subject to its vagaries, until about the end of the 1940s, and to a certain extent until much later, it managed to maintain itself as a sociologically viable entity. Castes, which often functioned as occupational guilds, *panchayats* (village councils), various forms of real or fictive kinship ties, and inter-caste functional interdependencies provided a degree of internal cohesiveness, the strength of which varied inversely with the degree of involvement in the market system. And such involvement had undoubtedly begun to occur during the last hundred years of British rule. Consumer goods produced by machine industries, such as cloth and umbrellas, were entering the rural market. At the same time, with the introduction of a plantation economy (tea, coffee, etc.) in south and northeast India, and of cash crops (particularly cotton) in west and central India, a part of Indian agriculture had already begun to assume some elements of capitalist farming and was subjected to international market forces. On the whole, however, it was a picture of a stagnant agriculture based on subsistence farming.

In most parts of India the village was largely insulated from the outside world, with little political, economic, or even cultural articulation with the wider society beyond its immediate region. Even government intervention seldom exceeded the collection of land revenue and the maintenance of law and order, with the exception of small relief measures in times of extreme calamity. What little industrial activity had already taken root in India had only limited ties with the agricultural sector. The surpluses extracted from the peasantry by the landlords did not, for the most part, take the form of capital. Even if the landlords lived in the cities, which many of them did, they used their income in conspicuous and wasteful consumption. As long as they could continue to extract this surplus, they had neither the need nor the desire to establish a capitalist growth pattern for agriculture. The label of "feudalism" to characterize the Indian agrarian system has been a subject of continuous debate among scholars.[31] It is true that the well-known categories of "Marxian feudalism" do not neatly apply to the Indian situation in modern times. Yet it contains

> enough of the characteristics of the declining feudal system to be called semi-feudal. Typical of the situation is the absence of a labor market in a large part of the rural sector; the personal subservence of the immediate producer to the landowner; the excessive importance of land rent; the underdeveloped marketing system resulting in little social division of labor, a low rate of accumulation, and the use of produce mainly to satisfy immediate needs.[32]

Although the Congress Party, which came to power in 1947, represented, by and large, bourgeois-landlord interests, conditions in rural India were so grim that it had no choice but to institute reforms. Furthermore, in order to facilitate much-needed industrial growth, agricultural productivity had to be boosted. Most important, however, were the rising, and to some extent organized, popular demands of the peasantry for immediate relief. A Kisan Sabha (Peasants' Organization) was formed as far back as 1936, and at its first conference it had demanded "the introduction of a system of peasant proprietorship under which the tiller of the soil is himself the owner of it and pays revenue direct to the government." [33] The 1940s saw some of the most militant peasant movements and uprisings in India: the Tebhaga movement in Bengal, the Telengana movement in Hyderabad, and numerous other uprisings in Madras and Kerala.[34] For all these reasons, pacification of the peasantry became one of the top items on the agenda for the new government, particularly when it had set out on the parliamentary path based on adult franchise.

A whole series of measures was instituted: land reforms, bureaucratic and administrative innovations, and the establishment of new institutions to provide credit, storage, marketing, and technical facilities to peasants. While it is impossible to detail these measures here, it is necessary to identify their salient features and to assess their effects on the formation of new class forces. Most of these measures, particularly those dealing with land relations, were ostensibly meant to alleviate the conditions of the weaker sections of the agricultural community and to curtail the exploitive powers of the landlords. What ensued at the end of roughly fifteen years was, however, far from these original intentions.

Land legislation went through three distinct stages. The first ran from about 1948–49 to 1951–52, when the various states of the Indian Union passed laws to abolish vast estates of the *zamindari* type, as well as to eliminate the various noncultivating, intermediate tenants who lived off the peasants' labor. The second phase, from about 1951–52 to approximately the end of the 1950s, involved numerous legislative measures which sought to regulate tenancy relations: to provide security of tenure, to fix rents, and in many cases to provide opportunities for the tenants to become owners by buying the land they tilled. In the third phase, running from the late fifties to the early sixties, attempts were made to put ceilings on the size of individual landholdings, with the hope of creating a pool of excess land that could be distributed to landless laborers or to small peasants.

Because of these numerous laws, because of time lags between their framing and their enactment (and even more, between their enactment and their actual "implementation"), and because of the widespread legal and constitutional battles that surrounded them, the 1950s was a decade of turmoil and uncertainty in rural India. The traditional village elite saw a deluge coming, and saw it in time to prepare to safeguard its interests. The primordial, village-based norms of reciprocity and interdependence soon disappeared—at least for those who held the economic and political power. The 1950s were characterized by double normative standards—deceit, false promises, political maneuverings, and bureaucratic manipulations—all of which concealed a massive power play. Even while the tenancy laws were still in the process of enactment, large-scale eviction of tenants occurred throughout the country; at the very least, tenancies were put on an oral, informal basis in order to prevent the tenants from claiming ownership when the laws were passed. In situations where such evictions could not be carried out for technical reasons, landlords invoked traditional norms to put pressure on tenant farmers: they appealed to them to uphold village solidarity, respect tradition, and maintain the status quo. All kinds of deceitful statements were made: all this was a temporary effort by undesirable elements to create discord in the village community; to avoid such discord, tenants should deny to the authorities that they were actually tenants; once the period of danger had passed, business would go on as usual and tenants would be allowed to cultivate the land as before. Unorganized, lacking a political base, fearful of severe reprisals if they opposed the landlords' wishes, and unequipped to defend their new rights in the courts, a vast majority of the peasants succumbed to these pressures. An amazing phenomenon occurred: countless numbers of erstwhile tenants "voluntarily surrendered" their new rights; those who did not succumb confronted awesome, expensive, and lengthy bureaucratic and legal battles. The odds were against them. More often than not they found that the revenue records on which they were to base their claims were either totally missing or had been altered to suit the interests of the landlords, who undoubtedly possessed far greater means to oil the bureaucratic machine. Physical force, or at least the threat of it, also dissuaded some adamant tenants from carrying on their legal struggles.[35]

In such ways landlords in most parts of India were able to evade the land reforms. Indeed, they were often not obliged to resort to unlawful means, for in most states the laws themselves contained loopholes or outright provisions to safeguard the landlords' interests. Resumption of tenancy land for the landlords' "self-cultivation" was, for example, provided for in most state land reform laws as well as in the earlier Zamindari Abolition Acts—a provision widely used by both *zamindars* and lesser landlords to dislodge their tenants and retain large amounts of land under their own control. "Self-cultivation" could, moreover, mean anything from disguised tenancy to cultivation through hired. labor to mechanized farming. Again, landlords took steps, in advance of impending legislation on land ceilings, to divide their large holdings into small parcels and register them in the names of real or fictitious relatives. Partly for this reason, and partly because when the laws on land ceilings, after much opposition in the legislative assemblies and after long battles on the grounds of their constitutionality, finally did become effective, they contained within them so many loopholes and exemption categories, besides prescribing too high ceilings on the existing holdings,[36] that there was hardly any surplus land left to be distributed to the poorer farmers and landless laborers.[37] We shall return later to some of these exemption categories.

The "winds of change" did eventually pass, and by the early 1960s the structure of land relations in India had assumed a more or less stable form. The old *zamindari*-type landlords and the various intermediaries had certainly been eliminated, at least in their earlier forms. The diverse systems of land tenure had also been changed into more uniform, simpler ones. This was certainly the case insofar as ownership rights in land were concerned, because all owners were brought into direct relation to the state. However, the original intention of converting Indian agriculture into one primarily of peasant-proprietors (if this was in fact the intention) was far from achieved. Tenancy cultivation as a form of feudal exploitation of the peasantry has to date continued to remain a major feature of Indian agriculture—with concomitant high rents and insecure tenure.[38] Moreover, there did not occur any significant change in the highly skewed pattern of cultivation holdings or in the size of the landless work force. Data for 1960–61 show that

> . . . taking the country as a whole, nearly 36 percent of the rural households did not cultivate any land or less than half an acre each. Households cultivating no land or less than 2.5 acres each constituted 57.59 percent of the rural households and between them they operated only 7 percent of the total land. On the other hand, only 2.09 percent of the households had operational holdings of more than 30 acres each, but between them they operated nearly 23 percent of the total land.[39]

And thus the story goes: a record of dismal failure of land reforms as far as the alleviation of the conditions of the masses of rural people is concerned. Yet the fifteen years of the implementation of various land legislation did unmistakably create a class of rich peasants—kulaks—who by the mid-sixties were all set to embark upon capitalist agriculture. Mostly composed of former *zamindars* and other landlords, but also including the top stratum of peasant proprietors and some former tenants who enjoyed superior and permanent rights, this class of rich peasants had consolidated its legal rights to the land by about the middle of the sixties. The uncertainties of the past decade were gone; and despite continuing clamor by some politicians and intellectuals about the ineffectiveness of land reforms and the need for more effective measures, this class had begun to feel firmly secure in its position.

Its sense of security was not, however, a sufficient condition, although it was a necessary one, for this class to enter into capitalist farming. Other simultaneous institutional and structural developments provided some of the remaining preconditions. Some of these developments were generated by the working of the land reforms; others occurred separately.

First, the various measures to abolish *zamindari*-type landlords and other intermediaries, while allowing them to retain large parts of their estates for "self-cultivation," also provided them with heavy compensation for their losses in land revenue, as well as outright "rehabilitation grants." Exact estimates of the total amount thus payable to these semifeudal lords vary from one government document to another,[40] but roughly speaking it was about Rs. 6,000 million. By 1968–69 some Rs. 3,200 million had already been paid to them.[41] Although only about half of this has been in the form of cash (the rest was in the form of government bonds), it is still a substantial amount of money to have reached the newly emerging class of rich peasants. These compensation grants undoubtedly offered at least a part of the necessary capital for later mechanization and capitalization in agriculture. Some *zamindars* also managed to retain *all* their land under their control while still receiving large sums as compensation. For example, according to a recently unearthed story, a West Bengal *zamindar* who owned 1,000 acres jointly with his brother managed to transfer all the land into the names of his sons and nephews and their wives, who were then shown as his "tenants." When the law came into force, these sons and nephews and their wives were made the owners, and now paid land revenue directly to the government. The two *zamindar* brothers were granted Rs. 700,000 by the government as compensation for their "loss in revenue," but they retained within the family possession of all the land they originally owned.[42]

A parallel development during the last two decades has been the consolidation of landholdings. Fragmentation of landholdings has long been a characteristic feature of Indian agriculture; often a farmer's total land was divided into numerous and widely dispersed pieces. The British rulers tried to correct the situation, at least in some provinces, by promoting the exchange of plots between individual holders. But it has only been in the last two decades that consolidation of dispersed holdings has been accomplished on a large scale —often through special legislation making such consolidation compulsory.[43] Without this transference of the small, widely dispersed strips of land into compact units, mechanized, capitalist farming could not possibly have emerged.

The last phase of land legislation dealing with ceilings on individual holdings contained elements that tended to push the owners of large holdings toward capitalist agriculture. Debates on the question of ceilings had been going on throughout the fifties, and by the time such legislation became effective in the early sixties, most large owners had already divided their land among members of their families. Nevertheless, the various ceiling laws specified numerous categories of farms that were to be exempt, including "mechanized farms," "farms with heavy investments," "efficient farms," dairy farms, orchards, plantations, "farms in a compact block," cooperative farms, etc. The ceiling laws thus provided added both incentives and opportunities to large landlords to switch over to capitalist farming in order to avoid alienation of their lands.

"Cooperative farms," one of the exemption categories noted, are interesting for still another reason. Ever since the government began to encourage cooperation in farming—particularly after the Nagpur session of the ruling Congress Party in 1959—"cooperative farming societies" became a double-edged sword in the hands of landlords and rich peasants. By dividing their large holdings among relatives and then pooling the subdivisions in the form of a "cooperative farming society," they were not only able to avoid the possible alienation of their land, but, since they now belonged to a "cooperative farming society," they also became eligible for all kinds of special treatment from the government, particularly in obtaining large, long-term loans for capital investments.[44]

Apart from these mechanisms, which were inherent within the land legislation, rural India, ever since the launching of five-year plans in 1951, has been subjected to a wide range of administrative and institutional changes. The Community Development Program started in 1952. Although it went through numerous vicissitudes during the following decade and a half, it succeeded in pouring a vast amount of public resources into the villages to help construct new roads, schools, health and recreation centers, irrigation projects, wells, drainage systems, storage facilities and warehouses, soil conservation projects, etc. Further, the Agricultural Credit Societies, which had been in existence for quite some time, were greatly expanded. From 105,000 such societies in 1951, the number reached 212,000 a decade later, with a corresponding rise in the total amount of loans and advances from Rs. 229 million in 1951 to Rs. 2 billion in 1961. Moreover, the same period witnessed significant, though relatively modest, expansion in various kinds of marketing and distributive cooperative societies. There is almost unanimous agreement among the observers of the changing rural scene in India—whether local or foreign, or whether state-sponsored studies or those by independent scholars—that all these new measures have mostly benefited the richest stratum of the Indian peasantry.

Even more significant have been the developments in the economic and political articulation of the rich peasants and former landlords with the wider societal forces. As was pointed out earlier, in pre-independence days the *zamindars* and other big landlords had few, if any, ties with the urban industrial bourgeoisie. The surpluses expropriated from the peasants were used essentially in conspicuous, wasteful consumption. With the expansion of industrial and commercial activities in the country as a whole, this situation slowly began to change. By the early 1960s, rich peasants and landlords had already begun to invest their savings in wholesale trade in food grains, as well as in the rapidly expanding road transport system. As electric power began to reach the countryside, small-scale rice mills and wheat flour mills began to operate within the villages or in nearby towns. These were almost invariably owned by the rich peasants and landlords. As the construction industry expanded, many of the rural rich—particularly those near urban centers—started brick kilns to supply the ever-expanding demand for bricks. In areas where new sugar refineries were opened on the principle of cooperative ownership, it was the rich peasants and landlords who constituted the major membership of these cooperatives. In this way the rural elite greatly expanded its economic activity and was no longer content with the surpluses produced by the toiling peasantry. Under these changed conditions, agriculture itself tended to turn into a profit-oriented vocation. How much of the agricultural surpluses did in fact become part of the growing industrial capital cannot accurately be ascertained, but a link between the two sectors was clearly established by the early 1960s. That is why the Federation of Indian Chambers of Commerce and Industries severely criticized the agrarian policies of the Third Five-Year Plan, particularly the section on proposed land ceilings, while in its comments on the Second Plan it had completely ignored the agrarian policies of the government.[45] Another indication of the close link between the rural elite and the growing industrial bourgeoisie can be seen from the consumption pattern of industrial goods. A recent study, based upon National Sample Survey data, has estimated that in 1960–61 the richest 10 percent of the rural people provided a much bigger market for industrial consumer goods than did all the urban people put together.[46]

Politically, too, the village in India has increasingly been linked with wider, national forces; with the introduction of universal adult franchise, this kind of linkage could hardly be avoided. But with the institution, in 1956, of the three-tier system of democratic decentralization, the elected leaders of village councils, who more often than not came from the class of landlords and rich peasants, became directly involved with the local self-governments at the "block" [47] and district levels. By the end of the fifties, these linkages had begun to acquire distinct ideological overtones. In various parts of the country, numerous farmers' organizations emerged or were reactivated to represent the interests of the landlords and rich peasantry. It was mainly in relation to the question of ceilings on landholdings, as proposed by the Nagpur session of the Congress Party in 1959, that the Swatantra Party, supported primarily by ex-princes, landlords, and rich peasants, was founded that year. To date this party has continued to draw its main support from these groups.

In these diverse ways, rural India has undergone major structural and institutional changes over the past two decades. These changes have brought to the surface a stratum of Indian agriculturists who are much more secure in terms of legal rights in their vast landholdings, much more articulated—economically and politically—vis-à-vis the wider society, and much less committed to village-based norms of reciprocity and interdependence than were their predecessors of twenty years ago. Feudal elements in Indian agriculture are still widely prevalent, as has been pointed out, but this seems to be a matter of convenience rather than of institutional necessity. The increasing trend in the sixties has been toward capitalist agriculture. And it is in the context of these structural and institutional changes that the recent successes of the green revolution must be seen. If the Ford Foundation had not exported the new technology to India, the new class of Indian kulaks would sooner or later have imported it from wherever it was available.

It is, moreover, these very changes which lie at the root of the rising politicization and militancy of the weaker sections of the Indian peasantry. Objectively, their conditions were bad enough twenty years ago; over time they have become worse, both absolutely and relatively. In 1960–61, 38.03 percent of all rural households (consisting mainly of agricultural laborers and cultivators of small holdings) lived below the extreme poverty line, based upon a very conservative estimate of a minimum of Rs. 15 per capita per month in consumption expenditure (1960–61 prices). The percentage rose to 44.57 in 1964–65 and to 53.02 in 1967–68.[48] In other words, more than 50 percent of the rural population was barely managing to survive in 1967–68. This is one of the most glaring objective realities on which the green revolution has been thriving. Dozens of field studies from many parts of the country in recent years have, uniformly and convincingly, demonstrated that the gap between the rural rich and rural poor is fast widening—not only between agricultural laborers and landowners but also between small and medium farmers, on the one hand, and rich farmers on the other.[49] The absolute daily wage of farm laborers has undoubtedly risen considerably in recent years, but their actual conditions have deteriorated, mainly because the rise in wages has been outstripped by the rise in the cost of living, but also because, in some places, there is a declining demand for wage labor resulting from increase in mechanization.[50]

Accompanying these hard realities in the objective conditions, there has been a marked change in the subjective forces since the early 1960s. For a whole decade (the fifties), the weaker sections lived under the illusion of impending structural reforms which never materialized. They saw a gradual erosion of traditional village norms—rather, they saw themselves victimized by those very norms, since promises made in the name of these norms were never fulfilled. At the same time, they saw fake cooperatives of one kind or another constituted by the rich to evade losses or to draw added resources from the government. They witnessed, at close hand and helplessly, how the big landlords, deceitfully and often with the full knowledge of government officials, divided their large estates to avoid the impending legislation on land ceilings. They saw these fellow villagers getting richer every year, with no discernible improvement in their own conditions. By the end of the decade they saw this rich rural elite firmly entrenched in seats of economic and political power. By this time they also fully realized that they had been cheated and that there was no possible solution to their miseries within the given framework. Increasing politicization and militancy of the poorer peasantry in these conditions were hardly surprising.

This process of politicization was further helped by the changed political climate in the country as a whole. The decade of the fifties in India was essentially "apolitical," with the almost total hegemony of the Congress Party under Nehru's leadership and with an almost total absence of ideology in the nation at large. On the one hand, such rightist forces as existed were more or less contained within the Congress Party. On the other hand, the Communist Party of India remained both discredited and ineffective—discredited because of the support it had extended, against the predominant national sentiment, to the Allied forces in World War II, and ineffective because after the abrupt withdrawal in 1951 of its support to the massive peasant uprising in Telengana, it had more or less settled, under the direction of the Communist Party of the Soviet Union, for constitutionalism as a means of peaceful transition to socialism. Even the Kisan Sabha, a militant organization of peasants, had been declared illegal by the government in the early fifties.

The situation began to change at the end of the decade. The rich peasants and the big landlords crystallized their position by rallying behind the Swatantra Party. At the same time the Communist Party of India began in the late fifties to undergo serious internal ideological debates, mostly centered around its assessment of the Indian situation and correct revolutionary strategy. These debates culminated in the vertical split in the party in 1964.[51] A large section of the movement began to be directly concerned with the peasant question. The Kisan Sabha, too, had come out in the open and was active in many parts of the country. Ideology had made a firm entry on the political scene of India. The Indo-Chinese border conflict of 1962 and the short-lived war with Pakistan in 1965 somewhat weakened the growing polarization in rural India because of opportunities they provided for the ruling Congress Party to stir up nationalist hysteria. But their effect did not last long, as was demonstrated by the debacle of the Congress Party in the general elections of 1967, when its hegemony was broken for the first time in twenty years. And since Naxalbari in 1967 there has been continuous growth in peasant militancy and peasant uprisings. Even before Naxalbari, Maoist-backed peasant rebellion had long been going on in the vast Srikakulum area of Andhra Pradesh.[52] It was, however, the Naxalbari revolt of 1967, and the events that have followed it, including the formation of a third, Maoist, Communist Party—Communist Party of India (Marxist-Leninist)—that put the Indian peasantry on the revolutionary map of the world.[53]

Both the green revolution and the increasingly class-oriented polarization of the Indian peasantry are thus the outcomes of a long, continuous process of major structural and institutional shifts in rural India; both phenomena came to the surface in the second half of the sixties. The former is only aiding the acceleration of the latter. Metaphorically speaking, one can say that the present situation in rural India is like a watermelon—green on the outside and red inside. Whether the watermelon rots and eventually bursts, with all the redness wasted, or whether it is cut at the appropriate time depends upon effective Left leadership, the prospects for which do not seem very promising at the moment.

Notes

1. Dr. Norman E. Borlaug, an American scientist, has spent twenty-seven years in Mexico as a staff member of the Rockefeller Foundation, working on a "wheat research and production program" at the International Maize and Wheat Improvement Center.
2. In the Oslo lecture delivered while accepting the Nobel award on December 10, 1970, Dr. Borlaug said, "If you desire peace, cultivate jus-

tice, but at the same time cultivate the fields to produce more bread; otherwise there will be no peace." The lecture, entitled "The Green Revolution, Peace and Humanity," was printed by the Population Reference Bureau, Washington, D.C., in its Selection No. 35, January 1971.

3. Clifton R. Wharton, Jr., "The Green Revolution: Cornucopia or Pandora's Box?", *Foreign Affairs*, April 1969, p. 464.

4. Borlaug, op. cit., p. 3.

5. Ibid., p. 4.

6. Editorial, *Economic and Political Weekly* (Bombay), April 17, 1971, p. 806.

7. According to a recent statement of the Minister for Food and Agriculture, the government intends to stop food imports after 1971. (Ibid.)

8. Borlaug, op. cit., p. 4.

9. Gunvant M. Desai, "Factors Determining Demand for Pesticides," *Review of Agriculture*, December 1970, p. A182. (Issued as a supplement to *Economic and Political Weekly*, December 26, 1970.)

10. Francine Frankel, "Agricultural Modernization and Social Change," *Mainstream* (New Delhi), January 3, 1970, p. 17.

11. For reports on these other districts, see the November 29 and December 13, 20, and 27, 1969, issues of *Mainstream*.

12. The production no doubt rose: from 54.9 million tons of food grains produced in 1950–51, production rose to 82.0 million tons in 1960–61 and to about 89.0 million tons in 1964–65, thus recording a 3.1 percent per annum growth rate during the fifteen-year period. However, much of this growth was due to an expansion in the cropped area. The rate of growth in per acre productivity during this period was only 1.33 percent per annum. For an excellent analysis of these and other patterns, see Martin E. Abel, "Agriculture in India in the 1970's," *Review of Agriculture*, March 1970, pp. A5-A14. (Issued as a supplement to *Economic and Political Weekly*, March 28, 1970.)

13. The incident occurred in December 1968 and was widely reported in the newspapers. The above account is based on eyewitness reports from the surviving members of the community whom I visited in early 1970. The charred hut still stood there as a sad reminder of the fateful night. But it was more than that: it had a new thatched roof and had been turned into a "shrine," with a red Communist flag flying on top.

14. Even in terms of brutality and size of toll, the Venmani incident is no longer an isolated case. A similar case of mass murder recently occurred in the Purnea district of Bihar, where all the forty-five houses of Santal sharecroppers in a village were burnt down one night by the landlords' armed thugs. At least fourteen people were reportedly killed and thirty-five others injured. For a full account, see N. K. Singh, "The Murder and After," *Frontier* (Calcutta), February 5, 1972, pp. 10–11.

15. *The Statesman* (New Delhi), March 20 and 25, 1971. Cited by Francine

Frankel, "The Politics of the Green Revolution: Shifting Patterns of Peasant Participation in India and Pakistan," paper presented at the workshop on "A Widened Perspective of Modernizing Agriculture," Cornell University, June 2–4, 1971, mimeographed, p. 23.

16. This happened at the 1969 Annual Conference of the Akhil Bharitiva Sarva Sewa Sangh, the national organization of the movement, meeting in Rajgir, Bihar, in October of that year. The controversy started with the distribution of a paper entitled "Gramdan Movement: A Turning Point," by one of the most respected leaders of the movement, Shankarrao Deo. The paper not only questioned seriously the claimed achievements of *bhoodan* (voluntary donations of land) and *gramdan* (voluntary collectivization of village land), but also called for a more militant approach to resolve structural and class inequality in the villages.

17. Quoted in *Mainstream*, December 5, 1969, p. 7.

18. At the time of independence there were more than 600 princely states scattered throughout India, covering 45 percent of the pre-partition territory. About 24 percent of the total population lived in these states. The rest of the country, known as British India, was divided into nine provinces. In internal administration the princely states enjoyed almost total autonomy. Most of these states were rather small in size, but some were as large as any of the British provinces. Regardless of size, however, these states represented the most extreme form of feudal exploitation of the peasantry in India.

19. These represented the three major land-revenue systems gradually evolved by the British to suit local conditions. For a brief yet adequate description of the three systems, the areas they covered, and the form of feudal relations, see Grigory Kotovsky, *Agrarian Reforms in India* (People's Publishing House, New Delhi, 1964), Chapter 1.

20. Government of India, Ministry of Labour, *Agricultural Labour Enquiry: Rural Man-Power and Occupational Structure* (Delhi, 1954), pp. 522–523; and *Agricultural Labour Enquiry: Report on Intensive Survey of Agricultural Labour* (Delhi, 1955), Vol. 1, Appendix VII.

21. Kotovsky, op. cit., p. 19. Kotovsky's estimates are based upon the government of India's Agricultural Labour Enquiry Reports of 1954, as well as on the census reports of 1951.

22. Ibid.

23. Following the Agricultural Labour Enquiry Report, Kotovsky lumps tenant farmers and laborers into one category, comprising 71 percent of the total agricultural population (ibid., p. 19). However, it is important to separate the two groups because of the different relations they have in the productive process. Since 28 percent of the agricultural population was classified as agricultural laborers in the census, about 42 percent is estimated to be composed of tenant farmers.

24. Government of India, Ministry of Food and Agriculture, *Agricultural Legislation in India* (Delhi, 1955), Vol. VI, p. v.
25. *Agricultural Labour Enquiry: Rural Man-Power and Occupational Structure*, op. cit., p. 521.
26. H. D. Malaviya, *Land Reforms in India* (Indian National Congress, Delhi, 1954), pp. 52, 103–104; *Report of the United Provinces Zamindari Abolition Committee* (Allahabad, 1948), Vol. 1, p. 354.
27. The per capita income for agricultural laborers in 1951 was Rs. 104, compared to the national per capita income of Rs. 265.2 for the same year—which in itself was one of the lowest in the world. See Charles Bettelheim, *India Independent* (Monthly Review Press, New York, 1968), p. 25.
28. Reserve Bank of India, Report of the Committee of Direction, *All India Rural Credit Survey*, Vol. II: *The General Report* (Bombay, 1954), pp. 277–278.
29. Ibid., p. 167. Also see Kotovsky, op. cit., p. 26.
30. S. J. Patel, "The Distribution of the National Income of India," *The Indian Economic Review*, Vol. III, No. 1, 1956, p. 7. (Quoted by Kotovsky, op. cit., p. 27.)
31. For a recent debate see S. A. Shah, "Class and Agrarian Change: Some Comments on Peasant Resistance and Revolution in India," and the rejoinder by Kathleen Gough in *Pacific Affairs*, Fall 1969, pp. 360–368. See also the essays by Hamza Alavi and Saghir Ahmad in this volume.
32. Bettelheim, op. cit., p. 23.
33. Quoted by H. D. Malaviya, *Land Reforms in India*, op. cit., p. 59.
34. For descriptions and analyses of these movements and uprisings, see Hamza Alavi, "Peasants and Revolution," in this volume; Kathleen Gough, "Peasant Resistance and Revolt in South India," *Pacific Affairs*, Winter 1968–69; and Mohan Ram, *Indian Communism: Split Within a Split* (Vikas Publications, New Delhi, 1969), Chapter 1.
35. Scores of field studies by independent scholars in different parts of the country, as well as numerous government reports, are filled with evidence which sufficiently testifies to these observations. Attention is especially drawn to the various five-year plan documents of government of India; to the numerous special reports issued by the Planning Commission of the government of India (e.g. *Reports of the Committee of the Panel on Land Reforms* [New Delhi, 1959]; *Progress of Land Reforms* [New Delhi, 1963]), and to the numerous independent studies sponsored by the Program Evaluation Organization of the Planning Commission, six of which were collectively reviewed by V. M. Dandekar in *Artha Vijnana* (Poona), December 1962, pp. 291–330. In addition, the following references are useful: H. D. Malavija, *Land Reforms in India*, op. cit.; Daniel Thorner, *Agrarian Prospects in India* (University of Delhi, 1956); Bhowani

Sen, *Evolution of Agrarian Relations in India* (People's Publishing House, New Delhi, 1962); G. Kotovsky, *Agrarian Reforms in India*, op. cit.; and the files of the *Indian Journal of Agricultural Economics* (Bombay), particularly its January–March 1962 conference number, which was mainly devoted to land reforms.

36. The level of ceilings varies in different states, in different regions of the same state in some cases, and for different classes of land. In Andhra Pradesh, for example, a holding could be anywhere between 27 and 324 acres, depending upon the quality of the land. In Rajasthan the range was 22–336 acres; in Tamil Nadu, 24–120 acres; and so on. For a state-by-state chart, see Government of India, Ministry of Information and Broadcasting, New Delhi, *India 1969: A Reference Annual*, p. 253.

37. For a state-by-state description of the ceilings acts and the poor performance on the acquisition and distribution of "surplus" land, see V. M. Dandekar and Nilakantha Rath, "Poverty in India. II: Policies and Programmes," *Economic and Political Weekly*, January 9, 1971, p. 118.

38. Many of the tenancy relations in present-day India are, for obvious legal reasons, concealed. But their existence is widely known and was acknowledged even by the government of India in a recent unpublished report by the Ministry of Home Affairs: *The Causes and Nature of Current Agrarian Tensions*, 1969. Even in Punjab, where capitalist farming is the most advanced in India, as many as 46 percent of all cultivators are reported to be taking some land on lease, mostly on a crop-sharing basis, and are at times paying as much as 70 percent of the harvested crop to the landowners. See F. Frankel, *Mainstream*, January 3, 1970, p. 23.

39. V. M. Dandekar and N. Rath, op. cit., p. 115. The data are based upon the Seventeenth Round of the National Sample Survey.

40. For example, in *India 1961: A Reference Annual* (New Delhi), p. 263, it was reported to be Rs. 6,700 million, whereas in *India 1969: A Reference Annual* (New Delhi), p. 249, it is reported to be Rs. 5,700 million. H. D. Malaviya, in a recent publication, suggests that the total payable compensation was Rs. 6,042 million: *Implementation of Land Reforms: A Review and an Immediate Programme* (Congress Forum for Socialist Action, New Delhi, 1969), p. 8.

41. *India 1969: A Reference Annual*, op. cit., p. 249.

42. *The Statesman*, April 3, 1968, cited by H. D. Malaviya in *Implementation of Land Reforms*, op. cit., p. 37.

43. The program is far from completed. By the end of 1968–69 only 29.5 million hectares had been consolidated. During the Fourth Five-Year Plan it is expected that an additional 28.3 million hectares will be consolidated (*India 1969*, op. cit., p. 254).

44. For an example of one such "cooperative farming society," see Hari P. Sharma, "Land Reform in a Village in the Union Territory of Delhi," in M. S. Gore (ed.), *Problems of Rural Change* (University of Delhi, 1963), pp. 111–112. For a general description of such societies, see A. M. Khusro and A. N. Agarwal, *The Problems of Cooperative Farming in India* (Asia Publishing House, New York, 1961), pp. 38–42; also the Special Conference Number of *Indian Journal of Agricultural Economics*, Vol. XIII, No. 1.

45. Federation of Indian Chambers of Commerce and Industries, *Draft Note on the Second Five Year Plan* (New Delhi, 1955), and *Draft Outline of the Third Five Year Plan: An Analysis* (New Delhi, 1960), pp. 5–6, cited by G. Kotovsky, op. cit., p. 93.

46. Ranjan Sengupta, "Festival of the Ten Per Cent," *Frontier* (Calcutta), September 4, 1971, pp. 8–9.

47. An administrative unit, comprising about 100 villages, which was created by the Community Development Administration in the early fifties.

48. P. Bardhan, "Green Revolution and Agricultural Labourers: A Correction," *Economic and Political Weekly*, November 14, 1970, p. 1861. This is a corrected version of his lengthy article, "Green Revolution and Agricultural Laborers," *Economic and Political Weekly*, July 1970 (Special Number), pp. 1239–1249. For similar yet more comprehensive data, see V. M. Dandekar and N. Rath, "Poverty in India. I: Dimensions and Trends," *Economic and Political Weekly*, January 2, 1971, pp. 25–48.

49. See F. Frankel, "Agricultural Modernization and Social Change," op. cit., and "The Politics of the Green Revolution," op. cit.; M. E. Abel, "Agriculture in India in the 1970's," op. cit., pp. A9–A13; Ian R. Wills, "Green Revolution and Employment and Incomes," *Review of Agriculture*, March 71 (published as a supplement of *Economic and Political Weekly*, March 27, 1971), pp. A2–A10; G. Ojha, "Small Farmers and H.Y.V. Programme," *Economic and Political Weekly*, April 4, 1970, pp. 603–605; B. K. Chowdhury, "Disparity in Income in the Context of H.Y.V.," *Review of Agriculture*, September 1970 (published as a supplement of *Economic and Political Weekly*, September 26, 1970), pp. A90–A96.

50. Most of the references cited under note 48 also refer to the problem of wages and demand for agricultural workers. In addition, see P. Bardhan, "Green Revolution and Agricultural Labourer," op. cit.; W. Ladejinsky, "The Green Revolution in Punjab: A Field Trip," *Economic and Political Weekly*, June 28, 1969; W. Ladejinsky, "Green Revolution in Bihar—The Kosi Area: A Field Trip," *Economic and Political Weekly*, September 27, 1969.

51. For a detailed description of the background and the final split, see M. Ram, *Indian Communism*, especially chapters 4 and 5, and also Ram's essay in this volume.
52. For a description of the Srikakulum struggle, see Mohan Ram, *Maoism in India* (Vikas Publications, New Delhi, 1971), Chapter 4, as well as his essay in this volume.
53. On the whole, political leadership to guide the growing peasant unrest does not seem to be in a very happy situation at the moment. Not only is the entire Maoist movement divided in various factions and often engaged in divisive conflicts; there have also been serious interparty conflicts, often violent, in the past few years. It was mainly due to this inability of the Left forces in India that Indira Gandhi's Congress Party was able to stage the massive landslide victory in the mid-term national elections of February 1971.

4. Some Trends in India's Economic Development

Paresh Chattopadhyay

The following work tries to analyze, in an extremely short space and within a necessarily simplified framework, the main trends of India's economic development over roughly the last two decades. Our analysis is confined to the basic spheres of production: agriculture and industry. The first and second sections discuss, respectively, the broad developments in these two spheres; the third and fourth sections analyze, respectively, the role of the state and of foreign capital in India's economic development; the fifth section shows some of the consequences.

I

We start with agricultural production. With 1949–50 = 100, the index of production rose from 95.6 in 1950–51 to 161.8 in 1967–68, falling to 158.7 in 1968–69.[1] This shows that the growth rate of agricultural production has been rather slow, exceeding slightly the growth rate of population, which is about 2.5 percent per year. Even this modest rate of growth seems, however, quite high compared with that during British rule. Between 1900 and 1924 food grain production in India seems to have increased at an annual rate of only 0.3 percent, and from 1924 to 1948 it declined at an annual rate of 0.02 percent,[2] whereas the compound annual rate of growth of food grain production in India between 1949–50 and 1968–69 has been 2.79 percent.[3] A part of this growth is explained by the extension of the area of cultivation, but from the mid-1950s this seems to have played a comparatively minor role. In fact, since that time the dominant

An earlier version of this article appeared in *Frontier* (Calcutta), December 25, 1971, and January 1, 1972.

trend is that of higher yield from the acreage cultivated. Increasing application of better inputs to agriculture seems to have been an important factor in this growth, although favorable weather conditions were also undoubtedly important. The area under irrigation increased from 51.5 million acres in 1950–51 to 96.9 million acres at the end of the Third Plan in 1965.[4] With regard to agricultural machinery, the increases are indicated in Table 1. As regards fertilizers, the consumption of nitrogenous and phosphatic fertilizers from 1956–57 to 1965–66 rose from 130,636 tonnes to 540,803 tonnes (1 tonne equals 1.1 tons) and from 21,967 tonnes to 156,489 tonnes, respectively.[5]

Table 1
Inputs in Agriculture
(in thousands)

	1951	1956	1961	1966
Tractors	8.6	21	31	53.97
Oil engines	82	123	230	441
Sugarcane crushers	526	568	624	587
Electric pumps	8.5	47	160	366

Source: *Indian Livestock Census*, 1956, Vol. I, p. 4; *Indian Agriculture in Brief*, 1968, p. 53.

It follows that this development of production and the forces of production—by all evidence much faster than that in the pre-1947 period, though far from satisfactory considering our requirements—could not have been achieved on the basis of a totally stagnant agrarian structure. Let us now see what modifications this structure has undergone and in which direction.

The Indian bourgeoisie, which by and large had led the national movement against imperialism, was bent upon carrying India along an independent capitalist path. But this was out of the question as long as the countryside remained semifeudal, a state to which it had been reduced by imperialism. The Congress Party, the political party of the Indian bourgeoisie, was aware of this at the time of the transfer of power. In fact, the report of its Agrarian Reforms Committee, published in 1949, was quite a radical document from the bourgeois point of view. It recommended abolishing intermediary tenants, giving land to the actual tiller, protecting the tenant from rack-renting, and the commuting of rent in kind into cash. The Committee envisaged small- and medium-sized farms following the allotment of land to the tenants. The whole program seems to have envisaged full-fledged capitalism in agriculture based on peasant proprietorship and resembling, in important respects, what Lenin called the "American path of land distribution," in contrast to the "Prussian path," which led to landlord-type capitalist farming.[6] But by the time the Congress governments in different states were enacting and later "implementing" the land legislation, the original program was greatly diluted in favor of rural vested interests as regards both heavy compensation and the wide definition of personal cultivation; the latter resulted in the intermediate tenants' taking on huge amounts of land by evicting millions of tenant-cultivators.[7]

There were several factors behind this step backward. The local and state leaderships of the ruling party were much more seriously compromised with the landed interests than was the national leadership. Secondly, the widespread mass struggle in the country at the time of the transfer of power, especially the armed struggle of the Telengana peasants that preceded the land legislation, had a dual effect on the bourgeoisie, as did the Chinese Revolution and the first phase of the national liberation struggle in Vietnam. On the one hand, the Indian bourgeoisie felt the necessity of undertaking land reforms to a certain extent to eliminate the stark exploitation in the countryside; on the other hand, it feared to go too far in this lest it antagonize the powerful vested interests in the rural areas, who could be its allies in the face of a popular upsurge. Consequently, the land reform measures did not amount to much; they did, however, result in some modifications of the old mode of production, although unevenly as between different states. For example, in the state of Saurashtra a sample study among 124 *girasdars* (landlords) showed that whereas before the land reforms they held 4,455 acres of self-cultivated land, after the reforms they held 5,764 acres of self-cultivated land, 26 *girasdars* having secured additional lands under *khudkasht*[8] allotments—all of which was effected by dispossessing the previous tenants from the land. On the other hand, in Rajasthan the *khudkasht* area held after the reforms was 26.4 percent less than the pre-reform operational holdings of the intermediate tenants.[9]

The success of land legislation regarding abolition of subletting or leasing of land was also mixed. In Andhra, for example, leasing increased from 8.8 percent of owned lands before the reforms to 10.7 percent after the reforms, while in Uttar Pradesh the extent of sub-tenancy, including sharecropping, was estimated to have declined from 13.98 percent to 10.50 percent of the total cultivated area of the sample villages.[10] On the whole, as a competent student has observed, "There is no evidence to show that the tenancy practices changed for the better as a result of the abolition of the intermediaries though the former tenants became owners *under the law*." [11] The ceiling on land offers us more or less the same story. The law in various states fixed the ceiling on existing holdings in such a way that it would preserve the middle holders and rich peasants; for with more than 60 percent of landholdings in India under five acres, the ceiling fixed by the different states ranged from 14 to 300 acres.[12] At the same time the intermediaries were able to retain huge amounts of land by underhand means. In West Bengal between a quarter and a third of the land ostensibly available under the legally fixed 25-acre ceiling went to the landlords through *mala fide* transfers.[13]

We shall say a few words here about usurious capital. It is well known that usurious capital, often connected with merchant capital and manifested through private moneylending, has historically preceded the capitalist mode of production.[14] But neither usurious nor merchant capital leads ipso facto to the capitalist mode of production. Everything depends on the particular stage of historical development.[15] However, it is perhaps not too much to say that usury, even if it does not per se strengthen the feudal or semifeudal mode of production, does at least retard its dissolution and the corresponding transition to commodity production and capitalism.[16] In our country about 54 percent of the rural households are indebted, and the share of private moneylenders in the total farm credit is 62 percent.[17] There has, however, been some, though modest, progress here over a decade. Table 2 shows that the grip of private moneylenders has to some extent diminished and that the share of government and cooperatives in total farm credit has somewhat increased over a decade.

One of the first things that strikes a student of India's agrarian situation is the extreme differentiation among the peasantry as regards both the size of landholdings and the value of assets possessed. Table

Table 2

Share of Various Credit Agencies in the Whole Farm Credit

Credit agency	Percentage share	
	1950–51	*1961–62*
Government and cooperatives	6	15.4
Traders	6	7.2
Agricultural and professional moneylenders	70	62.0
Relatives	14	6.4
Landlords	2	0.9
Commercial banks	Less than 1	Less than 1
Others	Balance	Balance
Total	100	100

Source: *All India Rural Credit Survey* (1950–51); *All India Rural Debt and Investment Survey* (1961–62).

Table 3

Household Operational Holdings and Area Operated by Size (All India)

Size of groups (acres)	% of holdings	% of total cultivated area
Up to 0.49	8.55	0.32
0.50–0.99	8.58	0.95
1.00–2.49	21.94	5.59
2.50–4.99	22.62	12.32
5.00–7.49	12.84	11.73
7.50–9.99	6.96	8.97
10.00–12.49	5.05	8.25
12.50–14.99	2.90	5.95
15.00–19.99	3.75	9.58
20.00–24.99	2.29	7.39
25.00–29.99	1.31	5.38
30.00–49.99	2.18	12.05
50.00 and above	1.03	11.60
Average size 6.49 acres.		

Source: *National Sample Survey*, 17th Round, September 1961–July 1962.

3 shows the distribution of operational holdings in Indian agriculture as it prevailed in 1961–62.

On the basis of Table 3 we know that a little less than two-thirds of all the operational holdings are less than 5 acres each—which is well below the average of 6.5 acres—and hold about a fifth of the total area operated, whereas the very top 3 percent of the households have more than 30 acres each and about a quarter of the total area operated. As regards the assets at the disposal of the peasantry, their distribution also shows great differentiation, as is indicated in Table 4.

Table 4

Distribution of Cultivator Households According to Value of Assets
(All India)

Asset group	% of households	Aggregate value of assets (Crores of Rs.)*	
Less than Rs. 500	6.5	99.4	(0.3)
Rs. 500–1,000	9.7	366.3	(1.1)
1,000–2,500	24.8	2,124.1	(6.3)
2,500–5,000	23.3	4,215.9	(12.5)
5,000–10,000	18.6	6,587.8	(19.5)
10,000–20,000	10.7	7,498.6	(22.2)
20,000 and above	6.4	12,885.6	(38.1)
All asset groups	100.0	33,777.6	(100.0)

* One crore equals 10 million rupees. Figures in parentheses are percentages of total assets for each asset group.
Source: *All India Rural Debt and Investment Survey*, 1961–62, Table I, in *Reserve Bank of India Bulletin*, June 1965.

The same trend is seen in fixed capital formation in farm business (for the data, see Table 5).

Both the cause and the consequence of the differentiation among the peasantry are reflected in the data concerning profit and loss per acre as the size of the holding increases. Farm management data from different states studied by the Ministry of Food and Agriculture show that loss decreases and profit increases per acre as the size of the holding increases. Table 6 indicates the figures for Punjab. With

Table 5

Fixed Capital Formation in Farm Business (All India)

Asset group (Rs.)	Proportion of cultivator households reporting (%)	Average per household (Rs.)	Aggregate (Crores of Rs.)	
Less than 500	10.1	3.4	1.1	(0.7)
500–1,000	13.1	4.2	2.0	(1.2)
1,000–2,500	16.9	6.7	8.4	(5.1)
2,500–5,000	22.2	12.9	15.1	(9.2)
5,000–10,000	27.5	30.9	28.9	(17.6)
10,000–20,000	33.3	65.4	35.3	(21.4)
20,000 and above	49.3	229.5	73.9	(44.9)
All asset groups	23.3	32.7	164.7	(100.0)

Figures in parentheses show the percentage contribution of each asset group to the total for all asset groups.
Source: *All India Rural Debt and Investment Survey*, 1961–62, Table XVII, in *Reserve Bank of India Bulletin*, June 1965.

Table 6

Profit and Loss per Acre on Crop Production
(Average of 1954–55 to 1956–57)

Holding size group (acres)	Profit or loss per acre (Rs.)
0–<5	−39.33
5–<10	−16.99
10–<20	−7.33
20–<50	−0.02
50	+16.3

Profit or loss has been derived by deducting the value of input from the value of output. A minus sign precedes loss; a plus sign precedes profit.
Source: *Studies in the Economics of Farm Management in the Punjab*, Combined Report, 1963, Table 4.10.

minor definitional differences and some minor internal variations, this picture is basically confirmed by more recent data on larger farms in the same state, as Table 7 on the next page indicates. This implies that small farmers find it increasingly difficult to continue

Table 7

Per Gross Acre* Sales Receipts, 1967–1968

Size of groups (acres)	Net cash receipts (in Rs.)**
20–25	179.92
25–30	162.15
30–40	174.10
40–50	194.71
50–75	164.22
75–100	182.98
100–150	255.78
150	591.52

* "Gross acre" derives from "gross area sown," which equals all area sown more than once.

** Net cash receipt is arrived at by deducting total cash expenditures from total sale receipts.

Source: Ashok Rudra, *Big Farmers of Punjab*; Table 17 in *Economic and Political Weekly*, Bombay, December 27, 1969.

farming. They first try to supplement their land income through nonfarming occupations, but ultimately swell the ranks of landless agricultural laborers. An official report in the early fifties already spoke of the first phenomenon.[18] Normally we should expect that the process would first lead to an increase in agricultural wage labor as a percentage of the active agricultural population, and ultimately to an increase in landless agricultural labor as a percentage of total agricultural labor. The reality, however, does not present us with such a straightforward answer. On the basis of available data it seems that forces are moving in two opposite directions. Thus, according to the census reports, the total active agricultural population of cultivators, excluding agricultural laborers, increased from 70 million in 1951 to 99.5 million in 1961, an increase of 43 percent, whereas agricultural laborers increased only from 28 million to 31.5 million during the same time, a rise of only 14 percent.[19] There may be several reasons for this apparently paradoxical phenomenon. To start with, the definition of the particular categories of the agricultural population differed in the two censuses.[20] But a more important reason seems to be a gradual, though slow, lessening of inequality in the size of operational holdings among agricultural households. If we compare the

national sample survey data for two years, 1953–54 and 1961–62—
that is, roughly speaking, those taken before and after the implementation of land reform legislation—we see that whereas according to
the earlier data about 71 percent of the households at the bottom
had less than 5 acres and operated 15.6 percent of the area, according to the later data about 61.7 percent of the households had less
than 5 acres and operated about 19 percent of the area.[21] (We shall
later give some indication of crop-sharing in the different states of
India.) Then, again, we should also try to see to what extent small
and impoverished cultivators are migrating to other occupations in
the rural or urban areas—a phenomenon which, unfortunately, we
cannot go into here for lack of comprehensive data. We must not,
however, forget that even under full-fledged capitalist agriculture
small-scale farming, while on the whole technically inferior to large-
scale farming, has a strong tendency to persist and act as an obstacle
to the proletarianization of the peasantry, also for reasons we cannot
go into here.[22] Of course, we do not doubt that the accentuation of
the process of the formation of agricultural labor, like other manifestations of transition to commodity production and capitalism, has
also been seriously hampered by the old mode of production which is
still very strong in our countryside. On the other hand, as the figures
in Table 8 indicate, we get a clear picture of the increase in landless
labor as a percentage of total agricultural labor.

Table 8

Percentage of Agricultural Labor Households (All India)

	1950–51	1956–57	1963–64
With land	49.94	42.87	38.83
Without land	50.7	57.13	61.17
Total	100.00	100.00	100.00

Source: *Agricultural Labour in India*, Labour Bureau, Department of Labour and
Employment, Government of India, 1968, Table 2.12.

There is an important consequence of this disintegration of the
peasantry. If we refer to the data on the size of distribution of operational holdings, we find that on the supposition that 7.5 acres constitutes an economic holding (striking a balance between the 5 acres

suggested by Nanavati and Anjaria and the 10 acres suggested by Professor Dantwala), about 70 percent of the area cultivated is already organized into units above the size of the economic holdings operated by a quarter of the households. It should be obvious that the bulk of the produce from this area is meant for the market. In other words, it appears that commodity production prevails in about two-thirds of the area cultivated in India. That the extent of commodity production has in fact been growing is also seen from the data on comparative growth rates of food grains crops and non-food grains crops as well as on the respective areas under them. Thus the compound growth rates per annum of production of food grains crops and the area under them between 1949–50 and 1964–65 have been, respectively, 1.34 percent and 2.98 percent. The corresponding figures for non-food grains crops are higher: 2.52 and 3.61 percent, respectively.[23] Our argument is further strengthened by the figures of interstate movement of cereals by rail and river: 3.20 million tons of cereals moved in 1955–56, and 9.25 million tons in 1966–67.[24]

It appears that there is a definite, though slow, trend toward the disintegration of the old mode of production in agriculture. But can we say that the capitalist mode of production already prevails in agriculture? The most definitive evidence of the degree of capitalist penetration should be the extent of wage labor in agriculture.[25] According to the census figures, roughly one-fourth of the active agricultural population in India consists of agricultural laborers, which compares favorably with the U.S. and German figures at the turn of the century.[26] Secondly, as we have already noted, there has been an increase in the percentage of landless laborers among agricultural laborers. Thirdly, the share of wage income in the income of agricultural labor households rose from 76 percent in 1950–51 to 81 percent in 1956–57.[27] However, as against these "advances"—in the objective, historical sense—there were some retreats. The ratio of attached to casual labor increased between 1950–51 and 1956–57 from 10.90 to 27.73.[28] Secondly, the share of cash in wage payment declined from 56 percent to 49 percent in the same period.[29] Finally, we should mention that according to the calculations of the Soviet author G. Kotovsky the area cultivated wholly or mainly by hired labor in the mid-fifties was 25 to 30 percent, which enables us to posit that a quarter of the area cultivated was then under the capitalist mode of production.[30]

On the whole, one must not be left with an exaggerated idea about the dissolution of the old mode of production—basically semi-feudal [31]—and the development of the capitalist mode in Indian agriculture. It is here, more than anywhere else in India, that "le mort saisit le vif." First, despite some undoubted progress—qualitative and quantitative—in the instruments of production in the post-1947 era as compared to what prevailed before, it does not come to much if we take the absolute picture. After a decade of economic development, the total value of the equipment used in farm business, excluding transport equipment, was on the order of Rs. 4,860 million, constituting a paltry 0.3 percent of the total value of tangible assets of the cultivator households of India, which was on the order of Rs. 332,750 million.[32] Secondly, even after the "implementation" of land reform legislation, survivals of the old system are still very strong. Unfortunately, exact data on tenancy, sharecropping, and lease of land are very difficult to come by. Still, some idea can be had from the accounts given by a report of the Planning Commission concerning different states: "In Andhra where substantive areas were cultivated through tenants and sharecroppers . . . they were not recorded. The Andhra Tenancy Act has been ineffective." In Assam "large areas are cultivated through tenants-at-will and sharecroppers. According to the 1961 Census 37 percent of cultivators were either tenant-cultivators or part-owner–part-tenant cultivators." In Bihar "crop-sharing is widely prevalent. According to the Census of 1961 about 25 percent of cultivators were part-tenant and part-owner cultivators and another 7.5 percent were pure tenants. The tenants usually pay half the gross produce." In Madhya Pradesh the "Tenancy Law which was soundly conceived had become ineffective due to lack of adequate steps for implementation—the law prohibits leasing (except by disabled persons). In practice, much leasing goes on in the form of crop-sharing and the sharecroppers are generally not recorded." In Madras, "in several districts large areas are cultivated through tenancies, mostly oral leases. There was much concealed tenancy." In Mysore, "in several parts of the state large areas are cultivated through sharecroppers and other tenancy arrangements but land records do not contain information about them." In Orissa "there is a fairly common practice of cultivating land through sharecropping. The sharecroppers have no security of tenure in practice. They were being evicted at the will of the landlords. The rents paid by them amounted in many cases to half of the gross produce." In Uttar Pradesh "the law prohibits leasing but permits partnership in cultivation. In practice, leasing or crop-sharing is increasing. The sharecroppers usually pay half the produce as rent. They are not allowed to remain on the land for any length of time lest they claim tenancy rights. Such arrangements are not generally recorded, and the sharecroppers are unable to claim any rights under the Law." In West Bengal, "according to the 1961 Census about 34 percent of cultivators were pure *bargadars,* that is, sharecroppers (13.4 percent) or part-owners and part-*bargadars* (21%). Between 25 to 46 percent [of the] area in different districts is cultivated through sharecroppers. The rent payable is 50 percent of the produce if the landlord provides plough cattle, etc. and 40 percent in other cases," etc.[33]

Thirdly, we have seen earlier that while there has been some progress as regards rural indebtedness, more than 60 percent of the total farm credit in India still comes under the usurious practices of private moneylenders. Worse still, interest paid by the agriculturists— excluding agricultural laborers—more than doubled over the period between 1951–52 and 1960–61 from 4.7 percent to 10.3 percent of the total income from agriculture.[34]

From the foregoing it follows that there were no real agrarian reforms in the countryside, some of the reasons for which we already referred to. The result was that the overall growth of the economy began to be seriously hampered by the lagging agricultural sector. The planners were practically convinced by the static agricultural level between 1960–61 and 1963–64 that the state of agriculture was seriously undermining the industrial development of the country. In 1964 the planners announced "a fresh consideration of the assumptions, methods, and techniques as well as the machinery of planning and plan implementation in the field of agriculture."[35] Two points were emphasized: (1) development efforts would be concentrated in areas having assured supplies of water—about a quarter of the total cultivated area; and (2) within these areas there would be a systematic effort to extend the application of science and technology. In October 1965 the new policy was put into practice under the so-called Intensive Agricultural Areas Program (IAAP). A model for this already existed in 15 districts "under the so-called Intensive Agricultural Development Program (IADP), which had begun in 1961. This new approach, which under the so-called High-Yielding Varieties Program (HYVP) would later be called the New Agricultural

Strategy, in essence emphasized the necessity of providing the culti-vator with a complete "package of practices"—including credit, modern inputs, price incentives, marketing facilities, and technical advice—in order to increase yield. Shorn of all verbiage, this "new strategy" boils down to accelerating the growth of capitalism in agri-culture *without* basic agrarian reforms—a modified version of what Lenin called "the Prussian path," a path that was followed, though in a different context, by Stolypin in prerevolutionary Russia. Though the full effects will take time to appear, there is no doubt, on the basis of available evidence, that there has been an accentuation of class differences in the districts operating under the "new strat-egy." [36] As is to be expected, the big farmers, and to some extent the middle farmers, have increasingly taken advantage of official assist-ance in relation to credit and new inputs in modern investments in production and in relation to high prices for agricultural products and low taxes. After a careful survey of the "green revolution" in four districts in widely separated parts of India, Francine Frankel comes to the following conclusion:

> The gains of the new technology have been very unevenly distrib-uted. In Ludhiana [in Punjab] where the majority of cultivators have economic holdings of 15 to 20 acres or more . . . the benefits of the new technology have been most widely, albeit still unevenly, shared. Prob-ably only the bottom twenty percent of farmers, holding ten acres or less, have experienced a serious relative deterioration in their economic position for want of sufficient capital to invest in indivisible inputs, nec-essary for profitable adoption of the new techniques. Yet, Ludhiana is atypical even for Punjab and much more so for large parts of the wheat growing belt. For example, in Bihar and Uttar Pradesh, both major wheat growing areas, over 80 percent of all cultivating households op-erate farms of less than eight acres. It is therefore not unreasonable to assume that the relative percentage of cultivators who have received significant benefits from the new technology compared to those who have been left out is almost exactly the reverse in these areas than in Ludhiana. Certainly, this has so far been the case in the rice growing region where the overwhelming majority of the cultivators have uneco-nomic holdings of two and three acres.[37]

Ladejinsky also comes to the same conclusion:

> The green revolution affects the few rather than the many not only because of environmental conditions but also because the majority of

the farmers lack resources or are "institutionally" precluded from taking advantage of the new agricultural trends. . . . The situation of the
multitude of tenants is even more difficult than that of small farmers.
. . . The old squeeze whereby tenants are reduced to sharecroppers
and eventually to landless workers is being accelerated as more of the
bigger owners become involved with the new technology. The basic
provisions of tenancy reforms are less attainable than before the advent
of the green revolution. . . . The new type of agriculture is labor-inten-
sive. . . . However the technology is both labor-absorbing and labor-
displacing. . . . Looking ahead, additional employment and better
wages are not forever, for new farm practices are bringing in a host of
labor-saving devices. . . . Thus the outlook is for an overcrowded, low-
wage farm market regardless of the scope of the green revolution.[38]

II

Next we turn to industry. The pattern of industrial development
in the postindependence era shows interesting features from the
point of view of the development of capitalism in India. We note first
that industrial production has grown at a fairly rapid rate, much
more rapidly than agricultural production, thereby widening the
differences between the town and the countryside at almost all levels
(Table 9 gives some idea of this). If we omit the years 1966–67
and 1967–68, which were exceptionally bad years for Indian industries, the index of industrial production rose from a level of 74 in
1951 (1956 = 100) to 182 in 1965—an increase of 146 percent in 14
years.[39]

At the same time the index of factory employment of labor rose
from 93.9 in 1951 (1956 = 100) to 136.5 in 1966.[40] Also, total productive capital—that is, fixed plus working capital—in large-scale
industries increased from Rs. 5,095 million in 1949 to Rs. 12,147 million in 1958, and from Rs. 17,374 million in 1959 to about Rs. 65,000
in 1965.[41] This picture does not, however, give any definite idea of
the structural changes that the industrial sector has undergone. First,
not all industries grew at the same rate: during the period under
consideration the large-scale (i.e., factory) sector grew faster than the
small-scale (i.e., non-factory) sector. In 1950–51 the ratio of large-
scale to small-scale was roughly 38:62. In 1968–69 it reversed itself to
approximately 60:40.[42]

Secondly, we have two important indices of increasing capital in-

Table 9
Production in Selected Industries

Industries	Unit	1950–51	1955–56	1960–61	1965–66	1967–68
Pig iron	Mill. tonnes	1.69	1.95	4.31	7.09	6.91
Finished steel	Mill. tonnes	1.04	1.30	2.39	4.51	4.00
Machine tools	Mill. rupees	3	8	70	294	283
Railway cars	Thous.	2.9	15.3	8.2	23.5	11.9
Diesel engines	Thous.	5.5	10.4	55.5	101.2	115.3
Electric motors	Horsepower (thous.)	99	272	728	1,753	2,029
Nitrate fertilizers	Thous. tonnes	9	80	101	232	367
Soda ash	Thous. tonnes	45	82	152	331	370
Jute textiles	Thous. tonnes	837	1,071	1,097	1,302	1,156
Cotton cloth	Mill. meters	4,215	6,260	6,738	7,440	7,509
Cement	Mill. tonnes	2.73	4.67	7.97	10.82	11.5
Sugar	Thous. tonnes	1,134	1,890	3,029	3,510	2,249
Tea	Mill. kgs.	227	299	320	373	383
Electricity (generated)	Bill. kwh	5.3	8.8	17.0	32.0	39.4

Source: Government of India, *Economic Survey 1969–70*.

tensity in Indian industries. In the first place, the ratio of total productive capital to wages plus salaries and other benefits rose from about 3 in 1949 to about 4.5 in 1958, and from about 4 in 1959 to about 6.6. in 1965.[43] In the second place, electricity consumption per factory worker rose more than 2.5 times between 1949 and 1958 and 1.5 times between 1959 and 1965.[44] Thus it seems that the organic composition of capital in the industrial sector is rising. Next, within the large-scale sector itself, consumer goods industries have in general shown a lower growth rate than capital goods industries:

whereas, for example, food manufacturing, beverages, textiles, and leather products show, respectively, 3.2, 6.1, 2.0, and 3.0 percent growth rates, electrical machinery, nonelectrical machinery, chemicals, and petroleum products show, respectively, 14.9, 17.7, 9.1, and 20.8 percent growth rates in the years between 1951 and 1966.[45] The same conclusion is reached by another calculation. The share of consumer goods in total industrial production declined from 67.9 percent in 1950–51 to 34.0 percent in 1965–66 while the share of nonconsumer goods rose, correspondingly, from 32.1 percent to 66.0 percent during the same period.[46] Again, this shows that one is growing much faster than the other.

The figures cited above on the growth rate of industries should not lead to an exaggerated notion about the extent of industrialization of India. The share of industries, including mining, in the Net National Product (at 1948–49 prices) actually *fell* from 17.1 percent in 1948–49 to 16.6 percent in 1960–61, while it rose only slightly (at 1960–61 prices) from 20.2 percent in 1960–61 to 22.4 percent in 1967–68.[47]

There is conclusive evidence that the progress of industry has strengthened the bourgeoisie. First, there has been a steady rate of increase in the industrial profits of the joint-stock companies over the third plan period. According to the Reserve Bank of India, between 1950 and 1956 (1950 = 100) the gross profits of joint-stock companies rose by 65 percent, while in the subsequent two periods—between 1955 and 1959 (1955 = 100) and between 1960–61 and 1965–66 (1960 = 100)—the gross profits of public limited companies rose by 42 percent and 55 percent, respectively. The comparable figures for private limited companies during the latter two periods were, respectively, 65 percent and 67 percent.[48] On the other hand, as regards the real earnings of factory workers earning less than Rs. 200 per month, the index rose from 100 in 1951 to 123.7 in 1955 and then gradually declined to 104.6 in 1964.[49] In fact, an official report has admitted that "during 1951–64, real wages have shown little improvement, while in 1964 there has been a substantial decline."[50] The report adds that "the provisional data for 1965 and 1966, now available, don't indicate any change in the trend."[51] Then, again, the paid-up capital of joint-stock companies increased by about five times from 1947–48 to 1965–66.[52] The particularly rapid expansion of large companies confirms that the big bourgeoisie has reaped the greatest advantage from this development. As Professor Hazari has shown, the four largest groups of capitalists—Tata, Birla, Martin Burn, and Dalmia Sahujain—increased their share of capital in nongovernment public companies from 18 percent in 1951 to 22 percent in 1958.[53] An official report listed, as of 1963–64, the top 75 groups of monopolies, which, while owning less than 6 percent of nongovernment nonbanking companies, held about 47 percent of their total assets.[54] In 1967–68 the share of these groups in the total assets of nongovernment nonbanking companies, of which they owned about 8 percent, rose to about 54 percent.[55]

III

Who are the agents behind the development of capitalism in India? We have seen that the Indian bourgeoisie wanted to carry India along an independent capitalist path. The most mature bourgeoisie in Asia outside of Japan, they were conscious of the difficulties faced by a backward capitalism, and were aware that private enterprise alone could not deliver the goods. There were two nonexclusive alternatives: intervention by the state—their state—in the economy at an accelerated pace, and collaboration with foreign capital.

That the Indian bourgeoisie opted for a large public sector is clear from Nehru's account of the role played by big business in the Congress National Planning Commission,[56] as well as from the fact that the so-called Bombay Plan, formulated toward the end of World War II by Tata, Birla, and six other big capitalist groups, provided for a considerable extension of state ownership and management of the economy. An examination of the government of India's Industrial Policy Resolutions of 1948 and 1956 shows that the state has agreed to step in only where for various reasons private enterprise cannot do the job alone. The intervention by the state in the Indian economy was meant *primarily* to create conditions for the rapid development of capitalism, and *secondarily* to prevent excessive concentration and monopoly of economic power, the latter being promoted by the exigencies of parliamentary democracy and the necessity of not alienating the small and middle bourgeoisie from the big bourgeoisie—in other words, in order to serve the interests of the capitalist class as a *whole* even at the cost of the interest of *particular* capitalists. As to the secondary purpose of the state intervention, we have seen that it had very little negative effect on the growth of concentration and monopoly.

The primary purpose of state intervention is proved by the essentially capitalist character of the state intervention itself and by the growth of the private sector during the planning period. As regards the first objective, it is enough to list the measures of nationalization effected so far, including the much-vaunted bank nationalization. If we consider the nationalization of air transport in 1953, of the Imperial Bank in 1955, and of life insurance in 1956, we see that each was undertaken with some specific goals in view and none formed part of any concerted anti-private enterprise strategy; the same holds true for bank nationalization in 1969. In the first case the resources at the disposal of air transport were insufficient; in the second case there was the necessity of extensive credit well beyond the scope of private moneylenders; in the third case, there was the uncertainty of mopping up savings for large industrial investments as well as the need to clean up an industry that was inefficient and corrupt; in the fourth case, there was the need to extend credit and banking facilities to agriculture so as to widen the basis of capitalism in the countryside.

Obviously the basic question involves who holds the state power. Since this power is essentially held by the big bourgeoisie in alliance with the landlords, the character of state intervention cannot but be capitalist. Even the share of the state in the economy cannot make one enthusiastic: two decades after independence, 88 percent of the domestic product is still at the disposal of the private sector, and the share of the government rose by only about 5 percent during the period.[57]

Also noteworthy is the rapid growth of the private sector in the course of the planning period, a growth that has been facilitated by the activities of the public sector. We have already cited some data in support of this contention. As an ex-cabinet minister has observed, "The private sector could not have achieved the expansion that it has but for the public sector investment in economic overheads and heavy industries." [58] We also know that the state has helped the private sector by extending long-term credit to big industries through such financial institutions as the Industrial Finance Corporation, the National Industrial Development Corporation, and the State Finance Corporations.[59]

IV

Thus, based on the evidence, India is following the capitalist path of development. We have already seen the impossibility of following such a path in the "classical" way, that is, by depending on private enterprise alone. The Indian bourgeoisie had to create a state capitalist sector for the purpose. Indeed, the private sector plus the state capitalist sector was at first considered sufficient to take India along the capitalist path of development, without *substantially* depending upon foreign capital. As a matter of fact, until the mid-fifties the Indian bourgeoisie was not very enthusiastic about the *fresh* inflow of foreign capital into India lest it jeopardize the very purpose for which the bourgeoisie had fought against British rule: independent capitalist development. This fact is reflected in the remark by an American observer that "until the late fifties the total inflow of foreign capital into India was sluggish. The inflow of American private capital amounted to little more than a trickle." [60]

But toward the end of the Second Five-Year Plan India's economic development began to show alarming trends. The growth of industrial production slowed considerably, investment fell off, and India faced its worst balance-of-payments crisis. The stage was set for a marked shift in the whole trend of foreign capital inflow. Whereas between 1953 and 1958 the book value of outstanding foreign business investments in the private sector—the sector involving commercial and industrial undertakings, including state-owned enterprises —increased by Rs. 135 crores, between 1958 and 1963 it increased by Rs. 244 crores.[61] At the same time, of the total number of foreign collaboration agreements approved—2,200 between 1948 and 1964—1,900 were effected between 1956 and 1964 alone.[62] Then, again, as a proportion of total investment in India, the net inflow of capital rose from 6 percent in 1954 to about 23 percent in 1964–65.[63]

However, one should not look merely at the quantitative aspect of foreign investments in India. More important is the *character* of foreign investments as revealed, first, in their national sources and, second, in their industrial distribution. On both these counts the character of foreign investment has undergone a vast change in the last two decades. In the first place, whereas the U.K. share in total foreign investment in the private sector was roughly 80 percent in 1948, it fell to 54 percent in 1965 and 48 percent in 1967. The corresponding figures for the U.S.A. were 4 percent, 22 percent, and 25 percent.[64] In other words, the change broadly reflects the shift in the balance of forces in world capitalism. Secondly, the composition of foreign investments in 1948 showed a "classical" colonial pattern: if we exclude services and concentrate on the productive sphere alone, we can see the overwhelming preponderance of the nonmanufacturing sector (excluding petroleum) as compared with the manufacturing sector (including petroleum). Two decades later the balance is completely reversed. (See Table 10.)

Table 10

Private Sector: * *Outstanding Long-term Foreign Business Investments* **
(Rs. millions)

Industry group	End of June 1948	End of December 1958	End of March 1967***
Plantations	522	951	1,114
Mining	115	118	101
Petroleum	223	1,184	1,649
Manufacturing	707	2,149	6,309
Services	1,079	1,223	3,133
Total	2,646	5,625	12,306

    * Excludes banking and insurance.
    ** Book value of investments.
    *** At the pre-devaluation rate.
Source: *Reserve Bank of India Bulletin*, August 1969.

Within the manufacturing sector itself the growth of foreign investments has been much higher in capital goods—including the most technologically sophisticated ones—than in consumer goods, is shown in Table 11. Similarly, of the total number of effective foreign collaboration agreements, as opposed to total number of approvals— amounting to 1,050 by 1965—the number of agreements in manufacturing alone was 1,006, and an industrywide classification reveals that machinery and machine tools, electrical goods, and chemicals

Table 11

Private Sector: Outstanding Foreign Business Investments in Manufacturing
(Rs. millions)

Items	End of June 1948	End of December 1958	End of March 1967
Food, beverages, etc.	101	304	406
Textile products	280	211	521
Transport equipment	10	57	657
Machinery and machine tools	12	59	363
Metals and metal products	80	760	1,166
Electrical goods and machinery	48	171	521
Chemicals and allied products	80	259	1,838
Miscellaneous	96	328	837
Total manufacturing	707	2,149	6,309
Total (all industry groups)	2,646	5,625	12,306

For explanations and source, see footnotes to Table 10.

together accounted for 55 percent of the total effective agreements.[65] Nothing illustrates better imperialism's control of the "commanding heights" of the Indian economy. The capitalist path that India is following is essentially a *dependent capitalist path*. This conclusion is further strengthened by the fact that foreign assistance—loans and grants, excluding foreign business investments—has increased over the three Plan periods, as Table 12 data indicate.

Table 12

External Assistance to India
(Rs. millions)

	Authorizations	Utilizations
Until end of First Plan	3,817.5	2,016.7
During Second Plan	25,311.4	14,301.9
During Third Plan	29,359.1	28,675.2

Source: Government of India, *Economic Survey, 1968–69.*

At the same time the share of the national resources in the investments made by the state capitalist sector has dwindled, as is seen
from the fact that the share of foreign assistance in total public sector
outlays has grown from 9.6 percent in 1951–56 (First Plan period) to
44.99 percent in 1967–68.[66] The lion's share of total foreign assistance—it goes without saying—is provided by the U.S.A., and has
amounted to more than $9,000 million between 1951 and 1969, an
amount that is higher than all the rest of foreign assistance over the
period.[67]

Last but not at all least, it should be emphasized that the "new agricultural strategy" referred to earlier has been directly inspired and
promoted by the U.S.A., through both technical and financial
means. According to an official handout,

> At present agriculture accounts for 40 percent of the technical assist-
> ance expenditures of the USAID Mission [in India]. Five years ago the
> figure was only 24 percent. U.S. foreign exchange assistance for Indian
> agricultural development exceeds Rs. 525 crores. In addition the U.S.
> has extended to agricultural development loans and grants totalling
> Rs. 750 crores from the sales proceeds of commodities supplied under
> PL 480. Some 125 American agricultural specialists are now serving in
> India at the request of the Indian Government.[68]

It must be pointed out here that the increasing Soviet economic
and military aid to India in no way alters the situation. This aid,
while strengthening the Soviet position in India vis-à-vis the American, at the same time strengthens the Indian ruling classes at the cost
of the emerging revolutionary forces inside India and serves the Soviet Union's global strategy of isolating China.

V

The consequences for India of following the *dependent capitalist path*
are plain for all to see. We shall touch upon the broadest economic
indicators.

National income and, still more, per capita income, in real terms,
have shown extremely moderate rates of growth. Thus, at 1948–49
prices, national income showed an annual growth rate of 3.5 percent
during the First Plan and 3.8 percent during the Second Plan. The

corresponding rates for per capita income were 1.6 percent and 1.7 percent. During the Third Plan the growth rates of national and per capita income, at 1960–61 prices, were a paltry 2.8 percent and 0.1 percent.[69] In fact, their index numbers, using 1960–61 prices and with 1960–61 as base, showed increases, respectively, of only 27.4 percent and 4.9 percent over a period of eight years (1960–61 to 1968–69).[70] Similarly, the annual growth rates of industrial and agricultural outputs (at 1960–61 prices), which were, respectively, 7.9 percent and 3.1 percent from 1954–55 to 1964–65, declined to 4.1 percent and 0.1 percent from 1964–65 to 1969–70.[71] Net investment as a proportion of national income—according to the Reserve Bank estimates—increased from 8.5 percent in 1954–55 to 14.0 percent in 1964–65, and thereafter showed a continuous decline to 9.3 percent in 1969–70. On the other hand, the annual growth rate in wholesale prices rose from 4.7 percent between 1954–55 and 1964–65 to 7.4 percent between 1964–65 and 1969–70.[72] Thus the Fourth Plan's assumption of relative price stability, on which all its estimates are based, is fast proving illusory. Again, giving the lie to the Indian government's proclaimed goal of eradicating unemployment by the mid-sixties, various Plan documents estimated the number of unemployed to have increased from 5.3 million at the end of the First Plan to between 9 and 10 million at the end of the Third Plan. By all accounts these were gross underestimates. The Fourth Plan document has given up all attempts to estimate the unemployed. Finally, India's external debt has grown alarmingly over the years: from Rs. 320.3 million at the end of 1950–51 to Rs. 10,013.7 million at the end of 1960–61, to Rs. 31,521 million at the end of 1965–66, and to Rs. 60,305.6 million at the end of 1967–68.[73]

The economic policy pursued by the ruling classes has already affected the standard of living of the people in a significant way. Taking a conservative estimate of Rs. 15 per capita per month (at 1960–61 prices) as the minimum standard of living in a rural area, a recent study using the National Sample Survey data has shown that the percentage of people below the minimum level in rural India went up from 38.03 in 1960–61 to 53.02 in 1967–68, thus registering a rise of about 40 percent in less than a decade.[74] Another recent study, taking about the same minimum standard of living for a rural area, has estimated that 40 percent of the rural population remained below this minimum in 1960–61, but that the percentage remained

the same in 1967–68. However, taking Rs. 22.5 as the minimum for
the urban area, the same study has estimated that 50 percent of the
urban population remained below this minimum in 1960–61 and
that the condition of the bottom 20 percent of the urban population
had deteriorated by 1967–68. "Thus while the character of rural
poverty has remained the same as before, the character of urban
poverty has deepened further." [75]

The serious difficulties the Indian economy has been facing regarding the growth of the national product and an all-round improvement in people's living conditions do not, in the main, arise
from any natural or technical deficiencies. They stem from the particular path of economic development that India has been following.
The choice of this path was primarily due to the incapacity and unwillingness of the Indian bourgeoisie—given its relative weakness
and its solidarity with the semifeudal elements in the countryside in
the face of growing mass struggle—to effect radical agrarian reforms
and thereby remove the obstacles to the development of productive
forces for the immense majority of the Indian people. It is only when
the poor and landless peasants, the majority of the rural people, directly take politics into their own hands that the indispensable agrarian transformations can be effected, the main obstacles to economic
development removed, and India's dependence on imperialism
ended. This, however, is unthinkable without the seizure of political
power by the proletariat in alliance with the peasantry.

Notes

1. Government of India, *Indian Agriculture in Brief* (1968), pp. 118–121; Government of India, *Fourth Five Year Plan (1969–74)*, p. 117.
2. Cited by S. R. Sen in *Commerce*, Annual Number, 1967, p. 43.
3. *Fourth Five Year Plan*, p. 117.
4. Government of India, *Third Five Year Plan*, p. 382; Government of India,
   Fourth Five Year Plan: A Draft Outline, p. 9.
5. *Indian Agriculture in Brief*, op. cit., p. 189.
6. Two important references are his *Agrarian Program of Russian Social Democracy in the Democratic Revolution* (1907) and Preface to the second edition
   (1907) of *Development of Capitalism in Russia* (1899).
7. Thus, a keen American observer of the Indian agrarian scene, Daniel
   Thorner, pointed out that in the state of Bihar the landlords, taking advantage of the definition of personal cultivation as given in the legisla-

tion, could retain 500–700 and even 1,000 acres of land in the post-"reform" era. See Daniel Thorner, *The Agrarian Prospect of India* (1956), p. 34.

8. *Khudkasht* signifies land under the personal cultivation of the landlord.
9. See the consolidated study by P. T. George in *Indian Journal of Agricultural Economics*, July–September 1968.
10. P. T. George, op. cit., and Singh and Misra, *Land Reforms in Uttar Pradesh* (1964), p. 160.
11. P. T. George, ibid. (Emphasis added.)
12. *Third Five Year Plan*, pp. 236–238.
13. Basu and Bhattacharya, *Land Reforms in West Bengal* (1963), p. 82.
14. Marx, *Das Kapital*, Vol. III, p. 607, in Marx-Engels, *Werke*, Vol. 25 (1964).
15. Ibid., p. 608.
16. Lenin, *Development of Capitalism in Russia*, Chapter XIII.
17. *National Sample Survey Report*, No. 95 (July 1960–June 1961); and Reserve Bank of India, *All India Rural Debt and Investment Survey*, 1961–62.
18. See *All India Rural Credit Survey* (1954), Vol. II, Chapter 30.
19. *Census of India*, 1961. Paper No. I of 1962 Appendix III.
20. See the reference already cited.
21. *National Sample Survey*, 8th Round, 1953–54, and 17th Round, 1961–62.
22. See K. Kautsky, *La Question Agraire* (1900), Preface to the French edition and Chapter VII; also Lenin, *Capitalism in Agriculture* (1900), first article, Sec. III.
23. Government of India, *Growth Rates in Indian Agriculture* (1966).
24. *Indian Agriculture in Brief*, Table 6.2.
25. See Lenin, *New Data on Laws of Development of Capitalism in Agriculture* (1914–1915), Part I, Sec. 16.
26. Cited by Lenin, ibid., Sec. 5.
27. *Report of the Second Agricultural Labour Enquiry* (1960), Appendix IV.
28. Ibid.
29. Ibid.
30. See G. Kotovsky, *Agrarian Reforms in India* (People's Publishing House, Delhi, 1964), p. 158. The existence of wage labor, while perhaps the most definitive evidence of the capitalist mode of production, is not its *only* evidence, at least in agriculture. Plowing back profits for further production is also important evidence. Lack of sufficiently disaggregated data on capital accumulation in relation to the farm size in India prevents us from any measurement in this regard.
31. Here we follow Bettelheim's characterization of India's agrarian structure as being not fully feudal but showing such features of a declining feudalism as absence of a labor market over a large part of the rural sec-

tor, the personal subservience of the immediate producer to the land-owner, the excessive importance of land rent, the use of produce mostly to satisfy immediate needs, and the underdeveloped social division of labor (*India Independent* [Monthly Review Press, New York, 1968], p. 23).

32. *All India Rural Debt and Investment Survey 1961–62*, Table II, in *Reserve Bank of India Bulletin*, June 1963.

33. Government of India Planning Commission, *Implementation of Land Reforms* (1966), pp. 2–13.

34. S. A. Shah and M. Rajagopal, *Economic Weekly* (Bombay), October 12, 1963.

35. Government of India Planning Commission, *Memorandum on the Fourth Five Year Plan* (1964), p. 26.

36. See, among others, Francine R. Frankel, *Agricultural Modernization and Social Change* (mimeographed), USAID, New Delhi, September 1969; W. Ladejinsky, "Green Revolution in Punjab," in *Economic and Political Weekly*, June 28, 1969; "Green Revolution in Bihar," ibid., September 27, 1969; and "Ironies of India's Green Revolution," *Foreign Affairs*, July 1970. See also Hari Sharma's essay in this volume.

37. F. Frankel, op. cit.

38. *Foreign Affairs*, July 1970.

39. Government of India Planning Commission, *Fourth Five Year Plan: A Draft Outline*, p. 10.

40. Government of India, *Indian Labour Statistics* (1968).

41. Government of India, Central Statistical Organization, Department of Statistics, Cabinet Secretariat, *Census of Manufacturing Industries* and *Annual Survey of Industries*. CMI data refer to the period up to 1958 with a much narrower coverage of industries than the ASI data, which refer to the period beginning with 1959. For details see the Introduction to the *ASI*.

42. Our calculation based on data given in *Statistical Abstract*, India, 1962 and *Estimate of National Product*, 1970 (Central Statistical Organization).

43. Calculated on the basis of data given in *Census of Manufacturing Industries* and *Annual Survey of Industries*. The 1959 ratio, while seemingly smaller, is not strictly comparable to 1958 ratio for the reasons already given.

44. Calculated on the basis of data given by CMI, ASI, and Central Water and Power Commission (Ministry of Irrigation and Power).

45. Calculated from Government of India, *Economic Survey* (1968–69).

46. Calculated from *Fourth Five Year Plan: A Draft Outline*, p. 10.

47. *Economic Survey* (1968–69). In the latter so-called "revised" estimate, as between 1960–61 and 1967–68, construction and electricity were added to industries and mining.

48. *Statistical Abstract*, India (1958–59, 1962, and 1968).

49. *Indian Labour Statistics*, 1968.

50. *Report of the National Commission on Labour* (1969), p. 189.
51. Ibid.
52. *Statistical Abstract*, India (1958–59 and 1968).
53. *The Structure of the Corporate Private Sector* (1966), p. 305.
54. *Monopolies Enquiry Commission Report* (1965), pp. 121–122.
55. B. Datta, "Growth of Industrial Houses," in *Company News and Notes*, May 1 and 16, 1970 (Department of Company Affairs, Ministry of Industrial Development).
56. *Discovery of India* (4th ed.), p. 404.
57. *India: A Reference Annual* (1966), p. 150; *Estimates of National Product* (August 1970).
58. Manubhai Shah, in *Eastern Economist*, July 21, 1967.
59. For a fuller analysis of the role of the state in India's economic development, see P. Chattopadhyay, "State Capitalism in India," *Monthly Review*, March 1970.
60. J. P. Lewis, *Quiet Crisis in India* (1962), p. 211. For a good summary of the evidence see M. Kidron, *Foreign Investments in India* (1965), pp. 65 ff.
61. *Reserve Bank of India Bulletin*, August 1969.
62. Reserve Bank of India, *Foreign Collaboration in Indian Industry* (1968), p. 4.
63. Our calculation, based on the RBI data.
64. Reserve Bank of India, *India's Foreign Liabilities and Assets* (1961), *Survey Report* (1964), and *Bulletin* (August 1969).
65. Reserve Bank of India, *Foreign Collaboration in Indian Industry* (1968), p. 102.
66. Planning Commission, as given in *Records and Statistics, Quarterly Bulletin of the Eastern Economist*, November 1968.
67. United States Information Service, *Fact Sheet: U.S. Economic Assistance to India* (1969).
68. Ibid., June 1951–January 1970.
69. *Economic Survey*, 1969–70.
70. *Estimates of National Product*, August 1970 (Central Statistical Organization).
71. *Reserve Bank of India Bulletins*, April, June, and October 1969 and September 1970.
72. *Reserve Bank of India Bulletins*.
73. Ministry of Finance, as given in the Planning Commission's *Basic Statistics Relating to the Indian Economy*, December 1969. India's external debt at the end of 1967–68 amounted to about U.S. $8,440 million.
74. P. Bardhan, "Green Revolution and Agricultural Labourers: A Correction," *Economic and Political Weekly*, November 14, 1970.
75. Dandekar and Rath, "Poverty in India: Dimensions and Trends," *Economic and Political Weekly*, January 2, 1971.

5. Neocolonial Alliances and the Crisis of Pakistan

Hassan N. Gardezi

When we speak of a crisis in Pakistan, a number of things come to mind. In the economic sphere we can see a continuation of the grinding poverty of the masses, alongside the accumulation of extraordinary riches by a few; an almost total and abject surrender of the national economy to U.S. advisers, planners, and investors, who have secured the country in a debt trap amounting to billions of dollars (Pakistan now owes about $5 billion to the lending countries, mainly the United States, and spends about 30 percent of its total export earnings as interest payments on these loans).[1] On the political side, the country has witnessed the suspension of two constitutions; extended periods of martial law and governor's rule; repeated suppression of mass media and political parties; incarceration of political workers; and servile alignments with Cold War manipulators. In the broader social sphere, such critical problems as corruption, illiteracy, inadequate housing and sanitation, abuse of manual workers, injustice toward children, women, and the depressed classes in general, and misuse of bureaucratic privilege and authority continue to aggravate the people. And at the moment (October 1971), the rulers are faced with a formidable secessionist movement in East Bengal, traditionally the most exploited region.

All these problems are tragic and take their daily toll of human happiness, dignity, health, and life. However, they are only the surface eruptions of a deeper crisis that afflicts Pakistani society, worsening over time. If we examine these problems in isolation from one another and as conditions of an autonomous society, our analysis will be limited to the level of symptoms. Indeed, there will be those who

An earlier version of this article was published in *Pakistan Forum*, December 1970–January 1971. The article was revised in October 1971 during the East Bengali resistance struggle against the armies of Yahya Khan.

will have us believe that these conditions are only the accidental and unfortunate by-products of "progress," and that there is nothing basically wrong. This view of the country's problems will preclude an analysis of the underlying process which creates the instruments for exploitation of people and the demeaning of their lives. And so long as we see these problems as by-products of an otherwise healthy society, we will not ask for radical change. Thus, as in the past, each overt crisis will be followed by minor readjustments that do not significantly disturb the status quo. These surface readjustments, now quite familiar to Pakistani people, may include emphasis on law and order, suspension of civil governments, reshuffling of administrative officers, temporary crackdowns on corrupt practices, and minor educational, legal, political, and economic reforms proposed by hurriedly convened commissions and implemented in the heat of the moment; or massive military retaliation may be undertaken in case of continued popular insurgency, as is being witnessed in East Bengal today. Such measures may succeed in managing the overt crises, but cannot be expected to eliminate the structural conditions responsible for their creation and perpetuation. Each time such minor readjustments are undertaken, there is a temporary containment of tensions and conflicts that are followed by ever more serious eruptions.

The Basic Crisis

In order to diagnose the basic crisis of Pakistan we must start with the most obvious socioeconomic reality. This consists of a historically widening gap between the ruling classes and the large masses of poor and powerless people. The most obvious manifestations of this gap are economic—extremes of poverty and affluence; equally important, however, is the system of power and privilege that operates on both the national and international level, and points to certain historical processes that began with the imperialist colonization of the Indian subcontinent. The end result of these processes is an operation through which the resources of the country and the labor of the vast majority of its people can be exploited by internal and external representatives of imperialist capitalism. A prerequisite for such exploitation has been the creation of particular kinds of small elite groups. Historically, these groups have had to become systematically alienated from the majority of their people—culturally, politically, and psychologically—before they could be instrumental in exploiting their own society.

In Pakistan the creation and progressive alienation of these elites began with the establishment of colonial rule in the subcontinent, and continued after the attainment of independence as part of a broader process of neocolonialism.

The Making of the Elite: The Landlords

The contemporary class structure of Pakistan owes its origin primarily to the colonial policy pursued by the British. As the administrative and economic needs of their empire dictated, the British superimposed on the indigenous stratification systems of the Indian subcontinent small groups of functionaries and privileged classes whose orientations and interests were deflected from the common concerns of their own people to serve the interests of the empire.

From the beginning these groups constituted several levels of title-holders to landed estates, who often maintained custodial armed detachments on behalf of the colonial authorities. Permanent land settlement programs were also used by the British viceroys to reward "loyal" subjects in the form of huge land grants. Large tracts of land were in some instances awarded to persons who were ruthless enough to indenture masses of laborers to dig a canal or build a strategic road. These landowning gentry came to be known as *zamindars, talukdars, jagirdars, mansabdars, nawabs,* and so forth.

Administrators, Professionals, and Lesser Functionaries

As the British acquired a stronger hold over the land, the local systems of administration, justice, trade, and commerce were gradually replaced by those obtaining in England. This necessitated the recruitment and training of administrative and technical functionaries to man the lower-level positions in various government departments. Thus an educational system was established, along the lines of British schools and universities, where some vocational and professional instruction was imparted to the natives along with a heavy emphasis on learning the English language, customs, manners, political and moral ideas, arts, and literature. These institutions produced masses of clerical workers and technicians as well as minor administrators and some professionals, such as lawyers, college teachers, medical doctors, engineers, and accountants. In the famous words of Lord Macaulay, these functionaries were to be "a class of persons, Indian in blood and color, but English in taste, in opinions, in morals, and in intellect." [2] Once through the new system of education, the majority of these classes were just enough removed from their indigenous culture to become socially and psychologically marginal to their own society. During the later period of colonial rule, when some of the local functionaries were permitted to enter the higher provincial and central government services—the so-called "superior" services—care was taken to drill them thoroughly in the British style of thinking and acting. They were sent to exclusive academies in the subcontinent and in England, where instruction ranged from observance of British table manners and horse-riding to techniques of maintaining law and order. A basic mechanism of maintaining law and order was to impress upon the people that the higher administrator was a superior being. He not only knew the routine of his office, but was initiated into the folkways of the ruling aliens and was thus entitled to the same deference and respect. His psychic and cultural distance from the people was maintained by providing him with retinues of attendants dressed in the courtly costumes of the Mughal kings. While the landed gentry and the professional classes were relatively free to maintain contact with the people, the senior administrators had few such opportunities. They were inbred in exclusive "civil lines" colonies that were well removed from the fret and struggle of the common man's life. With rare exceptions the senior civil servants of Pakistan maintain this style of life to this day.

The Capitalists and Businessmen

A third dominant class that began to emerge at the turn of the century consisted of big businessmen and industrialists. When the British first established their foothold in the subcontinent, they found the area rich in raw materials and manufactured goods. These raw materials soon became a major source of supply for the large-scale manufacture which had commenced in England as a result of the Industrial Revolution. On the other hand, indigenous industries and commerce were seen as having no value except the negative one of reducing the Indian market for manufactured goods coming from England, and competing with the mother country's products in foreign markets. Thus, throughout the eighteenth century and the early part of the nineteenth century, local commercial and manufacturing activity was undermined, first through outright plunder and later by calculated neglect and the use of discriminatory tariff restrictions.[3]

At the same time, however, the British were drawing on Indian revenues to foot the bills of administration both in India and in the Colonial Office in England. By the 1920s, as a result of the systematic depletion of agricultural revenues and the almost total lack of major indigenous commercial and industrial activity, government revenues had declined to the point where the administration of India was no longer very profitable. In 1920, for example, India's net annual exports by sea amounted to £16,313,490, while during the same year £17,532,298 were paid toward the Secretary of State's bill in the India Office in England.[4] Regular verbal battles were fought over the sharing of revenues between the viceroys of India and the India Office in England.[5] As a result, the British belatedly started paying attention to the industrial and commercial development of the subcontinent. This commercial and industrial activity was promoted in the best traditions of capitalism: the 1930s witnessed the emergence of a sizable class of local industrialists and entrepreneurs whose mode of production and related social philosophies were imported ready-made from England.

The Military

The British Indian army was from the beginning an instrument of imperial conquest and repression. After the "mutiny" of 1857 the development of the armed forces took certain directions which explain their past and current performance. Earlier reliance on the local overlords for the supply of detachments at times of crisis was abandoned in favor of recruitment of a centralized army with direct allegiance to the British crown. Through emphasis on professionalization, attempts were made to neutralize the social consciousness of the soldiers. When they were not on the front lines of the British wars in East Asia, the Middle East, Africa, and Europe, they were barracked

in carefully guarded cantonments. Their domestic role was to periodically suppress the popular uprisings and localized riots.

Recruited mostly from the "more loyal" northern provinces, the
regiments were organized on ethnic lines. When faced with a popular uprising, the regiments employed for repression belonged to ethnic groups other than those found in the area of conflict. Chauvinistic and racist stereotypes were openly promoted among the ranks as
well as the civilian population. Thus the Punjab was the "sword arm
of the British Empire." Sikhs, Baluchis, and Gurkhas were the "martial races." The army in general was "more civilized" than the civilian population.

The commanding ranks in the army were mostly held by British
officers during colonial rule. However, the need to recruit native Indians to the officer ranks became increasingly acute with the two
world wars and the needs of British imperialism to police its enclaves
of influence around the world. As a result, some native Indians were
handpicked for initiation into the officer ranks. These recruits,
mostly descendants of the elite groups mentioned above, were
trained, groomed, and brainwashed in Sandhurst-type academies established in the subcontinent and in England.

These directions of recruitment, training, and socialization of the
armed forces continued during the postcolonial period. In the case of
Pakistan, the source of inspiration, training, and material help simply shifted from England to the United States. The collapse of parliamentary democracy also provided the military with the opportunity to bring the country under its rule. The performance of the
military regime from 1958 is described in the following pages. The
civilian elite had no difficulty in coalescing with the military rulers
in pursuit of their mutual class interests. The elite rule, conjoined
with the oppressive power of the military, only sharpened the class
contradictions in the country, thus generating the conditions for
eventual bloody confrontations.

Elite Groups and the Working Class

When the struggle for independence began, the basic class apparatus of the capitalist system of production and political control was already created. Among the elite groups the categories with dispropor-
tionate shares of political and economic power were the large

landlords, the owners of large capital and industry, the senior administrators, and the professionals. Below them there was a somewhat larger, heterogeneous "middle class" of clerical and technical workers, craftsmen, small shopkeepers, writers, poets, teachers, and religious scholar-functionaries. At the bottom of the class structure were the masses of manual workers and peasants. The basic cleavage of orientation and interest within this class structure was between the top elite and the masses of peasants and workers. The middle groups, because of their socially and economically marginal position, were by and large unable to identify consistently with either the top elite or the masses of people.

The Transfer of Political Power to the Elite

As the struggle for independence gained momentum from the 1930s on, most of the spokesmen against foreign rule, who were both articulate and also recognized as such by the British rulers, emerged from the ranks of upper class professional and independently wealthy men of high caste and "known families." The broader sections of the population had already become restive after more than a century of colonial exploitation, several acute famines, involvement in two major foreign wars, and a severe depression. Militant protests, bombings, and sabotage of government operations had become very common. The British saw that the choice before them was either to wait until the masses rose in popular revolts, thus effecting a final break with their erstwhile colonizers, or to talk and eventually to transfer government to the newly emerging elite classes of professionals, landowners, and industrialists who had come in touch with Western ideas of nationalism, parliamentary democracy, and industrial development. More than one Western commentator has acknowledged that the timing and manner of the transfer of power were effected with a view to ensuring that the leaders of the new states of India and Pakistan would share the political language and ideology of the British rulers, and would thus be willing to prevent a popular socialist movement from materializing after the end of colonial rule.[6] Gunnar Myrdal maintains:

> Because of its decision to relinquish its political hold in the area, Britain was able to preserve all its financial, industrial and commercial

positions in India and Pakistan practically intact. It also maintained much of its political and cultural influence in these two countries. . . .[7]

Never before had the British found the political scene in the subcontinent dominated by an array of independently wealthy groups of professionals, high-caste pundits, religious scholars, landlords, titleholders, and industrialists. All of these were fairly safe candidates for inheriting the imperial political power, and by their very class composition were incapable of posing a real threat to the essential continuity of colonial policy in the postindependence period.

Betrayal of the People

While before independence these elite groups had managed to keep their positions on the basic questions of economic freedom and social justice fairly vague, after the creation of Pakistan they could no longer evade these issues. No matter how much the understanding and social consciousness of the ruling elite were confounded by their class interests, the meaning of independence for the working class people was quite clear: it was an opportunity to free themselves from hunger, disease, ignorance, and oppression. In fact, it was the realization of being an underprivileged socioeconomic community that made the Muslims of the subcontinent rally behind the demand for an independent homeland, separate from India. Those Muslims who regarded themselves primarily as a religious community were opposed to the idea of Pakistan. Among the major religiously based parties which opposed the creation of Pakistan were the Jamiat-ul-Ulema-e-Hind, Jamaat-e-Islami, and Ihrar. The founder of the Muslim League, as well as many workers in the movement, portrayed the struggle for independence from colonial rule as freedom from exploitation by the big-city financial and capitalist interests. For some time after the creation of Pakistan, those who succeeded the British rulers continued the rhetoric of freedom, equality, and prosperity for all. However, as has been shown, they are incapable of grasping the significance of the people's participation in politics and nation-building. On the contrary, their social origins and experience dispose them to serve the needs of an internal and external capitalism which thrives on inequities of wealth and privilege.

This precisely is the basic crisis of Pakistan. It explains the reluctance of the successive governments to seek electoral support for their policies. It explains repeated resort to the forces of law and order and to military retaliations, suspensions of the civil rights of people, and the banning of political parties with socialist programs. It explains repeated expressions of suspicion and contempt for the political judgment of the working classes by the elite, both inside and outside the government. While the newly empowered elite struggle and scramble for political positions, and in the process knock each other in and out of political office, they blame the failure of parliamentary democracy on the "irresponsibility" of the "uneducated" electorate.[8] Above all, the socioeconomic character of the elite explains the recent intensification of the people's struggles in various parts of Pakistan against the repressive regime. To understand these struggles we need to expose the nature and extent of exploitation to which the people of Pakistan have been subjected in the postindependence period.

Economic Exploitation

The ruling elite's lack of responsiveness to the needs and aspirations of its own people contrasts sharply with its eagerness to serve the international neocolonial hierarchy with its own special brand of industrial, financial, and monetary institutions. This international system is recommended to the local elite through elaborate mechanisms of powerful salesmanship, individual enticement, brainwashing (guided tours to America and scholarships for training abroad), and militarist infiltration and pressure. The case of Pakistan is a classic example of how these mechanisms have been used, ostensibly to modernize the country, but in effect to acquire total control of its political economy and social policy. It is instructive to review Pakistan's postindependence economic and political evolution in this context.

Despite many prophecies to the contrary, within a few years after independence Pakistan emerged as an economically solvent nation. Until 1956 the country produced substantial surpluses in its balance of payments.[9] With the exception of the year 1952–53, when there was a crop failure, the country was practically meeting its total needs for staple food (grain, pulse, and flour). This situation lasted until

1956, when food imports started escalating to phenomenal proportions.[10] Beginning as an importer of textiles, within seven years Pakistan was exporting substantial quantities of cloth.[11] While in 1953–54 Pakistan was spending almost five times less on imports of machinery than in 1959–60, its annual rate of growth, originating in manufacture, registered increases of as much as 29.6 percent[12]—a record performance that was never matched during the so-called development decade. Furthermore, these levels of performance were achieved with a minimum of foreign assistance. Prior to 1959–60 Pakistan received only nominal economic aid from the United States, and had a much smaller contingent of foreign advisers, experts, and consultants.

Approximately after 1958, and with the advent of Ayub Khan's regime, dependence on foreign aid increased to enormous proportions, with the process of economic planning becoming completely dominated by foreigners—particularly a large contingent of Americans from Harvard University—and Pakistan moved rapidly into the position of a new type of economic colony. The insidious takeover of the Pakistan Planning Commission is described in detail by Albert Waterston, a member of the inner circle of American advisers.[13] The role of foreign advisers and planners was only the beginning: Pakistan became one of the biggest employers of foreign technicians, with no check on their qualifications or on their knowledge of local environmental conditions. In 1967 the number of such technicians in water and electric power departments alone was reported to be more than 1,000.[14] At the same time that this invasion of highly paid foreign technicians was taking place, large numbers of Pakistani technicians and scientists were being forced to leave the country because of a combination of factors—unemployment, misemployment, low salaries, delays in the processing of applications, arrogant behavior of the Pakistani officialdom, and phony objections to the qualifications of candidates for jobs (for example, being married to a foreign wife). To meet the costs of foreign personnel and goods, reckless borrowing of foreign capital was inevitable. This is shown by the fact that the flow of aid to Pakistan, primarily as interest-bearing loans, increased from $455.8 million from 1950 to 1955 to about $3.4 billion from 1960 to 1968.[15]

All this was being done, according to Ayub Khan, his advisers from abroad, and the gentlemen of the higher civil service, in order to rescue the country from the economic "disaster" of the preceding years. By the late 1960s the spokesmen for the regime were characterizing the period of their ascendancy as an era of "miraculous" and "dramatic" economic growth.[16] Evidence of the "progress" is cited in terms of the growth of Pakistan's Gross National Product and per capita income by a few percentage points. However, behind this numbers game lie the stark realities of the social and economic exploitation of the large masses of people. Since these realities are rarely expressed in the official statements of economic progress, it is worthwhile to highlight them here.

Even if we accept at face value the official calculations showing an increase of a few percentage points in the annual GNP, it tells us nothing about the benefit to the people at large. There is evidence that after allowing for increase in the cost of living, the real wages of rural and urban workers declined over the period under consideration.[17] Furthermore, the enormous concentration of wealth in the hands of a few created a vast gap between the rich and the poor. According to official reports, 80 percent of bank funds and 87 percent of insurance funds in Pakistan are now controlled by twenty families.[18] Furthermore, 82 percent of total advances made by Pakistan's commercial banks are concentrated in only 3 percent of total accounts.[19] Whereas about 85 percent of the country's population lives in rural areas, 70 percent of commercial bank loans are being utilized in three urban centers.[20]

The worst victim of this lopsided economic policy was the East Bengal region. The West Pakistan-based industrial elite, and their co-planners in the civil service and foreign advisory groups, were able to reduce East Bengal to a client colony. East Bengal remained largely a producer of raw materials for the world market and for West Pakistan's factories, and served as a protected market for consumer goods made in West Pakistan and sold at arbitrary prices. The region also lost its edge over West Pakistan in gross domestic product because a large part of its export earnings was used to finance the growth of capitalists in West Pakistan.

The real damage to the country's political economy during this period was done by its conversion into a hinterland controlled by capitalist interests abroad. Pakistan's heavy dependence on aid now makes it possible for the lending countries to regulate its basic policies governing taxation, prices, distribution of income, and national and international political commitments. Methods used to acquire control over the recipient country's political and economic life have been described by U.S. Senator Frank Church.[21]

While the country and its people as a whole share the burden of aid loans, the real benefits are monopolized by a small fraction of the Pakistani elite and the lending country's own interest groups. Most of the aid has gone, and continues to go, to pay for "establishment" charges, that is, to pay for the transportation, salaries, offices and residences, commissaries, and servants of AID personnel. Another large sum is spent on arranging training and "orientation" trips to America for the government elite. Almost 95 percent of the amount spent to buy machinery and other capital goods must be spent in the donor country, which is usually the United States. This condition forecloses those sources of supply where the same goods could be bought and transported at much smaller cost. Having installed expensive American machinery, Pakistan becomes forever dependent on that country for the supply of spare parts. Furthermore, American machinery is made for a capital-intensive system of production, whereas Pakistan has an abundance of labor. Manufacturing of this type, though profitable for the capitalist, does little to expand jobs for the growing population.

The capitalist prescription under which this kind of borrowing and investment was adopted by Pakistan aims at increasing GNP and investment profits. This is done largely by making consumer goods for Pakistan's upper classes and international markets. It has little to do with the needs of the masses of deprived people, for whom the "decade of progress" has produced nothing but more poverty and more frustration. One of Pakistan's influential economists of the "decade of development" openly proclaims that expenditures on the provision of such social services as housing, health, and social welfare are "not economic" and therefore must be "resisted." [22] In other words, Pakistani planners should serve only the goals of international capitalism and its palace slaves—the tiny Pakistani elite. If the Pakistani elite have behaved as "robber barons" in order to accomplish the "miracle" of capitalist development, we could hardly expect otherwise. As Gustav Papanek, one of the Harvard economists who had a major role in planning Pakistan's economic development, observed, how else could an economy develop without accepting the "social utility of greed"? [23] What Papanek overlooks is that in the United States the practice of greed by the captains of industry may not affect members of his own class; but for the poor people of his country as well as for large masses of people in the Third World, the greed of the capitalist profiteers cuts into the bare minimum of subsistence that keeps people alive.

Alternative for Pakistan

In view of the above-mentioned developments, Pakistan is now structurally trapped in the institutional constraints of the international capitalist system. The basic problem we have outlined is not amenable to any solution other than a drastic redistribution of wealth and power in the country and the uprooting of local and foreign vested interests. By their social origin, training, outlook, and material interests, the country's ruling elite, as a class, are incapable of responding to the needs and aspirations of the majority of their people. If not for their narrow class interests, the recolonization of Pakistan after independence, particularly during the Ayub regime, would not have taken place. Any further reliance on this class, its foreign alliances, or its theories of economic and social development will simply mean the prolongation of the poverty and exploitation of the people at large.

Those of Pakistan's elite who—in the name of their less fortunate compatriots—still have their palms extended in the direction of the capitalist countries, particularly the United States, are not so naive as to ignore completely the struggles of the oppressed minorities within these affluent countries. They also know that the capitalist prescription of development based on so-called "free trade and aid" has not produced a single case in the Third World countries where general levels of literacy, health, housing, nutrition, and employment were raised to meet even the minimum standards of human life and dignity. On the contrary, capitalism, by sanctioning the egotistical exploitation of man by man ("free competition"), has provided instruments of discrimination and plunder of those very groups in society who need the greatest help and protection—racial and regional minorities, the poor, the sick and disabled, and even women, children, and the aged. In the case of Pakistan these groups constitute an overwhelming majority of the population. It is not possible for a small minority to thrive at the expense of these people for very long. On the other hand, active involvement in the struggles of these people against all kinds of privations and discrimination is the only experience that will engender a just and viable strategy and a philosophy of rational human development.

To initiate such a program and philosophy of development will inevitably be a revolutionary effort. It will require the creation of new institutions of public service, a new plan of living for all sections and classes of society, a remobilization of the natural and human resources of the country. It will be predominantly a program of self-reliance, a reinvolvement of people in the central tasks of development, requiring a total break from the present vicious circle of class interest, class alienation, and class exploitation. We can draw upon the experience of a few Asian, Latin American, and African countries such as China, Cuba, and Tanzania, which have managed to bring about radical changes in their societies. But this experience will have to be interpreted and utilized in the context of Pakistan's society and its economic realities. Some specific elements of this program are suggested by the preceding analysis of the crisis of Pakistan. Others will emerge through participation with the people in a common struggle to eradicate historical forms of exploitation.

Notes

1. Embassy of Pakistan, *Pakistan's Five Year Plan, 1965–1970*, Report Series, December 1969, p. 1; A. T. Chaudhri, "Pakistan's Crippling Burden of Foreign Debt," *Atlas*, November 1970, reprinted from *Statesman* (Karachi).
2. Quoted in G. M. Young (ed.), *Speeches by Lord Macaulay with His Minutes on Indian Education* (Oxford University Press, London, 1935), p. 350.
3. Rajani Palme Dutt, *The Problem of India* (International Publishers, New York, 1943); see also an extract from the same author's book, *India Today*, in M. D. Lewis (ed.), *British in India* (D. C. Heath and Co., Boston, 1966), pp. 41–53.
4. B. B. Misra, *The Indian Middle Classes* (Oxford University Press, London, 1961), pp. 219–222.
5. Ibid.
6. E. W. R. Lumby, *The Transfer of Power in India* (George Allen and Unwin, London, 1954), pp. 260–261. Lumby worked in the India Office for a long time and was on the staff of the British Cabinet Mission to India in 1946.
7. Gunnar Myrdal, *Asian Drama: An Inquiry into the Poverty of Nations*, Vol. 1 (Pantheon Books, New York, 1958), p. 152.

8. Ayub Khan, Field Marshal, *Friends Not Masters* (Oxford University Press, Lahore, 1967), pp. 188–189.
9. R. D. Campbell, *Pakistan: Emerging Democracy* (D. Van Nostrand Co., Toronto, 1963), p. 26 (based on data published by the Government of Pakistan).
10. Government of Pakistan, *Pakistan Statistical Yearbook, 1964* (Government of Pakistan Press, Karachi, 1966), p. 152.
11. Gunnar Myrdal, *Asian Drama,* Vol. 1, p. 322.
12. Government of Pakistan, *Pakistan Statistical Yearbook, 1964,* p. 163; Gustav F. Papanek, *Pakistan's Development: Social Goals and Private Incentives* (Harvard University Press, Cambridge, Mass., 1967), p. 7.
13. Albert Waterston, *Planning in Pakistan* (The Johns Hopkins Press, Baltimore, 1963).
14. Embassy of Pakistan, *Pakistan's Third Five Year Plan, 1965–70,* Interim Report Series, December 1969, p. 2.
15. Ibid., p. 1.
16. Papanek, op. cit., p. 6.
17. A. R. Khan, "What Has Been Happening to the Real Wages in Pakistan," *Pakistan Development Review,* Autumn 1968; S. R. Bose, "Trend of Real Income of the Rural Poor in East Pakistan, 1949–1966," *Pakistan Development Review,* Autumn 1968.
18. *Pakistan News Digest,* Karachi, June 15, 1970, p. 10.
19. Ibid.
20. Ibid.
21. Frank Church, "Gunboat Diplomacy and Colonial Economics," *Transaction,* Vol. 7, No. 8, 1970, pp. 25–31.
22. Mahbubul Haq, *The Strategy of Economic Planning: The Case of Pakistan* (Oxford University Press, Lahore, 1963), p. 35.
23. Papanek, op. cit., Chapter VIII.

6. The State in Postcolonial Societies: Pakistan and Bangladesh

Hamza Alavi

The object of this article is to raise some fundamental questions about the classical Marxist theory of the state in the context of postcolonial societies. The argument is premised on the historical specificity of postcolonial societies, which arises from (1) structural changes brought about by the colonial experience and alignments of classes and superstructures of political and administrative institutions established in that context, and (2) radical realignments of class forces which have been brought about in the postcolonial situation.

The argument is stated in terms of an account of recent developments in Pakistan and Bangladesh. While there are, necessarily, some particular features that are specific to that context, the essential features of the situation which invite a fresh analysis are by no means unique. The focus of the analysis is on the special role of the military-bureaucratic oligarchy which has become all too common a phenomenon in postcolonial societies. This role is interpreted in terms of a new alignment of the respective interests of the three propertied exploiting classes: the indigenous bourgeoisie, the metropolitan neocolonialist bourgeoisies, and the landed classes, under metropolitan patronage, which, in my opinion, is also not unique to Pakistan. The argument is that a weak and underdeveloped indigenous bourgeoisie is unable at the moment of independence to subordinate the relatively highly developed colonial state apparatus through which the metropolitan power had exercised dominion over it. However, in addition, given a new convergence of interests of the three competing propertied classes, under metropolitan patronage, the bureaucratic-military oligarchy mediates their competing but no

This article was first published in *New Left Review*, No. 74, July-August 1972. Copyright © 1972 by Hamza Alavi.

longer contradictory interests and demands. By that token it acquires a relatively autonomous role and is not simply the instrument of any one of the three classes. Such a relatively autonomous role of the state apparatus is of special importance to the neocolonialist bourgeoisies because it is by virtue of that fact that they are able to pursue their class interests in postcolonial societies.

A fundamental distinction can be seen between that situation and the situation subsequent to the bourgeois revolution in European societies on which the classical Marxist theory of state is based. A distinction may also be made between cases such as that of Pakistan (which experienced direct colonial rule) and other countries (which experienced colonial exploitation under indirect rule). My analysis is confined to an example of the first type. Comparative analysis will throw light on the similarities and differences between it and cases of the other type. Such comparative and critical studies are needed before we can hope to arrive at a general theory of the state in postcolonial societies. The purpose of this article will have been served if it focuses on fresh questions that require examination in relation to postcolonial societies.

The questions will be raised primarily with reference to the classical Marxist theories of the state. What Miliband calls the primary Marxist view of the state "finds its most explicit expression in the famous aphorism of the *Communist Manifesto*: 'The executive of the modern state is but a committee for managing the common affairs of the whole bourgeoisie,' and political power is 'merely the organized power of one class for oppressing another.' " [1] Miliband adds: "This is the classical Marxist view on the subject of the state and it is the only one which is to be found in Marxism-Leninism. In regard to Marx himself, however, . . . it only constitutes what may be called a primary view of the state . . . for there is to be found another view of the state in his work. . . . This secondary view is that of the state as independent from and superior to all social classes, as being the dominant force in society rather than the instrument of the dominant class." This secondary view of the state in Marx's work arises from his analysis of the Bonapartist state. Miliband concludes: "For Marx, the Bonapartist state, however independent it may have been *politically* from any given class, remains, and cannot in a class society but remain, the protector of an economically and socially dominant class." In the postcolonial society, the problem of the relationship be-

tween the state and the underlying economic structure is more complex than the context in which it was posed even in the Bonapartist
state or in other examples that arose in the context of the development of European society. It is structured by yet another historical
experience and requires fresh theoretical insights.

The military and the bureaucracy in postcolonial societies cannot
be looked upon, in terms of the classical Marxist view, simply as instruments of a *single* ruling class. The specific nature of structural
alignments created by the colonial relationship and realignments
that have developed in the postcolonial situation have rendered the
relationship between the state and the social classes more complex.
The two patterns of historical development are quite different. In
Western societies we witness the creation of the nation-state by indigenous bourgeoisies, in the wake of their ascendant power, to provide
a framework of law and various institutions that are essential for the
development of capitalist production relations. In colonial societies
the process is significantly different.

The bourgeois revolution in the colony—insofar as it involves the
establishment of a bourgeois state and the attendant legal and institutional framework—is characterized by the imposition of colonial
rule by the metropolitan bourgeoisie. In carrying out the tasks of the
bourgeois revolution in the colony, however, the metropolitan bourgeoisie has to accomplish an additional task that was specific to the
colonial situation. Its task is not merely to replicate the superstructure of the state which it has established in the metropolitan country
itself; it must also create a state apparatus through which it can exercise dominion over all the indigenous social classes in the colony. It
might be said that the "superstructure" in the colony is therefore
"overdeveloped" in relation to the "structure" in the colony, for its
basis lies in the metropolitan structure itself, from which it is later
separated at the time of independence. The colonial state is therefore
equipped with a powerful bureaucratic-military apparatus and with
governmental mechanisms that enable it, through routine operations, to subordinate the native social classes. The postcolonial society inherits that overdeveloped state apparatus and its institutionalized practices through which the operations of the indigenous social
classes are regulated and controlled. At the moment of independence, weak indigenous bourgeoisies find themselves enmeshed in bureaucratic controls by which those at the top of the hierarchy of the

bureaucratic-military apparatus of the state are able to maintain and even extend their dominant power in society, having been freed from direct metropolitan control.

The essential problem of the state in postcolonial societies stems from the fact that it is not established by an ascendant native bourgeoisie but, rather, by a foreign imperialist bourgeoisie. At independence, however, the direct command of the latter over the colonial state is ended; yet, by the same token, its influence over the state is by no means brought to an end. The metropolitan bourgeoisie, now joined by other neocolonial bourgeoisies, is present in the postcolonial society. Together they constitute a powerful element in its class structure. The relationship between neocolonial bourgeoisies and the postcolonial state is clearly of a different order from that which existed between the imperialist bourgeoisie and the colonial state. Hence the class basis of the postcolonial state is complex. In view of the power and influence of the neocolonial bourgeoisie, it is not entirely subordinate to the indigenous bourgeoisie. Nor is it simply an instrument of any of the latter, which would have the implication that independence is a mere sham. Neither bourgeoisie excludes the influence of the other, and their interests compete. The central proposition I wish to emphasize is that the state in the postcolonial society is not the instrument of a single class. It is relatively autonomous and it mediates the competing interests of the three propertied classes—the metropolitan bourgeoisies, the indigenous bourgeoisie, and the landed classes—while at the same time acting on behalf of all of them in order to preserve the social order in which their interests are embedded, namely, the institution of private property and the capitalist mode as the dominant mode of production.

The multiclass relationship of the state in the postcolonial societies calls for specific explanation and for an examination of its implications. In this situation the military-bureaucratic oligarchies, the apparatus of the state, also assume a new and relatively autonomous *economic* role, which is not paralleled in the classical bourgeois state, because the state in the postcolonial society directly appropriates a very large part of the economic surplus and deploys it in bureaucratically directed economic activity in the name of promoting economic development. These are conditions which differentiate the postcolonial state fundamentally from the state as analyzed in classical Marxist theory.

The state apparatus does not, however, consist only of the bureaucratic-military oligarchy. Where democratic forms of government operate, politicians and political parties also form a part of it. Where political leaders occupy the highest offices in the state, formally invested with authority over the bureaucracy and the military, the role of the bureaucratic-military oligarchy cannot be evaluated without a clear understanding of the precise role of politicians and political parties in the state, as well as the extent of their powers and limitations. Politicians and political parties stand at the center of a complex set of relationships. On the one hand, they are expected (ideally) to articulate the demands of those from whom they seek support; they are supposed to attempt to realize those demands by their participation in the workings of government. On the other hand, they also play a key role in manipulating public relations on behalf of those who do make public policy, to make it acceptable to the community at large. Toward that end they channel public grievances and seek to promote an "understanding" of public issues and thereby diminish potential opposition. Their relationship with the bureaucratic-military oligarchy is, therefore, ambivalent; it is both competitive and complementary. The ambivalence is greater where politicians who occupy high public office can influence the careers of individual members of the bureaucracy or the military.

There are many variants of the distribution or sharing of power between political leadership and bureaucratic-military oligarchies in postcolonial societies. Political parties at the vanguard of the movement for national independence inherit the mantle of legitimacy and the trappings of political power. Nevertheless, in a large number of postcolonial countries there has been in evidence a progressive attenuation of their power and, correspondingly, an expansion in the power of bureaucratic-military oligarchies, which has often culminated in an overt "seizure" of power by the latter. In general, however, there has been both accommodation and tension between political leadership and bureaucratic-military oligarchies, with the former serving a useful purpose for the latter by conferring the mantle of political legitimacy on regimes and, through the charade of democratic process, absorbing public discontent and channeling grievances. The role of political parties does not necessarily rule out the relative autonomy of bureaucratic-military oligarchies. The essential issue is that of the relative autonomy of the *state apparatus as a whole* and its mediatory role as between the competing interests of the three propertied classes—the domestic bourgeoisie, the metropolitan bourgeoisies, and the landowning classes. Insofar as a political leadership participates in the performance of that mediatory role and in the preservation of the relative autonomy of the state apparatus, it is valuable for the purposes of the bureaucratic-military oligarchy; it becomes their partner, a third component of the oligarchy. It is only where political parties seriously challenge that relative autonomy and the mediatory role of the bureaucratic-military oligarchy that conflicts arise in which, until now, the latter have prevailed.

We have yet to see a clear case of unambiguous control of state power by a political party in a capitalist postcolonial society. The case of India comes closest to that. But even in India the situation is ambiguous. The ruling Congress Party is by no means a party of a single class; it participates with the bureaucracy in mediating the demands of competing propertied classes, while at the same time participating with it in using state power to uphold the social order that permits the continued existence of those classes, despite the socialist rhetoric of the Congress Party. Even with regard to foreign capital, the actual performance of the government of India is very different from the rhetoric of the Congress politicians.[2] What is crucial to the present analysis is that, behind the apparent power of Congress politicians, the Indian bureaucracy does enjoy a very wide margin of autonomy (as attested to in recent research).[3]

To understand how relationships between the bureaucratic-military oligarchies and politicians have evolved in India and Pakistan, one must examine the historical background of the development of their mutual relationship and, in particular, the institutionalization of a wide measure of bureaucratic and military autonomy. Before independence, members of the bureaucracy and the military were the instruments of the colonial power. One of their principal functions was to subordinate the various native classes and to repress the nationalist movement on behalf of their colonial masters. During the freedom struggle, they were on opposite sides of the political barricades from the leadership of the nationalist movement. After independence, the same political leaders whom it was their task to repress were ensconced in office, nominally in authority over them. A new relationship of mutual accommodation had to be established. The experience of partial transfer of power by stages during the

1920s and the 1930s had, however, already institutionalized procedures by which the bureaucracy could bypass the political leaders
who had been inducted into office on sufferance under the umbrella
of British imperial rule. These procedures were extended and consolidated by the proliferation of bureaucratic controls, as well as by the
fact that, by and large, members of the public have extensive direct,
routine dealings with the bureaucracy, and these dealings do not
admit of mediation by political parties. An exception occurs only
when individual politicians seek favors from officials for some of their
supporters, in which case their relationship vis-à-vis the bureaucracy
is weakened rather than strengthened. Politicians are reduced to
playing the role of brokers for official favors. The mediation between
the public and the bureaucracy is one of the important sources of political power in India,[4] as in other similar cases. But since the politician can ill afford to lose the goodwill of the official, this influences
the overall balance of their collective relationship. The strength of
the bureaucracy rests in the extensive proliferation of administrative
controls and in the direction of a vast array of public agencies engaged in a variety of activities.

The actual pattern of the evolution of relationships between political leaders and bureaucratic-military oligarchies varies from country
to country according to differences in historical background and in
the evolution of political forces. In Indonesia, for example, a long period elapsed before the emergence of the overt power of the bureaucratic-military oligarchy after the overthrow of Sukarno. The underlying factors in that case are complex, but a part of the explanation
must be that the bureaucracy and the military in Indonesia had to
be radically restructured after independence and it took time for the
oligarchy to be consolidated. In India and Pakistan, by contrast,
powerfully organized bureaucratic and military structures were inherited. In Pakistan the military was, it is true, in bad shape at the
time of independence, but the organization and bases of political
parties were still weaker. The ruling Muslim League party leaned
heavily on the stature and authority of its leader, Quaide Azam Mohammad Ali Jinnah, who died soon after independence. By that
time the Muslim League had begun to disintegrate and its leadership had become isolated from its bases.

In Pakistan two facts stand out in sharp relief in its twenty-five-
year history. One is the dominant position of the bureaucratic-mili-

tary oligarchy in the state: it has been in effective command of state power not, as is commonly believed, after the coup d'état of October 1958 but, in fact, from the inception of the new state. In the first phase, politicians and political parties, who provided a façade of parliamentary government, were manipulated by them and were installed and expelled from office as it suited the bureaucratic-military oligarchy. When in 1958 the prospects of the impending general elections appeared to pose a challenge to the supremacy of the oligarchy, those who already held the reins "seized power" by abolishing the institutions of parliamentary government through which the challenge was being mounted. Despite this, the bureaucratic-military oligarchy needed politicians, who fulfill a complementary role, and by 1962 the politicians were put to work again in a parody of democratic politics under Ayub Khan's system of "Basic Democracy." That phase ended in 1969 with the fall of Ayub Khan after a great national political upheaval. Nevertheless the reins of power were left securely in the hands of the bureaucratic-military oligarchy. The latter still needed politicians to fulfill a complementary role in government. President Yahya Khan promised restoration of "constitutional government" subject to his own veto. The election of December 1970 ended in the political crisis that culminated in the secession of Bangladesh. (It is a complex history which I have examined in some detail elsewhere.[5]) In its first phase, the period of "parliamentary government," the true role of the bureaucratic-military oligarchy was obscured by the political fiction under which it operated. After 1958, its dominant and decisive role became manifest. What remains problematic is the social character, affiliations, and commitments of the oligarchy, or those of different sections of it, vis-à-vis the various social classes in Pakistan and its different regions, including the metropolitan bourgeoisies that have reappeared, in the plural, after British colonial rule was ended.

The second outstanding fact about Pakistan's political history is that the most powerful challenges to the dominant central authority of the bureaucratic-military oligarchy came primarily from political movements that drew their strength from people of underprivileged regions and voiced demands for regional autonomy and for a fuller share for the regions in the distribution of material resources as well as in state power. It was not only from East Bengal, but also from Sind and Baluchistan and the North West Frontier Province

(NWFP, the land of the Pathans), that such challenges were mounted. Support for regional autonomy became an article of faith with the radical and left-wing political groups—indeed, most of them were embedded in regionalist movements. It appeared, on the surface, that the radical politics of Pakistan were conditioned primarily by ethnic or linguistic solidarities rather than by class solidarities stretching across regional boundaries. True, radical challenges were directed against class privileges, but such privileges were identified primarily in regional terms. Politically the demands of radical and left-wing movements were for a federal parliamentary system of government and for representation in the upper echelons of bureaucratic (and military) appointments of people from underprivileged regions. These two outstanding facts about Pakistan politics—the dominance of a bureaucratic-military oligarchy and the regional basis of challenges directed against it—are essentially two aspects of a single reality of the political situation in Pakistan which centers around the role of the bureaucratic-military oligarchy.

Until 1958 the bureaucratic-military oligarchy in Pakistan made and unmade "governments" with a succession of prime ministers. In 1956 it even instigated the creation of the Republican Party. A new type of constitution was introduced by Ayub Khan in 1962 after his 1958 "seizure of power" through a coup d'état. Politicians were put to work again; under Ayub Khan their manipulation was perfected to a fine art. But what is significant here is the anxiety of the military leaders to retain a façade of political government. Thus, after the reimposition of martial law in 1969, President General Yahya Khan was very keen that a political leadership should be installed in office as soon as possible, although under the hegemony of the bureaucratic-military oligarchy. He promised elections for that purpose and immediately installed a chosen group of civilians as interim ministers. Some of his most influential military advisers were particularly insistent that without politicians in office the military would become directly the object of public disaffection, that it would lose its mantle of political legitimacy, and that as a consequence its assumed right to intervene at every moment of crisis would be jeopardized. It would be simplistic to take for granted that the bureaucratic-military oligarchy necessarily prefers to rule directly in its own name; it often prefers to rule through politicians so long as the latter do not impinge upon its own relative autonomy and power. For the bureaucratic-military oligarchy in Pakistan the elections of December 1970, however, had disconcerting results: the crisis of 1971 ensued, resulting in the secession of Bangladesh.

The assumption of power by President Bhutto after the defeat of the Pakistani army in Bangladesh can be seen in a similar light. Here was a traumatic moment of crisis, a moment when the oligarchy more than ever needed a political leadership that could manipulate an explosive political situation. Bhutto's political position in the country, and the fact that his services were indispensable for the oligarchy, gave him a degree of freedom. Nevertheless, his dismissal of a clutch of generals after the assumption of power should not be taken simply as evidence of a final defeat of the bureaucratic-military oligarchy, for Bhutto is closely allied to powerful factions in the oligarchy and his actions reflect the demands of those factions. Bhutto "dismissed" General Yahya Khan and his associates and appointed his friend General Gul Hassan as the new Commander in Chief of the army, having himself assumed the office of President. But it would be a mistake to assume that General Gul Hassan was a political nonentity whom Bhutto installed in office simply as his own nominee. The General in fact belonged to a powerful faction in the military establishment. As early as October 1968, before the massive political agitation against President Ayub Khan (which occurred a month later), it was already being whispered in the corridors of power in Rawalpindi and Islamabad that Ayub would be removed and that his most likely successor would be General Gul Hassan, who was then Corps Commander at Multan, one of the two senior field appointments in the Pakistan army. In anticipation, President Ayub outmaneuvered the faction being aligned against him: he resigned and handed over the presidential office to someone of his own choosing, the man he had appointed as his Commander in Chief—General Yahya Khan. In turn Yahya Khan successfully protected Ayub Khan from the retribution being demanded not only by an angry public but also by powerful elements in the army itself. With Yahya Khan's fall, events had turned full circle.

In the crisis after the military debacle in Bangladesh, intervention by the political leadership was indispensable for the military-bureaucratic oligarchy. At this moment the political leadership did assume some weight. The fact that the critical struggle for power still lay within the military-bureaucratic oligarchy was, however, soon made manifest when Bhutto had to dismiss General Gul Hassan from the post of Commander in Chief and install in his place the powerful General Tikka Khan, a leader of the "hawks" in the army who had masterminded the military action in Bangladesh. It could not but have been an unpalatable decision for Bhutto, for the appointment was most inept in the context of the political necessity for Bhutto to negotiate with India and Bangladesh for the repatriation of Pakistani prisoners of war, but the supremacy of the army junta was evidently decisive.

Factions in the military are based on personal groupings and allegiances, but there are underlying structural factors that influence the gravitations of groups into broader alliances. One can therefore distinguish, on the one hand, "conservative right-wing" generals. They come from the wealthier landed families or they (or their very close relatives) have made substantial fortunes in business. Others have made money in collusion with foreign businesses and foreign powers. Big businessmen in Pakistan have adopted the practice of awarding profitable directorships to retiring generals, and therefore attempted to establish relationships with factions in the army. As regards dealings with foreign powers, a remarkable fact about the political situation in Pakistan has been the ability of the army to have direct dealings with foreign powers (notably the U.S.A.) over the heads of the government in office. These varieties of affiliations and interests have resulted in powerfully entrenched positions within the army on behalf of the various vested interests. The case of the bureaucracy is parallel, for many bureaucrats come from landed families and have acquired extensive business interests; some have become millionaires.

There is, however, another influence in the army that tends to promote radicalism, but this is potentially radicalism of the Right as well as of the Left. The evidence so far, in fact, suggests that ultra-right radicalism is the preponderant element in this group, and derives from the fact that the army is recruited from one of the most impoverished and congested agricultural regions of the country, the unirrigated area consisting of the Rawalpindi division of the Punjab and parts of the North West Frontier Province. Whereas big farmers in some parts of the country, such as the Canal Colony districts of the Punjab, have prospered enormously through the so-called "green revolution," the smallholders in the unirrigated region have not benefited. Their tiny unproductive holdings do not yield even a bare minimum for their livelihood, and their sons must find outside employment. Hence it is from these districts that the army draws its soldiers and junior officers. These men have strong social grievances, especially because of inflation and the deterioration of their economic situation in recent years, but they have little political education. In general they subscribe to a conspiracy theory of society and imagine, for example, that inflation is due simply to the greed of a few businessmen (the so-called twenty families); they fail to see the roots of the problem in the economic system itself. The solution, in their view, is not to be found in radical economic policies and a transformation of the social system but simply in the brutal punishment of "miscreants." The same idea of dealing with "miscreants" was applied by them in Bangladesh. Politically these men have been reared on the chauvinism and religious ideology of the extreme right wing. The influence of the Jamaat-e-Islami has been quite considerable among them. In recent years, however, the radical rhetoric of Bhutto's Pakistan People's Party has caught their imagination. Through them, Bhutto's political position is strongly rooted in the rank and file of the army.

There is also a group of generals who have close affinities and links with the above-mentioned second category of army officers and rank-and-file soldiers. They are the "army generals," for whom the interests of the army as such take precedence over other considerations. It is among them that one finds the "hawks." The concept of army "hawks" is not a psychological one, as suggested by Tariq Ali;[6] rather, the term describes commitments that are rooted in the objective conditions and interests of the army. The "hawks" have been able to exploit the grievances of the army rank and file and therefore have a powerful position in the army. They thrive on chauvinism, for only on the basis of an aggressively chauvinist ideology can they enforce increasing demands on national resources for a larger and better-equipped (and more privileged) army. The massive rearmament and reorganization of the Indian army in the last decade, following its confrontation with China, has altered the military balance in South Asia—a fact that was brought home to the Pakistani oligarchy in no uncertain terms after the debacle in Bangladesh. This will make the old policy of confrontation with India no longer credible. This confrontation has been a source of embarrassment to the two superpowers, the U.S.A. and the U.S.S.R., who have attempted for more than a decade to bring about a rapprochement between India and Pakistan. They will doubtless use their influence to restrain the "hawks" in the army and strengthen the hands of the "conservative right-wing" generals to this end. Nevertheless, the fact that the oligarchy has so far resisted the efforts of the two superpowers in this respect, despite pressure for over a decade, reflects its relative autonomy; this resistance occurred because such a rapprochement would encroach on the interests of the army.

Both the bureaucracy and the military in Pakistan are highly developed and powerful in comparison with their indigenous class bases. Capitalist development in Pakistan has taken place under the corrupt patronage and close control of the bureaucracy. Because of bureaucratic controls, business opportunities have been restricted to a privileged few who have established the necessary relationship with the bureaucracy, essentially based on the cash nexus. In the late sixties the chief economist of the government of Pakistan revealed that twenty privileged families owned 66 percent of Pakistan's industry, 79 percent of its insurance, and 80 percent of its banking; most of the remainder was owned by foreign companies. That revelation, in a pre-election year, is itself an indication of the ambivalent relationship between the bureaucracy and the indigenous bourgeoisie. Even so, the local monopolists do not control any political party which can be said to represent them as a class. Indeed, the bases of political parties are primarily rural. The influence of the business community on the conduct of public affairs is primarily through its direct contact with and influence on the bureaucracy itself.

Under parliamentary democracy, party politics are monopolized by the landowners, who hold sway over the countryside. They are elected to places in the national and provincial legislatures. (Even in East Bengal, where there are no big landowners comparable to those in West Pakistan, "Sardari lineages" of rich landholders control the local votes.) The bureaucracy and the army recruit their senior officers largely from rich rural families, thus affording the landowning classes a built-in position within the oligarchy. The bureaucrats have a direct stake in the privileges of the landed classes. This link has been greatly reinforced by the grant of land to civilian and military officers, who have thereby become substantial landowners in their own right when they were not already. As a result, landowners have been able to pursue their class interests effectively, despite occasional attempts by the indigenous bourgeoisie and the metropolitan bourgeoisies to alter that state of affairs. Agricultural incomes, for example, are exempt from income tax. For two decades the bourgeoisie and their foreign allies have pressed the demand that these huge incomes be taxed in order to raise resources for a larger development plan, in which their own interests lie. The landed classes have not only successfully resisted that attempt; they have also obtained large subsidies whose lion's share goes to rich farmers and big landlords. Nevertheless, landlords as a class, despite their close and effective links with the bureaucracy and their dominant role in party politics, cannot be said to have command over the bureaucracy. Many instances can be cited in which the interests of landowners as a class have been subordinated to those of the bourgeoisie—for example, the price policy for raw cotton has worked to the disadvantage of the landowners and to the benefit of the business magnates who own textile mills.

Foreign businessmen, like others, have been granted bureaucratic favors. In their case, private corruption is reinforced by governmental pressure; the greatest pressure is exercised by the government of the United States. I have examined elsewhere ways in which U.S. aid has been used to enforce policies in Pakistan in support of U.S. business to the detriment of domestic interests.[7] Competition exists not only between U.S. and indigenous business interests but also between competing metropolitan bourgeoisies—British, German, French, Japanese, Italian, and others. None of them has complete command over the bureaucracy, nor do they command it collectively. Neocolonialism is probably the greatest beneficiary of the relative autonomy of the bureaucratic-military oligarchy. It is precisely such a relatively autonomous role that renders the government of the postcolonial society sufficiently open to admit the successful intrusion of neocolonial interests in the formulation of public policy. That is why Western ideologues place considerable emphasis on the importance of the bureaucracy as an "agent of modernization." Every effort is made to influence the bureaucracy ideologically in favor of policies that are in conformity with metropolitan interests. This ideology is expressed in the form of "technique of planning" and is presented as an objective science of economic development. The Western-educated bureaucrat is regarded as the bearer of Western rationality and technology, and his role is contrasted with that of "demagogic" politicians who voice "parochial" demands. Considerable resources are devoted in the metropolitan countries to imparting training to bureaucrats of the postcolonial countries. But there are also more direct methods of influencing their outlook and policy orientations. International agencies and aid-administrating agencies who evaluate the viability of projects give advice on developmental planning and channel the policies of postcolonial governments along lines that suit the metropolitan countries. The influence on state policy through foreign aid, conjoined with the private corruption of bureaucrats, makes this possible even when some of the policies are blatantly against the interests of the country. Those who tend to assume the existence of mutuality in the processes of international negotiations, and who assume that if the government of a postcolonial country has agreed to a certain course of policy it must surely be in the interests of their country, should recognize this disjuncture between the interests of the country (however defined) and those of the corrupt bureaucracy and individual bureaucrats.

Pakistan's experience suggests that none of the three propertied classes in the postcolonial society—the indigenous bourgeoisie, the neocolonial metropolitan bourgeoisies, or the landowning classes—exclusively command the state apparatus; the influence and power of each is offset by that of the other two. Their respective interests are not mutually congruent or wholly compatible. They do, however, have certain basic interests in common—above all, preservation of the existing social order, based upon the institution of private property. But they make competing demands on the postcolonial state and on the bureaucratic-military oligarchy which represents the state. The latter mediates and arbitrates between the competing demands of the three propertied classes. This is a historically specific role of the military and the bureaucracy, who constitute the state apparatus in postcolonial societies. The reason for this distinctive role stems from the fact that, in contrast to the ascendant bourgeoisie in an independent capitalist state or the metropolitan bourgeoisie in a colony, both of which establish their dominance over other social classes, in postcolonial societies none of the three propertied classes exclusively dominates the state apparatus or subordinates the other two. This specific historical situation confers on the bureaucratic-military oligarchy in a postcolonial society a *relatively autonomous* role.

There are two senses in which the idea of "relative autonomy" of the elements of the superstructure (such as the state), in relation to the underlying "structure"—i.e., the economic foundations of society (the relations of production)—has been discussed in Marxist literature. This should be clarified at this point. One is a basic philosophical sense, namely, that historical materialism does not mean that elements of the "superstructure" are determined mechanistically by the underlying structure, but that the formative influence of the latter, although mediated in a complex way, is the ultimate determinant of the superstructure. This was emphasized by Engels in his well-known letter to Joseph Bloch in which he criticized mechanistic and deterministic interpretations of "vulgar Marxism." This fundamental—philosophical—issue should be distinguished from another —theoretical—issue. The idea of the "relative autonomy" of the superstructure is put forward in this second context as a theory, i.e., as an explanation of the relationship between the state and the underlying "structure" in certain (exceptional) historical situations. Marx's analysis of the Bonapartist state deals with the most extreme case of the relative autonomy of the state from among such historical examples analyzed by Marx and Engels. However, in classical Marxism, in the fundamental philosophical sense as well as in the specific theoretical sense, the idea of the "relative autonomy" of the superstructure (or the state) was conceived of explicitly within the framework of a society subject to the hegemony of *a single ruling class*. The issue in relation to the postcolonial societies is fundamentally different and should be distinguished clearly from the issues that underlay earlier discussions. The classical position is summed up by Poulantzas:

> When Marx designated Bonapartism as the "religion of the bourgeoisie," in other words as characteristic of all forms of the capitalistic state, he showed that this state can only truly serve the ruling class insofar as it is relatively autonomous from the *diverse* fractions of this class, precisely in order to organise *the hegemony of the whole of this class.*[8]

Such a proposition cannot apply to a discussion of postcolonial societies in which the problem arises not with reference to "diverse fractions" of a single class, the bourgeoisie, but rather with reference to three different propertied classes that do not constitute "a whole," for they have different structural bases and competing class interests.

In postcolonial societies the phenomenon of the relative autonomy of the state apparatus is therefore of a different order from that which is found in the historical cases on which the classical Marxist theory of the state is based. The role of the bureaucratic-military oligarchy in postcolonial societies is only *relatively* autonomous, because it is determined within the matrix of a class society and not outside it, for the preservation of the social order based on the institution of private property unites all the three competing propertied social classes. That common commitment situates the bureaucratic-military oligarchy within the social matrix. Nevertheless, the role of the bureaucratic-military oligarchy is relatively *autonomous* because, once the controlling hand of the metropolitan bourgeoisie is lifted at the moment of independence, no single class has exclusive command over it. This relative autonomy is not predicated on that negative condition alone. It derives also from the positive conditions engendered by the far-reaching interventions of the state in the economies of postcolonial countries, both by way of a network of controls, in which the vested interests of the bureaucracy are embedded, and by direct appropriation and disposition of a substantial proportion of the economic surplus. These constitute independent material bases of the autonomy of the bureaucratic-military oligarchy. Perhaps there are parallels here in the changing role of the state in metropolitan societies also, but we cannot pursue this question here. Yet it could be argued that, given the role of the state in "promoting economic development" in postcolonial societies, the difference between the two situations is of a qualitative order. This role, it should be added, is closely linked with imperialist interventions in postcolonial societies, especially through the administration of economic and military aid.

The mediating role of the bureaucratic-military oligarchy between the competing demands of the three propertied classes is possible in the postcolonial situation because the mutual interests of the latter and their interrelations are aligned in a qualitatively different way from that which is experienced in other historical circumstances, on which the classical Marxist theory of the state is premised. In the postcolonial situation their mutual relations are no longer antagonistic and contradictory; rather, they are mutually competing but reconcilable. In the colonies, the classical theory envisages a coalition between the metropolitan bourgeoisie, the native "comprador" bourgeoisie (composed of merchants whose activities complement those of the metropolitan bourgeoisie), and the "feudal" landowning class. The theory also envisages the interests of the rising native "national" bourgeoisie to be fundamentally opposed to those of the metropolitan bourgeoisie. The colonial liberation is therefore characterized as the inauguration of a bourgeois-democratic revolution, "anti-imperialist and antifeudal" in character, which is premised as a necessary historical stage in the development of the liberated colonial society. The postcolonial state is taken to be the instrument of the ascendant native national bourgeoisie through which its historical purpose is finally accomplished. Yet this is not what we have actually witnessed in postcolonial societies. This was noted, for example, by Paul Baran:

> Its capitalist bourgeois component, confronted at an early stage with the spectre of social revolution, turns swiftly and resolutely against its fellow traveller of yesterday, its mortal enemy of tomorrow (i.e., the industrial proletariat and the peasantry). *In fact it does not hesitate to make common cause with the feudal elements representing the main obstacle to its own development, with the imperialist rulers just dislodged by the national liberation, and with comprador groups threatened by the political retreat of their former principals.*[9]

It is true that unprecedented challenges from revolutionary movements constitute a most important element in the postcolonial situation in which the three propertied classes stand united in defense of the established social order. But their political unity would not be possible if they were still divided by irreconcilable contradictions. It *is* possible because of fundamental differences in the underlying structural alignments, which differentiate the postcolonial situation from other historical parallels. The suggestion by Baran that the new unity of the propertied classes for the defense of the established social order represents a retreat from and an *abandonment* by the native national bourgeoisie of its historic antifeudal and anticolonial role, because it fears the revolutionary challenge which it cannot confront alone, overlooks the fundamental differences in the underlying *structural* alignments in the postcolonial societies from those in the colonial situation on which the classical theory of the role of the native "national bourgeoisie" was premised.

An accommodation between the native bourgeoisie and the "feudal" landowning classes is now possible because the task of winning national independence is completed and the structure of the nation-state and the institutional and legal framework necessary for capitalist development—products of the bourgeois revolution—already exist, for they were established by the metropolitan bourgeoisie. The native bourgeoisie is not confronted with the historical task of the European bourgeoisie to subordinate feudal power for the purpose of establishing the nation-state. On the contrary, the "feudal" landowning class now complements the political purposes of the native bourgeoisie in the "democratic" running of the postcolonial state, because it plays a key role in establishing links between the state at the national level and the local-level power structures in the rural areas which it dominates. At that level it also "contains" potentially revolutionary forces and helps to maintain the "political equilibrium" of the postcolonial system.

As regards economic aspects too, the specific nature of the relationship between the native bourgeoisie and the "feudal" landowning classes in postcolonial societies, especially in the context of the growth of capitalist farming, under the auspices of the big landowners rather than in conflict with them, has made it unnecessary for the native bourgeoisie to seek the elimination of the "feudal" landowning class for the purposes of capitalist development. The position and the interests of the "feudal" landowning classes are, however, challenged both from within the rural society as well as from "radical" urban forces. In response to such pressures, perfunctory efforts were made in some countries, soon after independence, to introduce land reforms. By and large these measures were ineffective, but their ineffectiveness has by no means impeded the development of the native bourgeoisie. In recent years in South Asia, the so-called "green revolution," based on an elite farmer strategy, has further helped to resolve the basic problem (for the native bourgeoisie) of increasing the agricultural surplus required to sustain industrialization and urbanization as well as of expanding the domestic market for manufactured goods. Pressures for radical action have diminished, while those for mutual accommodation have increased. Contradictions remain, nevertheless, for the elite farmer strategy is having a disruptive effect on the fabric of rural society, and this may have consequences which reach beyond its confines. This growth of socially "disruptive" forces in the rural areas, which may contribute powerfully to a revolutionary movement, occasions concern on the part of the bourgeoisie, which seeks to consolidate the conservative alliance with the "feudal" landowning classes to preserve the existing social order rather than contribute to the forces seeking to overthrow the power of the landowning classes in the rural areas.

As regards the relationship between the metropolitan bourgeoisies and the indigenous or "national" bourgeoisies of the postcolonial societies, their mutual relationship is also quite different from that which is premised on the classical Marxist theory. The classical Marxist theory postulates a fundamental contradiction between the two. It therefore concludes that the "bourgeois-democratic" revolution in the colonies, of which independence is only the first phase and which continues in the postcolonial situation, necessarily has an "anti-imperialist" character. It is true, of course, that the native bourgeoisie plays an anti-imperialist role and contributes to the national independence movement against the colonial power, but only up to the point of independence. In the postcolonial situation there is a double reorientation of alignments, both of the indigenous bourgeoisie and of the erstwhile "comprador" class of merchants, building contractors, and the like. The latter, unable to compete on equal terms with giant overseas concerns, demand restrictions on the activities of foreign businesses, particularly in the fields in which they aspire to operate. They acquire a new "anti-imperialist" posture. On the other hand, as the erstwhile "national" bourgeoisie grows in size and aspires to extend its interests from industries which involve relatively unsophisticated technology (such as textiles) to those which involve the use of highly sophisticated technology (such as petrochemicals and fertilizers, etc.), they find that they do not have access to the requisite advanced industrial technologies. Their small resources and scale of operation keep the possibility of independently developing their own technology out of their reach. For access to the requisite advanced industrial technology they have to turn for collaboration, therefore, to the bourgeoisies of the developed metropolitan countries or to socialist states. This they do despite the fact that the terms on which the collaboration is offered are such that they hamstring their independent future development. As it grows in size and extends its interests, the so-called "national" bourgeoisie becomes increasingly dependent on the neocolonialist metropolitan bourgeoisies.

The concept of a "national" bourgeoisie which is presumed to become increasingly anti-imperialist as it grows bigger, so that its contradictions with imperialism sharpen further, is one which derives from an analysis of colonial and not postcolonial experience. The mutual relationship of the native bourgeoisie and the metropolitan bourgeoisies is no longer antagonistic; it is collaborative. The collaboration is, however, unequal and hierarchical because the native bourgeoisie of a postcolonial society assumes a subordinate—client—status in the structure of its relationship with the metropolitan bourgeoisie. The erstwhile "anti-imperialist" character of the native "national" bourgeoisie changes in the postcolonial situation to a collaborationist one. The metropolitan bourgeoisies value their collaboration with the native bourgeoisies of postcolonial societies because that provides a channel through which they can pursue their economic interests without political risks attendant on direct investments by themselves. Their agreements with the native bourgeoisie establish captive markets for their products as well as for their technologies.[10] The conditions underlying the collaboration between the native bourgeoisie and the neocolonial metropolitan bourgeoisies are therefore embedded not only in superstructural conditions—namely, the threat of revolutionary movements to which Baran refers—but also in structural conditions, i.e., the access to technology for their economic operations. It must be emphasized that even though the indigenous "national" bourgeoisie and the metropolitan bourgeoisies are brought together into a close collaborative and hierarchical relationship, they are by no means, by that token, merged into a single class. The concept of collaboration implies and describes the fact of their separateness, and hierarchy implies a degree of conflict between their interests and a tension that underlies their relationship. A convergence of their interests does not dissolve into an identity of interests. It is this element of mutual competition which makes it possible, and necessary, for the bureaucratic-military oligarchies to play a mediatory role.

Because of the powerful role of the bureaucratic-military oligarchy in postcolonial societies, positions in the oligarchy are of crucial importance, especially for aspiring educated middle class groups; and their political demands are focused on shares of positions in the oligarchy. Where the oligarchy is recruited from a narrow social or regional base, as for example in the case in Pakistan, the unprivileged educated middle class groups who are denied access to positions of influence and power in the oligarchy organize political opposition. "Moral" principles and ideologies are invoked by both the ruling oligarchy and the opposition to justify their respective interests and to rally public support in their own behalf. For this very reason, differences of caste, ethnic origin, religion, or language dominate the politics of postcolonial societies. Opposition groups raise slogans of cultural or linguistic identity. On the other hand, the particular ethnic or linguistic (or other sectional) group which has a dominant position in the ruling bureaucratic-military oligarchy invokes, in defense of its own particular privileges, the ideology of "national solidarity" and denounces the opposition as narrow-minded and divisive particularism. The campaign in behalf of this group is mounted by the bureaucratic-military oligarchy itself. Political issues arising out of the sectional or regional character of the bureaucratic-military oligarchy are therefore merged with broader issues of public policy as they concern different classes of people; and in the ensuing political debate, political questions which concern the underlying social and economic issues are often expressed in the idiom of cultural, linguistic, or regional demands.

In Pakistan the ruling, predominantly Punjabi, bureaucratic-military oligarchy has taken over and put to its own particular use the slogans of Muslim nationalism, the slogans of the movement on whose strength Pakistan was brought into being. It extols the virtues of "Islamic solidarity" and denounces linguistic or regional opposition movements as divisive provincialism. In this way, since the creation of Pakistan, the nature and political role of Muslim nationalism and the significance of its slogans have altered. Muslim nationalism in India propagated the cause of the underprivileged Muslim-educated middle classes in India, who were numerically small and educationally less advanced than those of the Hindus. The creation of Pakistan, the separate homeland of the Muslims, was the fulfillment of that cause. Therefore, after the state of Pakistan had been created, the raison d'être of that movement ceased to exist. At that point the Muslim League, the principal organ of the movement, disintegrated. The surviving faction, which appropriated the mantle of the Muslim League, then began to propagate its ideology on behalf of the privileged groups, especially the Punjabi oligarchs, in opposition to regional challenges. The ideology of Islamic unity was now employed to deny the validity of the claims and demands of the less privileged groups—the Bengalis, Sindhis, Pathans, and Baluchis—for recognition of their distinct identity and needs.

The aspirations of Bengalis who, among others, challenged the domination of the "Punjabi bureaucracy," were expressed in the secular idiom of the Bengali Language Movement, which began with the birth of Pakistan itself. It had its first martyrs in 1952. Although the focus of the movement was on the issue of national language, an issue which by its nature was closest to the hearts of students and the educated lower middle class, it was nevertheless instrumental in creating a radical consciousness that extended beyond the immediate interests of those who voiced the slogans of the language movement and gave it leadership. With an urban population that constituted only 5 percent of the total population, the educated middle class of Bengal is drawn overwhelmingly from villages and maintains a close contact with the rural society. Under conditions of widespread public discontent, the problems and demands of the impoverished rural population influenced the cadres and leaders of the movement and their slogans. But the aspirations of the leadership were concerned primarily with the issue of the regional share in government jobs, and especially with places for themselves in the bureaucratic establishment.

There were, therefore, two traditions in the Bengali movement: (1) a petty-bourgeois elitist tradition for those who hoped to rise to senior positions in the bureaucracy or to become members of the newly created business community in Bengal on the strength of governmental financial support and subsidy; and (2) a rural populist tradition that articulated the frustrations and aspirations of the long-suffering sections of the extremely poor Bengal peasantry. The two traditions were intertwined but remained distinct. The educated sons of rich peasants had other aspirations than those of the peasantry in general.

In the early 1950s the Bengali Language Movement embraced both traditions. At the vanguard of that movement was the Awami League in the form in which it was then constituted. At the head of the elitist faction of the Awami League was Suhrawardy, who aspired to public office at the cost of popular objectives. As Prime Minister of Pakistan he was an ardent supporter of imperialist powers and went to the extent of openly and vigorously supporting the Anglo-French-Israeli intervention against Egypt at Suez as well as the U.S. alliance. Sheikh Mujib was a protégé of Suhrawardy and was schooled by him in politics; his political commitments were firmly with the elitist group. On the other hand, there was a populist tradition in the Awami League, which flourished under the umbrella of Maulana Bhashani. The elitist leadership was largely concentrated in the towns and cities. The populists had large numbers of cadres in the field in villages. Since the Communist Party was illegal, there was also a solid core of Marxists in the Awami League. Under their influence many of the populist cadres had moved toward explicitly Marxist ideas. In February 1957, at the Conference of the Awami League at Kagmari, the conflict between the elitist leadership and the populist cadres was brought to a head on the issue of Prime Minister Suhrawardy's foreign policy. This led to a break and to the ouster of populist cadres in the Awami League and of their leader, Maulana Bhashani. They later formed the National Awami Party. The character of the Awami League, which was left in the hands of Suhrawardy and the elitist group and was deprived of its populist and Marxist cadres, was thus transformed. It is crucial to the understanding of the Awami League in its new form that, although its populist cadres were eliminated, its mass populist base among the rural people remained. By a mistimed and badly managed precipitation of the party crisis, it was the populist cadres who were isolated. In the retention of the party's hold over the masses, the role of Sheikh Mujib was crucial: notwithstanding his firm commitments to the elitist group, his rhetoric and even his personal style of life were populist in character. He was a man with whom the people could identify. He bridged the gap between the elitist leadership of the Awami League and its populist mass base.

As the Bengali movement progressed, reluctantly—but inevitably —the dominant Punjabi bureaucratic elite yielded some of the demands of the movement for a fair share of jobs and promotion. As a consequence, by the late 1960s, the provincial administration in East Bengal was almost wholly staffed by Bengali civil servants at all levels. Bengali progress was less remarkable in the central government. It was not until 1969 that for the first time a few Bengali officers were installed as secretaries to the central government, at the head of some minor ministries. The bastions of power—the Ministries of Defense and Finance, the Planning Commission, and the Establishment Division—were still retained securely in trusted West Pakistani hands.

The Bengali movement for equitable treatment reached a new

level when, in the late 1950s, demands began to be made for a fair and adequate share in the allocation of economic resources for development for East Bengal. East Bengali economists prepared excellent detailed studies to demonstrate the steady exploitation of East Bengal by West Pakistan. Their argument that there should be a radical reallocation of developmental resources and a realignment of economic policies, as well as their demands for bureaucratic appointments, replaced the issue of the language as the principal issue in the Bengali movement. There was also a progressive radicalization of the movement and socialist ideas began to gain ground.

In the sixties, President Ayub decided to foster in East Bengal a Bengali bourgeoisie which, he believed, would provide him with a political base in the province and counter the influence of socialist ideas. This endeavor was blessed and backed by the Pakistani bourgeoisie. But to create a bourgeoisie the regime had to put money into the hands of men who had too little of it. Two categories of people from East Bengal were drawn into the process of "capital formation" devised by the Ayub regime; we can refer to them as the "contactors" and the "contractors." The "contactors" were educated Bengalis with influential bureaucratic contacts (especially those who were relatives of bureaucrats or influential politicians); they were granted all kinds of permits and licenses, which had a ready cash value because they could be sold to West Pakistani businessmen who needed them to be able to engage in profitable business transactions. This process transferred money into the pockets of a parasitic group of people, at the expense of the ordinary consumer who ultimately paid for this corruption in the form of inflated prices. The "contactors" lived expensively, and few of them contributed to capital accumulation or built up industries.

But the "contractors" were different. They were small businessmen who were awarded construction contracts, etc., by the government at deliberately inflated rates. The excess profits made by them were plowed back into their businesses. They were later encouraged, by generous loans and official support, to become industrialists. For some industrial projects, for example, the Industrial Development Bank of Pakistan, which was set up for the purpose, would advance about two-thirds of the investment funds required and the East Pakistan Industrial Development Corporation would provide half of the remaining third. The final one-sixth of the amount had to be raised by the prospective industrialist from his own pocket (already filled with public money) or from the stock exchange. In fact a substantial part of this equity was also subscribed by the state-sponsored National Investment Trust and the Investment Corporation of Pakistan. To set up an industry, therefore, the budding Bengali industrialists needed barely 10 percent (or less) of the required capital. But profits were so high that it did not take long before they became sole owners of their industries and began to multiply their new-found fortunes.

The attitude of the newly created nucleus of the Bengali bourgeoisie toward the politics of Bengali nationalism was one of qualified support. They profited greatly from the pressures created by those politics; but at the same time they were apprehensive because of its leftward gravitation. Moreover, their extraordinary privileges were brought into existence because there was a central government which could be pressured. The continuance of their privileges in an independent East Bengal was perhaps a little problematic. Not all of them supported the movement wholeheartedly; they also supported right-wing movements in East Bengal and collaborated with the ruling oligarchy. They were particularly demoralized after the winter of 1968–69, when nationwide protest against the Ayub regime, which brought about his downfall, threatened to develop into a revolutionary movement, especially in East Bengal. Many of them transferred substantial amounts to safer investments in politically more "stable" West Pakistan or, illegally, abroad. While they supported a movement for regional autonomy and for the diversion of a larger share of economic resources to East Bengal, they also looked upon the bureaucratic-military oligarchy, which is based in West Pakistan, as a bulwark for the defense and protection of their own class interests. They therefore valued the link with West Pakistan. Thus the movement for the independence of East Bengal cannot be explained by reference principally to the aspirations of the Bengali bourgeoisie. Moreover, in assessing the class base of that movement, one must take into account the fact that the movement existed and flourished before the Bengali bourgeoisie was brought into being. The class base of that movement was essentially petty bourgeois.

The massive electoral success of the Awami League in the election of December 1970 was guaranteed by a third category of people who had jumped on the bandwagon—the rural elite in Bengal, which was previously divided into many factions. The countryside in Bengal is dominated by lineages of big farmers, the "Sardari lineages." Their wealth, status, and power, much of which is derived from moneylending, enable them to have access to the bureaucracy, on the strength of which they mediate on behalf of their factional supporters and thus further consolidate their local political power. These locally powerful rich farmers aligned themselves with the elitists of the Awami League; the latter were, after all, their sons who had been given a university education and who aspired to big jobs in the bureaucracy.

Despite the radical rhetoric of the elitists in the Awami League, their intentions vis-à-vis the West Pakistan-based oligarchy were quite ambivalent. This was because the elitist leaders were apprehensive about the radical aspirations of their own populist political base. While, on the one hand, they exploited the radical sentiments of the latter in order to generate some force with which to confront those who were in power in West Pakistan and to gain some concessions, they had little wish to allow the radicalism of their followers to overwhelm them and to threaten the social order to which their own elitist aspirations committed them. It is this ambivalence which explains the anxiety of Sheikh Mujib to continue negotiations with General Yahya Khan in the first few weeks of March 1971 for autonomy within Pakistan, notwithstanding the fact that, as a consequence of an effective general strike in East Bengal, he was already in *de facto* control of state power in the province; and that at a time when the Pakistan army was numerically weak and unprepared for the action that it later launched against the people in East Bengal. This was testified to by Tajuddin Ahmed, Prime Minister of the Bangladesh Provisional Government, who, on the eve of his return to liberated Dacca, told newsmen: "The original demand for *autonomy within the framework of Pakistan* had been raised by the Awami League as a whole but the demand for independence grew when Pakistan not only refused to grant autonomy but also unleashed a reign of terror on the people of East Bengal." [11]

Since the creation of Bangladesh, the confrontation between the elitist element in the Awami League and its populist base has reemerged on a new level. Whereas the elitist leadership found a safe haven in Calcutta, the populist and Marxist political cadres, who were once isolated, have now established a new relationship with the people in the course of their armed liberation struggle. The organization and strength of the armed resistance were not yet strong enough to overthrow the Pakistani army, but they were growing. Moreover, the position of the Pakistani army was reaching a point of crisis because the weak economy of West Pakistan could not sustain the long military campaign. The economic crisis in West Pakistan and the outbursts of public discontent opened up new prospects for the advance of the liberation forces in Bengal. It was precisely at that moment that the Indians chose to intervene, so as to forestall the liberation of Bangladesh by popular forces and to install the Awami League elitist leadership in power.

The picture in Bangladesh today is fundamentally different from that which existed in Pakistan at the time of its independence in 1947. The Bengali bureaucracy exists, and the Awami League regime has identified itself with it and with the privileged groups in the country, but the latter are not backed by substantial military forces. On the other hand, the populist forces have experienced armed struggle, in the course of which they have developed organizationally. Large quantities of arms are in their possession. True, "anti-insurgency groups" were also trained in India and were armed to prepare for the day after the liberation of Bangladesh. For the present, all the political skill of Sheikh Mujib is directed to persuading the popular forces to hand over their arms or to become integrated in the organized military forces of Bangladesh—but with little success. It may yet be that a new bureaucratic-military oligarchy with outside aid will in due course consolidate its position and power in Bangladesh. But it is equally possible that Bangladesh will be plunged into an armed revolutionary struggle, for the instruments of coercive state power at the disposal of the Awami League and the Bengali bureaucracy are weak and the economic crisis runs deep.

Notes

1. R. Miliband, "Marx and the State," in Ralph Miliband and John Saville (eds.), *The Socialist Register 1965* (Monthly Review Press, New York, 1965).
2. Hamza Alavi, "Indian Capitalism and Foreign Imperialism," a review of *Foreign Investment in India*, by M. Kidron, in *New Left Review*, No. 37, June 1966.
3. C. P. Bhambhri, *Bureaucracy and Politics in India* (Delhi, 1971).

4. This "middleman" role of politicians has been analyzed in numerous studies; see F. G. Bailey, *Politics and Social Change—Orissa 1959* (London, 1963).

5. Hamza Alavi, "The Army and the Bureaucracy in Pakistan Politics," in A. Abdel-Malek (ed.), *Armée et Nations dans les Trois Continents* (in publication). Written in 1966, this article was privately circulated and was published in abridged form in the *International Socialist Journal*, March–April 1966.

6. Tariq Ali, "The Struggle in Bangladesh," in *New Left Review*, No. 68, July–August 1971, footnote 21, p. 43.

7. Hamza Alavi and Amir Khusro, "Pakistan: The Burden of U.S. Aid," in *New University Thought*, Autumn 1962; reprinted in R. I. Rhodes (ed.), *Imperialism and Underdevelopment*, 1970.

8. Nicos Poulantzas, "Capitalism and the State," *New Left Review*, No. 58, November–December 1969, p. 74. (Emphasis added.)

9. Paul Baran, *The Political Economy of Growth* (Monthly Review Press, New York, 1957), pp. 220–221.

10. This development was analyzed in Hamza Alavi, "Imperialism, Old and New," in Ralph Miliband and John Saville (eds.), *The Socialist Register 1964* (Monthly Review Press, New York, 1964).

11. *The Times* (London), December 23, 1971.

7. Structure and Contradiction in Pakistan

Feroz Ahmed

> I am a believer in socialism; that is why, leaving my class and the government, I have come back to workers, peasants, students, and poor people. What can I get from my deprived people except love? I am the follower of socialism because I know that only in this economic system lies the salvation, progress and well-being of the people. No power on earth can prevent the establishment of this system of truth and justice, equality and human dignity, in Pakistan. This is the call of time and history. Come and see. Bearing the great revolutionary flag of socialism, I have come in the field to serve the people. I have no greed or lust for gain. I am a socialist and as an honest socialist I would fight for the revolution of the poor till my last breath.
>
> —Zulfikar Ali Bhutto[1]

A few days after Zulfikar Ali Bhutto took over as the President of Pakistan and declared that the "common man" would be the master of his destiny, inmates in Karachi and Multan jails, taken in by Bhutto's eloquence, demanded that they be given a chance to live as decent citizens in the new Pakistan. As government officials balked at the prisoners' demands and as their relatives gathered outside the prisons, chanting "Long live Chairman Bhutto" and "Long live the People's Government," [2] the prisoners lost their patience and attempted a jailbreak. The government answered the uprising with police gunfire. According to official reports, seven inmates were killed in Karachi and two in Multan.[3] The Minister for Presidential Affairs, Mr. J. A. Rahim, warned that any attempt on the part of the prisoners to take the law into their own hands would be met with force.[4]

This article was first published in *Pakistan Forum*, February and March 1972, under the title "Has People's Rule Arrived in Pakistan?"

Before political observers could sit down and begin to analyze the character of Pakistan's new regime, the prisoners of Karachi and Multan, inadvertently and at great risk to themselves, had laid bare the realities hidden behind the radical and populist rhetoric of the People's Party. Lest we be accused of being unsympathetic to the grave difficulties of the regime and of reading too much into the prison affair, we shall attempt to analyze the character of the present government of Pakistan and to provide perspectives on what lies ahead.

In order to be able to explain the current (January 1972) policies of the Bhutto regime and to offer a prognosis, one must discuss briefly the origins of the People's Party and recapitulate the events leading up to the downfall of the right-wing military junta in Pakistan.

Protégé of a Dictator Becomes the "People's" President

Zulfikar Ali Bhutto, a wealthy landlord of Sind and a minister in Ayub Khan's government since the military coup of 1958, fell out with his patron over the issue of the Tashkent declaration, signed by Pakistan and India in 1966 to end the hostilities in the region. Bhutto, accusing Ayub of a sellout in Kashmir, found an enthusiastic response among the West Pakistani people, who felt outraged at Ayub's capitulation before big-power pressure. After sounding out the existing left-wing National Awami Party (NAP) and finding it less than enthusiastic, Bhutto formed the Pakistan People's Party in 1967 and announced his candidacy for the scheduled 1969–70 presidential elections under the system of restricted franchise, euphemistically called "basic democracies." Ayub Khan threw Bhutto—as well as the East Pakistani leader, Sheikh Mujibur Rahman—into jail. A massive popular upsurge against the Ayub regime gripped the country from October 1968 to March 1969.[5] Bhutto was released because of popular pressure. While the old bourgeois opposition kept harping on the tune of a "return to parliamentary democracy," Bhutto spellbound the masses with his slogans for the abolition of feudalism and capitalism and the establishment of socialism in Pakistan. In March 1969, Ayub was forced to resign and hand over the reigns of government to Yahya Khan, Commander in Chief of the army. Yahya held the promised elections in December 1970 and Bhutto's party emerged as the majority party in West Pakistan, with 83 of the region's 138 National Assembly (NA) seats. When the military decided to ban the overall majority party, the Awami League, and unleashed genocide in East Pakistan, Bhutto thanked God for "saving Pakistan." However, when Bhutto demanded transfer of power to his party, the military refused. Bhutto then raised the slogan of "power or prison by November 1971." [6] When the army regrouped the right-wing political parties, distributed the Awami League seats to them, and nominated one of their members as the Prime Minister of Pakistan, Bhutto accepted the position of Deputy Prime Minister. When the Pakistani military surrendered to the invading Indian troops in East Pakistan and accepted the cease-fire in West Pakistan, the younger military officers forced Yahya's junta to resign and asked Bhutto to assume the presidency of Pakistan with the powers of Chief Martial Law Administrator. Today, Zulfikar Ali Bhutto occupies the Presidential Palace because General Gul Hassan and his colleagues want a civilian popular figure. In a truncated Pakistan, Bhutto would still head the government if a constitution were framed and parliamentary democracy restored.

Whatever part the Tashkent declaration, Ayub's blunder in arresting Bhutto, and Pakistan's military defeat in the war with India may have played in changing the fortunes of Zulfikar Bhutto, the man and his politics cannot be separated from the social forces that have been at work during the past thirteen years. An analysis of these forces and of the class interests Mr. Bhutto represents—and not of his personality and style—is fundamental for an understanding of the character of the present regime and its future.

Deepening of Contradictions During the "Decade of Development"

The scope of this article does not permit a discussion of the power structure inherited by Pakistan at the time of independence in 1947.[7] It will suffice to say that under the peculiar conditions of postcolonial Pakistan, the ruling oligarchy consisted not only of the propertied classes, such as the feudal aristocracy and the bourgeoisie (especially the big monopolist bourgeoisie), but also of the bureaucracy and the military, who in spite of being drawn from the propertied classes and in spite of being their defenders, retained a great deal of autonomy to pursue their specific interests, some of which were not complementary to the interests of the propertied classes.[8]

As a result of Pakistan's alignment with the United States and the flow of military and economic "aid"—accompanied by the militarization of Pakistan's political culture and the pursuance of a model of capitalist development—a handful of capitalist entrepreneurs came to control a large proportion of the country's wealth and the military became the paramount political force in the country. Pakistan, under Ayub Khan's rule, achieved significant economic growth and "political stability." However, the model of capitalist development had its contradictions, which were bound to negate the success achieved between 1958 and 1968.[9] In political terms, the "decade of development" not only sharpened the conflicts between the ruling groups and those outside the power structure, but created fissures within the ruling alliance itself.[10]

1. Conflicts Between the Rulers and the Masses. On the lands owned by the absentee landlords and not touched by the "green revolution," the peasants continued to groan under the traditional exploitation and oppression of the feudal lords. Population growth and increase in the prices of essential nonagricultural commodities, such as cloth, kerosene oil, and safety matches, added further impoverishment and misery to the lives of sharecroppers. During the later part of the Ayub era, the "green revolution" began to have its economic and social impact. The increase in agricultural production on the modernized farms and the consequent overall decline in farm prices adversely affected the poorer segments of rural society. An increasing number of agricultural laborers and sharecroppers were evicted from the land as a result of decreased demand for labor on the mechanized capital-intensive farms.[11] The small peasant-owner, who had not had the opportunity to modernize his farm, received less income for the same volume of production, while the landlord, who was responsible for the price decline, made up for it by producing and selling more. Because of their political influence and contacts with the bureaucracy, the landlords and the rich peasants were able to sell their products at the right time and price.[12] The governmental program of purchase, designed to stabilize prices, was also mainly used by the capitalist farmers and the big feudal lords. The poor peasants, sharecroppers, and agricultural laborers could see clearly that not only the landlords but government policies and law-enforcing agencies were responsible for the multiplication of their hardships.

Through a policy of virtual wage freeze and a ban on labor strikes, the industrial working class was pauperized in direct proportion to the enrichment of the capitalists. These policies, added to the official repression of workers trying to form unions or to defy the strike ban, made it evident to the industrial proletariat that their aims had to transcend "economism" and brought them into the forefront of political struggle.

Some members of those lower rungs of the petty bourgeoisie who engaged in trade were ruined by governmental policies favoring the big bourgeoisie and by the mounting inflation during the Ayub era. Students, minor government employees, and other low-income white-collar workers with fixed incomes were seriously hurt by inflation and by lack of job opportunities for their family members. Wholesale corruption and nepotism in the government and the absence of civil liberties had thoroughly alienated the segment of the population known in Pakistani parlance as the "educated middle class," which consisted of professionals, teachers, students, managerial personnel, clerks, and junior functionaries in the civil service. The shameful surrender at Tashkent had profoundly shocked this segment of the petty bourgeoisie, especially in Karachi and Punjab,[13] which had always stood up for everything identified with Pakistan-Islam, self-determination for Kashmir, the Urdu language, and Allama Iqbal.[14] The upper segments of the petty bourgeoisie were also disenchanted with the regime because of its policies favoring the development of monopolies and the control of financial institutions by a closed group of industrialist-financiers who denied credit to the petty bourgeoisie.

One of the larger "groups" in the urban areas consists of the unemployed, semi-employed, beggars, part-time beggars, pimps, prostitutes, thieves, jugglers, street messengers, sidewalk palmists, knife-grinders, shoe-shine boys, and other casual workers generally known as the lumpen proletariat. The shortage of urban employment, the population growth, the fragmentation of small landholdings, and the eviction of tenants by the "green revolution" constantly add to this growing group. According to official government figures, one-fifth of the civilian labor force was out of work at the time of Ayub's fall; the actual figures must have been much larger. Indeed, during my visit to West Pakistan in 1969 after five years' absence, the most startling change that I noticed was the stupendous growth of the beggar population and the enormous number of educated unemployed crowding cheap restaurants.[15]

2. *Conflicts Within the Ruling Circles.* The feudal lords, the richest class in the country at the time of independence, witnessed the growth of the urban bourgeoisie with envy. The feudal lords had joined the ruling coalition because of a lack of alternatives and were indebted to the bureaucracy and the army for keeping them in business; at the same time they resented the fact that the bourgeoisie always got preferential treatment from the army. The government policy of siphoning off agricultural surplus into private industries adversely affected not only the peasants, as pointed out by Richard Nations,[16] but also the landlords. The bourgeoisie, through its control of financial institutions, also prevented the landlords from becoming industrial capitalists. The feudal lords had one advantage over the bourgeoisie: they controlled a large population in the countryside because of their traditional power. The feudalists realized that that power could be harnessed at an appropriate time when the bourgeoisie faced a serious challenge from other segments in society.

Control of the commanding heights of the economy by twenty to twenty-five monopolist families was one of the most significant outcomes of the pattern of economic development pursued by the Ayub regime under American advice. The nonmonopoly sector, otherwise content with the regime's "pragmatic" policies and the inflow of American "aid," nonetheless resented the monopolistic control and therefore remained open to the possibility of alignment with groups that would challenge the monopolists. The swiftness with which they deserted Ayub's party after his fall and switched to the opposition parties was one indication of their uneasy alliance with the regime.

Although the bureaucracy had developed a symbiotic relationship with the bourgeoisie, a number of steps undertaken in the interests of the capitalists did not suit the interests of the bureaucrats. Many bureaucrats did not like the Ayub government's policy of "disinvestment," by which industries initiated at the expense of public capital were turned over to the private sector after their success. If these projects had remained under state control, the bureaucrats would have continued to be their directors. The capitalists could always win over the discontented bureaucrats by offering them jobs in their industries or shares to their family members. Nevertheless, the slogan of nationalization remained quite attractive for certain sections of the bureaucracy.

State capitalism had had a strong appeal for many young military officers who blamed the capitalists for the country's misfortunes. Influenced by the Arab military regimes, some of them even privately suggested exemplary punishment for industrialists and traders. The same officers also held the bureaucrats responsible for corruption, inefficiency, and demoralization, and wanted to curb the powers of civil servants. It is not without significance that after the removal of Ayub Khan 304 senior bureaucrats were dismissed from the service. Those military officers who had tasted power considered these bureaucrats a hurdle in their attempt to establish the military's hegemony.

These sentiments were, of course, reciprocated by the bureaucrats. Control of certain government departments and autonomous bodies —for example, the health department, the National Shipping Corporation, and the Bureau of Natural Resources—by military officers certainly did not please the bureaucrats. The bureaucrats also observed with displeasure the fact that the members of the bourgeoisie had begun to view the army as the "ultimate authority." An industrialist failing to obtain a necessary favor from a bureaucrat could turn to a leading man in the military and have the bureaucrat's decision overruled. After their retirement, many bureaucrats went on to become business executives thanks to the friendships they had cultivated with the capitalists during their term of office. These civil servants now saw retired military officers competing with them, basically through the same mechanism. In some respects the military was building a parallel bureaucracy against the entrenched civil servants. For this reason, the demand for a return to parliamentary democracy voiced by the opposition had many sympathizers within the ranks of the bureaucracy.

In addition to the conflicts within the national ruling oligarchy, there were antagonisms between the national power structure and regional power groups. The military, which was politically paramount, was drawn largely from the Punjab province. The industrial capitalist class consisted almost entirely of Punjabis and Gujarati immigrants, settled in Karachi itself. Most of the bureaucrats came from the Punjab and from among the Urdu-speaking refugees who had settled in Sind.

In order to operate as cohesive groups, the military and the bureaucracy pursued policies which kept the Sindhis, the Baluchis, and the Pathans away from influential positions in the military and the bureaucracy. Likewise, the business entrepreneurs from the minority provinces found it exceedingly difficult to obtain business and industrial licenses.

The feudal lords who had been co-opted into the ruling alliance under Ayub Khan were mainly Sindhi or Punjabi; but these feudalists were junior partners in the coalition. There were other landlords who were kept out of the national ruling oligarchy. Regionalism was the most convenient bargaining tool for these feudal lords.

The growth of capitalism had demanded an enlarged resource area and an integrated market. Thus, in 1955 it was decided to "integrate" the four provinces of West Pakistan into "one unit" and to concentrate power in the central government. These developments greatly aggravated regional tensions in the minority provinces. The petty bourgeoisie of Sind, Baluchistan, and Sarhad was particularly incensed by the policies of the central government, which denied them the opportunity to participate in the central civil and military services and systematically suppressed the regional cultures. The "intelligentsia" of Sind was particularly bitter about the regime's policies, especially that of eliminating the Sindhi language from the schools.

Thus, subordination of regional ruling groups to the national oligarchy, disparities in regional development, job discrimination against the petty bourgeoisie of the minority provinces, and the suppression of regional cultures led to the intensification of regional nationalism in Sind, Baluchistan, and Sarhad. Whereas Sind and Sarhad had their own sharp class conflicts and some representation in the national ruling oligarchy, nomadic Baluchistan had neither clear-cut class conflicts of its own nor any representation in the central government. As in East Bengal, all social strata of Baluchistan were united in their opposition to the national power structure. Led by the National Awami Party, the Baluchi nationalists were no less vehement in their demand for autonomy than the Bengalis of East Pakistan.[17]

Emergence and Growth of the People's Party

It is against this backdrop that the emergence and growth of the People's Party and the popularity of its leader, Zulfikar Ali Bhutto, must be viewed. Bhutto and the handful of his friends in Ayub's Convention Muslim League clearly saw the forces that were emerging in the country. Joined by a small number of Marxist and non-Marxist leftists who were disillusioned with the National Awami Party, they formed the Pakistan People's Party (PPP) in 1967 and adopted a program that represented the interests of the petty bourgeoisie while simultaneously providing enough radical rhetoric for the consumption of the masses.

At the end of 1967 the PPP, under the influence of these elements, drafted a document that very crudely described the party's social-democratic program for solving the people's problems.

The document unhesitatingly named the Scandinavian social democracies as a model and even went so far as to praise capitalism as practiced in the United States and Western Europe:

> In none of those [imperialist] countries is capitalism permitted to reign uncontrolled, and in several the public sector is very extensive indeed. Apart from that, they [the local apologists of capitalism] ignore what makes the Western countries attractive to the unbiased mind, which is the immense freedom enjoyed by the individual.[18]

For Pakistan, the PPP's recipe for "socialism" consisted of nationalizing the banks, insurance, heavy industry, the already partially nationalized communications, and energy resources. At the same time:

> As for the private sector, it ought to flourish under conditions proper to private enterprise, that is, of competition, and not behind the shelter of high tariff walls or disguised subsidies. Only in that way can the efficient running of private enterprise be assured and the consumer protected from exploitation by monopolists.[19]

Further:

> The private sector will play its own useful role in the kind of mixed economy envisaged, but will not be able to create monopolistic preserves.[20]

Once "socialism" has been established and the private sector has been given its rightful place, where does the worker fit in?

> The workers will be encouraged to participate in the efficient running of the factories by appropriate incentives and will by law have the right to share in the profits of companies in [the] private sector.[21]

Furthermore:

> It is obvious that the ILO principles which represent the decent norms of relations between the state, employers and employees, must be enforced, especially as they are in consonance with fundamentals of human rights.[22]

On the crucial land question, the single most important problem in West Pakistan, the party document made a sweeping remark that feudalism will be abolished "in accordance with the established principles of socialism," [23] but did not specify the maximum landholding it would allow.[24]

As the opposition to the Ayub regime intensified and the competition with the old opposition parties became fierce, the rhetoric of the People's Party also escalated. Enchanted by Bhutto's slogans and attracted by his financial resources, a growing number of leftist intellectuals, journalists, poets, writers, and student leaders flocked toward the People's Party. Others saw a distinct national bourgeois tendency in the PPP. Objectively the petty bourgeoisie was in conflict with the monopolists entangled with imperialist capital. The pursuance of its class interests required a confrontation with imperialism; Bhutto's outbursts against the United States and his pronouncements in support of national liberation struggles[25] were viewed in this context. The hostility of the Johnson administration and the liberal Western press toward Bhutto confirmed the thesis that Bhutto was a genuine anti-imperialist against whom the Pakistani reactionaries, in complicity with imperialists, had ganged up. A series of harsh actions against Bhutto by the Ayub regime, including a frame-up, an assassination attempt, and the disruption of his rallies, reinforced the myth surrounding him.

In Pakistan's political context, Bhutto and his petty-bourgeois supporters represented a progressive force. They had spoken for the end of dictatorship, feudalism, and monopoly capitalism; they had demanded restoration of the freedom of press; they had provided opportunities to the leftist intellectuals, suppressed for too long, to express themselves again; and, above all, they had legitimized the slogan of socialism, which had been taboo in Pakistan.

Those who did not believe in the socialist *bona fides* of Bhutto conceded that it was at least possible to bring about a bourgeois-democratic revolution in cooperation with the forces represented by Bhutto.

The task of organizing the party at the grass roots was shouldered mainly by these leftist political workers and by the new cadres recruited by them. They spread out in the countryside and in the urban *mohalas* (neighborhoods) to organize the party. Organization of the party and mobilization of support for it required intense political education. This function was effectively performed by the leftist journalists and writers whom Bhutto had won over. On the model of the right-wing Jamaat-e-Islami, the PPP undertook an extensive program of publishing books, pamphlets, and posters. A Lahore weekly, *Nusrat*, was acquired by the party and entrusted to an experienced leftist journalist.[26] The party's leftist-operated propaganda machinery effectively portrayed the miserable plight of the masses, exposed the injustices and oppression of feudalism and capitalism, debunked right-wing propaganda, and projected a revolutionary image of the PPP and its leader. Mr. Bhutto chose the title of "Chairman" rather than that of "President," as was customary in Pakistani political parties. His leftist supporters equated him with Chairman Mao. One issue of *Nusrat* carried a picture of Bhutto shaking hands with Mao Tse-tung. The caption read: "Asia's two great leaders, Chairman Mao and Chairman Bhutto." Even a $3\frac{1}{2}''$ by $4\frac{1}{2}''$ book of quotations of Chairman Bhutto was published.[27] A rather awkward-sounding slogan—"Islam is our faith. Democracy is our policy. Socialism is our economy"—was designed to appeal to the various hopes, fears, and prejudices.

As a result of the downfall of Ayub Khan and his own uncompromising stand against the Round Table Conference, arranged by Ayub to divide the pie with the opposition parties, Bhutto emerged from the crisis of 1968–69 with greatly enhanced stature and unmatched popularity. For the first time in West Pakistan's politics, cooptation was rejected and confrontation had succeeded. The laurels for this feat went to Zulfikar Bhutto.

Feudal Lords Join the PPP

The disintegration of Ayub Khan's coalition and the discrediting of his Convention Muslim League presented a serious dilemma to the feudal politicians who had supported him. The immediate reaction in the Punjab was to join forces with the old feudal-bourgeois Council Muslim League of Mumtaz Daulatana, then in opposition. In the minority provinces, feudal restoration was sought behind the slogans of the petty-bourgeois-oriented regionalist movements. This was especially true in Sind, where there were many displaced landlords as well as an intense movement for the breakup of the "one unit" and for regional autonomy. Many landlords previously associated with Ayub joined hands with the veteran Sindhi nationalist, G. M. Sayed, to form the Sind United Front (SUF), whose emotive slogan of *"Jeeye Sind"* (Long live Sind) had created a strong wave of chauvinism and frightened the large non-Sindhi minority in the province.[28] Others were simply marking time to determine which way the wind was going to blow.

General Yahya Khan's decision to dissolve the "one unit" administrative structure in West Pakistan and restore the four original provinces took the wind out of the sails of the SUF. The PPP in the meantime had made significant inroads among the Sindhi students and done some spade work at the local level.[29] Given these facts, plus the parochial rivalries in Sind, Bhutto's prospects of winning over a large group of landlords appeared bright. By the middle of 1970 the PPP's popularity in Punjab had become undisputed and many fence-sitters had begun to jump on the party's bandwagon. In Sind, the People's Party's big break came when one of the two principal *pirs* (spiritual leaders), Makhdoom Mohammad Zaman Khan of Hala, a big landlord and a poet, who uses the nom de plume of Talibul Maula, declared himself for the PPP. Soon most of the politically influential feudal lords, including Sind's former ruling family, the Talpurs, who (with the exception of Mir Rasul Bux) had supported Ayub Khan, joined the People's Party. The remaining major landlords mobilized around Makhdoom's rival, *pir* Sikander Ali Shah of Pagaro, who supported Qayum Khan's Muslim League.

The decision of the landlords to forge a united front with the Punjabi petty bourgeoisie under the banner of the People's Party cannot be fully explained either by the circumstances discussed above or by the vagueness of the PPP over the land question. There was at least one area in which the class interests of the landlords coincided with those of the petty bourgeoisie. Both were victims of the monopoly capitalists. Both wanted to have easy access to credit, foreign exchange, and licenses. Many landlords had already realized that feudalism had no future and that industries were a more efficient way of accumulating wealth. If they could seize state power, weaken the monopolies, exercise control over the financial institutions, and acquire industrial and trade licenses, there would be little to prevent them from transforming themselves into industrial capitalists. Given these desiderata, land reforms would be complementary, not antagonistic, to their interests since compensation received for the lands surrendered could be invested in more lucrative factories and businesses.[30] This process of voluntary liquidation of landed properties and conversion of landlords into industrial capitalists has already been witnessed in Latin America.

The PPP, the Military, and the Bureaucracy

Fear—real and imaginary—of India and the aim of "liberating" Kashmir have been the main rationalizations for the growth of the Pakistani military. Among the civilian leaders, none had advocated the military's case more intelligently than the PPP chief, Zulfikar Bhutto. During the 1965 war he had implored the people to continue fighting India for a thousand years and to eat grass in order to continue arming the military. His book, *The Myth of Independence*,[31] is essentially an exposition of his chauvinistic and jingoistic politics. In it, he wrote:

Pakistan's security and territorial integrity are more important than economic development. Although such development and self-reliance contribute to the strengthening of the nation's defence capability, the defence requirements of her sovereignty have to be met first.[32]

Bhutto's advocacy of establishing an "industrial war base"[33] and developing a "nuclear deterrent" against India[34] could not but fall on receptive ears in the military. In fact there was considerable support for the PPP among some in-service army officers, and a large number of retired officers had joined the party.[35] Bhutto's opposition to the Tashkent declaration won him many admirers among the junior military officers who, like the Punjabi public, felt very bitter at the fact that the top brass had had numerous majors, captains, and lieutenants massacred because of its own strategic blunders in the 1965 war and that it had no moral courage to stand up to the big powers.

The People's Party's slogan of nationalization was received enthusiastically by a good many bureaucrats who saw in this scheme an opportunity to exercise greater control over the means of production. Mr. Bhutto's jibes against the *kamora shahi* (bureaucracy) notwithstanding, the bureaucracy as a whole had nothing to fear from him.[36] A party whose lifeblood comes from the so-called "educated middle class" can never be averse to the bureaucracy. After all, the children of the bureaucrats join the ranks of the "educated middle class," and almost every male member of the "educated middle class" aspires to become a CSP (Civil Service of Pakistan) officer before reaching his twenty-fifth birthday. And, above all, state capitalism strengthens, rather than weakens, the power of the bureaucracy.

The New Coalition Replaces the Old

The People's Party thus succeeded in pulling together the forces alienated by the Ayub regime: the petty bourgeoisie of Punjab and Karachi; the "progressive" landlords of Sind, lower Punjab, and parts of Sarhad; and the disgruntled members of the military and bureaucracy. Not only was the party's program in their interest, but Mr. Bhutto gave repeated assurances to these groups that their vested interests would be protected. To the vast mass of the alienated and exploited people—the peasants, the workers, and the lumpen proletariat—the PPP was sold as a revolutionary socialist party that was bent upon "tumbling the thrones and tossing the crowns." [37] They were told that every trace of feudalism and capitalism would be eliminated, that the fields would belong to the tillers and the factories to the workers, and that every exploiter would have to be answerable to the people's court.[38] In short, there was no revolutionary slogan or cliché which was not used by the PPP leaders and cadres.

In Punjab, where the leftist cadres had done splendid work of grassroots organization and where there was no competing regionalist movement,[39] the masses, looking at their own objective conditions, at the brutal repression of the PPP by the ruling oligarchy, and at the sincerity of the party workers, were taken in by the radical rhetoric. They voted massively for the PPP and gave it a landslide victory in both the National and Provincial Assemblies. In Sind, where political education and organization of the masses had not progressed so well, the PPP owed its success to the traditional hold of the landlords over the peasants.

To ensure control by feudal lords and the petty bourgeoisie, democracy within the party was disallowed.[40] Top positions were arbitrarily assigned by Mr. Bhutto to the representatives of the propertied classes. The 18-member central committee, named by Bhutto, included only three persons—S. M. Rashid, Mairaj M. Khan, and M. Haneef Ramay—who could be considered leftist by any definition. Similarly, party tickets for the elections were awarded almost exclusively to the rich members. In Punjab, of the sixty-three PPP members elected to the National Assembly, only two, Sheikh Rashid and Mukhtar Rana, represent the peasants and workers. In Sind, all of the nineteen NA members from the PPP are either landlords or belong to aristocratic families.

The party's wealthy leadership also worked out deals with landlords of other parties whereby the PPP did not contest certain constituencies, or, if it did contest, did not campaign wholeheartedly in behalf of its own candidates. The most blatant exposure of such deals came when Mr. Bhutto went to Multan to campaign for himself but refused to visit nearby Vehari, where a new PPP stalwart, Taj Mohammad Lengah, was effectively challenging Mr. Daulatana, the old guru of the Punjabi feudal politicians.[41]

The Monopolists React

As has been noted, it was only the monopoly capitalists who had to fear the forces gathering under the banner of the PPP. Due to the peculiar conditions of postindependence Pakistan and as a consequence of the imperialist domination of the country, Pakistan's capitalists had progressed rather rapidly and without the paraphernalia of the bourgeois order. They had not even felt the need to build an effective political party of their own: the military and the bureaucracy had provided them the necessary cover. Now, when the military and the bureaucracy had yielded to the popular demand for the restoration of parliamentary democracy, the big monopoly capitalists panicked. They attempted to prevent the elections but failed. In the elections, although thirty right-wing candidates, over whom the big bourgeoisie could maintain some sort of control, were elected to an NA of 300 members, both members of the "big twenty-two" families who contested the elections, Saeed Haroon and Rafique Saigal, were soundly defeated. The immediate reaction of the bourgeoisie to the election results was to panic: the stock market declined, prices went up, and capital began to fly out of the country.[42] A series of actions by the big capitalists and their agents indicated that there was a conspiracy to prevent the restoration of democracy.[43] To many leftist critics of the PPP, this may sound pretty far-fetched. But an understanding of the narrow political base of Pakistan's big bourgeoisie, an appreciation of the nature of the conflict between the big bourgeoisie and the "emergent bourgeoisie" of the PPP, and an examination of the events taking place between December 8, 1970, and March 25, 1971, would confirm the assertion that Pakistan's big bourgeoisie felt seriously threatened by the specter of the West Pakistani petty bourgeoisie marching into its monopoly preserves.[44]

The Petty Bourgeoisie Retreats

Given a transfer of power under normal conditions, with industries still holding out the promise of big profit, the PPP, in all likelihood, would have made an earnest attempt to implement its social-democratic program. The result would have been a state-owned and state-operated economic infrastructure supporting the competitive capitalism of the petty bourgeoisie. In order to understand the dynamics of state capitalism we need not go very far: the experience of our neighbor, India, is an eye-opener (see the table on the next page).[45]

Unfortunately, Pakistan's industrial sector is not in a very happy state at the moment. In fact, the country as a whole rests on very shaky foundations. The bourgeoisie—both entrenched and emergent—is in the lowest of spirits. Pakistan's economy has never recovered since the uprising against Ayub Khan. The accompanying table summarizes the economic conditions which obtained at the time of the start of the Bengal genocide. The prolongation of the military occupation of East Bengal not only cost the exchequer an average

Economic Indicators

Gross National Product, 1969–70 (at present market exchange rate)	$5,000 million (approx.)
Total external debt at the time of Bengal operation	$4,600 million
Annual rate of increase in GNP, 1968–69	5.2%
Annual rate of increase in GNP, 1970–71	1.4%
Annual rate of population growth before the massacre	3.0% (approx.)
Foreign exchange reserves at the time of Bengal operation	$184 million
Foreign exchange earning, 1967–68	$800 million
Average annual flow of foreign economic aid	$500 million
Planned imports, 1970–71	$1,900 million
External debt service, 1968–69	$141 million
External debt service, 1969–70	$150 million
External debt service, due at the time of Bengal operation	$210 million
Debt service as part of foreign exchange earning, 1960–61	3.6%
Debt service as part of foreign exchange earning, 1969–70	20%

Sources: *Pakistan Yearbook 1969; Interim Reports of Pakistan Embassy in Washington*, September 1969 and June–July 1971; A. T. Chaudhri, "Pakistan's Crippling Burden of Foreign Debt," *Atlas*, November 1970.

monthly sum of $30–40 million but deprived West Pakistan of revenues, foreign exchange, and a market for its manufactured goods. The shrinking of markets and the shortage of foreign exchange seriously affected production in West Pakistan, where several thousand workers were laid off.[46] The military defeat at the hands of India and the de facto establishment of Bangladesh completed the severance of the parasitic link between West Pakistan and East Bengal. All West Pakistani assets in Bangladesh have now been nationalized.[47]

The major economic consequences of the separation of East Bengal for West Pakistan are:

1. The GNP has been reduced by at least 45 percent, not counting the downward economic trend in West Pakistan itself.

2. At least a 50 percent reduction in export earnings has occurred,

again not counting the reduced capacity for earning foreign exchange in West Pakistan. This means a drastic (at least 40 percent) reduction in foreign exchange available for the importation of capital goods and industrial raw materials. West Pakistan earned, at most, 50 percent of united Pakistan's foreign exchange and spent at least 70 percent of it.

3. The loss of East Bengal implies the loss of markets for Rs. 1.7 billion worth of West Pakistani goods annually, including approximately 40 percent of West Pakistan's manufactured goods. Even if alternate markets are found in the Middle East, there will be no incentive to expand such industries as cotton textiles.

4. It will be necessary to spend Rs. 550 million annually in foreign exchange to purchase tea, jute, and paper, assuming that no foreign exchange is spent on Rs. 200 million worth of other commodities that were purchased every year from East Bengal.

5. Repayment of the nearly $5 billion owed to foreign creditors of Pakistan must now come from West Pakistan's resources alone.[48]

6. West Pakistan must now bear a tremendous burden of military expenditure, the defense budget of undivided Pakistan being roughly 5 percent higher than the total revenues of West Pakistan.

7. Since the ratio of West to East Pakistanis in the civil service was more than four to one, about half the civil service personnel of West Pakistani origin are now surplus and must be re-absorbed in West Pakistan.

To all these must be added the economic disaster in West Pakistan, which was an inevitable outcome of the colonial type of relationship between the two parts of Pakistan and the incredibly stupid policies of the military regime.

Given this economic picture, plus the military and diplomatic vulnerability of a truncated, weakened, and demoralized Pakistan, Pakistan's new rulers will have to take great risks to implement their program. Aside from a revolutionary restructuring of the society, there is no way for Pakistan to pull itself up by its bootstraps. Such a change is certainly not in the interest of the classes in power. They must seek the easiest remedy for their troubles, i.e., imperialist "aid."

In order to put the West Pakistani economy back into shape, it will require as much as $1.5 billion per year in foreign "aid" for the next several years. The social consequences of this "economic recovery" are not likely to be very different from what Pakistan has already witnessed. Nevertheless, the petty bourgeoisie, true to its class character, cannot find a better way of coping with its problems.

Mr. Bhutto's comment that a new era in friendship with the United States has opened and that a new era in business relations with the U.S. is going to start,[49] in addition to the government's repeated assurances to foreign investors, is indicative of the dilemma of the "national" bourgeoisie, which had fed the people with anti-imperialist slogans during the elections. The same Mr. Bhutto who was incensed at America's failure to support Pakistan in 1965[50] has only praise for America when it did essentially the same thing while Pakistan was being dismembered in 1971. Today he appears reluctant to pull Pakistan out of SEATO and CENTO, against which he campaigned so vociferously between 1966 and 1970.

Domestically, the imperialist pressure and the "emergent bourgeoisie's" own lack of self-confidence will mean going back on its manifesto. Instead of nationalizing many industries and all financial institutions, as promised in the party manifesto, the government has taken over the management—not the ownership—of a handful of industries. Instead of breaking the monopolies, it has only attempted to curb the "political" influence of the big capitalists.[51] Instead of breaking the imperialist stranglehold over Pakistan's economy, it is inviting foreign investment.[52] Instead of forcing management to honor contracts made with the workers, it is urging the workers to desist from *gheraoing* (besieging) the bosses.[53]

Since the industries have lost their attraction—at least for the time being—the landlord faction in the PPP does not appear very enthusiastic about land reform. There are neither the investment opportunities of 1968 nor funds in the state coffers to pay immediate compensation for lands. The banks and insurance companies do not have sufficient deposits to advance much credit to the "emergent bourgeoisie." It is no accident that Bhutto, who is rationalizing martial law in the name of reforms, has had to wait three months to announce his much-publicized land reforms. It would be unwise to prejudge the land reform bill. It will probably be out before the publication of this article and should be analyzed carefully. At the moment, we must make two observations on the land reform question: (1) many landlords have already transferred some of their land to their relatives and loyal tenants; others are trying to complete their deals before the reforms are announced, and (2) the average maximum limit of 150 acres, proposed by the PPP during the elections, will hurt very few landlords and benefit few peasants.

The petty bourgeoisie's nervousness is manifested not only in its response to imperialism and in its economic policies but in its entire political conduct. During the past five years it vehemently opposed martial law and dictatorship, and demanded representative government. Today, when given the opportunity, it prefers to rule by martial law rather than by people's mandate. A year ago it opposed the idea of the majority party alone forming the central government on the grounds that the Awami League had no support in West Pakistan. Today, it attempts to rule all four provinces of West Pakistan when it has no mandate in two of them. Despite its proclamation about amnesty, it continues to hold political prisoners[54] and even makes fresh arbitrary arrests.[55] Instead of pardoning, or showing leniency to, the "outlaws" who want to surrender and live decent lives, it raises the price on their heads.[56] Instead of dissolving the notorious National Press Trust, as promised during the elections, it uses the Trust to its own advantage by installing its cronies in it.[57] Instead of purging the corrupt bureaucrats—which any liberal government would do to win the confidence of the people—it resuscitates the old hacks of the bureaucracy.[58]

It is difficult to think of an elected party anywhere in the world which so rapidly exposed its lack of faith in the people, which refused to rule by popular mandate, and which did not even make a feeble attempt to assert its independence and self-confidence. This nervousness about, and lack of confidence in, the democratic process also explains why, despite the exploding of the military's myth, only a handful of "fat and flabby" (read: anti-Bhutto) generals were fired and why the military as an institution escaped criticism, let alone firing. The nervous petty bourgeoisie's most reliable ally is the "new" military, which most likely will try to rebuild itself on a Nasserite or a Gaddafiite model. Pakistan's military vulnerability will again be used to justify the remilitarization of the country, unless the big powers, on whose "charity" the fate of Pakistan's capitalists depends, prevent it for their own reasons.

The performance of the Bhutto government must not be judged in terms of Bhutto's "dictatorial personality" or of the behavioral attributes of the "new breed" of politicans who surround him. What has happened so far and what is likely to happen must be viewed in the context of the class interests of the people in power, the specific conditions obtaining in Pakistan, the dilemma faced by the new rulers, and the options open to them. The ultimate limit to the options is set by their class interests.

Pakistan cannot become independent, united, and prosperous without eliminating the causes of dependence, disunity, and impoverishment. In order to eradicate the roots of these evils it will be necessary to destroy the social arrangements which institutionalize them and the social groups which perpetuate and profit from them. Such an undertaking is certainly not on the agenda of Pakistan's present rulers. What was originally on the agenda of the PPP cannot be fully realized due to the conditions created by the Yahya dictatorship and Pakistan's military defeat. To do so would exact a price from the "emergent bourgeoisie" which it is unwilling to pay.

One may then ask what specifically the new rulers will or will not do. Without making claims to prophecy or prediction, we can safely say that the new rulers *will not even attempt* to bring about the equality and justice they have repeatedly promised. They will not sever the links with imperialism or take an independent posture in foreign policy. They will not attempt to demilitarize Pakistan. They will not curb the privileges and power of the capitalists or the landlords—especially the kulaks, the military officers, and the bureaucrats. They will not do away with the repressive laws which allow detention without trial. They will not restore the complete freedom of expression which they have been demanding for themselves.

They will attempt to do a number of things in which they are not likely to succeed—for example, stopping the eviction of peasants and the victimization of factory workers, reforming the educational system, providing elementary education and basic health care to as many people as possible, reducing unemployment, and streamlining the judicial system.

The new government is likely to succeed in the following areas: collection of taxes from the super-rich, prevention of investment in luxury goods, equitable access to credit for all capitalists, prevention of further growth of monopolies, partial substitution of technocrats for generalist bureaucrats, and more effective government control over the banks and insurance.

Because of the pressure of the masses in the streets or of the PPP's probable coalition partners, the NAP and the Jamiat-ul-Ulema-e-Islam, many things may happen contrary to expectations. By and large, however, the above picture is likely to hold.

Notes

1. Z. A. Bhutto, "Address to the Hyderabad Convention, September 21, 1968," in *Let the People Judge* (Pakistan People's Party, Lahore, March 1969).
2. *Dawn* (Karachi), December 31, 1971.
3. *Dawn*, January 8, 9, and 10, 1972.
4. Voice of American broadcast, January 9, 1972.
5. For a graphic account of the events of 1968–69, see Tariq Ali, *Pakistan: Military Rule or People's Power?* (William Morrow and Co., New York, 1970).
6. *The Observer*, July 24, 1971.
7. For a general review of Pakistan's ruling structure at the time of its independence, see Tariq Ali, op. cit.; for an analysis of the military and bureaucracy as semi-autonomous forces in Pakistan, see Hamza Alavi, "Military and Bureaucracy in Pakistan," *International Socialist Journal*, March–April 1966 (revised version to be published).
8. The military's decision to unleash terror in East Pakistan, despite the West Pakistani capitalists' conciliatory attitude toward the Awami League, is the most glaring example of such conflicts; see Feroz Ahmed, "The Structural Matrix of the Struggle in Bangladesh," in this volume. Subordination of specialized technocrats to "generalist" bureaucrats is another example of the interests of the bureaucrat being given precedence over those of the capitalist, which demand the most effective employment of all available skills.
9. For an analysis of the contradictory aspects of capitalist development in Pakistan, see Arthur MacEwan, "Contradictions of Capitalist Development: The Case of Pakistan," *The Review of Radical Political Economics*, Spring 1971 (abstract published in *Pakistan Forum*, October–November 1970).
10. The conflicts between the West Pakistani rulers and the classes in East Pakistan will not be dealt with here; for a discussion of this, see Feroz Ahmed, op. cit.
11. *Pakistan Forum*, December 1970–January 1971, p. 11.
12. Mechanization of agriculture took place on the large farms of some of the feudal lords as well as on the lands owned by the rich peasants and retired military and civil officers who turned to farming. According to Alavi, the consequences of mechanization were much more severe on

the lands of the rich farmers than on those owned by the old big landlords; see Hamza Alavi, "Elite Farmer Strategy and Regional Disparities in the Agricultural Development in Pakistan," in Stevens, Alavi,
and Bertocci (eds.), *Rural Development in Pakistan* (to be published).

13. The petty bourgeoisie of the minority provinces of West Pakistan, like its
    counterpart in East Bengal, was preoccupied with regional nationalism
    and demanded regional autonomy, proportional allocation of resources
    and jobs to the provinces, and guarantees for the protection of regional
    languages and cultures. It has usually been sympathetic to the Bengalis
    and has been less vulnerable to religious bigotry.

14. The famous Urdu poet from Punjab (often compared with Nietzsche),
    who allegedly first dreamed of Pakistan.

15. An Association of Unemployed Graduates has recently been formed in
    Karachi, enrolling 1,000 members instantly; see *Dawn*, January 11,
    1972.

16. Richard Nations, "The Economic Structure of Pakistan: Class and Col-
    ony," *New Left Review*, No. 68.

17. Armed revolts were staged on a number of occasions by Baluchi nation-
    alists, but were mercilessly crushed by the Pakistan army. The major
    crackdown of Baluchi dissidents during Ayub's times was conducted by
    General Tikka Khan, who later acquired the notoriety of being the
    "butcher of Bengal" for the carnage he organized in East Pakistan. The
    reports of Baluchi insurrections and the army crackdowns never ap-
    peared in the Pakistani press. In Hyderabad (Sind), I had the occasion
    to talk with a physician who had examined the bodies of "dozens of tall,
    18- to 25-year-old handsome Baluchis." The doctor told me that these
    incidents had generated a wave of sympathy for the Baluchi resistance
    fighters and intense hatred for Ayub and his cronies in Sind.

18. Pakistan People's Party, *Foundation and Policy* (Lahore, 1968).

19. Ibid.

20. Ibid.

21. Ibid.

22. Ibid.

23. Ibid.

24. Throughout his election campaign, Mr. Bhutto, while constantly at-
    tacking feudalism and capitalism, cleverly evaded the land question. In
    his privileged election speech on television, he promised distribution of
    government land to the landless peasants but made no mention of the
    private lands (*Dawn*, November 19, 1970). The party manifesto was so
    ambiguous on the land ceiling to be allowed by the PPP that Mr. M. A.
    Kasuri, Vice-President of the party, issued a clarification that the maxi-
    mum landholding to be permitted was 150 acres, and not 50 acres as
    many PPP workers thought (*Dawn*, December 18, 1970).

25. Besides many public statements of this nature, his anti-imperialist pro-
nouncements appear in his two works: *The Myth of Independence* (Oxford
University Press, Karachi, 1969) and *Pakistan and the Alliances* (Pakistan
People's Party, 1969).

26. In the wake of the *Nusrat*'s success, the same journalist launched a daily
paper, *Mussawat* (Equality), which overnight became immensely popular. Several other daily and weekly publications were later started by
the PPP in different cities in West Pakistan.

27. Kaleem Nishtar (compiler), *Chairman Bhutto Ke Aqual Aur Afkar* (Sayings
and Thoughts of Chairman Bhutto) (Maktabe Alia, Lahore, 1969).

28. The fears of the non-Sindhi minority were exploited by the right-wing
pseudo-religious parties representing the interests of the colons who
were given lands as a reward for playing the fifth column for Ayub's
clique.

29. The People's Party took no effective stand against the "one unit." However, once it was dissolved, it accepted the fait accompli and tried to
take maximum advantage of the changed situation.

30. A number of landlord supporters of the PPP had already invested
money in industries and trade. For example, Hakim Zardari, who was
later elected to the National Assembly, owned several cinema houses in
Karachi and other urban properties. The Talpurs have a textile mill in
Hyderabad and other industrial assets. A detailed profile of the PPP
leaders—with information on their landed, business, and industrial assets—would be of great interest and use in explaining the policies of the
Bhutto regime.

31. Bhutto, op. cit.

32. Ibid., p. 152.

33. Ibid.

34. Ibid., p. 153.

35. Several retired colonels, majors, and captains were awarded PPP tickets
to run for the National and Provincial Assemblies. The People's Party's
popularity among the in-service officers could be judged from the fact
that a novice of this party defeated a former chief of the air force by better than a 2-to-1 margin in Rawalpindi city, headquarters of the Pakistan army. The PPP also captured most of the Provincial Assembly seats
in the Rawalpindi district, including the riding (administrative district)
of the military cantonment.

36. The tally of absentee ballots cast by the on-duty bureaucrats showed an
overwhelming vote for the PPP candidates. The only bureaucrat to join
a political party, Mr. Mazari, was to join the PPP. Mr. M. M. Ahmed,
who acted as Yahya Khan's Rasputin in the Bengal operation, was simultaneously Mr. Bhutto's adviser. He has been now given new responsibilities by President Bhutto. The new regime has so far not touched the

bureaucracy despite many utterances about the "conspiracies of the bureaucrats."

37. See, for example, the banner line of the December 5, 1970, issue of the
party's official organ, *Mussawat.*

38. *Mussawat,* December 7, 1970.

39. In the minority provinces the regionalists, using Punjab as a scapegoat,
were quite successful in channeling the militancy of the masses into the
nationalist movements. In Punjab, the age-old slogan of "Islam in danger" was used by the reactionaries to distract the masses from class struggle. By prefixing socialism with "Islamic," the People's Party effectively
defused the right-wing propaganda that socialism was the antithesis of
Islam.

40. The visible split in the People's Party at the local level all over the Punjab since March 1971 has been mainly over the issue of internal government and party elections. A small faction, led by MNA-elect Ahmed
Raza Qasuri, unsuccessfully attempted to challenge Bhutto's dictatorial
methods. The left-wing faction, led by MNA-elect Mukhtar Rana, has
recently launched a drive for democracy within the party and in the
country. As a result of these demands at the grassroots, Bhutto has increasingly been drawn toward the right wing of the party. In fact, in recent months, he has recruited dozens of reactionary tribal leaders in Baluchistan and Sarhad and assigned them the task of reorganizing the
party.

41. No such "adjustments" were, however, offered to the recognized leaders
of the working class and to other known leftist candidates. In Multan,
Mr. Bhutto decided to run himself rather than give the ticket to Babu
Ferozuddin Ansari, the leader of the weavers, despite the fact that Mr.
Bhutto was running from five other constituencies. In Lahore, the veteran leader of the railway workers, Mirza Ibrahim, was opposed and
soundly defeated by a rich engineer of the PPP, Dr. Mubashar Hassan,
who is now Finance Minister of Pakistan. In Karachi, because of rank-
and-file pressure, the party decided not to run a candidate against Mrs.
Kaneez Fatima, a militant labor leader. But I have been told on good
authority that the PPP workers campaigned for a right-wing candidate,
Mufti Mohammad Shafi, on the pretext that Kaneez Fatima had no
chance and that in order to ensure the defeat of another ultra-rightist it
was necessary to support Mufti Shafi. The revolutionary poet Habib
Jalib, running on the ticket of the NAP, was also opposed and beaten by
an unknown PPP candidate. In Sarhad province, the PPP's intransigence resulted in the defeat of the NAP and the victory of the right-wing
Muslim League in several constitutencies, despite the fact that the NAP
withdrew its candidate to enable the PPP province chief, Sherpao, to
win a seat in the provincial assembly.

42. *Pakistan Forum*, February–March 1971.

43. See, for example, reports appearing in Karachi's *Daily News*, January 11 and March 18, 1971, and an article by Mazhar Ali Khan in *Forum* (Dacca), January 16, 1971.

44. The intrigues against the People's Party did not stop on March 25, 1971. The Yahya regime's attempts to impose an artificial right-wing majority (see *Pakistan Forum*, October and November 1971) were undoubtedly received by the big capitalists with enthusiasm.

45. See Paresh Chattopadhyay, "State Capitalism in India," *Monthly Review*, March 1970.

46. According to a "conservative" estimate of the conservative Karachi daily *Dawn* (January 6, 1972), at least 45,000 workers were laid off in Karachi alone since the imposition of Yahya's martial law.

47. This action has affected almost all of Pakistan's big capitalists, including a PPP supporter, M. M. Ispahani, who had most of his capital invested in East Pakistan.

48. There is a good possibility that the petty-bourgeois government of Bangladesh, now desperately begging for imperialist "aid," may agree to repay a portion of this debt in return for fresh loans from the World Bank and other agencies. The international creditors, who are capable of exercising "leverage" on the Bangladesh government, will find this arrangement more practical—if not fair—in recovering the money owed by Pakistan.

49. *Dawn*, January 3, 1972.

50. Bhutto, op. cit.

51. Bhutto's interview with the Canadian Broadcasting Corporation, January 23, 1972.

52. *Dawn*, January 3, 1972.

53. *Dawn*, January 4, 1972.

54. Afzal Bangash and other leaders of the Kisan-Mazdoor Party, who were incarcerated by the Yahya gang, were not released by the new regime until a month after the release of other detainees, during which a nationwide campaign for their release was launched. Ghulam Jilani, a former Awami League leader, is still illegally detained.

55. Jam Saqi, a peasant leader of Sind, was recently apprehended under a martial law regulation (*Dawn*, January 15, 1972).

56. Mubeen Dahri, a peasant of Nawabshah district, who was driven to "banditry" by the cruelties and exploitation of the landlords, recently wrote to the President of the Sind People's Party that he would like to live a decent life if given amnesty (*Dawn*, January 14, 1972). The government replied by raising the price on his head from Rs. 5,000 to Rs. 15,000 (*Dawn*, January 16, 1972).

57. Yunus Saeed, editor of the People's Party's Karachi weekly, *Combat*, was made the chairman of the infamous Press Trust which controls several large daily papers.
58. Two notorious pro-American bureaucrats, Aziz Ahmed and G. Ahmed, brothers and former ambassadors to Washington, were among the first beneficiaries of the Bhutto regime; they were called from retirement to head the foreign office and to "reform" the police.

Part II

The Roots of Struggle in the Villages

1. Peasant Classes in Pakistan

Saghir Ahmad

> In a very short time, in China's central, southern and north-
> ern provinces, several million peasants will rise like a mighty
> storm, a force so swift and violent that no power, however great,
> will be able to hold it back. They will smash all the trammels
> that bind them and rush forward along the road to liberation.
> —Mao Tse-tung[1]

Twenty-two years later, Mao Tse-tung's unorthodox analysis and
prediction came true. The Chinese were the first to make a successful
peasant revolution. In later decades, their example was followed by
peasants of other countries, forcing the world to take cognizance of
their role in the vanguard of revolutionary change. In Barrington
Moore's words:

> The process of modernization begins with peasant revolutions that
> fail. It culminates during the twentieth century with peasant revolu-
> tions that succeed. No longer is it possible to take seriously the view
> that the peasant is an object of history . . . which contributes nothing
> to the impetus of change.[2]

But not all classes of peasants are agents of change. Mao recognized this when he wrote:

> But has this great revolutionary task, this important revolutionary
> work, been performed by all peasants? No. There are three kinds of
> peasants, the rich, the middle, and the poor peasants. The three live in
> different circumstances and so have different views about the revolu-
> tion.[3]

I am indebted to Kathleen Gough for her comments and criticisms of an earlier draft
of this paper. (Minor editorial changes have been made in this posthumously published paper. An earlier version appeared in the *Bulletin of Concerned Asian Scholars*,
Winter 1972—Eds.)

Much of the sociological literature on peasants concerns the roles of these various classes. In order to assess these roles, one must first delineate the classes clearly. In some of the literature there has been a tendency to mechanically apply a model of the Chinese class structure to other societies. Although peasant societies share common sociological characteristics, they are nevertheless marked by wide differences in culture, customs, and traditions. It is necessary to examine the relation between structural and cultural variables that have a bearing not only on class position but also on class consciousness. Here I will examine the class structure and its relation to other structural and superstructural variables, using illustrative data from a village in the Western Punjab.

The Village

The data were collected in 1965 from Sahiwal, a village in the district of Sargodha. Sargodha division, like Multan and Bhawalpur, is a canal colony area, such areas comprising about 70 percent of the cultivated land in West Pakistan. In contrast to the old settled districts, the canal colony areas were settled mainly after the introduction of irrigation works in the late nineteenth and early twentieth centuries. The systems of tenure in these districts are of two types: 1) peasant-proprietorship with small holdings of 5 to 25 acres, and 2) tenant farming with large areas owned by landlords. In recent years there has also been an increase in capitalist farming, with wage laborers employed to work on the farm. In 1965, at the time of this research, the land of Sahiwal was predominantly cultivated by tenant farmers.

The village land, whether cultivated, noncultivated, or uncultivatable, is divided between two landlord families, Haji and Khan, who also own two nearby villages. The land of the three villages, a total of 4,572 acres, was acquired in 1867 by a common ancestor of the present landlord families. Farmers from various regions of the Punjab were encouraged to clear and settle as much of the land as they wished. Settlement size was, however, restricted by technology. One pair of plow-oxen can adequately plow only 12.5 acres of land. Even today, when villagers are asked the amount of land they own or cultivate, they reply "one plow" or "two plows" of land, meaning 12.5 or 25 acres.

The settlers' primary obligation was to produce. Those who failed to fulfill the landlords' demands were subject to eviction. The landlords provided the agricultural and residential land and paid the land revenue. In return, the tenants paid half of all they produced and contributed *begaar* (unpaid labor) when this was demanded. All the expenses and energy involved in agricultural production were the responsibility of the tenants.

The settlers included *kammis,* those who manufactured and serviced the farmers' tools or performed other services, in some cases for the village at large. The duties and obligations of *kammis* were traditionally defined, as were the amounts of their payments in the form of annual shares of the produce.

Sahiwal has 1,590 people divided into 274 households. The household, headed by the eldest male, is the primary social, economic, and political unit. The following quantitative data, unless otherwise designated, refer to household heads.

Occupations and Status Groups

Status distinction occurs in terms of *quoms.* Different definitions and usages of *quom* have confused many students of Punjabi society. Some have equated *quoms* with castes, others with clans, and still others with occupations. Indeed, *quom* has elements of all. In my view, *quoms* are best explained as examples of Weber's "status groups." In Sahiwal the word *quom* has two meanings, which I shall refer to as "major" and "minor" *quoms.* There are two major *quoms:* Zamindars (traditional cultivators) and Kammis (traditional artisans).[4] Membership in these groups does not today specify one's actual occupation, for many Kammis are cultivators and a few Zamindars have become artisans. These two major *quoms* further subdivide themselves into a number of minor *quoms.* Twenty-three of the minor *quoms,* such as Doogal, Mattan, and Sheikh, belong to the major *quom* of Zamindars. Fifteen minor *quoms* belong to the major *quom* of Kammis. In contrast to the single traditional occupation of cultivation among the Zamindars, the Kammis have traditionally performed many different artisan or service functions, such as weaving, carpentry, haircutting, laundry work, etc. Accordingly, the names of the fifteen Kammi *quoms* indicate ancestral occupations—Carpenter, Barber, Weaver, Washerman, or Blacksmith—although, as with the major *quoms,* many people today no longer engage in the traditional occupation of their *quom. Quom* membership today accords a person a certain status in the traditional social hierarchy rather than actually determining his occupation.

Although there is no exact correspondence between *quom* membership and occupation, the two are still rather closely associated. In Sahiwal, 107 households claim to belong to Zamindar *quoms,* while 167 households identify with Kammi *quoms.* In reality, however, 131 (47.8 percent) of the heads of households are cultivators. This number includes 100 Zamindars and 31 Kammis. Seven Zamindar households work in jobs other than their traditional occupation. Of the 167 Kammis, only 61 (36.5 percent) work full-time in their ancestral occupation, while 47 (28.1 percent) work part-time in such occupations, and sometimes in other jobs as well. Thirty-one (18.6 percent) of Kammis have become farmers; the remainder (16.8 percent) are unemployed, semi-employed in nontraditional occupations, or working outside the village.[5] Altogether, only 75 percent of the Kammis can be said to be fully employed; the rest are either unemployed or partially employed.

Quoms have often been equated with castes, but such an equation is inappropriate, for most of the commonly accepted caste characteristics, such as birth status, traditional occupation, restricted social mobility, commensal and pollution rules, and endogamy do not apply to the *quom.*[6] Most of the structural, behavioral, and attitudinal differences among villagers are also not explained to references to *quom* membership. Hamza Alavi, who recently completed a village study in a different district of the Punjab, similarly concludes that "caste, insofar as it exists in rural Punjab, is a vestigial phenomenon and does not constitute a referent in social interaction."[7] We must, however, pay attention to one vestige of caste. Analogous to caste ranking in Hindu India, there does exist a hierarchy of *quoms.* Thus, when the residents of Sahiwal were asked to rank the various *quoms,* they universally agreed that all the Zamindar *quoms* ranked above all the Kammi *quoms.* They further ranked each of the minor *quoms* (23 among the Zamindars and 15 among the Kammis) within these major groups. The *quoms* of Syeds, descendants of the Prophet Mohammed, and Awans, descendants of converted Hindu Rajputs or feudal princes, were assigned highest status among the Zamindars, and the Miana *quom* (traditionally caretakers of mosques) among the

Kammjs. *Quom* status alone did not, however, appear to have great political or social significance. For instance, when the villagers were asked to name village influentials, none of the Syeds, Awans, or Mianas was named. Nevertheless, if a member of a high-status *quom* also possesses other valued characteristics, such as land, money, and/or a large patrilineal lineage *(biraderi),* he and his whole *quom* are likely to be viewed with greater respect and to be more influential than if the *quom* is of low rank. But unaccompanied by these other characteristics, the recognition accorded to a high-ranking *quom* is more a reflection of historical tradition than of political reality.

In Sahiwal there were cases of families which changed their *quom* name when changing their occupation. Indeed, a common Punjabi proverb is: "last year I was a Jullaha [weaver], this year I am a Sheikh [disciple of the Prophet Mohammad], and next year, if the prices rise, I will be a Syed [descendant of the Prophet Mohammad]." In other words, a rise in economic status or a change to a more valued occupation may lead to a change in status group membership, although this is not always immediately accepted by other villagers.

Problems of Class Structure

In analyzing classes among the villagers, one must take into consideration the nature and form of changes induced by growing industrialization and an increase in market relationships.

Because of the enactment of various land reform laws, and because of a desire to accumulate capital and invest it in industry (due to the recent opening up of opportunities for industrial investment), many Punjabi landlords have in recent years changed their previously tenanted land into capitalist farms or have emphasized the production of cash crops. Both changes have brought changes in the relations of production, and thus in the village class structure. Their net effect has been (a) to create tenants, artisans, and landless laborers who are linked to their landlords through cash payments that derive from the operation of market forces, rather than through the sharing of a subsistence crop; (b) to increase the proportions of laborers who are hired for short periods, as opposed to tenants and artisans having long-term ties to their landlords; and (c) to impoverish tenants, artisans, and landless laborers and widen the gap between their incomes and those of the more prosperous landlords.

To deal first with cash crops, the opening of a sugar mill twenty-five miles away gave impetus to the village landlord to grow more sugar cane. Previously, only a small amount of sugar cane was grown to feed the cattle or to make unrefined sugar for domestic consumption. Now more than one-third of the total land is planted with sugar cane, all of which is supplied to the sugar mill. The result is that the tenants are not only deprived of growing one of the traditional crops, but the customary relations between the cultivators and the *kammis* have been disturbed. Growing sugar cane involves greater wear and tear of farming tools, which means increased work for those artisans who are customarily responsible for repairs. But sugar-cane cultivation also means that the *kammi,* like the tenant farmer, ends up short of a portion of the wheat or cotton crop he would customarily have received and used for home consumption. In theory, tenants and artisans receive cash payments for the work they contribute toward sugar-cane production. In fact, however, the price of sugar cane is paid by the sugar mill to the landlords' agents, and by the time they have deducted for the tenant's seed, fertilizer, fines, and current loan to the landlord, only a few lucky tenants receive the rewards of their cash crop farming.

A further shift toward capitalist agrarian relations that impoverish the tenants and artisans has been caused by the enactment of land reform measures and the threat of more radical land reforms. This has led many landlords to put a certain portion of their land into "self-cultivating" farms, on which the land is in fact now cultivated by hired laborers rather than by tenants, as in the past. By 1965, the two village landlords had put more than 200 acres each into such farms in order to avoid having their land confiscated. This meant not only eviction of tenants but also loss of work for *kammis.* At the same time, the growing industrialization of the country in general, including the establishment of textile mills and shoe factories, has meant a loss of markets for such artisans as weavers and cobblers.

One problem in delineating classes among peasants involves the very definition of a peasant. Who is a peasant? Generally it is agreed that "peasant" refers to a cultivator and not, for instance, to a fisherman. Yet those who thus define peasants also refer to Indian and Pakistani villages as peasant villages, and, as we have seen in Sahiwal, which is typical of many Punjabi villages, more than 50 percent of the population are not cultivators. They are artisans, shopkeepers, village functionaries, etc. Are they peasants? If so, what is their class position? Are they rural proletariat? If so, how do the *kammis,* who are paid a customary share of the produce, differ from the landless laborers who earn a daily wage? In seeking an answer to these questions, we must briefly review some of the pertinent literature.

In his pioneering works[8] Mao Tse-tung analyzed the rural society of China as consisting of five classes: (1) landlords; (2) rich peasants; (3) middle peasants; (4) poor peasants; and (5) workers. The landlords possessed land, did not engage in labor, and lived by the exploitation of the peasants. The rich peasants generally owned land, but some owned only part of their land and rented the remainder; in all cases, however, they possessed abundant means of production. The people whom the rich peasants exploited were chiefly farm workers. Many middle peasants owned land; others rented all of the land they farmed. The middle peasant neither exploited the labor of others nor sold his own. As a rule the poor peasant had to rent land for cultivation and sell a part of his labor power. A worker had to make his living wholly by selling his labor power. In Mao's analysis, the middle and the poor peasants constituted the largest mass of the rural people. The "peasant problem" was essentially their problem.

Hamza Alavi, while recognizing the distinction between rich, middle, and poor peasants, argues that the "different strata arranged one over the other, in a single order . . . is misleading. The middle peasants, for instance, do not stand between the rich peasants and the poor peasants; they belong to a different sector of rural economy." Accordingly, he distinguishes between three sectors. The first sector is composed of the landlords and the sharecroppers or poor peasants. The second sector consists of independent small landholders or middle peasants, who do not exploit the labor of others. The third sector is that of capitalist farmers or rich peasants. Their farming is based primarily on the exploitation of the wage labor of the farm laborers. Thus there are *"capitalist farmers, independent smallholders, sharecroppers, and farm laborers."* [9]

Kathleen Gough finds that the rural population of Kerala and Tanjore in South India is divided into five classes in a manner similar to Mao's description of China.[10] There are landlords, rich peasants, middle peasants, poor peasants, and landless laborers. According to her analysis, the classes tend to be arranged one over the other in terms of production relations as well as wealth and social status, since middle peasants usually rent some land from landlords and employ some workers at peak seasons. In this sense, among others, she disagrees with Hamza Alavi.

Among the most recent analyses—and the one most pertinent to our case—is that of Tariq Ali.[11] Tariq Ali distinguishes five classes in rural West Pakistan: (1) big landlords, who own more than 100 acres of land; (2) rich peasants or kulaks, who own between 25 and 100 acres; (3) middle peasants, who own between 5 to 25 acres; (4) poor peasants, who own less than 5 acres; and (5) tenant sharecroppers, who own no land of their own, and rural proletariat (farm laborers who work for daily payments in cash or in kind).

I shall deal briefly with the points of view of the several writers.

Alavi's analysis does not appear to deal adequately with the problems of rural social stratification. Speaking of "certain common assumptions in all different theories of social class," S. Ossowski notes that "classes are components of a system of two or several groups of the same kind. . . . It means that any definition of any social class must imply relation of this class to other groups of the same system; . . . the notion of middle class implies again the notion of upper and lower classes." [12] In this sense I disagree with Alavi and follow a rather conventional definition. Alavi's formulation also tends to simplify the changing class structure: he separates landlords and capitalist farmers into two different classes, equating the latter with the rich peasants. This creates both theoretical and methodological problems. The two property owners of Sahiwal, like many others in West Pakistan today, rent part of their land to sharecroppers, while another part is cultivated by wage laborers. Are they both landlords and rich peasants? It appears to me a difficult proposition to treat the same group of people as members of two distinct classes.

Tariq Ali, on the other hand, reduces the whole problem of class differences to differences in the amount of land owned. He does not incorporate the notion of relation to the means of production. More importantly, all three—Alavi, Gough, and Ali—even while dealing with rural India or Pakistan, have neglected to incorporate the artisans into their analysis. Not being familiar with rural China, I do not know whether Mao can be criticized on the same count. But for those concerned with rural India and Pakistan, the neglect of artisans and other servants, who in some areas constitute nearly 50 percent of the population, is a serious oversight. Perhaps this problem can be resolved if we follow the Marxist definition of class and emphasize structural and relational rather than occupational criteria.

Classes exist in relation to the means of production. This relation defines the positions people occupy in the organization of production, which in turn refers to a hierarchy of a composite of social, economic, and political differences. "The classical Marxist three or four class scheme," Ossowski says, "is formed by the cross cutting of three dichotomic divisions based on different criteria: (a) those who possess and those who do not possess means of production, (b) those who work and those who do not work, (c) those who employ hired labor and those who do not." [13]

The exclusion of artisans from the definition of peasants obviously stems from placing primary emphasis on the nature of the occupation. Raymond Firth, for instance, finds that "the term peasant has primarily an economic referent. . . . The primary means of livelihood of the peasant is cultivation of the soil." [14] Similarly, Robert Redfield concludes that peasants are "people who control and cultivate their land for subsistence." [15] Potter et al., after an extensive review of the literature, conclude that the "emphasis on agriculture and self-sufficiency is implicit or explicit in many writings about peasants, yet we believe that stressing occupation and cultural content obscures the really important diagnostic criteria." These authors then define peasants in a manner that I find useful:

> We agree that peasants are primarily agriculturists, but we believe that the criteria of definition must be structural and relational rather than occupational. For in most peasant societies, significant numbers of people earn their living by nonagricultural occupations. *It is not what peasants produce that is significant; it is how and to whom they dispose of what they produce that counts.* [16]

Historically, artisans and other village servants have been essential components of rural India and Pakistan. Their specialized skills have helped in the development and survival of the village communities as more or less self-sufficient social and economic units. The work of cultivators has depended upon certain artisans, generally referred to as agricultural *kammis* or agricultural artisans. In rural Punjab the traditional reciprocal rights and obligations between cultivators and artisans take the form of the relationship of *seip*. The artisans serve their *seipi* (cultivators) with their particular skills, and the cultivators in return are obligated to pay their *seipi (kammis)* a proportion of the agricultural produce and to look after their welfare. Those artisans who are enjoined in the contractual relation of *seip*, and they constitute an overwhelming majority, cannot be treated as entrepreneurs for they do not run a business concern. Their economic fortune is tied to those of the cultivators they serve. This is not to imply that some village artisans are not entrepreneurs. The most striking example of a village entrepreneur is the goldsmith, who, at least in modern times, is not part of the system of *seip*. Others, too, can break their contractual relations and become entrepreneurs, but this, as is discussed below, entails structural changes.

Like the cultivators, the artisans are also divisible into classes that are defined by their relation to the means of production. The changes in the "modes of production and of exchange" affect their structural positions as they affect those of cultivators. For instance, when a village landlord starts a capitalist farm or adopts modern farm machinery, both sharecroppers and artisans lose their economic base and become laborers.

Classes in Rural Punjab

Landlords/Capitalist Farmers. In West Pakistan, those who own 100 acres or more are frequently classified as landlords. Within this category, those who exploit wage laborers rather than sharecroppers and make use of advanced technology are regarded as capitalist farmers. Such distinctions are, I think, inaccurate and misleading.

Class position should be determined by one's relation to the means of production and not by the amount of wealth owned. In this sense, all those who own land, who do not themselves work to produce and live exclusively by the exploitation of others, should be treated as belonging to the class of landlords. Furthermore, the distinction between landlords and capitalist farmers is transitional rather than structural. In this period of transformation from a feudal-type economy to a capitalist economy, many traditional landlords have adopted new modes of production and new methods of capital accumulation. In Sahiwal, for instance, while most of the land is cultivated by sharecroppers, both owners have each put more than 200 acres into "self-cultivating farms." Since neither of the two owners lives in the village, both the tenanted and the "farm" lands are supervised by the owners' employees—the managers. The difference between the two is that in one case the tenants take half of all they produce, while in the other the laborers are paid wages for their work on the "self-cultivating farms." In both cases the ownership of the means of production is in the hands of two families, who never engage in productive activity. The transition from old-style landlord to capitalist farmer does, however, involve some changes in social relations and life style.

The relationship between the more old-fashioned landlords on the one hand, and tenants and other villagers on the other, is more "feudalistic" in nature. Although the sharecropper is exploited, his exploitation is nevertheless sweetened by customary norms. The traditional landlord, unsophisticated, uneducated, and well-versed in the customs and traditions of the area, easily mingles with the villagers even when (as in Sahiwal) he does not live in the village. He also provides protection to the villagers and helps them in times of crisis. By contrast, the growing number of capitalist farmers tend to be urbanized, educated, and unaware of the village customs. Their whole life is alien to the villagers. Thus, their method of exploitation appears harsher.

While traditional landlords indulge in more feudal pastimes, capitalist farmers are Westernized; many are invited by Americans to study advanced methods of farming or farm management in a university in the U.S.A. Many are financed by one of the American agencies to participate in leadership programs or 4-H activities in the U.S. These new developments have caused a cultural gap between landlords and capitalist farmers, but have not created any noticeable division in class interest.

Both the landlords and the capitalist farmers continue to exploit the villagers to maintain their superior life style, to entertain lavishly, and to spend money on securing elected positions that lead to the attainment of positions of authority and extended control in the larger society.

The demands of the larger society are, however, contradictory. On the one hand, society demands that the seeker of higher positions indulge in "conspicuous consumption." On the other, he is required to have the backing and support of many people. These contradictory demands lead to contradictory behavior on the part of this class. The need for money leads to exploitation and oppression of the villagers in general and of cultivators in particular. The usual means to extract the maximum are beating, forced labor, fines, eviction or the threat of it, refusal to extend credit, and refusal to help against harassment by outsiders. But such behavior is limited by an equally important need to secure and ensure the continuing allegiance and support of the villagers, which is not only necessary for certain types of success but is also indicative of one's status. This was exemplified in the 1964–65 elections when both of the landlords were interested in elective offices for themselves or their candidates. They competed with each other in generosity and kindness toward the villagers to secure their votes.

It is in this context that one must understand the Punjabi peasants' attempt to create competition, or to keep old factionalism alive between their landlords, for the peasants benefit from such rivalry and disputes. I was amazed and amused at the villagers' constant attempts to create dissension between the landlords, between the landlords and managers, and between managers. The results are, of course, limited, for the landlords make up the ruling class. By controlling the land on which the people live and from which they draw their subsistence, the landlords have some control over every villager. They set the tempo of village life and the standards of right and wrong.

The Rich Peasants. In Sahiwal there were no rich peasant cultivators, i.e., independent small landholders who owned their own land. Hence the following comments are of limited generality, based primarily on my observation of village entrepreneurs—the goldsmiths, two carpenters, the village Hakim (wise man) and a few shopkeepers.

The distinguishing feature of this class is that they, like the small landholders, own the means of production; unlike the landlords, however, they do not live primarily by the exploitation of others. The cultivators in this class hire labor only at the peak of the season; in addition, some have one or two house servants. The only kind of labor the village entrepreneurs exploit is that of apprentices or trainees. In contrast to other classes, they are fairly well-off and are able to maintain a decent standard of life.

On the basis of my limited observation, it seems to me that this class is one of the more conservative elements in the village society. The entrepreneurs in Sahiwal appear to be religiously orthodox, politically conservative, and extremely conscious of their social status. Although they are not regarded as of very high status, they nevertheless pretend to be and imitate the customs of the socially and economically superior group. For instance, while the goldsmiths are assigned a low rank among the *kammis,* they enforce strict *purdah* (wearing the veil) for their women, a rather uncommon practice among lower social groups. When asked for self-placement on a five-point hierarchical social scale, they placed themselves at the top. The rich peasants are the only group in the village which practices religion strictly. Among the five *hajis* (pilgrims to Mecca) in the village, four belonged to this class. In short, the class of rich peasants identifies with the landlords even though it does not have the means to engage in similar activities or to enjoy the same life style.

The Middle Peasants. The middle peasants own land, but not of sufficient quantity or quality to make an independent living. They are forced into supplementing their income by other means, most often by becoming tenants of the landlords. Their great hope is to become self-sufficient farmers.

In Sahiwal nearly 10 percent of the tenants belong to this category. They are reputed to be "good farmers" and they work hard, attempting to save enough to buy land of their own. Because their ambition is to become rich peasants, much of their social behavior is like that of rich peasants. However, given the reality of their economic situation, they are unable to practice the life style of their richer cousins. Thus, for instance, while higher classes advocate *purdah* for their women, the middle peasants are unable to practice it without hurting their aspirations; the women are needed to work in the field with their husbands or fathers. Unlike women of the poorer classes, the women of this class are generally considered of good moral character. While, however, the middle peasants advocate greater religiosity, their actual behavior does not conform to their ideal norms.

In contrast to other classes, the middle peasants spend more money for the ceremonial fund. They also conform more closely to the ideal Punjabi norm of hospitality and generosity.

In the village they are named as influential members of the community: they are called upon to settle disputes, to judge the merits of various cases, and to be advisers in familial and communal affairs. The landlords and their managers also respect the middle peasants. While others often receive harsh treatment, the middle peasants are always politely treated.

The Poor Peasants. The second largest group of rural Punjabis are the poor peasants. They include tenant farmers (sharecroppers) and artisans. The farmers depend exclusively upon rented land as their only means of subsistence. Some among this class may have better equipment or more and better animals, and may be richer than those who do not have these advantages. But poor or less poor, their livelihood depends upon rented land from which they can be evicted any time the owner finds it profitable.

The artisans depend upon the customary *seip* relation, whereby they receive a share of all that their patrons produce in return for their work. Their subsistence, like that of sharecroppers, depends upon the fate and whims of their patrons—whether they be rich, middle, or poor peasant farmers.

While the cultivators and the artisans occupy the same position in the organization of production and objectively have similar class interests, one often finds social divisions between the two groups. The tenants who belong to one of the Zamindar *quoms* conceive of themselves as socially superior to the Kammis. This social division is often exploited by the landlords to exacerbate conflict among the poor peasants. However, this contradiction appears to be an example of what Mao Tse-tung calls a nonantagonistic contradiction, i.e., in the opposition to the exploiting class, status differences are replaced by a unity around class interest. For example, when one of the landlords proposed the idea of buying harvesters, which would have enabled both the landlords and the tenants to make extra money by supplying wheat in the market ahead of others, the idea was rejected by the poor peasants. While the tenants knew they would make some extra money, they realized that this would mean an end to the customary share of the *mehnati-mussali* (winnower), and that if mechanization was approved it might also mean an end of tenancy over a period of time. Similarly, in the above-mentioned case of sugar cane, both the tenants and the artisans together demanded remuneration for the artisans, who were adversely affected by the increased sugar-cane production.

Mechanization and capitalization of farming hurt the artisans as well as the tenants; both are forced to become peasant proletarians. In this period of increasing emphasis on mechanization, artisans are worse hit; but since mechanization is only the first step in the emergent capitalist farming, the tenants will soon follow in the footsteps of the artisans.

The Peasant Proletariat. The members of this class are neither craftsmen nor tenants. They have neither a share of produce nor a fixed income. They are laborers, and they sell their labor power. They also contribute most to the semi-employed and unemployed. Historically, they are drawn from the ranks of middle and poor peasants. With the increasing mechanization and capitalization of agriculture, their number has been growing. The Planning Commission of Pakistan reports that mechanization of farms reduces the need for labor by 50 percent, and that with the arrival of the green revolution—i.e., tractors, tube wells, new seeds, fertilizers, pesticides, etc.—thousands of tenants have been evicted from land. It is needless to add that mechanization of farms affects not only the tenant farmers but, even more, the artisans.

In Sahiwal at the time of this study (1965), not many ex-tenants belonged to this class. Instead, it was dominated by the artisans. It was recently reported to me, however, that more land had been put into so-called "self-cultivating farms"; this could have been achieved only by evicting the tenants or decreasing their holdings, hence forcing them to work at least partly as laborers. Deprived of the means to earn a living either by farming or craftsmanship, they roam from village to village and from village to cities in search of jobs. They form the majority of the unskilled workers in the building and construction projects. I was told that the workers in the Rural Works Program are drawn primarily from this class, though they leave during the harvest seasons for the agricultural work they prefer (the Rural Works Projects then come to a virtual halt). Those unable to find work survive because of the generosity of their fellow villagers.

While they are conscious of the status differences among themselves between the ex-Zamindars and ex-Kammis, the recognition of difference is not acute.

Smoking, drinking, and rowdy and boisterous behavior are common characteristics of this class. The women of this class are often accused of having low moral character; from this class are drawn the largest number of prostitutes. Instances of elopement, runaway wives, and abduction are more common in this class. Objectively, this class is the most exploited, oppressed, and alienated.

Conclusions

In the foregoing analysis of peasant classes, I have incorporated the artisans as an integral part of the peasant social structure. This has been a departure from the established literature on peasants. The reason for taking this position is both structural and cultural. The artisans occupy positions equivalent to those of cultivators. Those who become village entrepreneurs with control over the means of production are, in behavior and position in the total economic structure, then analogous to the rich farmers. The difference is occupational rather than positional. Similarly, the position of share-croppers is shared by those artisans whose fortunes are tied to the cultivators. When the owners of land, who rent it to the sharecroppers, opt for capitalist farming, not only are tenants evicted but also artisans, who lose their jobs and means of livelihood. Similarly, when a rich peasant implements the mechanization of farming, such as the use of tractors or harvesters, the artisans, e.g., carpenters and blacksmiths, also lose their function. Technological developments in a capitalist mode of production lead to equal pauperization of artisans and cultivators in the class of poor peasants.

I have used the five-class schema, not only because it approximates the observed reality in Sahiwal but also because maintenance of the more or less accepted classification will aid future comparative analyses. Among the five classes, the class of landlords/capitalist farmers is obviously the dominant and the exploiting class. In the larger society and especially in the rural society, they form the ruling class. As the country changes from feudal to capitalist, and from agricultural to industrial modes, members of this class also change from landlords to capitalist farmers and to industrial bourgeoisie. This class is dominant and superordinate in relation to the rich peasants. In relation to the other rural classes, they are the exploiters. The rich peasants often collaborate with this class for mutual benefit, but in the long run those rich peasants who are unable to keep up with modern developments and increasing competition will be forced into the roles of exploited people.

The middle peasants suffer the most inconsistency of position.

First, their class interest is often confused. Being primarily tenants but also part-owners, their loyalties are divided. Psychologically, i.e., in terms of aspirations, they identify with and strive to become rich peasants; but structurally their position is more akin to poor peasants. Secondly, and linked to the above, is the problem of status inconsistency. While middle peasants resemble poor peasants structurally, they nevertheless enjoy a higher social status. This conflict between their status and class position creates ambiguity in their behavior; their behavioral and attitudinal responses are often extremist in that they tend to react strongly against exploitation, but at the same time they uphold traditional norms and customs.

The poor peasants and the proletariat form the largest mass in the rural population. They are also the most oppressed and exploited classes. Among the poor peasants of Sahiwal, the artisans are the most conscious of their class position. First, they suffer status discrimination; second, they constitute the largest proportion of the peasant proletariat. They, more than others, realize that any social or technological change will adversely affect their means of subsistence. A desire to change their living conditions is most evident among the artisans. The desire lacks any organized efforts, but the changes are evident in individual efforts. Of all the groups and classes, the younger generation of artisans has ardently pursued different avenues from the traditional occupations. In Sahiwal, with a total of 13 high school graduates, 11 come from the poor peasant artisan families and 2 from the poor peasant farmers. The only college graduate also belongs to this class. Of the five government servants employed outside the village, 4 are artisans. Those whose jobs have been eliminated—such as the *tobas* (well-cleaners), after the introduction of canal irrigation—have been quick to retrain and learn new occupations. In any organized activities for social change, I predict that the poor peasants, and especially the artisans, will form the most disciplined group.

Notes

1. Mao Tse-tung, "Report on an Investigation of the Peasant Movement in Hunan." *Selected Works of Mao Tse-tung*, Vol. 1 (Foreign Language Press, Peking, 1967), p. 23.
2. Barrington Moore, Jr., *Social Origins of Dictatorship and Democracy* (Beacon Press, Boston, 1966), p. 453.

3. Mao Tse-tung, op. cit., p. 30.

4. Because of the lack of complete correspondence between *quom* membership and occupation, I have adopted a usage common in the Indian literature and have capitalized the proper names of *quoms* (e.g., Zamindar or Farmer; Kammi or Servant, Carpenter, Blacksmith, etc.), as in the English surnames Smith or Miller, while using the lower case for actual occupations (*kammi*, weaver, etc.).

5. Sahiwal contains an unusually large proportion of households of traditional Kammi status groups by comparison with villages in the Indo-Pakistan subcontinent generally. A quick survey of representative village studies from West Pakistan and from North, Central, and South India shows that members of such traditional service groups tend to form between about 12 percent and 30 percent of the village. In Sahiwal, however, they form 60 percent, although the people actually engaged full-time today in such service occupations form only 22 percent, and those engaged either full-time or part-time in traditional Kammi occupations, only 40 percent of the total villagers. Since it is a recently settled area, it may be that the canal colony zone as a whole contains an unusually large number of people of artisan or other service groups, whose forebears lost their work in other regions because of the increasing population or the changing economy, and who moved to this area in search of work or land. (Eds.)

6. For a fuller discussion, see Saghir Ahmad, "Social Stratification in a Punjabi Village," *Contributions to Indian Sociology* (Delhi, 1971).

7. Hamza Alavi, "Clan, Caste and Class in Local Level Politics in the Punjab (West Pakistan)" (paper presented at Second European Conference on Modern South Asian Studies, Copenhagen, July 1970).

8. Mao Tse-tung, op. cit., Vol. 1: "Analysis of Classes in Chinese Society," pp. 13–21; "Report on an Investigation of the Peasant Movement in Hunan," pp. 23–59; "How to Differentiate the Classes in Rural Areas," pp. 137–143.

9. Hamza Alavi, "Peasants and Revolution," *The Socialist Register 1965* (Monthly Review Press, New York, 1965), p. 244. (Emphasis added.)

10. Kathleen Gough, "Peasant Resistance and Revolt in South India," *Pacific Affairs*, Winter 1968–69, pp. 527–544.

11. Tariq Ali, *Pakistan: Military Rule or People's Power?* (William Morrow and Company, Inc., New York, 1970).

12. S. Ossowski, "Old Notions and New Problems: Interpretations of Social Structure in Modern Society," in André Béteille (ed.), *Social Inequality* (Penguin Books, London, 1969), p. 80.

13. Ibid., p. 82.

14. Raymond Firth, *"The Peasantry of South East Asia,"* quoted in J. M. Potter,

M. N. Diaz, and G. M. Foster, *Peasant Society: A Reader* (Little, Brown and Co., Boston, 1967), p. 4.

15. Robert Redfield, *Peasant Society and Culture* (University of Chicago Press. 1956), p. 31.

16. Potter, Diaz and Foster, op. cit., p. 6.

2. Harijans in Thanjavur

Kathleen Gough

There are some 80 million Hindus of the Scheduled or "Untouchable" castes in India—about 15 percent of the population; they are usually darker in color than Hindus of higher castes. Until the mid-nineteenth century most Untouchables, like blacks in the United States, were slaves who did agricultural work on their high caste owners' estates. Those who were not slaves of particular families belonged to hereditary caste groups of village servants who were confined to such tasks as scavenging, leatherwork, black magic, and the care of graveyards and cremation grounds. In Hinduism such tasks are regarded as extremely defiling in a religious sense; because of this it was traditionally a grave sin for Untouchables and Hindus of higher castes to touch, or even to approach, each other.

Hindus who are not Untouchables (known as "caste Hindus") are themselves divided into numerous ranked castes. In South India, a single village of about 1,000 people may contain groups of families from up to 20 or more such castes.[1] Each caste was formerly, and to some extent is still, associated with one or more hereditary occupations. The castes of a region (usually a former kingdom) form a complex hierarchy based upon traditional relations of production and differential rights in the produce of land, as well as upon Hindu beliefs regarding the relative religious value of their occupations.[2] Throughout most of India, Brahmans, who are often landlords as well as priests, form a group of castes at the top of the hierarchy; Untouchables form a group of castes at the bottom. Between them fall a large number of mutually ranked castes traditionally involved in such occupations as cultivation, herding, fishing, trading, specialized crafts, and many kinds of service work. Even among caste Hindus, people of different castes did not traditionally eat with, live near, marry, or touch each other; if they did, it was believed that those of

222

lower caste would defile or pollute those of higher caste, bringing on both groups misfortune in this life or in some future birth. The social and religious gulf between Untouchables and caste Hindus was, however, far greater than that between different groups of caste Hindus.

During and since British rule, the development of new modes of production, the spread of capitalist relations, and associated modern legislation have undermined the traditional caste system, so that today large blocs of similar castes within each linguistic region are beginning to resemble the major ethnic groups in the United States rather than the tightly organized, mutually interdependent, feudal-like estates of the pre-British and early British periods. Large proportions of Hindus no longer work in their hereditary occupations; most are involved in market relations of production and distribution; geographical as well as social mobility occurs; marriages sometimes take place across castes; religious rules concerning occupational defilement are gradually losing their force; and socioeconomic class, to some extent crosscutting caste membership, increasingly determines collective behavior.

The Untouchable castes, too, have been affected by such changes. A small proportion, for example, now have wealth and education and are lawyers, doctors, and politicians. As the spiritual and political leader of the Indian bourgeois-nationalist movement, Gandhi in particular concerned himself with the social betterment of Untouchables, whom he renamed "Harijans" (Children of God). Although legally freed from slavery more than a century ago, and although nominally guaranteed equal civil rights and employment under the Indian constitution, most Harijans are still confined to their old tasks as landless agricultural laborers and village servants of low rank. Throughout most of India the vast majority still live in segregated settlements outside the villages occupied by caste Hindus. Socially and economically, most live in conditions little different from those of their forefathers. To orthodox Hindus, and indeed to most Indians, they are still outside the pale.

In this article I examine the social relations and politicization of Harijans in two villages of Thanjavur district in Madras state, where I did anthropological research in 1951–1953. The article was first written as a lecture in 1954. Except for footnotes and minor editorial changes, I have kept the original wording and conclusions in order to provide time-depth and a comparative study in relation to the article by Mythily Shivaraman which follows. Shivaraman's essay reports on a 1969 study of Harijans in villages of eastern Thanjavur very close to Kirippur, the second village I studied in 1953–1954. It is hoped that, together, the two essays will show changes and continuities in social relations, political consciousness, and the progress of the Communist movement among Thanjavur Harijans over a period of eighteen years. In what follows, the present tense refers to the period 1951–1953, when my study was made.

Thanjavur

Thanjavur district in Madras state (called Tanjore by the British) lies at the southeastern tip of India. It is a flat, green, fertile country, the delta of the Kaveri. The river enters the district in the northwest and becomes dispersed in a network of irrigation channels that finally reach the sea. The chief crops are wet rice and coconuts. Modern irrigation projects have removed some of the dangers of seasonal drought and flooding, but not entirely: thousands half-starved and some died in the dry season of 1952, and in December 1952 a cyclone and ocean-flooding devastated several hundred square miles of trees and grainfields in eastern Thanjavur.

Between 1891 and 1951 the population of Thanjavur almost doubled. Part of the increase is indigenous. As in other regions of India, it appears to result partly from the spread of modern medicine, particularly from the control of such epidemics as smallpox and cholera. In Thanjavur there has recently been an added increase through immigration from less fertile districts to the west during widespread failures of the monsoon rains in 1947–1952. Thus in 1951, with an area of 3,259 square miles and a population of nearly 3 million, Thanjavur was one of the most densely populated parts of India. Harijans are unusually numerous, constituting about 24 percent of Thanjavur's population and 18 percent in Madras as a whole.

Since almost no machine industries have been developed and since the traditional methods of food production have hardly changed at all, Thanjavur, even more than most areas of India, suffers from acute rural "overpopulation." This means that more people live in villages than are needed to produce the amount of food still being produced by traditional methods, and more than can adequately be

fed by such methods. In every village a small number are totally unemployed and unable to find work in the towns, while a majority are
underemployed by comparison with the work their forefathers did
and which they know they are capable of doing.[3]

Thanjavur has three broad sets of Hindu castes: Brahman, Non-
Brahman, and Harijan. (In addition, 5 percent of the people are
Muslims, and 4 percent are Christians.) The Brahmans (landlords
and priests) are only 8 percent of the people but own the land in one-
third of the villages. Non-Brahmans include, first, certain high castes
(Vellalars, Mahrattas, Naidus, Kallars) who own land and, like
Brahmans, administer villages; second, various lower castes of tenant
farmers (Padayacchis, Vanniyars, Muppanars, Porayars), artisans,
palm-wine tappers, fishermen, astrologers, musicians, dancers, enter-
tainers, laundry workers, and barbers, who own little land and serve
Brahman or Non-Brahman landlords.

Harijans in Thanjavur are called Adi Dravidas ("Original Dravi-
dians"), usually shortened to "A.D.'s." They comprise two main
castes, Pallas and Parayas. Their customs are similar but they do not
traditionally intermarry or eat together. Parayas rank below Pallas
and do certain things that Hindus regard as especially polluting:
they eat beef, drum at funerals, guard cremation grounds, and remove dead animals. But the chief work of both castes is agricultural
labor in the rice fields of the landlords.

Kumbapettai Village

Kumbapettai, where I worked in 1951–1952, lies about seventy
miles inland in the northwest of the district close to Thanjavur, the
capital town. It is a highly traditional village.

Kumbapettai contains 962 people. It is controlled by 42 households of small landlords, *mirasdars* of the Brahman caste, who number
323 and live in the center of the village on a street that is flanked at
each end by temples to their deities, Siva and Visnu. Sixty-six lower
caste households of Non-Brahman tenant farmers, cowherds, blacksmiths, carpenters, barbers, washermen, fishermen, and small traders
live in neighboring streets, a total of 270 people. These castes comprise the main village settlement. Across paddy fields, half a mile
away, lie five streets of Harijans arranged in two separate hamlets.
They are all of the Palla caste; they comprise 91 households and 369

people. Kumbapettai has no Parayas, but calls some from a village two miles away when they are needed for funerals.

The British conquest of 1799 did not at first affect the pattern of slavery.[4] Each Palla family was owned by one or another Brahman household, whose headman held the right of life or death over them. Even after the legal abolition of slavery in 1843, most Pallas, having no other work, stayed in the service of their former masters as tied laborers or *pannaiyals*. Today about one-fifth of Kumbapettai's Pallas still remain in the traditional production relationship as *pannaiyals*. Nowadays, landlords engage their *pannaiyals* by the year, but some tied laborers are in fact kept on by the same landlords indefinitely. A *pannaiyal* is paid daily in paddy (unhusked rice) and can be called to work at any time. On marriage, his wife becomes a servant of her husband's landlord, although she is paid separately. Children nowadays are engaged independently of their parents; formerly, servitude was hereditary. In addition to their pay, tied laborers receive one set of clothing per year and small cash sums at marriages and funerals— actually, loans more often than gifts. Laborers must also borrow from their landlords in the two dry months of May and June, when work and food are scarce. Once in debt, a laborer may not transfer to another landlord or leave the village unless his new employer pays off his debts and assumes the role of creditor. Tied always by debt, *pannaiyals* are in fact even today little more than slaves.

Pallas in Kumbapettai have no doubt increased in numbers over the past sixty years, although I do not know by how many. During this period the Brahmans have come from owning virtually all of the village land to owning only 56 percent of it, although 63 percent is still owned by village residents. (Small amounts have been bought by the better-off tenants and by incoming traders.) The rest now belongs to traders, white-collar workers, or bigger landlords of nearby towns and villages. More than one-third of the land is thus owned by absentee landlords. One result is that today only 22 percent of Pallas are tied laborers in the service of traditional masters. By contrast, 39 percent are now casual day-workers (coolies) for whoever cares to employ them. They are paid daily in cash and can be dismissed at any time. Such workers have no guarantee against the summer months of starvation, and are sometimes unemployed for about a third of the year.

In the past, Brahman owners customarily leased part of their land for cultivation by Non-Brahman sharecroppers. (Brahmans themselves are forbidden by religious law to touch the plow and do not work in rice fields, although a few do occasional garden work.) Tenants, or *kudiyanavar*—in Kumbapettai chiefly of the Cowherd caste—take the land on an annual lease (*kuthakai*) and pay a fixed rent after the two harvests. In a good year the tenant may retain up to two-fifths of the crop, from which he provides seed for the next year's sowing. In a bad year he may lose all. If the rains fail—as they had for five years before I arrived—he may even be in debt after his rent is paid. In such cases some landlords make concessions or lend money or paddy to tide the tenant over for a season. But not all do this, nor are they legally obliged to do so. Some tenants are also tied laborers and eke out their livelihood by gardening for the landlord, carting his paddy to market, tending his cowshed, or, in the case of children, grazing cattle or bathing them in the village bathing pool.

In the past ten years some Pallas have also begun to sharecrop land. This change results from the departure of educated Brahmans to work in the towns of the state. Indeed, eight Brahman houses now lie vacant while their owners are in urban work. In their absence, landlords lease their lands to kinsmen in the village, who in turn sublease them, often to those Pallas who were formerly tied laborers of the now-absent landlords. Some Muslim traders of the market town three miles away, who now own land in Kumbapettai but have no regard for caste customs, also lease lands either to Pallas or to Non-Brahmans. Thus, 38 percent of the Pallas are now small sharecropping tenants. Despite losses in bad harvests, they sometimes own their own oxen for plowing and are slightly less poverty-stricken than their fellows.

But in 1951–1952 all tenants and workers in Kumbapettai lived in direst poverty. Tenants' houses were thatched mud huts with two or three rooms and paneless windows. Those of Pallas were mostly windowless one-room hovels in which one could not stand upright indoors and into which one had to crawl through the entry. Most people owned only one piece of cotton clothing, which they washed daily while bathing in the ponds or irrigation channels. Male tied laborers earned three-quarters of a measure (about one liter) of paddy per day, worth about $0.10. Women earned half a measure, worth $0.05. I was told that in order to eat twice a day, three-quarters of a measure was needed for a family of four. The rest was exchanged for tea and betel leaf, areca nut, quicklime, and tobacco for chewing. Twice a year, at harvest time, wages did rise higher: both men and women were paid two measures a day and also received a small part of the paddy they threshed.[5]

Coolies received one rupee (about $0.14) daily, but their work was very irregular. Roughly calculated, the monthly incomes of Non-Brahman tenants and Harijan laborers varied, per family, from Rs. 20 to Rs. 100, with Non-Brahmans in most cases earning more than Harijans. The Brahmans, too, have felt impoverished in the last fifty years: their numbers have grown, they have lost some land, their wants have increased through contact with urban culture, and almost all are in debt to kinsfolk, bigger landlords, traders, or moneylenders. Even so, their monthly incomes ranged from Rs. 160 to Rs. 800.

Between 1947 and 1951 these conditions led to anger and rebellion among tenants and laborers. Their distress was aggravated by the immigration of thousands of destitute people from famine regions southwest of Thanjavur district; by the increasing number of absentee landlords who had no concern for their tenants; and by the rich living (in the district although not in this village) of a few wealthy landlords who owned up to 6,000 acres and continued to extract full rents in the period of monsoon failure.

In August 1952, just after I left the village, the Congress Party Chief Minister of Madras promulgated an emergency measure, the Tanjore Tenants' and *Pannaiyals'* Protection Ordinance, to meet the growing disturbance. The bill applied to landlords owning more than six and two-thirds acres (a *veli*) in one village. These had to increase the wages of laborers from three-quarters to two measures of paddy for a man, and from one-half to one measure for a woman. Sharecropping tenants were assured of a flat two-fifths of the produce of the land they tilled. Tenants and tied laborers might not be dismissed for a period of five years.

The bill evoked much opposition from landlords in Thanjavur. Even *The Hindu*, the chief English newspaper of the Congress Party in South India, roundly opposed it. It was dubbed a hasty individual act on the part of Chief Minister Rajagopalachari (himself a Brahman). It was widely publicized that it would disrupt the "benevolent paternal relationship" between landlords and tenants. But the bill carried, chiefly through the support of Communist and Socialist members of the Legislative Assembly and some Congressmen from outside the district. Actually, few A.D.'s in Kumbapettai gained from the bill: 39 percent were daily coolies whose position was unaffected, and fewer than twenty people in the whole of Kumbapettai worked for landlords owning more than six and two-thirds acres.

In Kumbapettai, since Brahmans still control much land, traditional rules of social intercourse are largely upheld. A.D.'s may not touch or be touched by others. They may not enter the houses of Non-Brahmans or the streets of Brahmans. They are paid from the back door of a Brahman house and, at the annual festivals of the village goddess, they assemble in the outer courtyard of the temple. In Non-Brahman teashops they have a separate space behind the shop and are served in separate glasses across a mud counter. Brahmans, in turn, may not enter the streets of A.D.'s. Not only would the Brahman be polluted, but it is also believed that the whole A.D. street would fall prey to disease and financial ruin. This rule affords the A.D.'s a privacy in their street which their landlords dare not infringe upon. The garden plots on which A.D.'s live are, however, owned by Brahmans, and from these they must carry produce to their masters whenever it is available and is required.

In spite of nationwide laws forbidding caste discrimination in public places, and in spite of the official Congress Party policy which opposes discrimination (whether private or public) in any form, rules of pollution are still strictly observed in Kumbapettai. This was brought home to me on my first day in the village. In the evening a crowd of Palla women and children, returning from work, flocked to the verandah of the house I had rented from a Brahman widow in the middle of a Non-Brahman street. I was accustomed to the Malabar Coast, where the Congress policy is now more widely observed, and so I called them indoors. Next day my cook (a Malabari and thus, of course, a foreigner) brought the news from my landlady that by inviting the Pallas I had polluted my house and my cook. He had then polluted her well, from which he had gone to draw water. If I wanted to stay in the house I must refrain from entertaining A.D.'s. That evening, a small deputation of Brahman elders arrived and

tactfully confirmed her judgment. Later, the Brahmans strongly opposed my visits to the Palla street, but I was able to get around this
by taking a plunge-bath in the irrigation channel before re-entering
the main part of the village. Trying to move equally in the Brahman, Non-Brahman, and A.D. streets created emotional, social, and
ethical problems that I was never able to solve.

With only four exceptions, the Brahman households belong to one
or another of six patrilineal lineages traditionally present in the village. Their members constantly intermarry, and in many contexts
form a highly unified group of close kin. As a united aristocracy, the
Brahmans are keenly aware of their hereditary rights in the village.
Thus, in spite of difficulties imposed by the emigration of some Brahmans, the impoverishment of others, the sale of land to outsiders, and
the immigration of new caste groups of tenants, the Brahmans still
try to administer the traditional laws of caste. Because they own
more than half of the land and their tenants and workers are largely
dependent upon them, they are able to do this to a considerable extent and even to defy or manipulate the police of the town three
miles away.

If a Palla is believed to have offended a man of higher caste, he is
reported to his own landlord, who punishes him. The first week of
my stay, a Kumbapettai Palla was accused of stealing a brass vessel
valued at six rupees from a Non-Brahman street in a village six miles
away. He was caught, bound at the wrists, and marched by Non-
Brahmans to his Brahman landlord in our village. This man called
an assembly of Pallas from the offender's street and, in the courtyard
of the village temple, heard the allegations against him. He returned
the vessel, fined the offender's kinsmen Rs. 10 (for the village temple
funds), gave his servant ten blows with a cane, and forced him to
drink a pint of cow-dung mixed in water—a customary punishment
for offenses in the tenant and A.D. castes.

Traditional administration is, however, made harder today by the
pressure of A.D.'s and Non-Brahmans, in their extreme poverty, for
greater stakes in the village resources. It is also weakened by a gradually growing disunity among Brahmans. Most of the more ambitious have left for the towns. Others, whose lands are depleted and
who fear the rebellious spirit of the tenants, shrink into apathy and
take little part in village affairs. A few, whose families have gained

new wealth in recent years, struggle for power over the lower castes and try to quell potential rebels by sporadic acts of violence. Later in my stay, for example, the gate of the village temple was broken open one night during the famine months; it was believed that someone wished to steal gold ornaments from the idol. The Non-Brahman priest, who lived next door, awoke to the commotion and drove off the marauder without recognizing his face or caste. Next day the village headman, a Brahman youth of twenty-two recently appointed by the government to collect land revenue, came to investigate. Seeing a Palla boy loitering by the temple gate, he summoned him and demanded to know what he had been doing the previous night. The boy said he was at the cinema in Tanjore, eight miles away. Perhaps annoyed that a Palla should be able to attend the cinema, the headman had him bound to a tree, flogged him, and left him to stand all day in the sun as an example to the village at large. Several Brahmans privately showed uneasiness at this incident, but when I broached the matter publicly in the Brahman street it was quickly hushed up. The headman had been harsh, it was said, and the incident was hard on the boy, but no punishment was too great for an attack on the deity.

Sometimes a whole street incurs punishment by infringing upon a law or the Brahman's wishes. When Prohibition came under Congress rule in 1947, the Pallas' lives were disrupted. All Palla men had been drinkers, often taking palm-wine instead of food at midday. One evening the Pallas could bear it no more and rebelled in unison. Large fires were built that night and huge pots of water, tree bark, French polish, lime fruits, and coconut flowers were boiled for several hours. All five streets were hilariously drunk for the next three days and totally incapable of work. When the bout subsided, the village headman called local police to the Palla streets to make selected arrests. The whole Palla population was then marched to the temple yard, harangued by Brahmans, and fined Rs. 200. The Pallas greatly resented this incident and, in their streets, grumbled that the Brahmans had become cruel and did not care for their servants.

Within each of their streets, Pallas elect officials of their own to administer affairs within their caste: a secular headman, a religious leader, and a treasurer who keeps the funds of the street. The headman is usually a man of thirty to forty, intelligent, and of strong character. His election must be ratified by the Brahmans, who may depose him at will. They had in fact recently deposed one headman because, in the drinking bout I mentioned, he had been heard to ask in public whether anyone could tell him what use Brahmans were to the village. The headman presides over the meetings of the married men of the street on the New Moon day of each month. At such meetings, caste disputes and offenses come up for judgment. These sometimes concern small thefts, unpaid debts, assault, or slander; more frequently they are cases of adultery and marriage disputes. Offenses are punished by fines which are kept by the treasurer to finance ceremonies of the Pallas' own street-shrine or to give a loan to needy families. Formerly, before Prohibition, after the trial of every dispute—including one ending in divorce—the opposed parties had to seal their agreement by buying drinks for all at the village palm-wine shop.

Occasionally, grave offenders against the morality of the street are expelled by its headman and elders. One such case happened during my visit. A man called Pattani had two younger sisters who brought their husbands to work in Kumbapettai where there were fields to be leased. One of the husbands, Kathiruvel, had been secretly distilling liquor. Fearing the police after the drinking bout, he went home for a time to his natal village. While he was gone his wife began to sleep with Perumal, her sister's husband. One day Kathiruvel suddenly returned and asked his wife to go with him to his village. She refused, and he began to drag her by the hair. Perumal ran and beat him with a stick, whereupon Kathiruvel drew a knife to stab him. Others intervened, of course, and the two were shut up in their separate houses for the night. Next morning the headman and the religious leader called a meeting of all five streets, which decided to expel both couples. The Brahman masters of both were approached and, seeing the seriousness of the case, decided to let the two families go. One landlord, in fact, forgave Perumal a debt of Rs. 30 to release him, and personally sent him off. Both men returned with their wives to their home villages.

Pallas show an almost fanatical passion for equality within their caste group. In fact, I found the equal and comradely style of life in the Palla street a great relief from the obsessive ritualism, hierarchy, and envy in the Brahman street. Palla egalitarianism seems to result from the fact that after about the age of fourteen all men are employed on almost equal terms by the Brahmans. Women, too, receive almost equal, though smaller, wages and are paid separately from their husbands. Brahmans ideally have patrilocal extended families in which married sons are subordinated to their fathers and women to their husbands. By contrast, Palla parents lose their authority over their children after the marriages of the latter and, as the head of a small autonomous dwelling group, each married man has equal rights with the rest. Women exercise almost equal authority in the family, although they play no formal role in street assemblies. Inside their street—which the Brahmans may not enter—the Pallas, like a large group of equivalent if somewhat rivalrous brothers, rely for order on their elected headman only in emergencies. Even then, the headman must express the will of the majority; otherwise, he is soon deposed. In everyday life, order is restored by the constant interference of the street in the lives of all its members. Privacy and individual choice are reduced to a minimum.

Toward the end of my stay, I was astonished by the extent of this intervention. A few Palla men learn to read, write, and play an instrument, and one of these wandered to Kumbapettai bearing notebooks of "dramas." These plays are composed by Non-Brahman authors and are based on some ancient religious story but incorporate local, modern, and typically low caste episodes. It was decided to put on a play about the marriage of Arjunan, the North Indian hero of the Sanskrit epic *Mahabharata*, to Alli, a queen of Madura, a town some fifty miles away. The instructor was to live for six months in one of the Palla streets. Each house would contribute equally to his food, and the parts were cast among the young men and boys. The whole street met every night for two months to admire the instructor's histrionics and to criticize the rehearsals. At the end of this time, the boy taking the part of the queen had still not learned his part and was too shy to act: the teacher's sarcasm and the streetmen's haranguing were almost breaking his nerve. At last he stayed away, stoutly refusing to leave his hut for the rehearsal shed. After a week of fruitless cajoling, the headman called a street meeting and it was decided to ostracize the boy's family. For a fortnight nobody spoke to them, entered their house, or showed the faintest awareness of their existence. Just as I left the village, I heard that the boy had capitulated and returned to practice his part.

A.D.'s react to their poverty (of which they are well aware) with a combination of anger, resignation, wryness, and humor. They laugh especially at humbug—their word for it is "Kumbakonam," the name of a famous Brahman religious center some twenty miles away. In Kumbapettai A.D.'s have their own street-shrines dedicated to their patron goddesses, about whom they tell various mythological stories and whose rites they observe rather carefully. But in general they are ignorant or skeptical of the religious beliefs that Brahmans spend much time discussing. One day, sitting in the A.D. street, I tackled a group of older Pallas on the subjects of death, duty, destiny, and rebirth of the soul. In my inadequate Tamil I asked them where they thought the soul went after death. One old man nudged another and said, "She wants to know where we go when we die!" The group collapsed in merriment—perhaps as much at my speech as at the question. Wiping his eyes, the old man replied, "Mother, *we* don't know! Do you know? Have you been there?" I said, "No, but Brahmans say that if people do their duty well in this life, their souls will be born next time in a higher caste." "Brahmans say!" scoffed another elder. "Brahmans say anything. Their heads go round and round!" More soberly, an old woman said she had heard, and it was her opinion, that a soul is born seven times in various bodies—as a pig, a rat, or a person of any caste—and then leaves the earth forever. I asked her whether she thought that one's virtue in this life determined one's birth in the next, and she answered abruptly, "No." Another woman thought that we might go to heaven (*swargam*) or hell (*naragam*) according to our sins or virtues during our human lives. A young man interposed that he did not believe in life after death at all. "The soul is like breath; it simply goes out of the body— whoosh." Others thought that only the souls of those who died violently hung about the living, haunting them as ghosts or demons (of which they gave graphic descriptions). Whatever they may have believed in the past, Thanjavur A.D.'s in general denied the orthodox Hindu theory—so reassuring to high caste landlords—that the performance of duty in a past life determines one's wealth and caste status in this one.

In the past, Pallas have been engaged in several different sets of crosscutting alliances and conflicts which served to uphold Brahman power in the village, but which also maintained certain minimal rights for the lower castes. First, they had unity within each street against other Palla streets with which they occasionally had disputes or fights. Second, in some contexts all Pallas united against all Non-Brahmans of the village, with whom they had few economic transactions and with whom they vied to obtain favors from the landlords. Third, Pallas felt collective unity against the Brahmans, whom they mocked in secret. Fourth, however, they had loyalties to the village they served and in whose collective ceremonies they shared. Urged on by landlords and helped by Non-Brahmans, they fought periodic battles with sticks and knives against neighboring villages, usually over rights to irrigation water or boundary disputes. It is noteworthy that these fights often took place at harvest time or at the annual festival of the village goddess, when the village boundaries were demarcated by ceremonial processions and when maximal cooperation was required between all castes *within* the village.

Fifth, each Palla tied laborer was ideally bound to his master by feelings of mutual loyalty, which some seem to have actually experienced at least part of the time. Even in these troubled times, I found affection between some Brahmans and their tied laborers of long standing. One Brahman, generally regarded as modest and kind, made a large cash gift outright at the marriage of "his" Palla's daughter. The following year he received back the voluntary gift of a cow. Another Brahman, who was unusually informal and rather popular with the peasants, told me that in spite of caste difference he liked and admired Pallas more than Brahmans, and some of "his" Pallas more than his relatives. Even in the past five years, two Brahmans had a bitter quarrel because each took the part of his own servant in a dispute between the servants over the wife of one of them. Similarly, Pallas of the same street have sometimes fought, with sticks, battles which arose as wars of words between their respective masters.

But increasingly in the past few years, Pallas in this village have been emerging as a united group of laborers whose interests are almost always opposed to those of their landlords, and who no longer feel strong ties with members of the upper castes. Movement between villages, the sale of village land to outsiders, and the growing population, poverty, and oppression have undermined traditional relationships. Short-term Palla tenants, tied laborers who change hands every year, and "coolie" workers, in particular, have begun to see themselves as an undifferentiated group of "poor people" with no loyalty except to other Pallas and with a common opposition to their masters.

In 1952 the Communist movement had not gained hold in Kumbapettai, although the landlords greatly feared it. But soon after I left, Communists arrived and helped the A.D.'s to organize themselves with Pallas and Parayas of four neighboring villages into a labor union. In the harvest of February 1953, the union threatened to strike unless all the Brahmans and other landlords agreed to pay tenants and laborers shares only slightly less than those laid down in the Tenants' and Laborers' Bill. When I went back to Kumbapettai on a visit in March 1953, the landlords had given in at least temporarily, and the red flag was flying in the Palla street. The Non-Brahman streets had not formally joined the union, but some of the Non-Brahman tenants and laborers were giving it their support and benefiting from its militancy.

Kirippur Village

Kirippur, where I worked in 1953, presents a further departure from traditional society. It lies off a main road eight miles from the port of Nagapattinam in eastern Thanjavur.[6] The village contains 806 people. Apart from one family of Brahman temple priests and the Brahman village clerk, all are Non-Brahmans or A.D.'s, with A.D.'s constituting 36 percent of the population. Ninety years ago the village contained only one small street of Non-Brahman (Vellalar) landlords, three streets of lower caste Non-Brahman tenants and village artisans, one street of Pallas, and one of Parayas. More than 60 percent of the people are of more recent origin. They include a new street of weavers, a street of small traders and peasants, and a new street of Pallas. Today, 44 percent of the land is owned by large or small landlords from outside the village, some of whom are businessmen in the town. The rest is parceled out in small holdings of one to ten acres between traditional and recent landlords and owner-peasants inside the village.

Of 84 A.D. men, 69 percent are tied laborers of landlords within or outside the village; 24 percent are daily coolies; 3 percent are sharecropping tenants; and 3 percent are ill and unable to work. Kirippur has many tied laborers in comparison with Kumbapettai, partly because the small Non-Brahman owners within the village are not absentees. They manage or even cultivate their own lands and need one or two men each on whom they can rely for at least a year. At the same time, the big landlords from other villages prefer to settle bailiffs on their estates to manage tied laborers rather than letting out their land to tenants, as town residents or traders might do. Ninety-four percent of Kirippur's A.D.'s are therefore landless laborers without tenancy rights, as against Kumbapettai's 62 percent. Kirippur's high proportion of tied laborers makes it in one respect more traditional than Kumbapettai; on the other hand, Kirippur's *pannaiyals* tend to change hands every year, while some of those in Kumbapettai still work for their families' traditional masters.

Kirippur shows two other main differences from Kumbapettai. First, the higher castes of small landlords inside the village are disunited. They comprise five small Non-Brahman caste groups who originally came from different parts of Tamil Nadu, as well as many isolated families of newcomers. These castes are no longer mutually ranked in a traditional manner, with differential rights in land, but compete with each other for the limited resources; there is much hostility between them. As a result, the traditional administration through a caste hierarchy has quite disappeared. A government-appointed village headman of the old landlord caste collects land revenue, but he has little formal authority. In disputes, influential villagers go to court against each other or summon police to arrest "troublesome" tenants or laborers. Sometimes those arrested are beaten in jail, held for a few days without trial, and then sent home. In the everyday administration of their affairs, the A.D.'s are left to themselves.

The segregation of A.D.'s has broken down in Kirippur somewhat more than in Kumbapettai, but so too has the sense of collective responsibility for the village's people. When the cyclone hit Kirippur in December 1952, the largest A.D. hamlet was flooded and all its dwellings and grain stocks destroyed. In addition, most of the trees were blown down and many houses damaged in the main, Non-Brahman, village; one peasant was killed by lightning. As the A.D.'s fled across paddy fields to the village, their clothes were blown off them, and they arrived almost naked and totally destitute. Non-Brahman peasants and artisans whose homes were damaged went to live and eat temporarily in those of kinsfolk, friends, or employers.

There was much private kindness; beyond that, each family repaired the damage to its own property as best it could. A few landlords and peasants gave cooked food to their own A.D. servants from the back doors of their houses—an act traditionally permissible and indeed morally obligatory in times of emergency. My own Non-Brahman neighbor, the wife of a fairly prosperous cultivator, fed all ten of her husband's A.D.'s, but grumbled that she hated doing it because of their upstart and "Communist" attitudes. All landlords and peasants gave the A.D.'s two days' holiday to rebuild their dwellings, but in the meantime no collective arrangements were made for shelter. Perhaps because they knew I had "Communist" leanings—as I had previously entered their huts—about 30 A.D. men, women, and children asked to stay for a week in the Non-Brahman house I was renting. There they occupied not only the outer verandahs (which they might have done by traditional caste custom) but also the small inner rooms and the big central courtyard. They chose, however, to cook on the front verandah to avoid "polluting" my kitchen. A young, high caste Non-Brahman landlord of left-wing persuasion approved the project and laughingly agreed to provide the rice for my "family" from his own granary. My peasant neighbors mocked me scornfully and I had a nasty argument with the village washerwoman, who thought I was sinning and polluting the village by inviting A.D.'s indoors. Since she was herself, however, of low caste, poor, and powerless, and since the landlords said nothing, she could not prevent the infringement of village custom. By contrast, Kumbapettai's orthodox Brahman landlords would not have allowed such irregular behavior. Instead, one of them told me later, in such an emergency they would have had the A.D.'s fed collectively from the village temple and ordered them to sleep on Non-Brahman tenants' verandahs. In Kirippur, the A.D.'s insisted on cleaning and whitewashing my house and mending the roof free of charge before they went back to rebuild their huts when the flood subsided. After this period of reciprocal aid they visited me freely and invited me to their New Moon meetings, a privilege that Kumbapettai A.D.'s had felt unwilling or unable to accord me.

Perhaps because traditional relations were more disturbed than in Kumbapettai, the Communist movement found ready supporters in Kirippur and had become powerful by 1948. For at least five years previously, rates of pay of laborers on large estates in the area were extremely low, and there was widespread unrest among them. Ugly stories are told of acts of brutality against struggling workers. In 1947 in a village six miles from Kirippur, a Non-Brahman landlord owning 1,000 acres seized a Harijan worker who led a party of A.D.'s demanding higher pay, and nailed his hand to a tree. The nail was removed some hours later and the man fled the district.

In 1947–1948 a district-wide Kisan (peasant) movement was formed to demand higher wages for workers and bigger shares of the crop for tenants. At first, Kisan leaders looked to the Congress Party and government for support. When this was not forthcoming and police were sent against them, many, especially in eastern Thanjavur, turned for help to the Communist Party, which already had two or three members in each of a number of villages. In 1948 at harvest time, a strike of tenants and laborers took place in much of Thanjavur. They demanded half the crop for tenants and doubled wages for workers. In a large area of eastern Thanjavur under Communist influence, tenants and workers took over the village government for several weeks, neutralized the police, and harvested the crops in their own behalf. There were armed attacks on the houses of grain-hoarding landlords and one or two of them were killed. In late 1948, however, the movement was crushed there, as elsewhere in India, and most of the Communists were jailed.

Since there were no big landlords in their village, Kirippur A.D.'s took no part in attacks on landlords' homes. In 1948, however, they raised the red flag in their streets and several times struck for higher wages, but were each time forced back to work. In February 1949, after the arrest of the Communist leaders, police arrived one day to enquire whether Kirippur landlords had any complaints. The village headman used the occasion to call the A.D. headman and impress on him the uselessness of further strikes. But men of the A.D. streets, hearing the command, thought their leader would be arrested and arrived with him in a body. The village headman became angry and ordered them to disperse. They refused, shouting that their lives were miserable, and asked that they all be taken to jail. Some climbed into the police trucks and made so much disturbance that thirty men were in fact arrested and driven a hundred miles to Trichinopoly jail, where they stayed for several months. Then the Kirippur landlords needed men for the farming, and so a deputation applied to the court and the workers were released to their former conditions of pay.

The A.D.'s look back with pride on the period spent in jail. They were housed four to a cell, but said they were beaten with staffs only when they accidentally broke the mud vessels in which they were required to eat. They refer to the jail as *mamanar veedu* (father-in-law's house), for they say that there one has no work and plenty to eat— but one does not feel quite at home. In jail they met Communists and other Communist supporters, learned Communist songs, and came back resolved to take up the fight again.

Occasional strikes and spontaneous stack-burnings continued for the next three years. Communist Party members were released from jail again early in 1952 before the first all-India general elections, seven months before I reached Kirippur. Village assemblies of A.D.'s were reorganized as labor unions based on the already existing street meetings for caste justice that I have described for Kumbapettai. Like the old street meeting, the labor union in each village met every New Moon day. Larger rallies were held, and a Communist member of the Madras Legislative Assembly was elected from the constituency. By 1953 the three A.D. streets of Kirippur were organized as part of a group of twelve villages. When I arrived the Tanjore Tenants' and Laborers' Ordinance had just been issued. The chief aim of the Kirippur and other unions was to prevent workers from scabbing and accepting wages lower than those stipulated in the bill. While I was in Kirippur they succeeded in doing this. Their unity at the time of the harvest of January 1953 forced all landowners and peasants, whatever the size of their holdings, to pay the stipulated amount.

Kirippur A.D.'s had thus already emerged as a united, organized group in open opposition to their employers, a state of affairs that A.D.'s in Kumbapettai were only gradually approaching. Changes in ideology and religious belief had accompanied this development. The two traditional streets of Pallas and Parayas still made annual offerings at the street-shrine of their patron goddess in a halfhearted manner, but took no part in the annual festival of the central village temple. In the third, more modern Palla street, I met blank faces when I first inquired about religion. At last one youth replied firmly, "Here we do not have any god. That all went five years ago. Now we are Communists."

Change had indeed occurred. Important were a much widened

range of relations and the ending of caste distinctions between Pallas and Parayas. They now dined freely together and had amalgamated their assemblies for caste justice. Both castes had made reforms in their customs in an effort to become worthy of equality with the higher castes. They had given up eating rats, small crabs, and carrion beef, although these were almost their only sources of meat. Young men of both castes traveled far beyond the village and often went to the cinema three miles away. Two boys had learned to write and kept the accounts of the monthly meetings.

In theory the Congress Party favors the abolition of caste distinctions and improved welfare for A.D.'s. Indeed, as soon as it came to power in 1947, it forbade caste discrimination by law. Since then, under a mandate from the central government, the Madras Congress government has effected other reforms. Since 1947 the state government claims to have removed 124,619 A.D.'s in Thanjavur from house sites owned by their landlords and to have placed them in new streets on government land where they own the produce of their gardens. Since 1949, 147 Harijan schools have been opened, with 10,000 children reported studying in them and receiving free midday meals. By law, no government school may now refuse access to Harijans, although many—including the one in Kirippur—do. Any Harijan who can obtain a high school education is assured of a job in government service.

But in Thanjavur at least, this is largely tokenism. The Congress Party is in fact mainly supported by landlords, most of whom formerly opposed the struggle for independence. In Kirippur, its nominal adherents were the traditional street of landlords, whose policy toward A.D.'s was the least progressive in the village. This street claimed one member of the Congress Committee of Thanjavur district, a man of about thirty-five. In my house he paid lip service to the ideals of Gandhi and held that Harijans must be slowly and gradually uplifted and admitted to schools. Cottage industries, he thought, might in time be introduced among them. But in the Harijan street he was hated and was known as one of those who most actively opposed the Tenancy Bill.

The Communist movement has been successful among Harijans of Thanjavur partly because they are relatively homogeneous both in their oppression and in their culture. They are almost all at one dead level of poverty, suffering similar exploitation from landlords and the same discrimination from caste Hindus. And although the content of this is changing, they share a common body of custom and belief.

The Communist movement might have failed, at least temporarily, if large numbers of Harijans had earlier become owner-cultivators, craftsmen, industrial workers, or white-collar employees. This was, in theory, the aim of the Congress government: to permit Harijans to lose their identity of oppression by dispersing them into more varied and lucrative occupations. But this aim was frustrated by the landlords' resistance, by the fears and rivalry of the Non-Brahmans, and above all by the fact that the economy is not expanding rapidly enough to provide avenues of upward mobility for more than a very few. It remains to be seen whether the Congress Party government can improve this situation, or whether the slow pace of economic development and the devotion of the Communists will gain them still more supporters among both Non-Brahmans and A.D.'s, as is already happening in some villages.

At present, village A.D.'s do not know much about international affairs. For them, equality and friendliness mean Communism, because it is from Communists that they have received equal and friendly treatment. For them, and indeed for most people in Thanjavur (especially the upper castes and the landlords), any person is a Communist who wants to abolish caste discrimination, to chat with A.D.'s in teashops, to raise the wages of landless laborers, or to see equal civil rights extended to all citizens.

This leads to some strange misunderstandings about international affairs. Although Communist Party members denounce Western imperialism in their speeches, the A.D.'s I met in Thanjavur showed little or no antagonism to the British. Many older people in Kirippur recall prewar British rule with nostalgia, chiefly because they associate it with cheap imports of rice from Burma. Some people believe that the monsoon has failed for five years because the British left. Some think that British people were more opposed to the caste system than are their Congress Party rulers, for they knew of individual British businessmen in the coast towns who paid no heed to caste distinctions, while they know of the Congress Party only through their landlords. Some older people believe that Communist rule in India would mean the return, from Russia, of white rulers similar to the

British. One old man, when I told him the British were not Communists, asked, "But is not Russia in London?" Many village Non-Brahmans, as well as A.D.'s, thought that America was part of England, and only a few sophisticates were aware of the Cold War between the U.S.A. and the Soviet Union.[7]

Because of such kinds of ignorance, landlords mock A.D.'s as blockheads and assert that they are led astray by the Communists, whom, it is said, they follow with blind devotion. In their own villages, however, where their experience lies, A.D.'s readily grasp the political realities: they know that no party financed and supported by landlords—as the Congress is—can bring them real economic or legal improvements.

Not only Hindu A.D.'s but also Christian converts from the Harijan castes are attracted to Communism. So are some younger Christians, as well as Hindus, of higher caste origin. Communism seems to them to uphold, in fact and not only in letter, the Christian demand for brotherhood and equality. A nearby Methodist high school, for example, had recently become a stronghold of Communist youths of many Christian and Hindu castes.

It is particularly necessary to emphasize the readiness of A.D.'s for change. Much has been written in the past about the conservatism of the Indian peasant, his slavish adherence to custom, his manifold superstitions, his suspicion of innovation. This is no longer true. I suspect that it has never been an accurate assessment of the lower castes, whose customs are more flexible than those of orthodox high caste Hindus and who have nothing to lose by change. Particularly since independence, the lowest castes throughout South India have awakened in an astonishing manner to the possibilities for education, economic advancement, and civil and social equality. And the Communists, at least, have impressive faith in the future. No Hindu fatalism or pessimism for them. The values they present to the peasants—equality and brotherhood—are dear to the A.D.'s because for centuries they have practiced them quite fanatically within their castes. But now the Communists are awakening them to the idea that these values can spread to society at large.

Notes (1972)

1. For a fuller discussion of caste in Thanjavur, see K. Gough, "Caste in a

Tanjore Village," in Edmund Leach (ed.), *Aspects of Caste in India, Ceylon and Pakistan* (Cambridge University Press, 1971). See also Dagfinn Sivertsen, *When Caste Barriers Fall* (George Allen and Unwin, London, 1963), and André Béteille, *Caste, Class and Power: Changing Patterns of Stratification in a Tanjore Village* (University of California Press, Berkeley, 1965).

2. See K. Gough, "Criteria of Caste Ranking in South India," in *Man in India* (1959).

3. This is not, of course, to say that there are too many people in an absolute sense; obviously many industrial regions of the world have a higher population density. The optimal population for Thanjavur under favorable circumstances cannot be determined until both its people and its capital have been mobilized for planned agricultural, industrial, and human development.

   Rural "overpopulation" is pronounced in all of India's irrigated coastal plains: in West Bengal, in the Telegu-speaking areas of eastern India, in the Tamil coastal regions north and south of Thanjavur, and especially on the southwest coast of Kerala. It is noteworthy that these are the regions where support for the Communists is strongest.

4. The word "slaves" rather than "serfs" is used because although servitude was hereditary and the bond servants do not seem to have been bought and sold often, they were not serfs in the sense of being allotted land of their own to cultivate or of owning their own oxen and plows. The Harijans' servitude seems therefore to have been more akin to slavery in the Marxist sense. That of the cowherds of Kumbapettai, and of other Non-Brahman tenants in Thanjavur as a whole, seems more to have resembled serfdom, for in addition to owing services to their masters and being tied to their masters' families, they received land to cultivate independently in return for crop shares, and they owned their own oxen and plows.

5. *Oru kuruni oru kottu*: "one wisp per hand-bundle."

6. Kirippur is in Nagai *taluk* (subdivision of a district) a few miles from Puducheri, which is mentioned by Shivaraman in the following article. I have used pseudonyms for both villages.

7. The tendency of A.D.'s to associate Communists and Russians with the British may have stemmed partly from the fact that during World War II, after the Soviet Union had been attacked by the Nazis, the Indian Communists supported the war effort in opposition to the Congress Party, which boycotted the war. While most prominent Congress members were therefore jailed in the war years, the British released the Communists, who became free to organize industrial and peasant unions. Most strikes and militant actions were, however, delayed until after the

war. The Communists· probably made their first appearance among Thanjavur A.D.'s during the war, when they began to organize them against the landlords, but abstained from direct action against the government and praised the war effort. Militant struggles against the police and the landlords occurred only in 1948, some months after the "landlord Congress" had come to power. For histories of this period see E.M.S. Namboodiripad, *India Under Congress Rule* (National Book Agency, Calcutta, 1967); for a "liberal" Western view, see Gene D. Overstreet and Marshall Windmiller, *Communism in India* (University of California Press, Berkeley, 1959).

When I returned to South India in 1964, Communist-supporting Harijans were far better informed about national and international affairs, at least in Kerala. A number of Harijan children could read and write in each village, and most Harijans heard the vernacular newspaper read aloud in the teashops each day. While Kerala has for centuries been more literate than Thanjavur, it seems likely that Harijans there, too, have increased their information thanks to growing literacy, political rallies, and village radios.

3. Thanjavur: Rumblings of Class Struggle in Tamil Nadu

Mythily Shivaraman

"Several heads would have rolled on the field, blood would have flowed like the Kaveri in flood, if only we had not been restrained by the higher-ups. But for that instruction from our leaders, we would have put real fear in their hearts. We would have shown them who we really are."

Adilingam, a thin man with bright, piercing eyes, seemed to relive that tense September day in 1968 as he continued:

"There were twelve police vans carrying hundreds of Madras Special Police forces. We *gheraoed* [1] the vans; they couldn't move an inch without killing several of us. We carried every bit of equipment we could get hold of, sticks, spears, sickles, kitchen knives. . . . Twelve of their men were wounded, not a single one on our side. The Superintendent of Police planted several white flags on the ground and asked for peace. We said, 'We will release one van if you go and bring our women you arrested last night like cowards under cover of darkness. Go, get them.' And our women were brought back in an hour's time from Kivalur station. For the first time in the history of our village, the police took orders from the laborers. It was a great day."

This was how a confrontation between agricultural laborers and landlords, backed by the police, was described to me by a leading participant.

It was the village of Puducheri in Nagai subdivision of eastern Thanjavur. The incident was part of a familiar pattern. In an area

Earlier versions of this article were published in *The Radical Review* (Madras), April 1970, and in the *Bulletin of Concerned Asian Scholars*, Winter 1972. Tamil Nadu is the area where the Tamil language is spoken; it is used chiefly to refer to the state of that name, formerly called Madras. There were about 33.5 million people who spoke Tamil in 1961, about one-tenth of them living in Thanjavur district.

where agricultural labor was organized and strong, laborers had asked for a wage increase of half a liter per *kalam*.[2] A landlord who refused to concede the demand had tried to bring in outside labor; local laborers said they would not let outsiders harvest the land they had cultivated. On the day of the harvest, the outsiders came to the field with police protection. Several local women laborers also came, despite attempts by the police to prevent them. When they had harvested about an acre, the police asked both local and outside labor to leave. They did; there was no further trouble. Early next morning, around 3 A.M., the police entered several streets in Puducheri and rounded up forty-two women, who were hustled away in a police van. Within a few hours several hundred Harijan laborers had gathered in Puducheri ready to fight the landlords and the police to the finish.

I talked to one of the women who had been severely beaten that night—a frail, anemic girl who couldn't have been more than twenty.

"A policeman pointed me out and said, 'That's the arrogant wretch who walked straight into the field not minding us one bit. She deserves a good thrashing.' I was pushed to the ground and a heavy-booted policeman kicked me repeatedly." She talked matter-of-factly, simply, not a muscle in her face moving. Was police brutality a routine experience for Kathamma?

The police stayed in Puducheri for three weeks "protecting" the landlords in the interests of "production"; the Harijans of Puducheri fled their homes. When they came back (and resettling them was a big problem for the local peasant union), they found that their paltry possessions—pots and pans, old trunks containing tattered shawls or wedding sashes—had vanished. Their "animal wealth" of a few goats, hens, chickens, and ducks had gone to supplement the three-course meals provided by the local trader—a landlord who so obviously needed protection—to feed the police.

The Puducheri incident was one of the more violent in a series of confrontations between the landed and landless of Thanjavur between 1966 and 1970. Landlord oppression found its classic expression in the village of Venmani, where forty-two Harijan women, children, and old men were burnt alive at the instigation of a local landlord a few months after the Puducheri episode.[3] The Madras daily newspapers, together with the scandal sheets, informed us that

Thanjavur was ridden with struggles between local and imported labor over the wage issue. As laborers persisted in demanding wage increases year after year, the landowners exercised their right to hire labor from wherever they liked. Consequently, local laborers attacked their competitors—the poor fighting the poor. What else could you expect from illiterate, uncultured laborers? The Madras English daily, *The Mail*, went to the extent of suggesting that in Venmani the "Communist laborers" had set fire to their own huts. This must have been an unparalleled case study in masochism!

What a base lie this was became obvious to me when I talked to two landlords in Alathambadi, not far from Venmani, in 1969. Not only did the laborers deny that the wage issue was basic to the troubles, but even the landlords shrugged it off as secondary. An emaciated old man, owner of about fifteen acres, lectured me on what he considered to be the source of the present problems: "Things used to be very peaceful here some years ago. The laborers were very hardworking and respectful. But now . . . the fellow who used to stand in the backyard of my house to talk to me comes straight to the front door wearing slippers and all. . . . And at 5:30 sharp he says, 'Our leader is speaking today at a public meeting. I have to leave.' His leader holds a meeting right next door to me and parades the streets with the red flag. These fellows have become arrogant and lazy, thanks to the Communists. They have no fear in them anymore."

Listening to several other landowners, including an important functionary of the DMK[4] party unit in Thiruvarur, was like hearing a broken record with the needle stuck. The monotony was relieved only by the vile abuse thrown at the Harijan laborers.

The root of the problem was easy to locate. It was the emergence of the new, fearless, politically aware Harijan laborer and his militant union. This was confirmed by my visit to Kovil Pathu in Nagai subdivision in 1969.

In the Harijan street of Kovil Pathu there are forty-five families. About four of them own one to three acres of land. The rest are landless laborers.[5] The *pannaiyal* is bound to the landlord throughout the year. He and his wife work on the land and in the master's house. In Kovil Pathu in 1967, all the laborers worked in the field of the local landlord, who was said to own about seven villages. According to the laborers, who should know, he controlled some 3,000 acres, although they conceded that there may not have been even an inch of land actually in his name.[6] "Why else would he build a school, a rest house, and a dispensary?" they asked. He was also the trustee of a big temple. The landlord lived mostly in Madras and his agent, "Iyer," managed the land.[7]

I had heard that Kovil Pathu had a long history of labor struggles. The absence of the red flag made me curious. Its story was told with a deep sense of bitterness. Not even a hint of this story and of similar ones I heard in several villages finds a place in the reviews and surveys of agrarian problems of Thanjavur which are now becoming popular with our press.

After some years of relative quiet, Kovil Pathu experienced a breakthrough in 1967. The landlord refused to implement a wage agreement. The *tahsildar* [8] came but nothing happened. Then the struggle took several forms: forcible harvesting by the rebelling laborers in opposition to scab workers (after all, who fertilized the land and planted the seedlings, and can we quietly watch someone else walk away with what is ours?); nonviolent civil disobedience, squatting in front of the landlord's house; a show of force by parading the streets in large numbers and shouting slogans. When the officials came to investigate the charge that local labor was denied work, the landlord justified it on grounds of laziness and poor performance. The struggle went on and the laborers managed to prevent strikebreakers from weakening their bargaining strength.

The landlord had tasted trouble and did not like its flavor. In September 1969, the CPI-M [9] organized an anti-tractor struggle.[10] Only five men from Kovil Pathu were asked to join it. On the day of the demonstration, the landlord, who normally used one or two tractors in that village, hired about ten tractors and lined them up in the field. In the true spirit of Thanjavur, the gauntlet was thrown. Even before the demonstrators approached the field, police arrested them.

After the incident all the laborers of the Harijan street—only five had participated in the demonstration—were denied work for about three weeks. The police station, which is only a stone's throw away, was overflowing with Madras Special Police contingents. During this period of unemployment, one night around 3 A.M. (a favorite time for the police), more than fifty policemen entered the street and pulled out the sleeping men from their houses. Severe beatings followed.

The raid was vividly described to me by Ayyakannu, a *pannaiyal* who had recently returned from two months in the hospital following the beating, and by others who still bore the marks of that night. The attack was totally unexpected; they had not participated in the demonstration and they had had no work for three weeks; many had eaten little during that period. The police came stealthily and began thrashing the men. Ayyakannu, who still has a gaping wound in his heel, was left unconscious when the police went off with their booty, thirty-three day-laborers arrested and in semiconscious state. The *pannaiyals* were left behind.

The thirty-three laborers were booked in a nearby village on charges of trespass. After their release on bail they had to walk to Thiruvarur, miles away, several times a week, to appear before the court. The case cost them about Rs. 200 each. By then they had been unemployed for quite some time. They found occasional jobs in distant villages, but the landlord's harassment persisted. When they were away the whole day, their cattle were stolen and occasionally their children were taken to the police station. The laborers could not afford the luxury of boycotting the landlord forever; they approached him for work. The landlord said, "Throw away the red flag before coming here. I want that flag removed from the *cheri* [Harijan street]. I should never see you again carrying that flag and parading the street." They were made to sign a declaration that they had quit the Peasant Union, that they would not attend New Moon meetings of the Union, that they would have nothing to do with the CPI-M. The men got their jobs back. There is no red flag in the street anymore.

"Down with Paraiyas, Down with Pallas!"

The labor union is the real target of landed interests. The independence of the laborer and the strength of his class are growing in the countryside; landlords know that their interests are threatened. The Vadivalam Desikars and Vadapadimangalams[11] are not foolish enough to risk a confrontation with laborers over a quarter or half a liter of paddy. They have correctly sensed the impending disaster and skillfully mobilized the support of lesser landlords, and even of many small fry, for their "Paddy Producers Association." As one

Alathambadi landlord told me, "Don't think it is only the agricultural laborer who has a union. We have one too and we can also parade the streets carrying flags and shouting slogans." And in one such parade in Puducheri, the slogan was *"Paraiyan ozhiga, Pallan ozhiga!"* ("Down with Paraiyas, down with Pallas!").

The fact that Thanjavur has had more than its fair share of "trouble" since 1966—and that, too, in places where the Red Flag movement has been strong—does not mean that agricultural labor struggles are new to this district. The history of such movements in pre-British India is very sketchy, but we have evidence to suggest that peasant uprisings against landlords, occasionally involving the killing of landlords and seizure of land, did take place during the British period. Beginning in the early 1940s, the peasants and agricultural laborers in Thanjavur were organized by the Communist Party.[12] The strongholds of the Communists were the Harijan streets. The only two parties which really had an impact on the Harijans were the Dravida Kazhakam[13] and the Communist Party. Although E. V. Ramaswamy Naicker's anti-Brahman rhetoric greatly enthused the Harijans, the DK failed to mobilize them in actual socioeconomic struggles. In Thanjavur, this was done for the first time by the Communists.

Yes, Gandhi and the Congress did open the famous temples to the Harijans and give them a new name. But it was the Communist Party which led the struggle to throw open the local teashops. In several Harijan villages where the party is strong now, its first struggle was against untouchability—against the Harijan having to drink tea in a cup reserved for Harijans while standing outside the shop. The people whom no political party would touch (while making sure it had one or two Harijans in prominent positions) became the staunch supporters of the Communists. In the rigid caste society of Thanjavur this worked against the Communists' attempts to broaden their party's base by winning over the poor and middle peasants across caste lines. The landed interests worked hard at branding the Communists as a "party of the Pallas and Paraiyas" *(Paraiyan-Pallan katchi)*. Using this caste weapon against the Communists, the landowners were to some extent successful in mobilizing the caste Hindu landless and small peasants on their side in disputes with the Harijan laborers. In the Puducheri struggle of 1968, the Harijans mentioned that many caste Hindu laborers had assisted the landlords in harvesting the land without their help. Puducheri is not the only instance of this disruptive landlord tactic. It is a familiar, universal game.

Apart from untouchability, the Communist-led laborers fought the primitive and barbaric punishments which were dealt them. The slogans used by the party at that time are very revealing: *"Sanipal kudukkade* ("Don't make us drink cow-dung milk") and *"Savukkadi adikkade"* ("Stop the whipping"). Other goals of the struggle were wage increases, fixing the land rent, and security of tenure.

The landlords, the press, and the government of Tamil Nadu have a stale story: the Communists are at the root of the trouble in Thanjavur. It is in their self-interest to create problems; by disrupting production and the normal functioning of life, they create the anarchy that is essential for a Communist takeover.

The *Census of India* (1961) offers a more serious explanation.[14] Two features about Thanjavur stand out: its iniquitous landownership pattern and the enormous proportion of landless labor.

Landownership Pattern. Fifty percent of the cultivating households own less than 2.5 acres each. Seventy-six percent of the cultivating households holding up to 5 acres own only 37 percent of the cultivated land, while about 25 percent of the cultivating households holding more than 5 acres own more than 62 percent of the cultivated area. Within this latter section, the ownership pattern is very much skewed: 3.85 percent of the cultivating households owning more than 15 acres own 25.88 percent of the cultivated area.

Agricultural Laborers. Within Tamil Nadu, Thanjavur has the highest proportion of agricultural laborers. In 1951, 86 out of every 1,000 persons (including women and children) were agricultural laborers. By 1961 the proportion had risen to 137 in 1,000, an increase of about 60 percent. Thirty-three percent of all workers of Thanjavur are agricultural workers, while the figure for Tamil Nadu state as a whole is 18 percent. For every ten cultivators in Thanjavur, there are nine agricultural laborers. The *Census* explains: "As most of the cultivators belong to the well-to-do class in this area, in many cases the actual cultivation is done by laborers hired on wage, while the landlords confine their activities to direction and supervision." It is doubtful that many landlords in the upper brackets "supervise" the land, for most of them have migrated to nearby towns or to Madras.

When laborers talk about *mirasdars* (landlords) they invariably refer to the agents who manage the land; the landlords are rarely seen. Although an accurate estimate of absentee landlordism in Thanjavur is not available, it must be one of the highest in Tamil Nadu. The extensive Hindu temple and monastic lands, which are managed by absentee landlords or by the government, also contribute to this.

Although it reveals the high proportion of agricultural laborers to cultivators, the *Census of India* comes to a curious conclusion about the nature of the agrarian economy in Thanjavur: "From the ratio of the cultivators to agricultural laborers it can be said that Thanjavur is an example of capitalistic farming, while Salem [another district in Tamil Nadu state] is an example of subsistence farming." That such a facile definition of capitalist farming should find a place in the census report probably reflects the wishful thinking of some section of the ruling class that the Congress reforms have already destroyed precapitalist relations in Indian agriculture.

Although we cannot discuss here in any depth the precapitalist relations prevalent in Thanjavur, the casual assertion by the *Census* calls for at least a brief rebuttal. Capitalist farming is not simply the hiring of labor to cultivate land as against leaving peasants to subsist by cultivating their own land. Hired labor is but one of many requisites of capitalist farming. The fact that in the past ten years agricultural labor increased by 60 percent in Thanjavur can be better explained by reference to the impoverishment of the small and middle peasantry, who have been forced to sell their land, and to the large-scale evictions of tenants resulting from inadequate tenancy legislation as well as from law evasion.

Furthermore, the exorbitant, illegal rents paid by tenants in Thanjavur, and their general insecurity in spite of nominal legal protection, can hardly be described as "capitalist farming." While the state average is 11 percent, 33.6 percent of the households in Thanjavur are exclusively tenants.[15] About 55 percent of the cultivated land is under tenancy. To enforce the legal rent and security against eviction is impossible, given the pressure of population on the land; hence the number of peasants ready to lease the land with or without a lease deed. Even according to the Madras government, the "extent under oral leases is not more than half the total under tenancy." [16] The Home Ministry's report of 1969 mentions that Tamil Nadu is one of several states where over 80 percent of the total number of tenants do not enjoy fixity of tenure.[17]

The tenurial conditions in Thanjavur have struck many a researcher, Indian and foreign. Wolf Ladejinsky, the Ford Foundation consultant to the government of India who studied the suitability of Thanjavur's tenurial conditions for the green revolution, concluded that it was "a district with one of the nation's worst tenurial systems. . . . If land tenure conditions were a part of the criteria for selecting a package [experimental] district, Thanjavur wouldn't qualify at all." [18] This was his second visit to Thanjavur in ten years, and he found that tenurial conditions had not improved as a result of the laws. If anything, they had worsened, because the landowner's right of resumption for personal cultivation had been freely exercised. Actual rents ranged from 60 to 65 percent of produce as against the legally fixed rent of 40 percent of the produce. Ladejinsky also concluded that a typical tenant of Thanjavur could hardly ever become an agent of the green revolution.[19] The unfair rent and insecurity of tenure left too little margin for investment; the tenant used only a fraction of the inputs of high-yield seeds, fertilizers, and other improvements prescribed by the government's experimental scheme. Moreover, little credit was available to the tenant since cooperative societies considered tenants on oral leases bad risks and the village-level workers appointed by the government refused to prepare credit plans without the approval of the landlord.

One of the criteria to determine whether capitalist relations exist in agriculture is the existence of a class of innovating and investing entrepreneurs using advanced techniques of production. The green revolution has attempted to create such a class by supplying well-to-do farmers with high-yield seeds, fertilizers, and credit. This has undoubtedly further enriched a small section of rich peasants and landlords, but there is no evidence to suggest that an entrepreneurial class is fast developing to replace the passive rent-receiving and money-lending landlords. The green revolution has grossly distorted capitalist development by crudely superimposing the advanced technology, usually associated with the capitalist stage of production—good seeds, chemical fertilizers, and machinery—on the existing precapitalist organization of production. Certainly the green revolution has left untouched the existing relationship between the tiller and the owner of the land, the high incidence of surplus agricultural labor and of insecure tenancies, the prevalence of sharecropping, and the power of parasitical elements, while inducing a small group of rich peasants to use modern technology in their methods of cultivation. The technique of cultivation is capitalist but the social organization of production is precapitalist.

The peculiar distortions brought about by the green revolution in the name of capitalist farming and increased productivity are now seen to be doing much more effectively what was considered the chief prerogative of the Communists, i.e., creating unrest. A Home Ministry report points out the two basic fallacies of the "new strategies" of the green revolution:

> Firstly, they have rested by and large on an outmoded agrarian social structure. The interests of what might be called the agricultural classes have not converged on a commonly accepted set of social and economic objectives. Secondly, the new technology and strategy, having been geared to goals of production, with secondary regard to social imperatives, have brought about a situation in which elements of disparity, instability and unrest are becoming conspicuous with the possibility of an increase in tension.[20]

After the Ladejinsky study of Thanjavur in 1964, a similar study was done by Francine Frankel for USAID in 1969. Frankel traced the roots of the Venmani tragedy to the progressive polarization between landowners and laborers, a trend that was accelerated by the green revolution. It had widened the economic disparities between big and small landowners and between landlords and landless laborers.

The political implications of this polarization were most visible in eastern Thanjavur. How did the new technology result in agrarian discontent, especially among the small and middle peasantry? Frankel found that the scheme had originally raised hopes in the peasant that all classes could participate in the green revolution. Nevertheless, she points out:

> An enquiry into the actual distribution of benefits showed that economic disparities between small and large farmers had substantially increased. Even when small farmers adopted the practice, the multiple handicaps under which they operated brought about a relative deterioration in their economic position. As for the laborer, added to the grow-

ing discontent caused by growing material deprivation, there was increasing resentment over the inequitable distribution of the benefits from the new technology." [21]

The Tamil Nadu government, however, betrays no awareness of the Home Ministry's warning or of academic studies like Frankel's. On every possible occasion, the ministers merrily reel off figures on area under double cropping, on high-yield seeds, on consumption of fertilizers, etc. As for "labor trouble,'" hasn't the government already enacted the Tamil Nadu Agricultural Labor Fair Wages Act? The "peace" in the district since the Act was adopted is presumed to testify to the justice done by the government to agricultural labor.

But the facts speak otherwise. In the Harijan street of Valiya Nallur, a little village in Nannilam subdivision, there are thirty families. Three are tenant families holding one to three acres of land; the rest are landless. For years landlords had claimed ownership of the laborers' homesites, but recently the laborers had heard the village clerk mention that the land was actually government-owned wasteland (*puramboke*).[22] The villagers seemed at a loss to verify this.

Were they getting the legal wage? They didn't think so, although they knew neither the legal wage nor how they were being cheated. After some questioning and calculating—theirs was a contract wage system, unlike the simpler system on which the Fair Wages Act was based—we found that a laborer lost about 7.5 *kalams* during the harvest period. The loss worked out to about 50 *paise* (half a rupee or about U.S. $0.10) per day during the cultivating season. The laborers didn't seem much surprised when we worked out the amount that was really due to them. They had known instinctively that they were being cheated, and the questions of how and how much seemed to them trivial details. Periodically, they had asked the landlord for wage increases, but they had never had a strike or any kind of struggle.

"Why? What's the use of going on strikes?" they asked. "If we refuse to work there are so many others, not only outsiders but even caste Hindu laborers of this village, who would be willing to labor at the existing wage rate. No, that won't work."

They didn't know what would work. Certainly, the Tamil Nadu Agricultural Labor Fair Wages Act had not worked. Casual chats with agricultural laborers whom I met in the fields and in buses and trains showed that Valiya Nallur is not an isolated instance. There are thousands of Valiya Nallurs in which the Fair Wages Act is violated.

What is the implementation machinery provided by this Act? A complaint of unfair wages can be made by an agricultural laborer to a Conciliation Officer, an official of the Revenue Department not below the rank of *tahsildar*. An appeal against the decision of a Conciliation Officer can be made to a Revenue Court. The District Court may in turn examine the proceedings of the Revenue Court and order annulment or reversal of such proceedings. In short, there is nothing new in this bureaucratic routine.

In several villages where wages were far below the legal minimum and other irregularities went on, I asked the laborers, "Didn't you report it to the *tahsildar* or the collector? Why didn't you do so?" I never found the laborers wanting in a sense of humor—they didn't sound annoyed at my naiveté but always laughed generously. In Ney Vilakku, a little Harijan village in Valivalam *panchayat*,[23] where the local landlord had been carrying out a vendetta against the entire village for more than a decade, a laborer explained the functioning of the Indian bureaucracy from his life's experience: "Oh yes, if we go and complain to the *tahsildar's* office a dozen times, he will come once—though he hasn't yet come to *our* street even once. He will go straight to the landlord's house and have coffee in a silver tumbler. He will sit in the swing and chat with the landlord for a while. After a good three-course meal he will send for us. We will stand near the gate while he comes and sits on the verandah. 'What's all the trouble you fellows are creating for us?' he will ask. 'I have discussed the matter with the Iyer. If you want to keep out of trouble, you'd better behave from now on!' " This anecdote has formed the subject of several doctoral theses and research projects. Scholars and critics, foreign and native, have reached similar conclusions in dull, staid volumes.[24]

No implementation machinery will be effective unless the predominant element in it is the people who are supposed to benefit from the law. This is the experience of the agricultural laborers of Thanjavur. In all the villages where the peasants' union (*kisan sangam*) was strong, the harvest wage was six liters even before the Fair Wages Act was adopted. Where the wage was below that level, it has been raised mostly in villages where the labor movement has become strong. In Puducheri, the familiar tactic of holding the wage line by threatening unemployment has been successfully resisted by a strong labor union using militant tactics to prevent the use of strikebreakers. It took several years of patient work by Communist Party cadres to help organize a people who had been rooted in servility and in acceptance of the natural law of oppression by the higher castes.

The laborers of Valiya Nallur just looked vacant when I asked, "Aren't you going to fight at least for what is legally yours? What are you going to do?" No, they had no tradition of struggle in their village. No doubt a Congress flag was flown there for years, a new one every five years. But a genuine labor movement, a strong political orientation—all this was foreign to them.

What it is that can revive human dignity in a long-oppressed and debased individual, that can make a man out of a human form, suddenly struck me when Vadivelu of Ney Vilakku village told me: "We will continue to fight even if every one of us in our village has to die. Ney Vilakku has always been the lone fighter against the landlord's oppression. No one but us has had the guts to fight back in this area. This is our land. Our forefathers cleared the forest here and leveled the land. We have worked here since our childhood. We will continue to live here and till this land; no one can drive us out. We will start our struggle again soon." Vadivelu gave me the story of Ney Vilakku.

The village had a long history of confrontation with the local landlord; the Communist Party had organized a union there. The residents, all Harijan tied laborers, had agitated for implementation of a wage increase in 1958. The local landlord was also the trustee of the temple land on which the laborers worked. Soon after the agitation, a cow belonging to the temple died. The Temple Trust, which in fact meant the landlord, filed a case against four men who had actively participated in the agitation, charging them with killing the cow. The case was decided in favor of the four. The Temple Trust then fired all eighteen of the village's tied laborers, as they had all helped finance the case. An appeal to the court under the Pannaiyal Protection Act failed. Since 1958, the *pannaiyals* have been denied work on the temple land.

Two years later, the temple was asked by the government to form a cooperative tenant farm.[25] The Harijans wanted to lease the land and went to pay the required deposit for membership in the cooperative. The panchayat President, Iyer, the agent of the landlord trustee, refused to receive their deposit. They had to go to Kivalur to hand over the money to the Registrar of Cooperatives. A few days later the money was returned and no explanation offered. The landlord formed a cooperative with all his personal servants and other "loyal" laborers as members. A woman, still enjoying what must be an old joke, said: "Even the salt-merchant is a member. Once in a while he goes to the Cooperative Society to apply for a loan. When he gives his loan money to the trustee, he gets a rupee. The merchant is mighty pleased." A few years later the society was dissolved, with arrears of 2,000 *kalams* of paddy from members. All of it had been going to the managing trustee's house. The society members lost their tenancy rights, which simply meant that they continued to till the temple lands as laborers. The trustee had proved that ignorant tenants could not work a cooperative successfully. Production was going down, and could any patriotic person tolerate this? The land reverted to the temple for direct cultivation.

The *pannaiyals* had lost many a battle against the landlord but the struggle continued. There was the government-owned wasteland of four acres in Ney Vilakku. Every year the trustee landlord would buy its cultivation rights at the government's annual auction.[26] When the laborers were denied jobs on the nearby land (most of it owned by the trustee landlord), they decided they too would bid for the wasteland. In the 1961 auction Iyer did not turn up (he was sure no one else would dare bid) and the *pannaiyals* got the land for Rs. 125. Twenty days passed and then came a notice that the land would be re-auctioned. No explanation.

On the day of the re-auction, Iyer came protected by his arms-bearing bodyguard. He got the land for Rs. 400. The *pannaiyals* pretended to retire peacefully, but after some time they found the Iyer returning home with a few men, caught them, and gave the Iyer a severe beating with their slippers. A case was filed against them. Seven of their houses—those of the more militant *pannaiyals*—were burnt. The Iyer's men saw to it that they did not come back to rebuild their huts. A few of the *pannaiyals* fled and never returned; others lived for some time under the trees; there was no point in putting up huts only to have them burnt down. After the Iyer became tired of this game they rebuilt their homes, but they have not been able to find work in the neighboring fields. Every day they walk to Tiruthurai Poondi subdivision to find work. The trustee continues to harass them in many ways.

Vadivelu ended this story with a challenge: "We will continue to live here and we will find a way to till this land again. We will start our struggle again very soon." Struggle was part of the proud past of this village, and Vadivelu its living symbol.

Every society has a period of "peace" when the exploited and the exploiters coexist. In parts of Thanjavur, this phase now belongs securely to the past. The agricultural laborer, idealized as the silent sufferer, the epitome of Hindu virtues, has at last begun to take seriously the Gandhian slogan of "Land to the Tiller" and to behave as if the law were meant to be implemented. Puducheri and Kovil Pathu, Adilingam and Vadivelu, prove that the "peaceful" past of Thanjavur can never be resurrected and that the future will be a long struggle sustained by the laborer's faith in a new social order, in which even the memory of his barbaric past will fade.

Puducheri and Kovil Pathu are, it is true, as yet only isolated pockets in Tamil Nadu; Adilingam and Vadivelu are by no means typical of their class. There are thousands of Valiya Nallurs in Tamil Nadu still untouched by ideas of independence, militance, and struggle. There are many laborers who still scratch their toes and look vacant when asked, "Aren't you going to fight at least for your legal rights?" The Communists have touched only the periphery of the problem in terms both of numbers in the laboring population and of politicization of those numbers. A visitor to Thanjavur receives the impression of numerous villages stagnating for want of leadership.

As I left Thanjavur, however, I felt hopeful: a spirit of struggle, the urge to fight back, was unmistakable in some of the villages I had visited, even villages like Kovil Pathu where the movement had suffered a recent setback. What the laborers there said as they bade me goodbye summed up this mood.

"When will the red flag fly here again?" I asked them.

"We can't do anything right now," someone said. "We have been without work for so long and we are dependent on the landlord for our livelihood today. But deep in our hearts we, every one of us, long to see the red flag in our street again. How can we just let it go? We have fought under it for so many years." A woman whose husband had been hospitalized for months after the police raid in Kovil Pathu added, "How can we take it lying down? It is not for nothing that we have suffered so much. No, we can't simply let it go. We shall be up on our feet again soon."

Notes

1. Surrounded and immobilized—a common tactic in mass struggles throughout India.

2. One liter is roughly equivalent to one U.S. quart; one *kalam* is somewhat more than 12 liters.

3. In the summer of 1970 a memorial built on the spot of the massacre of the Venmani martyrs was inaugurated by the Communist Party of India-Marxist leaders. Thousands of landless laborers had assembled. A young Harijan woman told me, "Can you imagine that the landlord, that murderer Naidu, is still freely gallivanting in the streets of Thanjavur!" She spat on the ground and continued, "Isn't there a single man among us? Why is that brute still alive? My heart won't be at rest until I skin him alive and make a roof for my hut with his skin." Recently, the court gave a life sentence to a laborer, a Communist, for having killed a hireling of the landlord Naidu; around the same time the court sentenced Naidu to ten years of imprisonment. The Communist is in jail while Naidu, who has appealed to the High Court, is still "gallivanting freely."

4. The Dravida Munnetra Kazhakam (Dravidian Advancement Party), formed in 1949. A Tamil nationalist and populist party led by wealthy people of Non-Brahman castes, it is opposed to North Indian economic dominance, the use of Hindi as a national language, and Brahman cultural dominance in Tamil Nadu. The party at first advocated a separate Dravidian state in South India, but modified this in the 1950s to demand greater economic and political autonomy for Tamil Nadu within the Indian constitution. The DMK won the elections in Madras against the Congress Party in 1967 and 1971. It has, however, faithfully followed Congress policies. The Land Ceiling Act it introduced had enough loopholes built into it to prevent any radical redistribution of land. A militant champion of social justice in its opposition days, it has now become the wildest cheerleader the green revolution ever had.

5. The *pannaiyal* is a vanishing phenomenon in Thanjavur, thanks at least partly to the Pannaiyal Protection Act of 1952. The act specified the wage to be paid and provided for compensation in case of dismissal. Many landlords preferred to get rid of their *panniyals* rather than abide by the law.

6. Landlords customarily avoid having to surrender surplus land under the land reform acts by putting it in the names of friends or relatives or by

nominally bequeathing it to charitable endowments of which they remain the trustees.

7. "Iyer" is the caste title of Smartha or Saivite Brahmans, used as an honorific term of address. Many bailiffs and village clerks are Brahmans.

8. The *tahsildar* is a government official in charge of a *taluk* or subdivision of a district. Under the Collector of the district, he collects revenue from the village headman and has certain magisterial powers.

9. The Communist Party of India-Marxist is the "Left Communist" parliamentary party which broke away from the "Right Communist" or pro-Moscow wing of the CPI in 1964. It has a strong following among poor peasants and landless laborers in Thanjavur.

10. In Thanjavur, where a laborer finds employment for only five to seven months a year, the introduction of tractors presents a further threat to his survival. The CPI-M protested against the use of tractors in the absence of basic land reforms. In view of the increasing numbers of tractor cheerleaders, including the Chief Minister of Tamil Nadu, the comment of an agro-economist is significant; "In India they [tractors] are not a high priority investment . . . they do not raise yields, they damage poor soils and they displace labor. . . ." (Doreen Warringer, *Land Reform in Principle and Practice* [Clarendon Press, Oxford, 1969]).

11. Local landlords of great wealth.

12. Some references to these peasant struggles are found in Kathleen Gough's article, "Peasant Resistance and Revolt in South India," *Pacific Affairs*, Winter 1968–69, pp. 526-644.

13. The Dravidian Association, formed in 1944 out of the old Justice Party by E. V. Ramaswamy Naicker, a notable advocate of independence for Tamil Nadu. The party lost strength after the departure in 1949 of its more progressive wing, the DMK, and more particularly after the formation of Madras as a separate Tamil-speaking state in 1956 and the shift of power within the Congress Party from Brahman to Non-Brahman leaders, which made the DK largely redundant.

14. *Census of India*, 1961, Vol. LX, Madras, Part X-V, District Census Handbook, Thanjavur, Vol. 1, pp. 241–242.

15. This figure excludes those who lease land to supplement the income from their holdings. Thanjavur has the highest percentage of tenant-householders in Tamil Nadu.

16. The government had an apology ready: "Many tenants prefer to keep their leases oral. . . . The Government does not consider it practical to resort to compulsion for execution of written lease deeds." The Madras government's indignant reaction to Ladejinsky's scathing criticisms of the tenurial conditions in Thanjavur is found in *A Study of Tenurial Condi-*

tions in Package Districts, by Wolf Ladejinsky (Planning Commission, Government of India, 1965).

17. The Home Ministry issued a 100-page report entitled *The Causes and Nature of Current Agrarian Tensions* in 1969. The report, apart from giving some valuable data on agrarian conditions in the various states, lists the factors "accentuating social tensions" in the Indian countryside. Concentration of landownership, insecurity of tenants, exorbitant rents, worsening conditions of agricultural labor, and high incidence of rural unemployment are some of the factors mentioned.

18. Wolf Ladejinsky, *A Study of Tenurial Conditions in Package Districts*, op. cit. The Census has this to say on the selection of Thanjavur as a package district: "The choice fell on this district because of its favorable agrarian conditions and abundant irrigation facilities."

19. Ladejinsky's proposal: "We conclude . . . that the problem facing the . . . full success of the package program is how to enable him to secure a firm footing on his cultivated acres. This presupposes more favorable rental arrangements which are real rather than imaginary, security of tenure, and whatever land ownership can be promoted among the tenants. The initiative for all this doesn't lie with the package program but with the government of Madras." (Ibid., p. 16.)

20. The report ruefully admits, after acknowledgment of the green revolution's "notable achievements," that "as an instrument of social transformation" its impact has been "disturbing."

21. *Indian Express*, February 16, 1970.

22. Each village has a number of sites, especially beside roads and irrigation channels, which are classified as wasteland by the state government and for which revenue is not assessed. In this case local landlords had claimed the wasteland as their private property and exacted rent from the tenants—a common practice. The government-appointed village clerk is usually threatened or bribed by the landlords not to divulge their fraud. In this instance the clerk seems to have been indiscreet.

23. A *panchayat* is a small cluster of villages, or sometimes one large village; it is the smallest modern administrative unit and is administered by an elected *panchayat* board and president.

24. Gunnar Myrdal in his *Asian Drama* concludes that the basic fallacy of Indian land reform is that implementation has been left to the existing power structure, of which the bureaucracy is an element. However, the government of India does not seem to share this opinion, as is evident in the most inane solution it has so far offered to this problem: a few training courses in remote hill regions on "how to serve the people." Implanting values unrelated to or in opposition to the economic realities of society cannot extend beyond the classroom.

25. Experimental cooperative farms have been tried in many parts of India over the past decade. In theory, they consist of groups of small owner-cultivators or cultivating tenants with tenure security, who work their lands collectively and together receive loans for equipment or capital improvements. In many cases (such as the present one), however, the persons registered as members of the cooperative are purely paper members, and the loans are used by a landlord or by one or two powerful peasant members for quite other purposes.

26. It is common for the cultivation rights in government-owned waste land, or its produce, such as coconuts, to be auctioned annually. A government servant from the Revenue Department comes to conduct the auction. Landlords often agree in advance on the buyer and price.

Part III
The Rise of Revolutionary Movements

1. The Songs and Revolution of Baharathi

David Ludden

When the people of colonial countries moved to end their own subjugation, they took art out of the hands of imperialist culture-makers and turned it to the social and political issues that were at the base of their powerless social position. It is in the interest of rulers to keep the theater, songs, poetry, and art in general as apolitical as possible, for this secures them in a position of unquestioned dominance. When art comes to those divested of political power, it by definition becomes political. Because it seeks to counter the cultural domination of traditional education, it implicitly represents re-education of the masses. And given its aim of re-education, its stated intention to undermine the established order, it is revolutionary.

I will discuss here the work of a particular artist in the initial phase of a nationalist movement. He is Subramania Bharathiyar, or simply Bharathi, a poet of Tamil, the language of thirty-three million people in South India. He lived between 1882 and 1921, during the first outbursts of the nationalist movement in India, when the groundwork was laid for a long struggle that ended not in revolution but in the capitulation of the imperialist power. The revolution never materialized as an armed conflict between legions of imperialists and nationalists; but in its early stages, before the main rash of twentieth-century colonial struggles, the Indian nationalist movement was indeed revolutionary—not in the tradition of Marx or Lenin but in the republican-nationalist tradition of Mazzini.

Bharathi's songs and poetry played a central role in the birth of the movement in South India. They exemplify forces working in the beginning of the revolutionary decolonization process and tell us something about the nature of the reforms of thought, self-image,

An earlier version of this article was published in *Concerned Theatre Japan*, Asia Printing Co., Ltd., Vol. 1, No. 2, Summer 1970.

and social organization that must take place before a subject people is ready, not to beg for but to assume—demand and gain—its independence. Bharathi's work illustrates not only that a revolutionary artist transforms his art into a medium of political education, but also that in the process he may alter the nature of his native culture and change the direction of his art form. Bharathi was a prime mover of the struggle for independence; at the same time he injected innovations into Tamil poetry, language, and song. He marked the beginning of the modern political age when India began to make history as a nation once again, as well as the beginning of modern Tamil literature.

Tamil is the central language of the Dravidian group in South India. Its heritage parallels that of the northern Sanskrit tradition in antiquity and refinement. However, during the period of British rule in India, English was the official language of government, business, and education throughout the country. To enter the mainstream of economic advancement, a student had to accept English discipline, thought, and patterns of behavior. In India there are at least sixteen major linguistic regions, but in the modern or colonial sector of the economy these were disregarded in favor of the administrative convenience of English. Newspapers, radio, movies, and modern publishing—all imports from Britain—were in English. The masses of Indian peasants and laborers, already isolated from the economic advantages of the colonial system, were thus doubly cut off by virtue of their ignorance of English. This dichotomization of the native population into Western-oriented and traditional-peasant sectors is universally characteristic of a colonial economic and social structure. In India, the fact that the Anglicized class was national in scope while the indigenous population was split into many language affiliations was an added barrier to the unification of the population against foreign domination. It is an obstacle even today to national solidarity in independent India.

A first step in the formulation of a nationalist movement was the disaffection of the educated class with imperialist cultural domination and their return to their native language as a primary means of expression. It was a move toward reunification with the masses. It is the Western-oriented native class that makes foreign rule of the colony possible; without the emergence of this class, administration of such a vast colony as India would have proven more expensive and time-consuming than the profit offered by the land could afford. This class was nurtured from the very beginning of foreign control by English schools, English media, and English systems of promotion and reward. Clearly, a movement away from the foreign system of education would be the first step in the mutiny of this all-important internal ruling class. In India, this meant a resurgence of vernacular languages among educated people. And in fact this is what happened: in various sections of the country, lawyers, businessmen, teachers, judges, administrators, and their peers became the prime movers of the Indian National Congress.

The next step in the formulation of a movement was to counteract foreign cultural domination at all levels of society. Mass re-education became a pressing need. Bharathi was the central figure in initiating this all-important re-education process in the south.

Bharathi was a rebellious son of the nascent Indian bourgeoisie. Born a Brahman, a member of the priestly caste, he was retained during his youth at the court of the Rajah of Ettapuram, who, like other regional princes during the period of British rule, maintained traditions of great pomp and pretense although he had lost the power enjoyed in earlier times. Bharathi was an absentminded boy who would literally forget to go to school when he was halfway there, books in hand. He was a belligerent truant throughout high school, but finally educated himself in English, Tamil, and Sanskrit at the holy city of Benares, where he lived with his uncle between the ages of fifteen and twenty. Bharathi's father wanted him to be a scientist, but the British and the thought of making good in their system repulsed him. When he came of age in Benares, he adopted manners of dress and speech that declared his rejection of the prevailing national servitude to British ways. His hallmarks were a scruffy beard, a big turban, and a long defiant mustache.

Bharathi's fame was as a lyricist, and Tamil is a language of song. Children learn their lessons by song; prayers are songs, as are stories and lovers' midnight whisperings. Every piece of literature cherished by Tamil culture is written in verse and sung. Traditional songs are primarily religious. They deal with myth, ritual, morality, and devotion to God (which is sometimes used as an image of the love of men and women). It was as a singer of devotional songs that Bharathi gained fame in the court and temples of Benares; throughout his lifetime he wrote and sang compositions in praise of the gods and saints.

And the rhyme and rhythm of devotional songs fill even his most po-litical works.

After returning from Benares to Madras, however, Bharathi be-came more and more a political figure. His devotion to God merged with his devotion to the goddess of India—a united, strong, and free India. He embodied the movement of Indian nationalism back into the heart of its own people, back into its native tongues. He wrote:

> From now on, I will speak only Tamil. I will write only Tamil, and I will think only in Tamil . . . I will strive to keep on writing, tirelessly.

And then his role became clear:

> Our work is poetry, working for country, and never growing lax, even when we blink.

He blended the ancient tradition of songs of devotion to God with songs of the nationalist movement. He was the first poet of Tamil—and perhaps of any Indian language—to take this traditional me-dium and turn it into a medium of mass political education.

Tamil

Among the tongues of men
there is none
I know
so sweet as Tamil.

Tell me
Is it right to live
like beasts, or idiots,
your land and
mother tongue
degraded in the world?
We must spread the sweetness
of Tamil
until it covers the globe.

Among all poets
there are none
like Kamban, Valluvar
and Ilango.
This is true,
and no mean boast.

We are living deaf
dumb
and blind.

You say you want
prosperity?
Then make the thunder
of Tamil
resound in every street.

We must
translate the wisdom of foreign lands
and recreate works of fame and grade,
in Tamil.

Our beloved
ancient tales
have lost their dignity.

There is no use
in whispering the glory of our past
among ourselves.

If our ancient tales are great,
then other lands will see
our artistry
and greet them with respect.

When a soul is born
of true light,
it shines in every word.

When art and poetry
grow
like a flood over the earth,
all the blindmen
will regain their eyes
and honor.

For they taste
the clear nectar
of Tamil song.

Here on earth
they know
the deathless glory
of the gods.

The first Tamil daily newspaper was begun in 1880. It was of necessity a conservative attempt to bring the political events of the day to the masses of Tamil people. It was founded by a patriot who sought to undermine the English monopoly on news presentation. In 1904 Bharathi joined the paper's staff as a translator of English speeches and news articles. In the next few years, political events were to give additional focus and a public outlet to his songs and poetry.

The partitioning of Bengal in 1905 by the ambitious viceroy Lord Curzon suddenly changed the political climate of India. Ironically enough, it was this move to obviate a coalition between Muslims and Hindus in India's traditionally most rebellious state that gave impetus to the first national organization of rebellion. A boycott of British goods was begun and a complementary effort made to revive *swadeshi,* the domestic production of goods for native profit only. In 1906 the Indian National Congress met, chaired by Dadabhai Naoroji, who analyzed for the members the exploitative process and the present crisis and declared for the first time the commitment of that body to *swaraj*—home rule. The phrase *Vande Matharam,* taken from a novel by the Bengali writer Bankim Chandra Chatterjee, became the rallying cry for the new nationalist movement. It meant "bow in worship to the motherland," and symbolized the combination of devotion to God and the country upon which the movement and Bharathi's poetry were based.

Also in 1906, as part of the Swadeshi Movement, Chidambaram Pillai founded the Swadeshi Steamship Company in Madras. It was the first native-owned and operated trading company in India since the landing of the East India Company nearly two and a half centuries earlier. It was subjected to constant harassment by the authorities and was eventually driven out of business. Two years later, Pillai was jailed for sedition and then sentenced to prison and exile at hard labor.

Indictment of Chidambaram Pillai by Governor Finch

> You
> have ignited the passion
> throughout this land.
> You stir coals into flame.

I
will break you,
starve your resolve
in prison.
I
will parade my power
indomitable.

You bring masses together
with a song of freedom.

You insult us,
defy the crown:
you have built a ship
and brought wealth to the people.

You spoke truth
to people chained in cowardice.
You broke the law:
You revealed the injustice
of poverty
slavery
death by decay.

You preach heroism
and give castrate slaves their manhood.
They cry out, "Enough suffering,"
and you heal them,
feeding desire
to cure anemic hearts.

These slaves were content
with their labor, but
you showed the way
to fame
through skill.

You have nurtured this longing
for self-rule
everywhere
you sowed the seed. . . .

But, can a rabbit do a lion's work?
Will you live to see it done?
I will sh- sh- shoot you down,
stab the heart of discontent.

I'll show you what wisdom is,
you'll find it
deep in prison.
Who can defy me?
I
will
have
revenge!

Chidambaram Pillai's Reply

In our land
we can no longer be slaves,
asleep.
We are no longer afraid.

        On this earth
        injustice multiplies
        with impunity.
        Does God have eyes?
        Will he not see?

We will sing
Vande Matharam
until life passes from us.
To the motherland we sacrifice
ourselves
in adoration.

Is it lowly for a living thing
to worship its only mother?
Is that so disgraceful?
Tell me:
Is our wealth stolen from us,
exploited
every minute of the day?

Should we continue
to die
sobbing silently to ourselves
forever?

        Or is life so sweet
        we dare not risk it
        for rebirth in freedom?

We are four-hundred million.
Are we dogs?
or children of dogs?

Is it only you
who are human?

> Sir, do I speak justly
> or is all this mere
> obstinacy?

Is it a sin to love freedom
until death?

Can you call this
worship of anger?

Is it a crime to end our suffering?
Is there hatred in that?

We have learned
the only way is unity.
That
we have learned well.

We will no longer be surprised
confused
separated
by your cruelty.

Our will is unshakable.

> If you slice my flesh
> into bits,
> will you lose your fear of us?
> your hunger for revenge?

> Will you gain your purpose?
> When my corpse is burnt
> my heart will not melt,
> for there is locked
> unsatisfied
> my life desire:

> freedom.

The imprisonment of Pillai was the beginning of the cycle of revolt and repression that fed the first flames of the independence movement and provided Bharathi with his initiation into real politics. Events demanded interpretation for the people, and two new media appeared: the underground or handout newspaper and the mass meeting. In Madras, both were centered around Bharathi. With private funding, he founded two leaflet papers, one in English and one in Tamil. The Tamil daily, *India*, handed out in the streets and at marketplaces and public meetings, was printed on red paper, and in its pages Bharathi's poems appeared publicly for the first time. The meetings were usually held on the long white beach in Madras city, bordering the Bay of Bengal. Speakers from all over the state and country came to the beach; they were often radicals who had come into public view as a result of recent events. But the real gathering force lay in Bharathi's songs. He sang and spoke and taught, and the people sang with him. Men on their way home from work stopped to listen to the music and found themselves learning of their own slavery. They confronted their first political analysis of the ills that they felt about them every day. That is the value of song as a medium, especially among a nonliterate people isolated from public events and with little awareness of their own plight.

In a colonial mine, plantation, or factory, the driving force of the laborers is fear. The people are cut off from wealth, power, advancement, and learning. Through fear they are cut off from each other. They cease to be a collective people at all and become so many individual wage-earners. They relinquish their manhood for the right to survive. They have no power as a race, a culture, a nation. All power is the foreigners', and it is they who make history in the colony. Natives have no pride, no courage, no will. And this image of themselves as lazy, heathen, barbaric morons is perpetuated by every word that issues from the mouth of The Man. It is this self-image that perpetuates their powerlessness and makes them so much easier for the colonialists to dominate. It becomes only natural for these people to be ruled, for they have become incapable of ruling themselves. They are degraded by their race, religion, language—by their very existence. And this degradation is taught them every minute of the day until it becomes an integral part of their minds. The rulers are white. South Indians are very black. Everything native becomes associated with backwardness and stupidity; everything English and

white becomes powerful, rich, educated, and worthy—even demanding—of emulation and adoration.

The Present State of the Indian People

My heart cannot bear
to think of people brought so low.
Fearing fear, afraid,
they are dying.
On this earth, for them,
nothing is without terror.

They cry out, "Cheating devils,
in the tree, the pond,
asleep in the hills."
Afflicted
maddened,
to think is to be afraid.

They call him witch doctor.
He turns their soul with a word,
and measures out their fear.
Black Magic.

How many thousand tortures?

Kings receive what is given
and protect the people—
that is the order of this world.
This government sows only fear.

Seeing its power
supernatural
they grow faint.

A soldier is coming
—the people are afraid.
The police
—poor hearts stop.
A man with a gun, still far off
—they run in the house,
to hide.
Someone is coming
—they see his clothes
and stand silently.

Their hands are folded,
weak and afraid
they moan
and live like housecats.

My heart cannot bear to
see men so degraded.

Are there yet a few differences
separating us?
Would, say, ten million
be too many?

If daddy says the snake has six heads,
the son, defiant, says five.
They split up, take sides,
and feud for years upon years.

They do not see the *Shastras,*
but, believing lying devils,
call their brothers heretics.

> Foaming at the mouth,
> "He's a Shaivite, he's a Vaishnava,"
> they fight among themselves.

And with one united greeting
they worship the lowly cheat
who turns their madness into gold.

My heart cannot bear it.
But they invite my soul
to pity,
not anger.

Bellies filled with air;
there is no porridge.
And they cannot see the reason.

> They weep and wail,
> "The famine is upon us,"

and daily starving
their frail life,
they die in the fields.

There is no way to end their suffering!
Their disease is countless.

They grow weak
as they rise,
and faint
as they walk.

Like blind children
bending,
following the touch
of a foreign hand,
they are trapped.

In this sacred land of a hundred million
sacred arts,
the people
line up
to live
like dumb and senseless animals.

This, then, is the mentality that a nationalist artist like Bharathi had to re-educate. In their emotional content, Bharathi's songs seek to return to the people their own manhood, to nullify their slave self-image. He seeks to restore confidence so the people can think, unite, and move to make history for themselves once again. He had to create within them the desire for freedom and sustain that desire by investing it with mystical significance, religious sanctity, and historical inevitability. The first step in this restoration of self-esteem was the reunification of the people with their own past. Bharathi teaches them of their own national identity by praising the glory of the Indian nation before the colonialists conquered the land. He praises great warriors, saints, India's literature, its languages. None of this is new to the people—the newness of Bharathi's historical songs is the pride they teach. He uses empathy with the forefathers to instill a sense of longing and a sense of shame at the present state of the land.

He makes identification national in scope. He praises Tamil land, history, and literature; but, most importantly, he unites a love for Tamil with a love for all India. Heroes of the past came from all over the nation—they were Bengalis, Punjabis, Nagas, Vaishnavas, Shaivites. Historically, there was no unified nation before the British conquest, but Bharathi's collective presentation gives a picture of the historic wealth that lay within the boundaries of what is now India. He shows that these people, essentially united by culture and geogra-

phy and dominated by no one, had created one of the greatest civili-
zations on earth. When he sings of the past and its glories, his songs
are joyous and boastful, filled with superlatives.

And then he speaks of the present. His songs are melancholic in
the extreme when he sings of the slavery, the fear, the poverty, and
the starvation that "reek like a corpse" across the land. He uses the
image of blindness: a blind nation, a blind people, "blind children
following the touch of a foreign hand."

Bharathi speaks of the means by which the people are kept in this
state. Their oppression comes from without and within, he says. The
people cling to superstition, crying out after devils and curses rather
than looking to the political realities that determine their slavery.
They are separated from one another by ten million petty feuds, yet
they are all persecuted by the same forces. They are fragmented,
each group clinging to its own life without thinking of the collective
power they have to improve their common condition. The people do
not see the greatness of their past or their present subjugation because they are blinded by lies and fear. They do not see the *Shastras*,
the ancient books of morality and social duty, which they all hold in
common, because they believe the witchcraft of the foreigner. They
are blinded by his cruelty and shackled by their own fear.

The foreigner becomes the object of catharsis. Ignoring whatever
good may have come to the people in the colonial age, Bharathi
makes subservience itself the demon, and the foreigner the one who
controls it. By restoring the glory of the national history of precolo-
nial times, he makes the colonial period seem an unnatural interrup-
tion of the people's own historical progress. Thus, he exhorts them to
remove the demon from their land and minds, and to continue to
once more develop their own culture, their own national history. He
shows how the movement of peoples to nationhood is a historical
process and how, in order to live among the nations of the world, the
Indians must carve out for themselves their own free nation. He
praises the national movements in Belgium and that of Mazzini in
Italy; he praises the Russians and the French. The movement of people to control their own destiny is as sure as time itself, and as irre-
sistible. The ruling British cling on in desperation, he says; they are
seeking to wreak their last revenge on the people who will soon rise
up and take their land back from the pillage of the white man. Free-

dom becomes a historical certainty, and the foreigners who fight against it are disparaged with the same wit and sarcasm they had used to denigrate the natives' character. The foreigner is portrayed as a loathsome, greedy, violent, barbaric devil who rules by the force of evil alone. The people are the vehicle of history's fulfillment, and they move toward freedom with the righteousness and indomitable strength of God.

The Glory of Freedom

He stands tall
heroic
and asks for freedom.
Will he be content
with less?

When a man craves ambrosia
will he bother his head
with cheap wine?

When he finds his own greatness,
his life duty,
all else becomes a lie.
Then,
can coolie labor
consume his mind?

If he knows
for every man born
death is certain,
will he forsake his pride
and believe
that clinging to life
is living?

When he sees the truth,
that it is difficult and excellent
to be born a man,
will he violate the soul of manhood
to save his flesh from the fire?

Will men sell the sun in the sky
and live by the light of fire-flies?

When freedom
—the sweeter eye—
is lost,
can you fold your hands
and live in servitude?

Hoarding joys of dirt,
desire,
will he lose the dream, the glory of freedom?

If you sell your eyes to buy a painting,
won't they laugh
and mock you in the street?

When he has sung: Vande Matharam,
and bowed in prayer to the motherland,
will he ever again fall
at the feet
of illusion?

Can he ever forget the one and only mantra?
Vande Matharam!

Thus, in Bharathi's songs, freedom for the Indian people becomes a matter of God's will. Bharathi wrote several translations of the Bengali song *Vande Matharam*. *Vande* is "to bow in worship and adoration"; *matharam* is from the same Sanskrit root from which "mother" derives—it means one's own mother; also motherland, as well as goddess, the Mother Goddess, Kali. Kali is the consort of Siva; she is at once the mother, protectress, and lover of all men, and the punisher, the vengeful destroyer of all that is evil. Kali is identified and equated in Bharathi's songs with Mother India. Protecting her people, she will nurse their infant courage and lead them into battle. Freedom will come with the grace of Kali and the people must become worthy through discipline, self-denial, and the performance of their ordained social duty—*dharma*. Worship is not only prayer but life. It is the duty of the people to reform their society in such ways that it will become strong and united against the evil that is subservience. Bharathi, more than taking the format of religious songs and adapting it to political themes, took the relation of a worshiper to his God that has come down through Hindu tradition and equated it with the relation of a patriot to his nation. Bharathi speaks to that heritage in the words of a religious mystic and makes it relevant to the modern context.

In this modern context, it is the duty of the patriot to eliminate all feuds and inequalities within Indian society that impede the unification of the country for the freedom struggle. The separation and inequality of caste, the slavery of women, the tradition of elitist rule, popular ignorance and illiteracy, and regional and religious rivalries—these are the elements that must be eliminated from the hearts and minds of every Indian. And yet it is these very traditions that are set off as auspicious, if not mandatory, in the *Shastra* literature. Caste differences and the lowly position of women in society are basic to *dharma* literature of the ancient period, but there are places in the Epics and in Tamil literature where these practices are criticized, and Bharathi cites these. His purpose was not merely to unite people with their historical past, with its political and religious forms. He meant, rather, to unite them with the very flow of their own history, which would carry them to freedom as a modern nation; and he meant to rekindle the flames of religious devotion and social duty, not in order to reinstate the forms of worship and social customs of the past but to bring people to the realization that devotion to a religious ideal—like a free India—entails concomitant social responsibilities. These social duties he teaches them directly, in words easily remembered and easily made an integral part of the social consciousness. At all times the duty to remove social inequities is placed in a religious-nationalistic context.

Song of Freedom

We will dance
and sing:
                  we have got sweet bliss
in freedom.   *(Refrain)*

The day is past for calling Brahmans "Sir,"
and white foreigners "Lords."
The day is gone when we revere beggars,
and do slave labor for cheats.

Everywhere the talk is "freedom," and
it is fact that we are equal.
We will shout our victory with a trumpet,
and let the whole world know.

The day is come when we are one,
and lies and deceit are chased away.
The day is come when good men are respected,
and "friends" who deceive are loathed.

We will worship farming and industry,
and condemn those who live fat in idleness.
We will no longer faint away, watering weeds;
and no longer waste ourselves, slaving for fools.

The land we live in is our own,
this we know,
and this is our right only.
On this earth,
we will be slaves of no man
but live to be slaves of God.

In the nationalist imagination of Bharathi, dedication to the nationalist struggle was a religious duty. All levels of personal, cultural, and political regeneration became integral parts of this duty. Bharathi's role as songster-poet was twofold in this regard: he wrote songs that educated the people as to their present condition, their past, and their necessary duties for the sake of nationhood; and he wrote songs that could serve as *mantras*, as hymns of the people in movement. His lyrics combine these educative and mantric qualities. He prepared the people for participation in mass movement toward nationhood, and also wrote songs they could sing as they moved.

Within the struggle for national selfhood lies the struggle for women to realize and assume their inherent place in the rejuvenation of Indian society. Bharathi saw the liberation of women from the restrictive roles prescribed for them in the ancient literature, roles imposed upon them throughout Indian history, as a prerequisite for a fully free, united, and strong India:

Among our two eyes,
shall we stab one out
and ruin our sight

As woman's knowledge grows
ignorance will disappear
from the earth.

Bharathi considered the liberation of the creative force of woman-kind in society to be as important to Indian national growth as the elimination of caste distinctions and economic exploitation. His lesson was no dry philosophizing, no academic sermon. Women will sing and dance in the joyful project of their own and their nation's liberation.

Women's Liberation Dance

Women will sing the joys of freedom.
The god that shines in our soul,
like the glow in our eyes,
He will protect us.

Beat the measure, that all
Tamil land may tremble.
Dance and sing:
        "The demons that trapped us
are gone, and we have found
prosperity."

Dance!

Those who said
it is evil for women to touch books
are dead.
The lunatics who said
they would lock the women in the house
cannot show their faces now.

They showed us our place in the home,
like we were bulls, bred
and beaten to do dumb labor.
We have ended that.
Sing this and dance!

He gets a good price for his dog,
does anyone ask the dog his thoughts?
Men put us in the same state.
Not brave enough to kill,
they found this crime.

Men say we must be chaste and true.
We will make them share that vow.

We will erase and crush
the marriage of girls
by force.

We have come to get degrees
and make the laws.
Look!
Women are no less wise than men.
Sing it loud and dance!

We will take lovers by the hand
and work beside them, whatever they do.
We will live to make
the ancient virtues of womankind
even more glorious.
Sing this and dance!

Bharathi's songs were more than an education, though. They are remembered and cherished as beautiful tunes. They are sometimes arrogant, sometimes sarcastic, witty, and crass. They utilize colloquial forms and simple, everyday language. These elements, completely new to Tamil song, opened a new era in Tamil literature and liberated the culture from the grasp of elitist Brahmin priests and court poets. Bharathi created a political medium, but only as he created a new secular literature. He invented the prose form in Tamil. Bharathi's songs are simple and lyrical. They are sung by little children and learned pundits today, and they form the basis of contemporary Tamil literary development.

Song to My Child

Run and play, my child.
Sitting still
will never suit you.
Join your friends
but never scold the little ones.

Like a tiny bird
turn
and fly to me.

Look at the bigger birds
full of color
and be glad in your heart.

The hen,
she pecks and turns
with measured steps.
Play with her, my love.

The crow swoops
to steal a grain of rice.
Have pity on her, my love.

The cow gives us milk
and is gentle.

The dog comes to you
wagging his tail.
He is man's companion.

The horse who pulls our cart,
the bull who plows our field,
the goat who abides with us,
just to live—
we must protect them
with love,
my child.

When you rise to the sun
go to your lessons,
and then,
the songs that bring your heart
to ripeness.

In the afternoon
play joyfully.
Spend your days like this,
my love.

You must never lie,
or worse,
make fun of anyone.
God is our aid,
no harm, no evil
will ever come to you,
my love.

If we see a man
sinning gravely,
it is no use to be afraid.
Knock him down
and trample him,
spit in his face,
my love.

When misery
and suffering
close in around you,
it does no good
to become weary.

There is a God full of love,
who will drive it all away.

Laziness is our ruin.
Don't defy your mother's call.

The child who cries,
gasping, stuttering,
is lame.

Take courage
and struggle,
my love.

Know that sacred Tamil Nadu
is the mother who bore you.
Join your hands in prayer to her.

She is the sweetness in ambrosia,
she is the land of your fathers.

Tamil is the greatness of words.
Learn your mother tongue
as a prayer.
Daily praise our India,
so full of wealth.

On the north, Himalayas.
In the south, Cape Kumari.
The endless ocean lies on the east and west.

This is the land of the Vedas,
and here heroism was born.
This unconquerable India,

worship her as your god,
my love.

There is no such thing as caste.
To say families are high,
or low,
is a sin.

The man full of love,
justice, wisdom, learning—
he is the great one,
my child.

You must show love
to all living things,
and know that God is Truth.
You need a strong heart.

This is the way to live,
my child.

In 1908 terrorism made its appearance in the Indian national movement—the first bomb was aimed at a British official and took the lives of two white women. The government moved to repress the revolt at its source. Introducing Law No. 144 into the Indian Penal Code, they forbade as unlawful the assembly of more than five persons and the incitement of individual emotions to disturb the peace in any public place. The songs and meetings on the beach in Madras had caused many incidents of violence between police and the people. The law obviously was aimed at these gatherings and at handout literature. A warrant was issued for the arrest of the editor of *India*, and the man whose name was registered as editor was arrested and imprisoned. Bharathi was persuaded to seek refuge in the French colonial territory of Pondicherry, within the borders of the Madras presidency, and to continue publishing *India* from the safety of exile. His poems and paper were banned in British India and confiscated on sight. Like Mazzini, he remained in exile for the bulk of his productive years, and he returned to his homeland after most of his songs and poems had been written. He died an ignoble death in an accident with a temple elephant in Madras in 1921. He never saw even a glimmer of his dreams fulfilled in political reality. But he left his message of hope.

References

Subramania Bharathiyar, *Mahakavi Bharathiyar Kavithaikal* (Shakti Publishing House, Madras, 1958).

P. Mahadevan, *Subramania Bharathi—A Memoir* (Atri Publishing House, Madras, 1957).

Frantz Fanon, *The Wretched of the Earth* (Grove Press, New York, 1963).

Mahakavi Bharathiyar Katturaikal (Collected Essays) (Aruna Press, Madurai, 1967).

Ponmolikal (Golden Sayings) (Arivalayam, Madras, 1960).

2. Peasants and Revolution

Hamza Alavi

> In colonial countries the peasants alone are revolutionary, for they have nothing to lose and everything to gain. The starving peasant, outside the class system, is the first among the exploited to discover that only violence pays. For him there is no compromise, no possible coming to terms.
>
> —Frantz Fanon[1]

The above view of the revolutionary potentiality of the peasantry was expressed by Frantz Fanon, ideologue of the Algerian revolution. From time to time, throughout the centuries, the peasant has indeed risen in rebellion against his oppressors. But history is also replete with examples of peasants who have borne silently, and for long periods, extremes of exploitation and oppression. At the same time occasional outbreaks of peasant revolt do raise the question of the conditions in which the peasant becomes revolutionary.

We cannot speak of the peasantry in this context as a homogeneous and undifferentiated mass. Its different sections have different aims and social perspectives, for each of them is confronted with a different set of problems. The constellation of peasant forces that participate in a revolutionary movement depends upon the character of the revolution, or, as Marxists would see it, the "historical stage" which it represents. Thus, when a revolutionary movement progresses from "bourgeois-democratic revolution" to "socialist revolution," the roles of the different sections of the peasantry no longer remain the same.

As a generalization about the revolutionary potential of the peasantry, Fanon's statement thus begs many questions. Equally ques-

---

An earlier version of this article appeared in *The Socialist Register 1965*, Monthly Review Press.

tion-begging are those generalizations which dismiss the peasantry as a backward, servile, and reactionary class, incapable of joining hands with forces of social revolution. The peasants have in fact played a role, sometimes a crucial and decisive role, in revolutions. The Chinese Revolution is a case in point.

The question that needs to be asked, therefore, is not whether the peasants are or are not revolutionary but, rather, under what circumstances they become revolutionary or what roles different sections of the peasantry play in revolutionary situations. These are questions which greatly interest socialist movements in countries with predominantly peasant populations. The main tradition of Marxist theory, until the turn of the century, took its stand firmly on the dominant, or even exclusive, revolutionary role of the industrial proletariat. But Marx and Engels were painfully aware of the fact that if the industrial proletariat was to fulfill its historic tasks by leading the forces of revolution, it would have to mobilize peasant support, especially in countries with predominantly peasant populations. For socialists, moreover, the question is not merely that of mobilizing peasant support as a *means* to achieve success in their struggle. The question is not just that of *utilizing* the forces of the peasantry. The free and active participation of the peasantry in transforming their mode of existence and giving shape to the new society must be an essential part of the socialist goal itself.

We propose in this essay to consider the roles played by different sections of the peasantry in the cases of Russia, China, and India. We shall examine the preconditions that seem necessary to bring about a revolutionary mobilization of the peasantry in the struggle for socialism, whether it be peaceful and constitutional or insurrectionary. We shall put forward hypotheses which, in our view, throw fresh light on certain aspects of the problem. These hypotheses require further consideration, especially in the light of the experiences of other countries.[2] We would like to emphasize at the outset that these propositions are being advanced tentatively and in order to open up a discussion on certain aspects of the problem that have so far been obscured.

Our hypotheses concern the respective roles of the so-called *middle peasants* and *poor peasants* and the preconditions that we find are necessary for a revolutionary mobilization of *poor peasants*. These terms have been defined in Marxist literature to refer to various classes of the peasantry. But they are fraught with ambiguity and, as we shall see later, they have sometimes been reinterpreted to alter their denotation to suit ideological exigencies of political tactics or the personal predilections of particular writers.[3] For a meaningful and scientific discussion of the subject, it is essential that the terminology used should be unambiguous. I have continued to use the above-mentioned terminology only because it is in common use. But, before we proceed further, the precise meaning of these terms should be clarified. This terminology appears to focus attention on relative differences in the wealth (or poverty) of various strata of the peasantry without any indication of the criteria by which the strata may be distinguished from each other as classes. Stratification on the basis of simple difference in wealth, on a single linear scale, is often the basis of differentiation of "classes" in academic sociology. But that is not the basis on which Marxists distinguish classes. The Marxist concept of class is a structural concept; classes are defined by relations of production. Where several modes of production coexist, classes cannot be arranged in a single linear hierarchical order because they must be structurally differentiated. The division of the peasantry into *rich peasants, middle peasants,* and *poor peasants* suggests an array of the peasantry with the different strata arranged one over the other, in a single order. This is misleading: middle peasants (i.e., independent peasant proprietors), for instance, do not stand *between* rich peasants and their employees, the poor peasants; they belong to a different sector of the rural economy.

In the transitional historical situations we shall deal with, a broad distinction may be made between three "sectors" of the rural economy, or three modes of production. In the first place, we have the sector whose essential distinguishing feature is that the land is owned by landlords who do not undertake cultivation on their own account. Their land is cultivated by landless tenants, mostly sharecroppers who are classed as *poor peasants.* The second sector is that of independent smallholders who own no more land than they cultivate themselves and enough of it to make them self-sufficient. They do not exploit the labor of others; nor is their labor exploited by others. They are the *middle peasants.* A special case of middle peasants was that of the allotment-holding peasants in Russia who were obliged to work for landlords because of various disabilities imposed upon them, as discussed below. A third sector is that of capitalist farmers, also described as rich farmers, who own substantial amounts of land and whose farming is primarily based on the exploitation of wage labor, although they may participate in farm work themselves. Unlike landlords, they undertake the business of farming and employ capital in it.

Farm laborers who are paid wages are referred to as the agricultural proletariat, but they are usually included with that other exploited section of the peasantry—the sharecroppers—in the term *poor peasant.* The use of the terminology makes it quite clear that the essential distinctions are those of relations of production and not simply those of relative differences in wealth or property. This is exemplified by the inclusion in the term *middle peasant* of an independent smallholder whose income may be very small but who does not work for others; whereas a sharecropper with a large holding, who may earn more than he does, is classified as a *poor peasant.* The terminology is clearly unsatisfactory. It would avoid a great deal of unnecessary confusion if we were instead to adopt structurally descriptive terms, such as *capitalist farmers, independent smallholders, sharecroppers,* and *farm laborers.* But in the statements and writings that we must discuss in this essay, the terms *rich peasants, middle peasants,* and *poor peasants* are widely used and for that reason we cannot avoid using them ourselves.

While using that terminology, we would like to emphasize the critical distinction between the class situation of the independent peasant smallholders, the *middle peasants,* on the one hand, and the exploiting and exploited sections of the rural population, namely, the *landlords* and capitalist farmers or *rich peasants,* and their sharecroppers and laborers, the *poor peasants,* on the other. The sector of *middle peasants* is characterized by their *economic independence* (from landlords and rich peasants), whereas in the other two sectors—sharecropping and capitalist farming—the mode of production is characterized by the exploitation of the poor peasants and their *economic dependence* on their masters. This distinction between the economic dependence and subordination of the *poor peasants* and the economic independence of the *middle peasants* is critical for our analysis.

We should qualify this threefold classification of the different sectors of the agrarian economy (or the different modes of production) by pointing out that there is a great deal of overlapping between these categories and the actual demarcation between them is by no means sharp and clear. In practice it is often the case that a person may enter into more than one relation of production. Ownership of his own patch of land does not by itself suffice to classify a peasant as a *middle peasant* if he also works as a sharecropper or a laborer to supplement his livelihood. The difficulty in classification is met (by Mao, for example) by attempting to determine the *principal* relation of production from which a person draws his livelihood. Thus a peasant who owns a tiny patch of land, but depends for his livelihood mainly on sharecropping for a landlord or on working as a laborer, is classed as a *poor peasant;* he is not classed as a *middle peasant* even though he owns some land. Again, a *middle peasant* who employs casual labor occasionally to cope with peak operations is classified as a middle peasant, for his livelihood does not depend principally on the exploitation of the labor of others. A similar problem arises in the case of a landlord who employs sharecroppers on part of his land and undertakes cultivation on his own account on another part of his land, say, by mechanized farming and wage labor. He engages in two modes of production at once. Lenin described such situations as "transitional." In Pakistan and India one finds that the two modes of production are not separate and simply coexistent; the two are structurally integrated because landlords who engage in mechanized farming retain sharecroppers on diminished holdings, insufficient for their livelihood, in order to have a tied source of the seasonal labor they require in the mechanized farm sector. The two modes of production are thus structurally integrated.[4] But we do not propose to pursue the question of transition from the one mode of production to the other. The relation that is essential to the analysis which follows is that of the economic exploitation and dependence of the poor peasantry, and this exists in either case. The crucial distinction we wish to reiterate is that of the economic independence of the middle peasant and the economic dependence of the poor peasant. We propose to examine their respective roles in the Russian and Chinese revolutions and in the peasant movements in India.

I

The peasants were given a definite place in the Bolshevik revolutionary strategy under Lenin's slogan of "Alliance of the Working Class and the Peasantry." However, the role of the peasantry in the

Russian Revolution is sometimes exaggerated out of all proportion. Thus, Lichtheim writes: "The uniqueness of Lenin—and the Bolshevik organization which he founded and held together—lay in the decision to make the agrarian upheaval do the work of the proletarian revolution." [5] Neither the facts of the Russian Revolution nor Lenin's theoretical formulations support such a judgment. It was in the towns and the cities that the Bolsheviks first seized power, for the class struggle in the countryside had not yet developed.[6] That was the conclusion Lenin reached after the October Revolution. His attitude toward the peasantry evolved continuously, in response to the developments taking place in the Russian countryside. From the point of view of the role assigned to the peasantry in Bolshevik revolutionary strategy, one can broadly distinguish three periods, in each of which we find a distinct theoretical stand. The first period was that up to the 1905 Revolution, although we can see the change in Lenin's views already beginning to take place after the peasant upsurge of 1902. The second period was between 1905 and 1917. The third period, one of reassessment, was after the October Revolution.

The central feature determining the perspective of the first period was Lenin's view of the dynamic growth of agrarian capitalism in Russia and the decay of the feudal economy. As early as 1893, young Lenin had begun to see the new economic developments in peasant life, which became the subject of the earliest of his writings to be preserved. In 1899 he published his first major work, *The Development of Capitalism in Russia*, two-thirds of which is devoted to a brilliant and thoroughly documented analysis of the capitalist revolution in the Russian countryside, the decay of the feudal economy, and the complex variety of transitional forms that had emerged. Without going into details of the rural economy of Russia at the turn of the century, we must, for our purposes, point out some of its salient features.[7]

A crucial factor that inflamed the Russian countryside, in 1905–1907 and again in 1917, was the peculiar problem, a legacy of the emancipation of 1861, of the allotment landholder, the Russian middle peasant. By the edict of emancipation the serf had received as "allotment" the land he had cultivated before, but with a portion of it withheld by the landlord; such withheld portions were called "cutoff lands." For Russia as a whole the proportion of "cutoff" land is estimated to have been about a fifth of the peasants' original holdings. The crucial fact, however, about the "cutoff lands" was not their relative size but the type of land that was taken away from the peasant and its role in the peasant economy. The peasant was deprived of meadows and pastures, water courses, and access to woods —all essential to the peasant economy. Moreover, the peasant was required to pay for the allotment land. He could do so by giving labor to the landlord or he could opt to make money payments, which considerably exceeded the rental value of the allotment lands. He could terminate his "temporary obligation" by making a "redemption payment," which again was in excess of the market value of the land; moreover, he had to borrow to make such a payment. The need to work off these obligations to the landlord, together with such surviving feudal laws and institutions as the commune, tied the peasant to the village and his land, and forced him to work for his landlord on unfavorable terms. This relationship between the middle peasant and landlord, a source of deep and direct conflict, was a feature peculiar to Russia.

Much of the landlords' land was, however, cultivated by sharecroppers—poor peasants—who had little or no land but who possessed some farm implements and horses. A distinction between the situation of such poor peasants and that of the middle peasants, as described above, is important. The middle peasant had a substantial allotment as well as access to communal grazing and woodland. His livelihood did not depend totally on the landlord, but his obligations to the landlord were an insufferable burden. In the case of the poor peasant, the sharecropper, his livelihood depended on his being able to get the land from the landlord for cultivation. Although he was exploited, he was too dependent on the landlord to be able to oppose him as the middle peasant could.

Some landlords' lands were cultivated by hired farm laborers—already a transition to capitalist farming. But it was the industrious kulaks, the rural bourgeoisie, who conducted farming as a business and employed the rural proletariat as wage labor. In the growth of agrarian capitalism in Russia, Lenin saw a powerful force for the bourgeois-democratic revolution which would open the door for the socialist revolution.[8] Plekhanov, and even more so some of the extreme Mensheviks, had looked exclusively to the growth of industrial capitalism for the maturation of the forces of revolution. This offered socialists the rather dismal prospect of an interminably long interlude of capitalist development before Russia could be ripe for the socialist revolution. The Mensheviks looked upon the peasantry as a conservative and reactionary force. Seen against the background of such ideas, the Narodnik view—that the peasant commune provided Russia with a unique opportunity for a direct transition to a socialist order—was not altogether without its attractions; even Marx and Engels were not altogether without sympathy for it.[9] Lenin rejected this idea as utopian. He saw the commune as a survival of the old feudal order which was to be swept away. The middle peasant, the mainstay of the commune, was disintegrating as a class. With the inexorable advance of capitalism, the middle peasant was being pauperized and the peasantry as a whole was being polarized into two classes, capitalist farmers and the rural proletariat. The immediate task, in Lenin's view, was to assist and speed up this process by fighting for the removal of those survivals of feudalism which tended to slow down the advance of agrarian capitalism.

Lenin thus looked to the classes in the capitalist sector of the agrarian economy, rather than to the disintegrating class of middle peasants, to provide the forces for the struggle against feudal survival and the completion of the bourgeois-democratic revolution. However, in 1901 he tended to discount even the rural laborer as an effective revolutionary force. In his *Iskra* article of April 1901, which set out the agrarian program of the Iskra-ists, he wrote: "Our rural laborers are still too closely connected with the peasantry, they are still too heavily burdened with the misfortunes of the peasantry generally, to enable the movement of rural workers to assume national significance either now or in the immediate future." [10] Thus, he argued, "The whole essence of our agrarian program is that the rural proletariat must fight together with the rich peasantry for the abolition of the remnants of serfdom, for the cutoff lands." [11] It was for the industrial proletariat to provide revolutionary leadership, while in the agrarian field it was the rural bourgeoisie who would provide the main force for the bourgeois-democratic revolution.

The central issue of the agrarian program was the demand for the restitution of the cutoff lands and the abolition of the remnants of serfdom. But Lenin overestimated the role of the rural bourgeoisie in this struggle and curiously ignored the role of the middle peasant, who was most directly concerned with it. The challenge of the kulak to the feudal system was economic—it lay in his greater efficiency, his ability to pay higher wages to the farm laborers, and his competitive strength in bidding for land available for buying or leasing. But he was outside the feudal sector and was not directly involved in conflict with the landowners. Although he resented being accorded an inferior social status by the nobility, this was not cause enough for him to engage in battle.

When the great peasant upheaval began in 1905, it was the middle peasant who provided its main force in the fight for cutoff lands. In February, soon after Bloody Sunday, January 9, 1905, the peasants rose in revolt. Peasant *jacqueries* flared up all over Russia and continued to inflame the countryside in 1905 and for two succeeding years, long after the revolution in the towns had been extinguished. The respective roles of the different sections of the peasantry in this revolutionary upsurge are described by G. T. Robinson:

> Such revolutionary leanings as existed in rural Russia had chiefly come out of the relations of small, land-short, farmers with large landholders rather than the relations of proletarians and "half-proletarian" laborers with capitalist cultivators. . . . Sometimes the better-off peasants joined with the rest in depredations upon the estates, and particularly in the cutting and carting-off of timber and in the illicit pasturing of cattle. However, there were at least a few cases in which the attacks of the peasants were directed against the richer members of their own class rather than against the landlords; and no doubt because of a fear of loss to themselves, the richer peasants . . . were often indifferent or openly hostile to the agrarian movement. . . . On the other hand the agricultural wage workers who had no land . . . were not usually the leaders of the agrarian movement in general or even of the labor strikes on the estates. . . . Indeed there developed in certain instances a definite hostility between the agricultural proletariat and those peasants who divided their time between the landlords' fields and their own." [12]

The kulak's role in the peasant uprising was ambivalent. He did not lead the attack on the landlords for the restitution of cutoff lands, for that was a matter which concerned the middle peasants. Indeed, as Robinson has pointed out, he was himself sometimes the target of attack and was often indifferent or openly hostile to the peasant uprising. On the other hand, he often found the tide too strong not to go along with it, and he participated in the attacks on landlords' manors and the looting that followed.

Until 1905 the Bolsheviks had looked upon the rural bourgeoisie, the kulaks, to provide the forces for the bourgeois-democratic revolution in the countryside. They had not paid much attention to organizing the broad mass of the peasantry themselves. In the *Iskra* article he had written in 1901, Lenin had virtually written off the rural proletariat as a force which was "still wholly in the future." He added that "we must include peasant demands in our program, not in order to transfer convinced Social-Democrats from the towns to the countryside, not in order to chain them to the village, but to guide the activity of those forces which *cannot* find an outlet anywhere except in the rural localities. . . ." [13] After the peasant upsurge of 1902, however, Lenin's outlook changed. He wrote: "The purely practical requirements of the movement have of late lent special urgency to the task of propaganda and agitation in the countryside." The basic strategy of the bourgeois-democratic revolution still was that "the rural proletariat must fight *together with* the rich peasantry for the abolition of the remnants of serfdom." Only the completion of the bourgeois-democratic revolution would lead to the "final separation of the rural proletariat from the landholding peasantry." [14]

By 1905 the bourgeois-democratic revolution was still far from being completed. But with the peasant uprisings of that year, the Bolshevik attitude changed fundamentally. Writing in March 1905, Lenin issued a call to organize the rural proletariat in the same manner as the urban proletariat had been organized. He added: "We must explain to it that its interests are antagonistic to those of the bourgeois peasantry; we must call upon it to fight for the socialist revolution." [15] Lenin subsequently repeatedly exhorted the Bolsheviks to organize the poor peasantry, but they had little success in doing so.

The basic unit of peasant organization was the traditional village assembly. Ordinarily, rich peasants—the kulaks—controlled collective decisions made by the assemblies. In revolutionary situations, in times of violent action, however, it was the middle peasants whose militant views prevailed in the assemblies; the poor peasant remained in the background. The peasants' organization at the national level was the All-Russian Peasants' Union, which was also largely under kulak influence. At its first congress in the summer of 1905, "the delegates themselves indicated that in most places the work of organizing the peasants had hardly begun as yet." [16] The political leadership of the peasantry was in the hands of the Social Revolutionaries, who primarily represented the rich peasants. The Bolsheviks never quite managed to get a firm foothold among the peasantry.

By 1917 we find Lenin more cautious and less certain about the possibility of organizing the poor peasantry independently. In his historic "April Thesis" he stated:

> Without necessarily splitting the Soviets of Peasants' Deputies at once, the party of the proletariat must make clear the necessity of organizing separate Soviets of Poor (semi-proletarian) Peasants, or, at least, of holding constant separate conferences of peasant deputies *of this class status* in the shape of separate fractions or parties within the general Soviets of Peasants' Deputies.

He was, however, by no means confident that this task would be accomplished; in the "April Thesis" he continues:

> At the present moment we cannot say for certain whether a powerful agrarian revolution will develop in the Russian countryside in the near future. We cannot say exactly how profound is the class cleavage within the peasantry. . . . Such questions will be, and can be, decided only by actual experience.[17]

The pattern of peasant upheaval which did develop in 1917 is rather complex. There were two sets of struggles—between peasants and landlords and among the peasants themselves—where the alignments cut across each other. The main peasant struggle in 1917, as in 1905–1907, was that of middle peasants against landowners for the cutoff lands and for the abolition of the surviving feudal restrictions. The intervening years had been relatively quiet. Now, once more, peasant struggle was precipitated by the decay of agriculture, the depletion of stocks and food shortages, and the high prices of goods. This time the struggle was more intense and violent than in the earlier period; in some respects, but only occasionally, it was more advanced in character.

A factor which possibly contributed to the greater militancy of the middle peasant in the second period was the fact that Stolypin's agrarian policy, in the intervening years, had loosened many of the feudal bonds which had tied down the middle peasant, thus giving him the taste of more freedom. Also, Bolshevik ideas had had a big impact on the soldier, the peasant in uniform, who participated with the industrial worker in making the socialist revolution. Deserters returning to the countryside from the front carried with them the ferment of new ideas and an attitude of militancy.

Now, as before, the struggle was concentrated on the meadows and forests; the most frequent forms of action consisted of seizures of hay and wood. More manors were looted and burned than before. An advance on the previous situation, however, was that in some cases village land committees (set up by the provisional government to mediate disputes between peasants and landlords) became vehicles for the seizure and distribution of land. Maynard suggests that "there was, paradoxically, a certain system, even a certain order, in the proceedings. Peasants did not seize the land which had not been cultivated by them or their forebears." [18] It is more likely that in actual practice the proceedings were not quite so orderly as Maynard imagines; there was little to stop the peasants from taking an optimistic view of their claims, except the competing claims of their fellows. However, the fact that the peasant, even in revolution, invoked only his claim to what was rightfully his reflects his conservative respect for private property and the fact that, in the main, the seizures of land were confined to the cutoff lands. Once again the middle peasant was in the forefront of the struggle. The attitude of the kulak remained, as before, a contradictory one: fear and even hostility combined with not-too-reluctant participation in sharing the loot. The rural proletarians similarly joined with the others in the looting, but did not emerge as an independent force and did not rise against their masters, the kulaks.

There was another, quite distinct, struggle in the rural districts, in which the middle peasant found himself mostly in conflict with the other two sections of the peasantry. This was the struggle of those who wished to preserve the communes against the "separators." During the inter-revolutionary years legislation had been promulgated providing for the dissolution of repartitional tenure in communes and for the establishment of hereditary holdings, which would make possible the establishment of individual farms free from communal restrictions. The pressure to break up the communes came from the enterprising "communal kulaks" (the other kulaks held their land outside the communes) who wished to be free from communal restrictions. It also came from the poor peasants whose tiny holdings served only to tie them to the village but gave them no livelihood. The middle peasant, however, had little to gain and much to lose by a breakdown of the commune. He staunchly opposed the "separators," and passions ran high. The middle peasants often resisted successfully the attempts to "separate," and in many cases peasants who had left were forced to return and pool their land again. Thus in these cases the middle peasants were once again the effective force in the village.

These divisions and conflicts among the peasantry evidently did not allow the formation of "revolutionary peasant committees," as Lenin had urged. The peasant Soviets, where they existed at all, existed at the county and provincial level and were mostly dominated by right-wing Social Revolutionaries, the spokesmen of the kulaks. The role of the peasantry in the revolution was an indirect one, though by no means an unimportant one. The Bolshevik formula was that they seized power in alliance with the peasantry as a whole. If the role of the peasantry must be called an "alliance," it was, from the side of the peasantry, undeclared, unorganized, and without a clear direction. Moreover, it could hardly be called an alliance with "the peasantry as a whole," for the peasantry was deeply divided. In a later controversy Stalin argued that the proletarian revolution was carried out by the proletariat "together with the poor peasantry." He supports this by quoting Lenin's repeated post-1905 calls for mobilizing the poor peasantry. As we have seen, this does not mean that the Bolsheviks actually succeeded in achieving that objective. Lenin's own postrevolutionary assessments make it quite clear that this was not so.

In October 1918, looking back on the experience of the Revolution, Lenin explained the Bolshevik failure to mobilize the poor peasants:

> Owing to the immaturity, the backwardness, the ignorance, precisely of the poor peasants, the leadership [in the Soviets] passed into the hands of the kulaks. . . . A year after the proletarian revolution in the capitals, and under its influence and with its assistance, the proletarian revolution began in the remote rural districts.[19]

But why did the Bolsheviks fail to break down the backwardness and ignorance of the peasantry, despite at least a decade of commitment to just that task? Lenin perceived that the true explanation lay beyond the subjective factor. He became aware of the existence of what we have referred to as the necessary preconditions for the mobilization of the poor peasantry—although he expressed it in a form which refers only to the Russian experience. Thus, in 1920, he referred to such preconditions as a truth which has been fully proved by Marxist theory and fully corroborated by the experience of the proletarian revolution in Russia, viz. although all the three above enumerated categories of the rural population (i.e. the rural proletariat, semi-proletarians and small peasants) . . . are economically, socially and culturally interested in the victory of socialism, they are capable of giving resolute support to the revolutionary proletariat only *after* the latter has won political power, only *after* it has resolutely dealt with the big landowners and capitalists, only *after* these downtrodden people see in practice that they have an organized leader and champion, strong and firm enough to assist and lead them and show them the right path.[20]

Lenin was generalizing here from the Russian experience; he was not elaborating a Marxist text. The Chinese experience, as well as examples from India, show us, however, that the prior seizure of state power by the proletariat is only one of several alternative forms in which the necessary preconditions for the mobilization of the poor peasantry may be realized.

II

The Chinese Communist Party set out on its revolutionary course in the Leninist tradition. But in the first few years of its life its work was concentrated largely on the urban proletariat and on students and intellectuals; very little was done among the peasantry. Jane Degras quotes a report of the Executive Committee of the Comintern according to which, in 1926, the working class membership of the CCP was 66 percent of the total and peasant membership no more than 5 percent.[21]

It was also among the industrial proletariat that Mao Tse-tung began his work, to use his own words, as a "practical Marxist." As secretary of the Hunan party he organized miners, railway workers, municipal workers, etc. He did very little work among the peasantry at the time, and it was not until 1925 that he became aware of their revolutionary potential. "Formerly," he told Edgar Snow, "I had not fully realized the degree of class struggle among the peasantry. But after the May 30 (1925) incident, and during the great wave of political activity which followed it, the Hunanese peasantry became very militant. I . . . began a rural organization campaign." [22] A new chapter had opened in the history of Chinese communism.

Peasant riots and uprisings were endemic in China at the time. Several factors had precipitated such a situation. Perhaps the most important was the constant civil war among warlords and the excessive taxes and levies extracted by them as well as by government tax collectors. Another factor of some importance was that in those "troubled times" many of the old "gentry" had moved to urban centers and were no longer present in the village to exercise their direct personal authority, which they had enjoyed by virtue of their wealth as well as traditional social status. The removal of the men who had exercised on-the-spot power loosened social control in the villages, enabled the peasants to gain more confidence, and allowed peasant militancy to develop. However, perhaps the most decisive factor lay in the operations of the Revolutionary Army, which had been established in 1923 by the Kuomintang government of Dr. Sun Yat-sen, with the support of the Chinese Communists and with help from the Soviet Union. In February 1925 the Revolutionary Army launched its First Eastern Expedition, the first of several against the warlords. This was followed by the Southern Expedition and, in the summer of 1926, by the famous Northern Expedition. It is significant that on the eve of the Northern Expedition nearly two-thirds of the nearly one million members of the peasant associations were in Kwangtung province,[23] one of the principal areas of operation of the Revolutionary Army during the Eastern and Southern expeditions.

The peasant movement was not created by the Communist Party or by the genius of one man. Mao was drawn into the peasant movement only after it had already begun. But Mao's organizing genius enabled it to reach new heights. In 1925 he began to train cadres for the peasant movement at the Institute of the Peasant Movement. At the end of the year he took his students to Hunan, established contacts with active elements among the peasantry, and set up peasant associations in the townships. A solid foundation was laid to provide leadership and organization for the peasant movement so that when it arose again in the following year, it arose with full force.

Mao summed up his experience of the peasant movement in two essays that are regarded as classics of Maoism. The first was an article entitled "An Analysis of the Various Classes of the Chinese Peasantry and Their Attitudes Toward Revolution,"[24] published in January 1926. The other was the celebrated "Report of an Investigation into the Peasant Movement in Hunan," written a year later. Stuart

Schram has pointed out what at first sight appears to be a rather curious "deviation" from the Marxist-Leninist orthodoxy in the original versions of these two texts. In the original versions the leading revolutionary role of the industrial proletariat is not specifically mentioned; appropriate references to that effect were not added until 1951. Does this mean that at this stage Mao had abandoned the basic principle of Marxism-Leninism, the principle of proletarian revolutionary leadership? In his analysis of Maoism, Isaac Deutscher has referred to the fact that "Mao . . . recognized more and more explicitly the peasantry as the sole *active* force of the revolution, until to all intents and purposes he turned his back on the urban working class." [25] But this, as Deutscher has shown, came later. It came after the defeat of the revolution when, following the autumn-harvest uprising of 1927, Mao and his comrades, with the core of what later became the Red Army, marched to the Chingkang Mountains and established a revolutionary base there. At first, as Deutscher has argued, the "withdrawal into the countryside" was thought to be only a temporary strategy, a marking of time until conditions for an urban insurrection revived. It was only "gradually [that Mao] became aware of the implications of his move." In 1926, thus, the point of departure of Maoism had not yet arrived. And it came two years later, not as a premeditated change of strategy but as one that was imposed by the logic of the situation.

To return to Schram's point, what explanation can we find of Mao's omission, in 1926 and 1927, of references to the leadership of the proletariat? Schram's explanation is that "Mao's position at this time constitutes neither orthodox Leninism nor a heresy *beyond* Leninism, but rather the gropings of a young man who has not yet thoroughly understood Lenin." He continues: "The Hunan Report is neither 'orthodox' nor 'heretical' Leninism; it is essentially a-Marxist." [26] Such a contention is quite untenable. It was his understanding of Marxism that led Mao, son of a peasant, to spend his early years of revolutionary work among the urban proletariat. Moreover, the issue of proletarian leadership in the revolution was a central issue in the CCP at the time. One cannot presume that the question was simply not in Mao's mind. However, two facts may suggest an explanation. First, if Mao had brought up the issue of the leadership of the revolution, he could hardly have avoided a frontal attack on the view then being put forward by the Comintern; evidently, young

Mao did not wish to take that course. Second, the two documents were written in the heat of a controversy in which Mao wished to establish "the agrarian revolution as constituting the main content of the Chinese bourgeois-democratic revolution and the peasants as its basic force." [27] He did no more in these documents than portray the revolutionary potentialities of the different sections of the peasantry. He did not engage in a theoretical analysis of overall revolutionary strategy. Moreover, it should be added that there is nothing in these documents to compare with the careful and detailed analysis Lenin made of the processes which were transforming Russian rural society. Mao learned his lessons in the field; the essence of his thought must be sought in his revolutionary practice rather than in writings, which do not always reflect accurately his own practice insofar as he had to pay lip service to Comintern orthodoxy in order to gain the freedom to follow the demands of the Chinese situation. Mao the "theoretical Marxist" had a role which did not always coincide with that of Mao the "practical Marxist."

The paradox of Mao is exemplified particularly by his attempt to make the facts of the Hunan Movement fit Comintern orthodoxy by the simple device of redefining categories, as we shall see below. In his Report Mao was at pains to demonstrate that both the leadership and the main force of the peasant movement came from the poor peasantry, which, in theory at least, made the facts of the Hunan Movement fit Stalin's conception of what was to be expected. But to appreciate the true character of the Hunan Movement, we must briefly consider the pattern of China's rural society and the main problems of the peasantry.

Capitalist farming had not yet developed in China, as it had in Russia. According to figures given by Mao, the size of the agricultural proletariat in China was less than 2 percent of the total number of peasants.[28] There were thus two main sectors of the rural economy. One was dominated by landlords, who controlled a large proportion of the land (Mao says 60–70 percent) that was cultivated by the poor peasants, i.e., sharecroppers, who had no land or very little land. Big landlords, those who owned more than 500 *mou* (i.e., 83 acres), were less than 0.1 percent of the rural population. Small landlords made up 0.6 percent of the rural population. The "semi-proletariat," who worked for them, consisted, according to Mao's classification, of: (1) semi-landholders (16 percent), who owned too little land for their subsistence; (2) sharecroppers (19 percent), who owned no land but owned the implements, etc., with which they worked the landlords' lands; and (3) the poor peasants (19 percent), who owned neither land nor implements. The other sector was that of the independent peasant landholders, i.e., the middle peasants (38 percent), whom Mao further classifies into three subclasses: (1) those with an annual surplus (3.7 percent of the total peasantry); (2) those who were just self-sufficient (19 percent); and (3) those who had an annual deficit (15 percent).

Three problems dominated the Chinese countryside. The first was that of putting an end to the exploitation of the landlords, or at least of easing its burden by reducing the share of the crop taken by them. Then there was the problem of rectifying the very uneven distribution of land among cultivators, providing secondary employment in order to relieve pressure of population on land, and improving the level of technique so that all cultivators could enjoy a reasonable livelihood. The solution to that problem would have to await the socialist revolution. Finally there was an immediate problem, one that in fact gave rise to the peasant movement and determined its character: the problem of the excessive demands made by warlords and tax officials on the peasantry. The aftermath of Yuan Shih-kai's unsuccessful attempt to restore the monarchy in 1916, the revolt of the generals which had thwarted it, and the constant imperialist intervention and intrigue resulted in a collapse of governmental authority. The warlords became a power in the countryside and began to dominate it. Before that time, prudence had restrained the landlords and the government from raising their demands on the peasantry beyond the limits of endurance, but there were no limits on the warlords. Everyone in the village was affected by their excessive demands, except for those big landlords who were in league with them.

Despite the continued extortions of the warlords, no major peasant movement arose to resist them until the various expeditions smashed the power of the warlords and their allies in the villages and the peasant uprisings began. The aims of the peasant movement that arose in 1926 went little beyond putting an end to the extortions by the warlords and their local allies. "The peasants attack as their main targets the local bullies, bad gentry and lawless landlords, hitting in passing against patriarchal ideologies and institutions, corrupt officials in the cities and evil customs in the rural areas." [29] In those words Mao gave the gist of the achievements of the Hunan Movement of 1926–1927, which he describes in some detail in his Report.

Of all the actions of the peasantry described by Mao in his Report, the weakest are dealt with under the heading of "Dealing Economic Blows Against Landlords." The central issue here, as we pointed out, was that of reducing, or indeed abolishing, the landlords' rent. Mao claims that the peasants' associations succeeded in preventing *an increase* in rent! Surely, in a revolutionary situation, there should have been no question of the landlords even thinking of increasing the rents further. Mao then adds that *after November* the peasants went a step further and began to agitate for a reduction in rent. But this was after the autumn harvest and the year's rent had already been collected. At that late stage, even if a demand for rent reduction was voiced by a few peasant organizers, it had no immediate practical value. The fact that the peasants' associations had not yet begun to challenge the fundamental class positions of the landlords is also indicated by Mao's reference to the fact that many landlords were trying to join the peasants' associations! Again, there is a suggestion made by Mao in his original essay, "Analysis of the Various Classes of the Chinese Peasantry," that some of the small landowners could be "led toward the path of revolution." [30] What kind of "revolution" could that be? It is clear that the movement aimed at little more than smashing the power of the warlords and their local allies, whose victims included, of course, the smaller landlords.

Landlords preserved not only their economic positions but also their armed forces. One of the achievements Mao claimed for the peasant movement in his Report is the "overthrowing of the landlords' armed forces." But what we actually find under this head is a tacit admission that, by and large, the landlords' militias continued to exist. What is said here is only that their armed forces had largely "capitulated" to the peasant associations and were "now upholding the interests of the peasants"! It is only with respect to "a small number of reactionary landlords" that the Report says that such forces would be taken over from them and "reorganized into the house-to-house regular militia and placed under the new organs of local self-government under the political power of the peasantry." It is evident that the continued existence of the armed power of the landlords, as well as their hold over the sections of the peasantry directly dependent on them economically—the sharecroppers, etc.—prevented the peasant movement from becoming a peasant revolution and brought about its subsequent collapse.

In the Hunan Report, Mao emphasizes repeatedly that both the leadership and the main force of the movement came from the poor peasantry. If the poor peasants had in fact provided both the leadership and the main force of the moment, it is inconceivable that such demands as the reduction and the abolition of rent would not have come to the forefront of the struggle. After all, that would not have antagonized the middle peasantry; indeed, it would have found support among them. And the landlords were only 0.7 percent of the rural population: in fact, it was their economic power and their hold over the poor peasantry which gave them power in the countryside. The demands put forward in the peasants' movement were those which affected the middle peasants far more than the poor peasants. The landlords, while exploiting the tenants to the limit, adopted a paternal attitude toward them and even afforded them some protection against extortions by such third parties as warlords and tax men. On the other hand, the independent smallholders, the middle peasants, stood exposed and weak, and were the principal victims of the warlords and tax men. More than the poor peasants, the middle peasants could squeeze out a surplus of income, and this marked them as the more likely victims of extortion.

In fact, when Mao uses the term "poor peasant" in the Hunan Report, he redefines it in such a way as to include some middle peasants. The original eleven categories of the rural population, as described in his January 1926 article, were, in the Hunan Report, compressed into three categories. In doing so, he included under the term "poor peasants" not only the peasantry directly exploited by the landlords, but also a section of the independent smallholders, the middle peasants. He says in the Hunan Report that the poor peasants were about 70 percent of the peasantry. This figure could be arrived at only by totaling the following categories, as described by Mao earlier: (a) farm laborers, 2 percent; (b) poor peasants, 19 percent; (c) sharecroppers, 19 percent; (d) semi-landholders, 16 percent; and (e) the poorer section of the independent peasant smallholders, 15 percent. But only the first three categories can be properly called poor peasants. The category of semi-landholders is an intermediate category, for their landholdings were too small for an independent livelihood and they had to depend on other sources to supplement their income. Peasants in the last category are middle peasants and not poor peasants.

Mao's redefinition of the term "poor peasants" is only implicit in his altered statistics; he does not describe his new categories in any detail. But by including a section of the middle peasants under the label of poor peasants, he gave at least a formal validity to his statement that the leadership and the main force of the movement came from the poor peasants. This only confused the issue. It is a spurious confirmation of his earlier prediction that the poor peasants were the most revolutionary, and is understandable only if we consider the fact that such a characterization of the movement made it acceptable in terms of Comintern (Stalinist) orthodoxy, which called for an alliance of the proletariat and the poor peasantry. The Report was written in the heat of party controversy, and evidently Mao was more preoccupied with the task of swinging party opinion on the subject than with formal niceties. Unfortunately, the supposed militancy and the leadership said to have been shown by the poor peasantry in the Hunan Movement have been made into a myth which glosses over the actual practice of the Chinese Communists and, indeed, Mao's own many statements in later years which contradict it. If anything is to be learned from the Chinese Revolution, we must turn away from this myth.

The poor peasantry were mobilized only after a new phase of the Chinese Revolution opened with the establishment of a red base in the Chingkang mountains, after the successful counter-revolution led by Chiang Kai-shek in 1927 forced the Communists to take refuge there. Under the umbrella of Red power, albeit in a very small area, the peasant revolution went a step forward. In the light of his new experience Mao came to the conclusion that "positive action is taken in the village against the intermediate class (i.e., small landowners) only at a time of real revolutionary upsurge, when, for instance, political power has been seized in one or several counties, *the reactionary army has been defeated a number of times, and the prowess of the Red Army has been repeatedly demonstrated.*" [31] Echoes of Lenin, 1920!

The creation of the Red Army was a decisive factor in the new situation. The Red Army did not, however, arise spontaneously out of the peasant movement, although its intimate relationship with the peasantry gave it its special character. The nucleus of the Red Army came from sections of the Kuomintang Revolutionary Army that had come over to the Communist side after the counter-revolution. Thus relatively well-trained, experienced, politically educated fighting units provided an essential core. One might contrast their situation with that of the armed forces of the Telengana Communists in India who were suppressed, after some brave fighting no doubt, by the Indian forces (who took three years to do it though). The Chinese Red Army was able to fight back against the far greater forces deployed against them.

Another factor which made possible the creation and the building up of the Red Army in China was that armed conflict had been endemic in China for at least a decade. In most villages there were armed units, although they were controlled by the landlords. Their importance and character are indicated by Martin C. Yang, a social anthropologist, in his description of a prerevolutionary village in Shantung province: "The first village-wide organisation [was] the village defence programme. . . . Wealthy families [were] expected to equip themselves with rifles . . . etc. . . . The very poor [were] asked for nothing except that they behave themselves and obey the defence regulations." [32] Although the village self-defense units were controlled by landlords, they had accustomed the peasants to the idea of arming themselves. Many of the village militias could also be taken out of the power of the landlords and absorbed in the Red Army. Moreover, the Red Army fitted easily into the rural setup. The people were accustomed to bear the burden of maintaining armies, and the burden of the Red Army fell lightly on their shoulders. It created conditions for the emancipation of the peasantry from extreme exploitation, and it drew its tribute from the exploiters rather than the exploited.

Finally, a factor of no mean importance was the collapse of central authority, which could not act immediately and swiftly to destroy the nucleus of the Red Army. When the blows finally came, backed with all the might and the resources of imperialism, the Red Army not only survived but was eventually victorious largely because of the existence of mass movements and the active support of the people. The actions of the proletariat in areas under Chiang Kai-shek, actions that impeded and sometimes disorganized his machinery of repression, were also no doubt of great value.

From the nucleus of the red base in the Chingkang Mountains the

revolution developed. With all its vicissitudes, it extended and deepened until it had transformed the whole of China. The progress of
the revolution and the precise content of the agrarian changes at its
different stages is a long and complex story that we can hardly attempt to survey in these pages.[33] But one crucial aspect needs to be
noted: land reform was implemented by peasant committees and not
by a Communist bureaucracy. Thus the implementation of the land
reform varied at different times and at different places; it reflected
the unevenness in the growth of revolutionary consciousness and in
the organization of the peasantry in different areas of the country, as
well as changes in the overall strategy of the Communist Party that
were determined by a number of factors, one of which was the rate at
which the revolutionary movement was going forward. But more
than the changing scope of the land reform at different stages, what
interests us particularly is the actual process by which it was carried
out.

The success of Mao and the Chinese Communists in bringing
about a revolutionary mobilization of the peasantry lay in their subtle dialectical understanding of the respective roles of the middle
peasants and the poor peasants. The task confronting them was to
raise the level of revolutionary consciousness of the poor peasantry, a
task that called for skill as well as much devoted effort. This was necessary precisely because the poor peasants were initially the more
backward section but were, at the same time, potentially the more
revolutionary section of the peasantry. On the other hand, Mao and
his comrades had to take full account of the fact that it was the middle peasant who was initially the more militant and his energies had
to be mobilized fully in carrying forward the initial thrust of the
agrarian revolution. Precisely because the middle peasants were not
a revolutionary class, the revolutionary initiative had to be maintained independently of them by the revolutionary leadership, while
fully utilizing their energies, and without antagonizing them. This
initiative was then to be carried forward to a second stage of the
agrarian revolution by the newly aroused poor peasants. Mao and
his comrades showed, in practice, a masterly understanding of this
dialectic. Yet in some of Mao's formal texts it seems to be missing altogether. The poor peasant is depicted as spontaneously and uncon-
ditionally playing a revolutionary role, a picture that obscures the
crucial role of the Communist Party as a party with a proletarian

revolutionary perspective, and of the Red Army which broke the existing structure of power in the village and prevented the Chinese revolution from degenerating into an ineffective peasant uprising.

It was during the period 1950–1953, with the consolidation of Communist rule, that a major wave of land reform set in motion a new dynamic in the rural society of China and transformed the face of the countryside. Embodying the lessons learned in the struggle, on the eve of this final phase the Agrarian Reform Law and related regulations were promulgated; these were explained in a report made by Liu Shao-chi.[34] While correctly emphasizing the need to mobilize the poor peasants, we see here a concern that the party cadres should appreciate the role of the middle peasants, especially at an early stage of the proceedings. The importance that was attached to the middle peasant was made even more clear in the speech of Teng Tse-hui, Director of Rural Work of the CCP, at the Eighth Congress of the CCP in 1956. He said:

> If we had confined our attention to relying on the poor peasants and neglected to unite with the middle peasants, if we had not firmly protected the interests of the middle peasants during the land reform . . . or, if we had not made efforts to draw the representative figures among the middle peasants into the leadership of the peasants' associations and cooperatives, *then our Party as well as the poor peasants would have been isolated* . . .[35]

A mere recognition of the role of the middle peasants, drawing them initially into the leadership of the peasants' associations and fulfilling some of their immediate demands, might not in itself have enabled the agrarian movement to develop further and enter the next stage, the stage of proletarian revolution. The success of Chinese agrarian policy lay precisely in following a dialectical strategy, ensuring at each stage that conditions were created for a further advance to the next stage.

The actual process by which this was achieved is described very vividly in two studies by social anthropologists, whose findings corroborate each other and are in turn corroborated by the general conclusions drawn by Teng Tse-hui in his above-quoted speech. One of the two studies is by David and Isabel Crook, pro-Communist Anglo-Saxons who work in China. The other is by an anti-Communist Chinese, C. K. Yang, who works in the United States.[36] Yang gives a picture of a village newly liberated by the Red Army: "Their first task was to 'set the masses in motion' in order to develop a situation of 'class struggle,' the basic step being to select 'active elements' amongst the peasants to serve as a core for the organization of the peasants' association and the new 'people's militia.'" Yang shows that middle peasants were initially selected to head the peasants' association and the militia "primarily because they had been active in village affairs." He argues, however, that "the selection of these [middle peasants] to lead the vital new peasants' association primarily on the basis of their active part in village affairs appeared to deviate from the official Communist policy of using only elements from the poor peasants and agricultural laborers as the core of the new village leadership." [37] This is precisely where Yang betrays his lack of understanding of Communist policy. It would have been all too easy for local party officials to nominate individual poor peasants to these posts and to issue directives in their name. But that would not have brought into being a vigorous peasant movement in which the poor peasants *as a class* could play an active role. Precisely for this reason, the regional and local authorities in China were under orders not to carry out land distribution by force or by mere orders, but only in accordance with the decisions of the peasants in each village and in conformity with local conditions. After peasant associations were established, initially under middle peasant leadership, Communist Party cadres encouraged poor peasants to press their demands, both through their representatives on the peasant associations as well as collectively through demonstrations, such as one described by Yang, when "noisy angry peasants appeared at the door" of the middle peasant head of the association with their demands. It was by means of this process that the level of consciousness of the poor peasants was raised to a point where they could take the initiative in local government. Otherwise the peasants' associations might have degenerated into merely an extension of the bureaucratic apparatus.

This sequence reveals a crucial underlying condition. The energies of the poor peasants were released only after the landlords and the rich peasants were isolated (which happened as a result of the coming of the Red Army and the Communist leadership) and finally eliminated as a class as a result of land reform. Only then was a new stage in the local struggle opened up; only then did the poor peasant leadership acquire a new perspective and a new confidence and begin to come forward to displace the middle peasants. This process is the vital process which transformed the agrarian upheaval in China into a proletarian revolution. It would not have grown as it did from its agrarian base but for the crucial role played by the Red Army and the Chinese Communist Party in releasing the revolutionary energies of the peasantry. Unfortunately, the mythology about the revolutionary leadership the poor peasant is supposed to have shown right from the beginning obscures this most important feature of the Chinese Revolution, one made possible by its special conditions.

In India, to which we turn next, we find that even those peasant uprisings in which, for a variety of reasons, the poor peasant had played an important part could not develop into a proletarian revolution.

III

The situation in India at the turn of the century was different from that of China. In India, inter-imperialist rivalry had long ended with the supremacy of the British. No warlords or private armies roamed the Indian countryside. The rising nationalist movement, with its modest constitutional aims, did not seek to arm itself as Sun Yat-sen's Kuomintang had done. Until the 1920s the nationalist movement stood isolated from the potent forces of the peasantry, although there had been much peasant unrest and occasional uprisings. Nor was there that crucial contact between the Indian nationalists and the Soviet Union which played such an important role in China, although the Russian Revolution had had a big intellectual impact on the minds of many young nationalists such as Nehru.

The radicalization of the nationalist movement in India just before and especially after World War I increasingly began to draw the masses into the movement. Gandhi, above all, who emulated the simple life of the peasants, spoke their language, and engaged in symbolic activities which captivated their imagination, played a vital role in mobilizing peasant support for the Indian National Congress. But if he made the peasant speak for the Congress, he did little to make the Congress speak for the peasant. When in 1921, during the first Civil Disobedience Movement, the peasant began to extend the struggle against British imperialism to a struggle against the landlord and the moneylender, Gandhi invoked the principle of nonviolence to call an abrupt halt to the movement. He was not prepared to do more than to back, at certain times, a call to the peasantry to refuse to pay taxes, a slogan which evaded the issue of class exploitation in the village but was strong enough to rouse the peasantry. But his most powerful appeal to the peasantry was through the millennial concept of "Ram Rajya" (God's Kingdom), which would be established in India after the expulsion of the British.

Gandhi's accent on the peasantry in his political language did, however, lead many middle class intellectuals to "go to the people," very much in the spirit of Russian populism. The effect of this is described by Nehru:

> He sent us to the villages and the countryside hummed with the activity of innumerable messengers of a new gospel of action. The peasant was shaken up and he began to emerge from his quiescent shell. The effect on us was different, but equally far reaching, for we saw for the first time, as it were, the villager. . . . We learnt.[38]

The growth of an urban working class movement, the new involvement with the peasantry, the ferment of new ideas—especially the impact of the Russian Revolution—and the disillusionment with the Congress after Gandhi's decision to halt the Civil Disobedience Movements of 1921 and of 1930, each time precisely when the movement was gathering momentum, caused many middle class intellectuals to shift leftward in their outlook. In 1934 the Congress Socialist Party was constituted within the parent organization. Several streams of ideas had influenced the young Socialists, but in its early stages the influence of Marxist thinking was strong. Although the Socialists had begun to take an interest in the problems of the peasantry, they concentrated on fighting within the Congress for a recognition of peasant demands rather than on mobilizing the peasants themselves to fight for their demands. Isolated peasant struggles did, however, develop from their local roots, and some assumed major importance. But little progress had yet been made to build up a class organization of the peasantry.

The Communist Party of India (a unified Communist Party began to take shape only in the thirties) had, in the twenties, concentrated mainly on organizing the industrial working class. The peasant upheavals of the 1920s did not produce a fresh orientation, as in China.

During the Civil Disobedience Movement of the thirties, when it could have developed peasant struggles, the Communist Party found itself crippled and isolated both because its main leadership was in prison, following the Meerut conspiracy case, and because the Comintern line at the time did not permit its participation in a movement led by the Indian bourgeoisie. Thus the Communist Party did very little work among the peasantry precisely at a time of ferment because of the economic crisis of the thirties and the impact of the Civil Disobedience Movement throughout the country.

In 1936 the Congress Socialist Party decided to admit Communists to membership. The coming together of the Left forces was the background to the setting up in 1936 of the All-India Kisan Congress, later renamed the All-Indian Kisan Sabha (Peasant Congress). Two other groups of peasant leadership also joined (and later contended along with the Socialists and the Communists in the AIKS). These two groups, along with the Socialists, spoke for the rich peasant and the middle peasant and eschewed struggle for the special demands of the poor peasants. Thus Professor Ranga, one of their leaders, spoke of a "common front to be put up by both the landed and landless *kisans*" and of the "common suffering of all classes of the rural public." [39] The Socialist Acharya Narendra Deva made this even more explicit in his presidential address to the AIKS Conference in 1938:

> Our task today is to carry the whole peasantry with us. . . . If romantic conceptions were to shape our resolves and prompt our actions, we would aspire to organise first the agricultural laborer and the semi-proletariat of the villages, the most oppressed and exploited rural class . . . but if we do so . . . the peasant in the mass would, in that case, remain aloof from the anti-imperialist struggle.[40]

If, for the Socialists in the 1930s, the postponement of the struggle for the poor peasants was a matter of political expediency because of the primacy, as they understood it, of the anti-imperialist struggle, after independence the ideologues of Indian socialism abandoned the struggle for the poor peasant altogether. Thus Ashoka Mehta, who was Chairman of the Praja Socialist Party (heir to the Congress Socialist Party) and its most influential ideologue, wrote:

> Should the Socialists, as the Communists are wont to do wherever they are in power, foment class conflict in villages even after land-

lordism is removed and use the wide array of tactics developed from
Lenin to Mao Tse-tung to use one section against the other? . . . If
that is the line chosen, democratic rights and socialist values cannot
survive. Then must come the whole complex of communist paraphernalia: people's courts, liquidation of kulaks, forced levies and the attendant violence. The other alternative is to help the village to recover
its community solidarity and foster autonomy of the village community. . . . The organic needs of village community cannot be met by
sharpening class conflicts or party rivalries.[41]

Such an outlook acquiesces in and perpetuates the exploitation of
the poor peasant by the rich peasant.

The Communists, on the other hand, did speak of setting up a separate organization of agricultural laborers, and in the Kisan Sabha
they put a special emphasis on the organization of the poor peasantry. But in practice several factors stood in their way. First, after
the mid-1930s they were guided by the "popular front" line of the
Comintern and were not inclined to force the issue with their colleagues in the AIKS. Secondly, Indian Communists took an essentially "Menshevik" view of the revolutionary perspective in India. In
the "Joint Statement" of eighteen Communist leaders issued at the
time of the Meerut trial, an important statement of Communist policy, it was argued that because of an insufficiently developed industrial base, an indefinite period would elapse between a "bourgeois-democratic revolution," which was the immediate objective, and an
eventual "socialist revolution" in India. In effect this meant that the
task of organizing the rural proletariat and the poor peasants did not
have any special urgency. Finally, the Communists, like the others,
had to face the fact that the poor peasants, desperately exploited and
literally starving, were nevertheless too strongly dominated by their
masters to be able to emerge, in the political context of the time, as
an independent force.

Thus the main direction of Communist practice was similar to
that of the Socialists and their other colleagues in the Kisan Sabha.
They concentrated on agitation for broad peasant demands, especially for security of tenure, debt relief, and cheaper credit facilities,
etc., and sought to influence government policy rather than to bring
about direct peasant action. This tradition largely continues to this
day. But the Communists did lead many local struggles, some of
which assumed proportions of major uprisings. We shall examine

very briefly two major peasant uprisings, particularly with a view to throwing light on the respective roles of middle peasants and poor peasants.

The two major peasant uprisings occurred toward the end of World War II and in the early postwar years, with the Communist Party providing the leadership in both. Apparently, they were both movements of poor peasants and therefore could be cited as examples that contradict the thesis advanced in this essay about the role of middle peasants. However, a closer examination of the two movements shows the crucial role played by middle peasants in each case, both in providing their initial thrust and in their eventual collapse. We must point out, however, that the published material available on these movements at the moment of writing is rather limited and insufficient for an adequate historical account. But their salient features are clear enough to provide a basis for an interpretative essay such as this.

The first of these two movements was the Tebhaga movement, which arose in North Bengal, including the districts of Dinajpur and Rangpur in East Bengal and Jalpaiguri and Maldah in India; it was concentrated mainly in the region which became East Pakistan. The slogan of the movement was the demand for reduction of the proprietors' share of the crop from one-half to one-third. The "proprietors" of the land, the *jotedars*, were "occupancy tenants" who possessed transferable and heritable rights to the land, and paid a fixed money-rent to the *zamindars*, the great landlords. Over the years, the fixed money-rent had become a relatively small part of the value of the crop so that, in course of time, the *jotedars* appropriated the largest share of the crop which they extracted from the cultivators of the land, the sharecroppers. The latter were called *adhiars* or *bargadars*; the number of landless in Bengal has been variously estimated at between a fifth and a quarter of the rural population. But the Tebhaga movement enveloped the bulk of the peasantry in the areas in which it arose. The vast majority of the Bengali peasantry consists of small peasant proprietors with tiny holdings, many of whom supplement their incomes by sharecropping. The bulk of them are under a heavy burden of debt, the lenders generally being the rich *jotedars;* and any analysis of class conflict in the Bengal countryside must especially take into account the effects of usury on the situation of the middle peasants. The situation of most of them is precarious, for they live from hand to mouth and a crop failure or the death of a farm animal may easily overwhelm them. *Jotedars* are only too eager to seize their lands when they are unable to meet their liabilities. As Bhowani Sen, a Communist theoretician and leader of the Tebhaga movement, expressed it: "The middle peasant of today is the sharecropper of tomorrow." And the peasant is painfully aware of this prospect. The situation of the middle peasant in Bengal is far more precarious than in many other regions. He was, therefore, only too willing to throw in his lot with the sharecroppers in the struggle against *jotedars*.

In fact, the movement did not begin as a movement of sharecroppers: initially it was a movement of middle peasants in their own behalf, and later drew in the sharecroppers. According to Bhowani Sen, the origins of the peasant unrest which eventually led to the Tebhaga movement can be traced back to 1939. The first movement began in Dinajpur district and it was not about sharing the crop. It arose on the issue of the illegal imposts levied by the *jotedars* and their manipulation of produce markets to the detriment of the small peasants. According to Bhowani Sen:

> In this movement the *jotedar's* share of fifty-fifty was not challenged. Only illegal exactions were challenged; and by their successful struggle they put an end to them. A big victory. That happened in 1939, against the background of the War and a spontaneous rumor that the Government was going to collapse, which gave confidence to the peasants. Prices had also begun to rise. The movement was very big but did not develop further; it subsided after winning some concessions. Things were then quiet until 1943.[42]

In 1943, 3.5 million peasants perished in the great Bengal famine. Bhowani Sen points out that because the rich *jotedars* were also the principal hoarders of food grains, hatred against them was intense and universal. He writes how he was struck by the contrast between the acquiescence and resignation of the starving peasantry during the famine, when millions died without a struggle, and the later militancy of the same peasantry during the Tebhaga movement. But he does not attempt to analyze the reasons for that difference, merely ending with the comment that "the intolerable conditions of the *adhiars* (sharecroppers) awakened them to a new sense of solidarity."[43] Their condition could not have been more intolerable than in 1943 during the famine, but the Tebhaga movement started later.

According to the CP it did not start (officially) until 1946, although in fact the movement had been gathering momentum since 1945.[44] Local Communist and Kisan Sabha cadres participated in these early actions; but the Communist Party did not put its full weight into the movement until the end of the war with Japan. When they did so in 1946, the movement went forward with overwhelming force.

Although the great famine found the peasantry unprepared and unable to rise up against profiteers and food hoarders, and much food had already vanished into the cities or military stocks, many of the unique features of subsequent years which helped the rise of the Tebhaga movement arose as a consequence of the famine. First, the weak peasant organizations were disrupted and disorganized by the overwhelming calamity of the famine. The Bengal peasant, used to semi-starvation, was helpless in the face of the disaster and evidently proved too weak to fight back. When the Kisan Sabha units recovered from the initial blow, they were quickly drawn into famine relief work. It was only in the following years that a new determination gave impetus to their organization. Secondly, large numbers of students and people from the educated middle classes were drawn into the voluntary relief work during the famine and into large-scale medical relief in the following year. This brought about a new contact between the peasantry and educated youth, provided social education for both, and was a very important factor in creating new cadres for the Communist Party and the Kisan Sabha. Third, a factor of vital importance, was that, following the famine, the Kisan Sabha renewed its drive against hoarders and black marketeers of food with fresh vigor. Now its hands were stronger inasmuch as the authorities also began to view the activities of the hoarders with a fresh concern because of the magnitude of the famine as well as the fact that in the spring and summer of 1944 the Japanese had invaded Assam and parts of East Bengal. The *jotedar*, who had the food to hoard and sell on the black market, could no longer count on the connivance of the authorities. The power of the *jotedar* was thus seen by the peasant to crumble in the face of the Kisan Sabha leadership, which gave the peasant a new confidence in that leadership and in the possibility of fighting back against the *jotedars*. An additional factor was that some tribal people, such as the Hajangs of North Mymensingh, who have a long tradition of militant struggle, participated in the movement. A further significant factor was that there developed a change in the bargaining power of sharecroppers. During the famine more sharecroppers had died than peasants of any other class, because they had the least reserves with which to get through the famine. Apart from the millions who died, large numbers had drifted to towns and cities in search of work and food and did not come back. The reduction in their numbers created a relative shortage of labor. The invasion of Assam and parts of East Bengal by the Japanese and the consequent large-scale military operations in the region also opened up alternative avenues of employment for sharecroppers. Their bargaining position vis-à-vis the *jotedars* was strengthened.

In the end, however, it was the role of middle peasants that was crucial, according to the account given by Bhowani Sen. The movement had begun in Thakurgaon subdivision of Dinajpur district as a middle peasant movement against the oppression of *jotedars*. During the 1939–1940 movement, these middle peasants had been politicized and the CP had recruited many of them. The intervening years had forged them into an effective political cadre. The sons of middle peasants had little difficulty in persuading their people that their fight against the *jotedars* could succeed only if they rallied the entire rural poor. They espoused the cause of sharecroppers, which was also their own cause, for many of them supplemented their incomes by sharecropping. According to Bhowani Sen, most leading members of Tebhaga committees were middle peasants and not poor peasants, but all participated in the movement. It was difficult, he said, to hold meetings of cadres because "everyone turned up. Meetings were held in somebody's house and everyone in the village came to know, with the result that every meeting tended to become a mass meeting."

The crucial battles of the Tebhaga movement were fought at harvest time, when the crop was shared out. But the fight did not always end then because the sharecroppers had to resist attempts by *jotedars*, with the support of the police, to deprive them of their gains. This continuing struggle was led by peasant committees, which became a power in the villages. They legitimized their authority in the name of a "new Raj." As Bhowani Sen put it:

> Peasants are not happy about doing anything illegal. When they were told that *a new authority* existed, namely that of the Kisan Sabha, they came to the *Kisan Sabha* and applied for a Red Flag to be given to

them so that they too could proclaim the authority of the *Kisan Sabha* in their village and enforce the demands of the Tebhaga movement. They even "arrested" police parties in the name of the Kisan Sabha. They understood that there was now a new Raj and no longer the old one.[45]

The peasant committees began to administer the affairs of the village and to administer justice. The Muslim League government of Bengal, with the connivance and support of the Congress, tried to repress the movement and eventually succeeded. On the other hand, the League was also compelled to make the gesture of introducing a bill in the Provincial Legislature in January 1947 to legalize the two-thirds share for the sharecroppers. The bill did not become law; the *jotedars*, through both the Congress and the Muslim League, fought back.

By the summer of 1947 the movement collapsed. Bhowani Sen called to the peasants not to launch direct action that year, pleading that after independence the new governments of India and Pakistan were to be given an opportunity to fulfill their pledges to the people. It was clear to all that those promises would not be fulfilled. Bhowani Sen's call merely formalized the fact that the Tebhaga movement, which he described as "one of the biggest mass movements of our time," had come to an end.

In his article, Bhowani Sen, with much candor and political courage, lists the "Main Failings of the Leadership" in the movement. In his self-criticism he argues that the failure of the movement was due to its inability to win the support of the "middle class" and the working class. Working class "support" could have been little more than a gesture of solidarity, for its practical contribution under the circumstances of the time could not have amounted to much. His remarks about antagonizing the "middle class" are significant, for both in the beginnings of the movement, as well as in its ultimate collapse, the role of the middle peasants proved to be crucial.

Concerning the role of middle peasants, Bhowani Sen wrote:

> Many of them are poor and petty *jotedars* who, while they recognise that the system is bad, feel that they would be done for if the system is liquidated without at the same time opening other avenues for their employment. . . . We should have advised the *adhiars* (sharecroppers) to exempt petty *jotedars* from the operation of Tebhaga and concentrated against the richest and the biggest.[46]

As it stands, this argument is somewhat unrealistic. What Sen says about the plight of the small *jotedar* is only too true. But if the movement had been strong enough to force the biggest *jotedars* to accept a one-third share of the crop, it would have been very difficult indeed to dissuade the sharecroppers who tilled the lands of small *jotedars* from demanding the same. However, Bhowani Sen's argument does point to the narrow base of the movement; it failed to generate slogans that could have sustained the active participation of middle peasants who had not been unsympathetic to the movement insofar as it had challenged the power of the landlords and rich peasants.

Two major changes in the situation also made it no longer possible for the Tebhaga movement to continue. First, with the end of the war with Japan, the authorities were no longer interested in supporting the anti-hoarding drives which had weakened and demoralized the *jotedars*. The full force of the government's machinery of repression was turned on the peasantry; and the movement, with its limited class base in the village, was not able to fight back effectively. Second, a deciding factor in the situation was that whereas the peasantry in the area in which the Tebhaga movement arose, both *jotedars* as well as sharecroppers, were mostly Muslim, the cadres of the Communist Party and of the Tebhaga movement were mostly Hindu. With the approach of independence, the full force of Muslim nationalism was sweeping through Bengal, as through other areas with a Muslim majority in India. This tended to isolate the Hindu cadres. With the establishment of Pakistan, most of the Hindu cadres went over to India and the movement was virtually decapitated.

The other great peasant uprising in India since the war was the Telengana movement. In character and political objectives, it was the most revolutionary peasant movement that has yet arisen in India. The movement began rather modestly in 1946 in the Nalgonda district of Hyderabad state, which was ruled by the Nizam under British suzerainty. The movement then spread to the Warrangal and Bidar districts of the state. The Hyderabad state was dominated by a backward, oppressive, and ruthless aristocracy. The initial modest aims of the Telengana movement reflected the broad demands of the whole of the peasantry against illegal and excessive exactions of the feudal lords, the Deshmukhs and the Nawabs. One of the most powerful slogans of the movement was the demand that all peasant debts be written off.

The repression let loose by the feudal lords and their government was met by armed resistance by the peasantry. The movement then entered a new revolutionary stage. Local Communists had participated in it vigorously, although it did not receive the official sanction of the Communist leadership until later. By the time of the Second Congress of the CPI in March 1948, the Telengana movement had already entered its revolutionary phase and was one of the factors that influenced the leftward swing in the Communist Party line at the Congress.

By 1947, the Telengana movement had a guerrilla army of about 5,000. The peasants killed or drove out the landlords and the local bureaucrats, and seized and redistributed the land. They established a government of peasant "Soviets" which were regionally integrated into a central organization. Peasant rule was established in an area of 15,000 square miles with a population of four million. The movement of the armed peasantry continued until 1950; it was not finally crushed until the following year. Today the area remains one of the political strongholds of the Communist Party.

There are several special factors in the Telengana situation which at the time favored the rise of a militant peasant movement and its subsequent transformation into a revolutionary movement. The political situation in Telengana in 1946 provided the right political climate for such a movement. With the independence of India in sight, the future of the Hyderabad state and its place in the Indian Union became a dominant political issue in the state. The nationalist movements in the subcontinent of India had looked to the eventual absorption of the "princely states" in free India or Pakistan, as the case may be. Hyderabad was the largest and the richest of them all. The majority of the population, which was Hindu, as well as its geography, favored Hyderabad's union with India. The feudal aristocracy, both Hindu as well as Muslim, favored the idea of an independent Hyderabad. So did the small Muslim middle class, which had enjoyed a favored position and had fears about its future in the Indian Union. They organized armed bands, called Razakars, to fight for an independent Hyderabad under the Nizam. Kasim Rizvi, leader of the Razakars, was looked down upon by the feudal lords, who considered him to be an upstart, but they used the Razakars against the peasants when the movement arose. The leadership of the Telengana movement, in its first stages, had supported the idea of Hyderabad's union with India; the Nizam's rule and the idea of an independent Hyderabad were identified with the feudal aristocracy of the state. The peasant movement at that stage thus drew great strength from the Indian nationalist upsurge in the state. But later, when union with India seemed to be inevitable and it became clear that the government of India would deploy far larger and more effective forces against them, the Telengana leadership, in panic, switched their political allegiance to the support of the Nizam and the demand for an independent Hyderabad. The Communist Party in Hyderabad was legalized for the first time, and Communists and Razakars fought together against Indian troops. Now the movement was aligned with the forces which it had fought in the past, and it was running counter to the nationalist sentiment. This created a great deal of political confusion and split the Communist leadership of the movement. Nationalist sentiment, a powerful factor in the rise of the Telengana movement, thus became an important factor leading to its eventual downfall.

Another factor which contributed to the initial success of the movement was that the feudal aristocracy was demoralized by the fact that union with India seemed inevitable, despite its desperate bid for autonomy. The state apparatus was corrupt and inefficient. On the other hand, there was general political unrest. The peasant movement, directed against the ruling aristocracy, drew much popular support and was able to withstand repression. But later, confronted with a more powerful army of India, it also lost popular support.

The movement developed its initial momentum from the fact that its demands were broad-based and it drew in the middle peasant as well as the poor peasant. Later, when the peasant "Soviets" were established and land was redistributed, conflicts of interest between different sections of the peasantry came to the surface. Some Communists argue that this was a hasty and ill-thought-out policy which the Telengana leadership sought to impose from above, instead of preparing the ground carefully and helping the peasantry to advance the movement from below. The disruption of their peasant base proved disastrous when they were under heavy military attack.

Among the special factors which favored the rise of the Telengana movement are those which favored the guerrilla struggle. Telengana is a very poor area, much of it covered by thorny scrub and jungle, interspersed with relatively more prosperous settlements in a few favored basins with tank irrigation. It also has a substantial tribal population, among whom there is a greater sense of solidarity and fighting spirit than there is among the stratified peasant societies in richer areas. Thus when an attempt was made in 1948 to extend the movement to the neighboring rich delta region of Andhra, it failed. However, it should be added that this failure was due also to the fact that by that time the movement had moved away from its broad slogans, had become sectarian, and thus lost the support of the middle peasant. By that time the movement was also running counter to the nationalist sentiment on the Hyderabad issue.

The Tebhaga and the Telengana movements had both risen from local roots rather than from any initiatives by the Communist Party, although the Communists provided the leadership and played a vital role in both. After the Communist Party Congress of 1948, the party was committed to launching insurrectionary forms of struggle but was not able to organize any movement on the scale of the Tebhaga or Telengana movements. Between 1948 and 1952 the Communist Party was banned in many states. On the peasant front, as on other fronts, party workers were subjected to severe repression. Most AIKS workers were either in jail or underground during this period, and the organization virtually ceased to function. Despite that, local peasant unrest continued to manifest itself throughout India; but it remained localized and limited in scope. It was clear that peasant insurrections could not be launched merely by party decisions, but required certain preconditions before they could develop.

In the period that followed 1952, the Kisan Sabha and the Communist Party moved away from the idea of direct peasant action except for demonstrations and agitation. Instead, they put the emphasis on exerting pressure on the Congress government for implementing effective land reforms and on parliamentary political struggle for the Communist Party, which, if brought to power, would itself reform. At the Congress of the Communist Party in 1958 at Amritsar, the party adopted a program of "peaceful road to socialism"; at the Congress in 1961 at Vijaywada it proposed the concept of "*national democracy* as the most suitable form to solve the problems of national regeneration and social progress along the *noncapitalist path* of development." Thus the CPI now seeks to replace the present government of "*bourgeois democracy* in which the leadership of the national bourgeoisie is decisive" by a government of national democracy. The latter is to be distinguished also from "*people's democracy* in which the leadership of the working class is decisive, that leadership having won the support of the overwhelming majority of the people." National democracy is distinguished from these two other concepts by the fact that in it "the proletariat *shares* power with the national bourgeoisie." [47] This conception does not appear to be very different from that of the Praja Socialist Party, which is also prepared to share power with the Congress in the hope of consolidating the Congress's "left wing." The fundamental differences between the Praja Socialist Party and the Communists now seem to lie almost entirely in the field of international relations rather than in domestic policy. The effect of this realignment of political forces has been to limit the peasant movement to agitation about government policies instead of undertaking any direct action.

Both the Communists and the Socialists are largely in agreement with the principles of land reform adopted by the Congress. Their main criticism is directed at the manner of its implementation, which defeats its objectives. The Report of the Congress Land Reform Committee, published in 1949, is a radical document. It took as its guiding principles the elimination of exploitation and giving the land back to the tiller. It sought to establish independent peasant landholdings and, on that basis, to develop a cooperative system of agriculture. That document, however, reflected the views of the Congress's "left wing" rather than those of the main body, much less the views of the various state governments which were to undertake the land reforms. The character of the land reforms, as implemented rather unevenly in the various states over the last decade, is very different indeed from the recommendations of the Agrarian Reforms Committee. The actual result of the land reform is the subject of some controversy. The Chinese view[48] is that it has "abolished only the *political privileges* of some of the local feudal princes and *zamindari (tax farming) privileges* of some landlords," but that "the Indian feudal land system as a whole was preserved." Such a view underestimates the profound changes which have in fact taken place in the Indian agrarian economy over the last decade. Land reform in the different states of India has, in varying degrees, eliminated or limited exploitation by noncultivating landlords and has encouraged the growth of capitalist farming. The changes in the different states are too numerous and complex to permit an attempt to present them here even in outline. Moreover, although numerous studies have examined the changes in detail, an overall statistical picture of the present situation is still not available. Sulekh Gupta points to the fact that, in 1953–54, 75 percent of the peasant households operated holdings of less than 5 acres. On the other hand, 65 percent of the land was farmed by 13 percent of the households; of the latter, at the top, 3.6 percent of the households possessed 36 percent of the land.[49] Gupta points to the increasing disparity between the growing prosperity of capitalist agriculture and the stagnation and bankruptcy of the small peasant economy, in which the vast mass of the peasantry live in increasing poverty. Gupta perhaps overestimates the extent of the capitalist sector. This picture is qualified by Bhowani Sen, who, while recognizing the trend toward the growth of the capitalist sector, also points out that "the *upper limit* of employment in India's capitalist cultivation is 16 percent of the rural labor force (40 percent of the agricultural workers—the rural proletariat)."[50] The many survivals of the old system are pointed out by Sen, as well as by Kotovsky and Daniel Thorner, whose works provide a very useful survey of the land reforms.[51] The existence of survivals of the old system is also indicated by the continued emphasis in official documents, such as the Mid-Term Appraisal Report on the Third Five-Year Plan, on such questions as the problems of tenancy reform, security of tenure, regulation of rents, etc.[52]

Two aspects of land reform have a direct bearing on the question of political mobilization of the peasantry. First, an upper stratum of tenants was able to acquire ownership of land and have become employers of labor. Kotovsky argues: "Before the reforms, this stratum of tenants energetically advocated abolition of the *zamindari* system; it played an important role in the peasant movement. . . . After the reforms were put through it withdrew from active peasant movement."[53] Second, one of the principal results of the land reform has been the mass eviction of tenants, on an unprecedented scale, by landowners taking over land for "self-cultivation." These peasants, deprived of their land and livelihood, might have been expected to have become an explosive force in the countryside. The issue did greatly agitate some local Kisan Sabhas and provoke some local demonstrations, but it did not develop into a militant movement. The peasants did not launch direct action to resist eviction. Indeed, from 1955 to 1958, when the land reforms were in progress, "there was a temporary decline of the organized peasant movement." [54] In criticizing the Congress land reform, the Communist Party has criticized its bureaucratic method of implementation, which resulted in widespread evasion. The party advocated instead the implementation of the land reform through peasant committees. But their appeal was evidently directed only toward the Congress government, for they took no steps to organize direct action by the peasants for this purpose.

The prospect that is being held out to the Indian peasantry today by the Communist Party of India is one of "revolution from above" rather than "revolution from below." Although the CPI distinguishes between the "peaceful realization of the socialist revolution" and "the parliamentary way of the reformist conception," it is clear that its commitment to a constitutional struggle leaves it with few alternatives of struggle beyond agitation against the existing Congress government to mobilize electoral support. On the question of the ruling classes relinquishing power, the CPI takes this view:

> Everything will depend on whether the force of peaceful mass struggle, isolating the ruling classes, compels them to surrender or whether they hit back with their armed might. . . . The class aspect (of the struggle) consists in *exposure* of capitalism . . . *showing how* the class aspirations of the national bourgeoisie conflict with the national aspirations. [55]

As far as the peasant masses are concerned, however, the policy of agitation and "exposure" of the Congress government has met with little success and has failed to mobilize a majority of peasant votes for the Left in the several elections that have been held in the decade and a half since independence. Nor has the agitational struggle generated a force which may isolate the ruling classes and compel them to surrender. This has been the situation, notwithstanding the fact that the Communist Party has, from time to time, launched massive demonstrations in towns and in the countryside on such issues as rising prices and tax relief. Thus, one of the most successful mass demonstrations launched by the Kisan Sabhas in recent years was the 1959 struggle in the Punjab against the "Betterment Levy," a tax that was levied on the enhanced value of land which has benefited from new irrigation. But if the Kisan Sabhas have had some success in launching such *"mass* struggles," they have had little success in launching any *class* struggles of the exploited peasantry. Moreover, success in such struggle, involving the entire peasantry, has not brought in its wake any substantial increase in electoral support. The reasons for this lie in the power relationships which operate in the rural society and in the structural conditions governing the political behavior of the peasantry; these cannot be changed merely by an "exposure" of the ruling Congress Party.

The pattern of political behavior of the peasantry is based on factions that are vertically integrated segments of the rural society, dominated by landlords and rich peasants at the top, and with poor peasants and landless laborers, who are economically dependent on them, at the bottom. Among the exploited sections of the peasantry there is little or no class solidarity. They stand divided among themselves by their allegiance to their factions, led by their masters. Political initiative thus rests with faction leaders, who are owners of land and have power and prestige in the village society. They are often engaged in political competition (even conflict) among themselves in pursuit of power and prestige in the society. The dominating factions, who by virtue of their wealth have the largest following, back the party in power and in turn receive many reciprocal benefits. The opposition generally finds allies in factions of middle peasants who are relatively independent of the landlords but often find themselves in conflict with them. Many factors enter into the factional picture: kinship, neighborhood ties (or conflicts), and caste alignments affect the allegiance of particular peasants to one faction or another.[56] But broadly speaking, it does appear that in one group of factions the predominant characteristic is that of the relationship between masters and their dependents, while other factions are those of independent smallholders. The number of votes that the Left can hope to mobilize depends primarily not on the amount of agitation it conducts (although this must affect the situation partly), but on the relative balance of the factions. Above all, the decisive question here is that of winning over the votes of the large number of poor peasants and landless laborers who are still dominated by their masters. This cannot be done unless the factional structure is broken, for the allegiance of the poor peasants and the farm laborers to their masters is not merely due to subjective factors such as their "backward mentality," etc. It is based on the objective fact of their dependence on their masters for their continued livelihood. Thus it seems hardly likely, in the absence of any direct action by the peasantry or any action by a government which might break the economic power of the landlords and rich peasants, that effective electoral support can be won by the Left. This is a paradox of the parliamentary way, and a dilemma for a party which renounces direct action.

We have raised a number of questions in the above analysis. There is, however, one theme which runs through our discussion: the respective roles of the middle peasants, the independent peasant smallholders, on the one hand, and the various categories of poor peasants on the other.

We have found that the poor peasants are *initially* the least militant class of the peasantry. Their initial backwardness is sometimes explained in purely subjective terms, such as servile habits ingrained in the peasant mind over centuries or the backward mentality of the peasant, etc. But in fact we find that when certain conditions appear, the peasants are very quickly liberated from such a servile mentality. Clearly, the subjective backwardness of the peasantry is rooted in objective factors. There is a fundamental difference between the situation of the poor peasant and that of the industrial worker. The latter enjoys a relative anonymity in his employment and a job mobility which gives him much strength in conducting the class struggle. (Where the industrial worker's relative independence is reduced by such devices as tied housing, etc., his militancy is also undermined.) In the case of the poor peasant, the situation is much more difficult. He finds himself and his family totally dependent upon his master for their livelihood. When the pressure of population is great, as in India and China, no machinery of coercion is needed by the landlords to keep him down. Economic competition suffices. The poor peasant is thankful to his master, a benefactor who gives him land to cultivate as a tenant or gives him a job as laborer. He looks to his master for help in times of crisis. The master responds paternalistically; he must keep alive the animal on whose labor he thrives. When, in extreme and exceptional cases, the exploitation and oppression are carried beyond the point of human endurance, the peasant may be goaded into killing his master for this departure from the paternalistic norm, but he is unable to rise, by himself, against the system. His dependence on his master thus undergoes a paternalistic mystification and he identifies with his master. This backwardness of the poor peasant, rooted as it is in objective dependence, is only a relative and not an absolute condition. In a revolutionary situation, *when anti-landlord and anti-rich peasant sentiment is built up by, say, the militancy of middle peasants, his morale is raised and he is more ready* to respond to calls to action. His revolutionary energy is set in motion. When the objective preconditions are realized, the poor peasant is a potentially revolutionary force. But the inherent weakness in his situation renders him more open to intimidation, and setbacks can easily demoralize him. He finally and irrevocably takes the road to revolution only when he is shown *in practice* that the power of his master can be irrevocably broken; then the possibility of an alternative mode of existence becomes real to him.

The middle peasants, on the other hand, are initially the most militant element of the peasantry, and they can be a powerful ally of the proletarian movement in the countryside, especially in generating the initial impetus of the peasant revolution. But this social perspective is limited by their class position. When the movement in the countryside advances to a revolutionary stage, they may move away from the revolutionary movement unless their fears are allayed and they are drawn into a process of cooperative endeavor.

Our hypothesis thus reverses the sequence suggested in Maoist texts—although it is in accord with Maoist practice! It is not the poor peasant who is initially the leading and main force of the peasant revolution, with the middle peasant coming in only later when the success of the movement is guaranteed, but precisely the reverse. Evidently, a correct understanding of this sequence and of the nature of the conditions required to mobilize the poor peasants must be vital to the formulation of a correct strategy vis-à-vis the peasantry.

Finally, we would like to conclude by emphasizing again that our conclusions are purely tentative and are intended to open up a discussion of the problems by raising several questions rather than suggesting cut-and-dried answers. The answers will no doubt be forthcoming from a fresh spirit of inquiry and, above all, from actual experience; and they will be proved by the success of those who lead the peasant struggle.

Notes

1. Frantz Fanon, *The Wretched of the Earth* (New York, 1963), p. 48.

2. Since the initial publication of this article, these hypotheses have been corroborated by the findings of various writers. They have been re-affirmed, in particular, by Eric Wolf in his article, "On Peasant Rebellions," in UNESCO's *International Social Science Journal*, Vol. XXI, No. 2, 1969, and reprinted in T. Shanin (ed.), *Peasants and Peasant Societies* (London, 1971). Wolf has corroborated the theses in the light of the experiences of a number of other countries in his *Peasant Wars of the Twentieth Century*, 1969.

3. In the present version of this article, I have slightly elaborated, in this and the two following paragraphs, on my original statement so as to clarify this important issue which has been misunderstood by some—for example by Saghir Ahmad, whose article appears elsewhere in this volume. It is essential to emphasize that, in defining social classes, Marxists do not participate in the apparent consensus among "social scientists" which Saghir Ahmad assumes; for the Marxist concept, unlike that of academic sociology, is a "structural" concept. Secondly, Saghir Ahmad's redefinition of the terms "rich peasants" and "poor peasants," which departs, for example, from the usage adopted by Lenin or Mao, illustrates the looseness of the terminology, which lends itself to such arbitrary and idiosyncratic redefinitions. If everyone were to choose his own definition, meaningful debate would become impossible and we would have semantic chaos.

4. See Hamza Alavi, "Elite Farmer Strategy and Regional Disparities in West Pakistan," in R. D. Stevens, H. A. Alavi, and P. Bertocci (eds.), *Rural Development in Pakistan* (to be published).

5. George Lichtheim, *Marxism, a Historical and Critical Study* (London, 1961), p. 333.

6. V. I. Lenin, *Selected Works*, Vol. II (Moscow, 1947), pp. 456–457.

7. For a fuller picture readers should consult the following works: Lenin, *The Development of Capitalism in Russia* (Moscow, 1956); G. T. Robinson, *Rural Russia Under the Old Regime* (New York, 1949); and Sir John Maynard, *The Russian Peasant* (New York, 1962).

8. See J. Stalin, *Problems of Leninism* (Moscow, 1953), pp. 213–236.

9. Marx and Engels, Preface to the Russian edition of *The Communist Manifesto*, in *Selected Works* (London, 1950), Vol. I, p. 24.

10. Lenin, *Collected Works* (Moscow, 1961), Vol. IV, p. 424.

11. Ibid., Vol. VI, p. 444.

12. Robinson, op. cit., pp. 206–207.

13. Lenin, *Collected Works*, Vol. IV, p. 427.

14. See "The Agrarian Program of Russian Social Democracy" and "Reply to Criticism of Our Draft Program," ibid., Vol. VI, pp. 109–150, 438–453.

15. Ibid., Vol. VIII, p. 231.

16. Robinson, op. cit., p. 161.
17. Lenin, *Selected Works*, Vol. II, p. 37.
18. Sir John Maynard, *Russia in Flux* (New York, 1962), p. 332.
19. Lenin, *Selected Works*, Vol. II, pp. 414–417.
20. Ibid., p. 647.
21. Jan Degras, *The Communist International—Documents* (London, 1960), Vol. II, p. 336.
22. Edgar Snow, *Red Star Over China* (London, 1963), p. 157.
23. Ho Kan-chih, *A History of the Modern Chinese Revolution* (Peking, 1959), p. 100.
24. The article included in the *Selected Works of Mao Tse-tung* (London, 1955), as "Analysis of Classes in Chinese Society," and dated March 1926, is a revised and consolidated version of two articles which appeared in *Chung-kuo Nung-min* in January and February 1926. Much of value in the original article has been lost in the revised version. Our references are to the translation of the original article, as given by Stuart Schram in *The Political Thought of Mao Tse-tung* (New York, 1963), pp. 172–177.
25. Ralph Miliband and John Saville (eds.), *The Socialist Register 1964* (Monthly Review Press, New York, 1964), p. 19.
26. Schram, op. cit., pp. 28 and 33.
27. Ho Kan-chih, op. cit., p. 139.
28. The percentage figures of the various classes of the Chinese peasantry are derived from the data given by Mao Tse-tung in the original article referred to in note 25.
29. Mao Tse-tung, *Selected Works* (London, 1955), p. 23.
30. Schram, op. cit., p. 173.
31. Ibid., p. 88. (Emphasis added.)
32. Martin C. Yang, *A Chinese Village* (London, 1947), p. 143.
33. See Chao Kuo-chun, *Agrarian Policy of the Chinese Communist Party* (London, 1960).
34. *The Agrarian Reform Law of the People's Republic of China* (Peking, 1950).
35. *Eighth National Congress of the CCP*, Vol. III (Peking, 1956), pp. 182–183. (Emphasis added.)
36. David and Isabel Crook, *Revolution in a Chinese Village* (London, 1959); C. K. Yang, *A Chinese Village in Early Communist Transition* (Cambridge, Mass., 1959).
37. C. K. Yang, op. cit., pp. 143–145.
38. Jawaharlal Nehru, *The Discovery of India* (London, 1956), p. 365.
39. N. G. Ranga, *Revolutionary Peasants* (New Delhi, 1949), p. 89.
40. Acharya Narendra Deva, *Socialism and the National Revolution* (Bombay, 1946), pp. 46–47.
41. Asoka Mehta, *Studies in Asian Socialism* (Bombay, 1959), pp. 213–215.

42. Bhowani Sen, "The Tebhaga Movement in Bengal," *Communist*, September 1947, p. 130.

43. Ibid.

44. Ibid., pp. 124 ff.; also All India Kisan Sabha, *Draft Report for 1944–45* (Bombay, 1945), pp. 9–13.

45. Bhowani Sen, op. cit., p. 130.

46. Ibid.

47. G. Adhikari, "The Problem of the Non-Capitalist Path of Development of India and the State of National Democracy," *World Marxist Review*, November 1964.

48. "More on the Philosophy of Pandit Nehru," *People's Daily*, October 27, 1962.

49. Sulekh Gupta, "New Trends of Growth in Indian Agriculture," *Seminar* (New Delhi), No. 38, October 1962.

50. Bhowani Sen, *Evolution of Agrarian Relations in India* (New Delhi, 1962).

51. G. Kotovsky, *Agrarian Reforms in India* (New Delhi, 1964); Daniel Thorner, *The Agrarian Prospect in India* (Delhi, 1956) and *Land and Labour in India* (London, 1962).

52. Government of India, Planning Commission, *The Third Plan, Mid-term Appraisal* (Delhi, 1963).

53. Kotovsky, op. cit., p. 80.

54. Ibid., p. 82.

55. Adhikari, op. cit., p. 39. (Emphasis added.)

56. For reasons of space we are unable to enlarge on this question, which deserves more attention than it has received so far from the Left. The following works provide a useful introduction to this subject: Ralph Nicholas, "Village Factions and Political Parties in Rural West Bengal," *Journal of Commonwealth Political Studies*, November 1963; Oscar Lewis, *Village Life in Northern India* (Urbana, Ill., 1958), Chapter IV; T. O. Beidelman, *A Comparative Analysis of the Hindu Jajmani System* (New York, 1959); and Frederick Barth, *Political Leadership Among Swat Pathans* (London, 1959). Since the original publication of this article, we have analyzed this question further. See Hamza Alavi, "Politics of Dependence: A Village in West Punjab," *South Asian Review*, January 1971, in which we commented on Nicholas' "pluralist" thesis.

3. The Communist Movement in India

Mohan Ram

The Indian Communist movement, in existence for forty-five years, is now fragmented. It has witnessed two major splits since 1964 and presently comprises two non-Maoist parties—the pro-Moscow Communist Party of India, or CPI, and the independent Communist Party of India-Marxist, or CPI-M—a Maoist party, the Communist Party of India (Marxist-Leninist) or CPI-ML,[1] and several Maoist groups which are not parties as yet, notably the Andhra Pradesh Revolutionary Communist Committee.

Individual Maoists, as well as those belonging to Maoist organizations, have come to be known as "Naxalites," after the peasant uprisings in Naxalbari in 1967. This article attempts to sketch the development of the Maoist perspective in India, to examine the differences within the Indian Maoist movement, and to assess the prospects for a Maoist revolution.

The first split in the Indian Communist movement occurred in 1964 in the wake of the Sino-Indian border war of 1962, and was simultaneous with the international Communist schism of 1963–1964. Yet neither the Sino-Indian border conflict nor the Sino-Soviet ideological dispute was the primary cause of the split in the CPI, although the two disputes interacted, first with each other and then with an existing pattern of dissension within the CPI, thus hastening the split. The split did not, however, represent a straight Moscow-Peking polarization, for it was not directly related to issues of ideology: it had more to do with differences within the CPI over issues of program, strategy, and tactics for the Indian revolution.[2]

The CPI-M, founded in 1964 as a result of the split, was not Maoist. The Maoist perspective in the Indian Communist movement

An earlier version of this article appeared in the *Bulletin of Concerned Asian Scholars*, Winter 1972.

was developed three years later, in 1967, resulting in a split within the CPI-M itself when a large number of Maoist-oriented cadres either left the party or were expelled from it. These Maoist groups and individuals did not at first form a party of their own, but functioned within loosely knit committees. In 1969 this incipient Maoist movement in turn experienced a major split when a section formed a party (the CPI-ML), excluding, among others, the most powerful Maoist formation in the country, the Andhra Maoists.[3]

The two non-Maoist parties, CPI and CPI-M, have different bases of support. The CPI's following is widespread rather than strongly localized. Its 1971 representation of 24 in the 525-member federal parliament came from eight of India's seventeen states, including the populous and backward states of Uttar Pradesh and Bihar. The CPI-M's seats were won from the three coastal states of West Bengal (2), Kerala (4), and Andhra Pradesh (1). These states are also CPI bases, but the CPI-M is the leading party in West Bengal and Kerala, while the CPI is far smaller by comparison in these two states. In Andhra Pradesh, once a stronghold of the Communist movement, the two parties are of roughly equal strength. The CPI-M's bases are now virtually limited to West Bengal and Kerala, where support is extensive and where it has acted as a regional party by strongly espousing local issues. In these two states it stands a fair chance of winning power through the ballot box, with the help of other parties or without it. In contrast, the CPI's constituency, although limited, is spread over a larger part of the country.

In the country as a whole, the CPI has a better hold over the organized trade union movement than does the CPI-M. The CPI's following among the peasantry is nationwide, while the CPI-M has powerful peasant bases only in the two states which are its strongholds. When the CPI split in 1964, the urban elite, most of the intellectual leaders, and the trade union functionaries stayed in the CPI, while most grassroots leaders who had live links with the masses joined the CPI-M.

The basic differences between the two parties stem from their attitudes toward India's ruling class alliance and their views of the stage and proper strategy of the revolution. More specifically, they differ over the composition and leadership of the front for achieving India's democratic revolution. The approaches of the two parties are, however, similar in important ways. Both advocate peaceful transition to socialism and both participate in the country's bourgeois parliamentary system. While the CPI's commitment to peaceful transition is unconditional, the CPI-M places the burden of such transition on the class enemy; that is, it is willing to attempt peaceful transition to socialism but does not rule out the possibility that India's governing classes may, through violent repression, drive the people and the party into militant resistance. The CPI-M places greater emphasis on extra-constitutional methods than does the CPI. The contradictions between the two non-Maoist parties are nonantagonistic in that both participate in the parliamentary system and believe in peaceful transition. Similarly, the contradictions within the fragmented Maoist movement are also nonantagonistic in that all the Maoist formations reject the parliamentary system and agree on the need for a Maoist model of revolution in India. Their differences relate to the specifics.

The CPI and the CPI-M

The origins of the CPI split of 1964 date back to the party's confused understanding of the significance of India's attainment of independence in 1947. At the inaugural meeting of the Cominform in September 1947, Zhdanov made a famous speech in which he characterized the world as divided into two hostile camps and called on Communists to lead movements to oppose "the plans of imperialist expansion and aggression along every line." [4] The Indian Communists misinterpreted the Zhdanov statement to mean that in every nonsocialist country the bourgeoisie had gone over to the camp of the Anglo-American imperialists and that this new alignment of forces had created two camps facing each other in irreconcilable conflict in every nonsocialist country. The Indian Communists went further than Zhdanov and embraced the view of Kardelj, a Yugoslav speaker at the Cominform meeting, who argued that the democratic and socialist revolutions must "intertwine" and that Communists must attack not only the big bourgeoisie but the bourgeoisie as a whole. Adopting this "Tito-ite" view, the Indian Communists concluded that India was already a capitalist country (rather than semifeudal and semicapitalist) and that they should link the two stages of the revolution (democratic and socialist) into a single stage through an attack on the whole of the Indian capitalist class.

This CPI conception came under attack from the Communists of the Andhra region in south-central India, who had been leading a peasant partisan war in the Telengana districts since 1946. The Andhra Communists invoked Mao Tse-tung's *New Democracy* to justify their strategy for a two-stage revolution in India, involving a four-class alliance for agrarian revolution.[5] In fact, the first recorded debate on the legitimacy of Mao Tse-tung's teachings as part of Marxism-Leninism took place in India between the CPI's central leadership and the "peasant Communists" of the Andhra region.

In the late 1940s the Cominform had no clear line for the CPI and the Southeast Asian Communist parties, which had embarked on a series of insurrections following their own interpretations of the Zhdanov statement of 1947. But as the Cold War began to replace class struggle on the Soviet agenda, the Cominform sought a broad peace front against U.S. imperialism. In 1950 the Cominform intervened to persuade the CPI to accept a strategy of a two-stage revolution based on a four-class alliance. This was in a sense a vindication of the Andhra Communists, as opposed to the all-India leadership's anticapitalist struggle, based primarily on urban insurrection and the general strike. The Andhra Communists thus found themselves leading the CPI in 1950, and went ahead with their peasant partisan war in Telengana. Soviet foreign policy interests, however, required that the CPI abandon armed struggle in favor of peaceful constitutionalism. The Kremlin wanted to stabilize Nehru as a nonaligned ally in the peace front against imperialism, and so in 1951 the Cominform once again intervened, this time to force the CPI to abandon armed struggle.

The CPI therefore gave up armed struggle in 1951, and in 1952 took part in the country's first general elections with universal adult franchise. Its success was most spectacular in Telengana and in the adjoining Telegu-speaking districts of what was then part of Madras state, where it had recently led peasant warfare. In Hyderabad state, where Telengana lay, the CPI was illegal at the time of the elections and over 2,000 of its active cadre were in jail. Nevertheless, having contested only 42 of the 98 Telengana seats, it won 36, clinched the victory of the 10 Socialist Party candidates it had backed, and obtained about one-third of the total vote. The Congress Party, which contested all 98 seats, received about the same percentage of the vote as the CPI and won only 41 seats, 25 of which were in districts where the CPI did not run candidates. In neighboring Madras state the CPI contested only 75 out of 140 seats, yet won 41 seats and polled 25 percent of the vote; while the Congress Party, although contesting all 140 seats, polled only 30 percent of the vote. In Hyderabad and Madras alike, the CPI gains were most spectacular precisely where the party had provoked the heaviest police and military repression by leading peasant partisan warfare or guerrilla squad actions. If the vote meant anything at all, it was a clear vindication of the Andhra Maoist line of armed struggle.

Immediately after the elections the CPI found itself divided in its attitude toward the Congress Party and the Nehru government. Should it fight the Congress all-out, or should it forge a united front with "progressive sections" to fight the rightist reaction that was growing both within the Congress Party and outside it? A united front would mean supporting Nehru's foreign and domestic policies against his critics both inside and outside the Congress Party.

Soviet policies at the time had much to do with the CPI's dilemma. When, in the early 1950s, Nehru showed an anti-West orientation and strove for closer ties (including economic aid) with the socialist camp, the Soviet Union supported India as a nonaligned ally in the peace front. The CPI backed Nehru's nonalignment policy without hesitation because it served Soviet foreign policy interests. But the party remained divided on Nehru's domestic policies. Amidst this continuing CPI controversy, Moscow began seeing progressive features not only in Nehru's foreign policies but also in his domestic policies. With this shift in the Soviet attitude, India became the pivot of Soviet policy for Asia. The CPI's 1951 program had assumed that India was a semicolonial and dependent country ruled by a big bourgeois-landlord government which was collaborating with British imperialism. This formulation now came under attack from a pro-Soviet section of the CPI; it insisted that Nehru had abandoned collaboration with imperialism and had taken to peaceful cooperation and coexistence with the socialist camp. This group argued that India needed a national united front as the prelude to a government of democratic unity. Such a policy would require an emergency alliance with the Congress Party to resist the "pro-imperialist and pro-feudal" offensive.[6]

This line of thinking was later to be developed into a slogan for a "national democratic government." In December 1955, a few months before the Twentieth Congress of the Communist Party of the Soviet Union, CPI General Secretary Ajoy Ghosh outlined a program of "uniting with and struggling against the Congress" to build a national democratic front. This program implied not only the peaceful transition to socialism (a concept that was to be proclaimed at the Twentieth Congress of the CPSU in February 1956), but also the concept of national democracy (proclaimed formally through the Moscow statement of 81 Communist parties in 1960). The CPI had thus anticipated two of the most controversial formulations which were later to be commended to the international Communist movement by the Soviet leadership. The same concepts became the major ideological issues in the Sino-Soviet dispute.[7]

The Moscow declaration (1960) described the national democratic state as a form of transition to socialism, especially in the nonaligned countries of the peace zone, in which the national bourgeoisie played an objectively progressive role and deserved socialist economic and diplomatic support. The national democratic state was one that had achieved complete economic independence from imperialism and was ruled by a broad anti-imperialist front that included the national bourgeoisie. The working class was to evolve as its leader only gradually. The concept of national democracy was a corollary of the concept of peaceful transition, and India was one of the countries of the peace zone where, in the Soviet view, peaceful transition via a national democratic state was possible.[8]

The "national democracy" concept added a new dimension to the CPI's continuing struggle for a program to replace its 1951 program. As Nehru's domestic policies shifted to the right and tension mounted on the Sino-Indian border, the attitude toward the Congress Party and the Indian bourgeoisie continued to be the central issue of debate within the CPI. The debate took a predictable form: national democracy versus people's democracy. The right wing of the CPI, with Soviet backing, contended that India's bourgeois democracy could metamorphose into a national democracy. It placed heavy reliance on Soviet aid as the instrument to secure national democracy. To this the left wing countered that the bourgeoisie was compromising with domestic reaction and with imperialism, and that Soviet aid, though necessary, was being used by the bourgeoisie to bargain for more aid from the West. Rival draft programs were presented at the CPI's Sixth Congress in April 1961, and a split was averted only by the intervention of Mikhail Suslov, who headed the high-level CPSU delegation to that Congress. Suslov, anxious to preserve unity, managed to salvage the rightist line and to maneuver the Congress into shelving the issue of a new CPI program. The conflict continued behind the scenes until the CPI split of 1964.

The crucial difference between the post-split CPI and the breakaway wing which constituted itself into the CPI-M concerns the class character of the Indian state. The CPI holds that the state is the organ of the national bourgeoisie as a whole, in which, however, the big bourgeoisie is powerful and has links with the landlords. This gives rise to a reactionary tendency within the ranks of those holding state power. The CPI-M holds that the state is in the hands of both the bourgeoisie and the landlords, but that it is actually led by the big bourgeoisie, which increasingly collaborates with foreign finance capital in pursuit of the capitalist path of development.

The CPI maintains that in order to embark on the socialist road, India must complete its present anti-imperialist, antifeudal, and national democratic stage of revolution. Its program proposes an intermediate stage, the "noncapitalist path of development," as distinct from the capitalist path now being traveled by the Indian ruling classes. This stage is to be realized through a national democratic front composed of the working class, the peasantry, the rising classes of urban and rural intelligentsia, and the national bourgeoisie (excluding the monopoly bourgeoisie). The leadership of the front will be shared by the national bourgeoisie and the proletariat. This dual hegemony implies a negation of the principle of proletarian hegemony in the revolutionary front.

The CPI-M is for a narrower, people's democratic front. Its formulation is as follows: India must undergo a people's democratic phase of revolution in order to achieve radical agrarian reforms and to expel foreign capital from the country. Agrarian revolution is the axis of the people's democratic revolution. The front that will achieve the revolution, to be led by the party, will comprise the working class and the peasantry. It will have in its ranks agricultural labor and poor peasantry, and an attempt will later be made to include middle peasants. Even rich peasants may be won over through suitable tactics. Secondly, the urban and other middle classes are to be recruited to the front. From the bourgeoisie, an attempt will be made to win over the nonmonopoly section as an ally.

The character of the revolution, the starting point, is thus the same for both parties (anti-imperialist, antifeudal, antimonopoly, and democratic), but they differ over the class composition of the front for revolution. Is the national bourgeoisie a part of the front? The CPI's answer is "yes," in keeping with its commitment to the concept of national democracy. The CPI-M holds that the imperialists, the feudalists, and the monopoly bourgeoisie are all in the enemy camp. The working class, the peasantry, and the petty bourgeoisie are in the camp of the revolution. As for the nonmonopoly bourgeoisie, this section may not be wholly in the enemy camp, for it has its own conflicts and contradictions with imperialism, with feudalism, and even with monopoly capitalism. The nonmonopoly bourgeoisie cannot, however, be regarded as a "stable" partner of the revolutionary front.

The CPI maintains that the present Indian state is virtually headed by the democratic non-big bourgeoisie, but the CPI-M holds that the maturing democratic movement will come to a head-on clash with the state power of the monopolists and the landlords.

Despite their differences, the two parties have much in common and have stakes in India's bourgeois parliamentary system, in which they have chosen to function. In the short run, however, there is antagonistic contradiction between the two.

Maoism in India

Except for the brief Maoist interlude in the late 1940s in Telengana, the Maoist perspective in the Indian Communist movement did not develop until 1967. The Naxalbari peasant uprising in 1967 and a revolt by the Andhra Pradesh state unit of the CPI-M in 1968 catalyzed a split in the CPI-M and gave rise to a Maoist movement in the country.

The 1967 general elections deprived the Congress Party of its electoral monopoly. It lost office in eight of the seventeen states and could retain office at the federal level only with a greatly reduced majority in parliament. In Kerala and West Bengal, the CPI-M was the dominant partner in coalition ministries which also included the CPI. The peasant revolt in Naxalbari, led by CPI-M radicals in West Bengal, placed the CPI-M in an awkward dilemma: if the coalition ministry did not crush the uprising, it would invite dismissal by the federal government for failure to maintain law and order; but if it crushed the revolt, the party would lay itself open to the charge of compromising with the bourgeois parliamentary system and subordinating class struggle to the compulsions of survival in office.

The West Bengal government smashed the Naxalbari uprising, with CPI-M power-holders playing an active part in the suppression. As a result the CPI-M found itself at odds with the Communist Party of China, which hailed the Naxalbari revolt,[9] and the party became internally polarized over the questions of peaceful transition to socialism and participation in the parliamentary system. A large number of Maoist dissidents left the party, but did not form a new party immediately. They functioned through loosely knit district, state, and national committees which coordinated their activities. The Maoists wanted to build a party through Naxalbari-type struggles all over the country.

While being confronted with this challenge to its leadership, the CPI-M had another problem on its hands: it had to come to grips with the ideological issues that were dividing the Indian Communist movement as a whole. Since its founding, the party had delayed taking a stand on these issues, while the CPI simply adhered to Soviet positions in the dispute.[10] In August 1967, under pressure from its ranks, the CPI-M leadership took up the ideological issues and produced a draft resolution for party discussion.

This resolution covered the entire range of issues in dispute: (1) the class assessment and evaluation of the "New Epoch," (2) the issue of war and peace, (3) the concept of peaceful coexistence, (4) forms of transition to socialism, (5) the fundamental contradiction of the present epoch, (6) the contradiction between imperialism and national liberation movements, (7) the assessment of Stalin's place and role, (8) the character of the Soviet state, (9) material incentives in the Soviet Union, and (10) Soviet proposals for unity of action with the Chinese in Vietnam.

The draft rejected as revisionist the Soviet positions on all the issues except one: cooperation in Vietnam. But this antirevisionist stance did not imply acceptance of Chinese positions on the issues, which, apart from the question of unity of action in Vietnam, were not examined. In spite of its opposition to Soviet positions, the CPI-M's stance could still be seen as revisionist from the Chinese point of view.[11]

When the CPI-M leadership placed the draft before the party for ratification, there was widespread dissent. The Jammu and Kashmir unit and the Andhra Pradesh unit rejected it outright. At the all-India plenum, where the draft came up for ratification, the powerful Andhra Pradesh unit spearheaded an attack on the leadership and demanded that the issues be examined afresh in the light of Chinese positions in the dispute.[12] When the national leadership tried to discipline the Andhra Pradesh unit, the dissenters broke away, deciding to become independent and function through a state-level coordination committee. Thus, while the Naxalbari revolt catalyzed the Maoist revolt against CPI-M participation in the parliamentary system and posed the issue of armed struggle in a new perspective, the Andhra revolt crystallized Indian Maoist support of the Chinese line in the international Communist movement.

The Indian Communist movement thus witnessed its second split in four years. Shortly after the Naxalbari uprising, in November 1967, an All-India Coordination Committee had been set up within the CPI-M to accelerate the struggle against revisionism and to launch mass struggles. After leaving the CPI-M, this committee became the All-India Coordinating Committee of Communist Revolutionaries in June 1968. The AICCCR, which was committed to building a Maoist party through Naxalbari-type peasant struggles, converted itself into a party, the Communist Party of India (Marxist-Leninist)—CPI-ML, in April 1969.[13] It excluded the Andhra Maoists and many others who thought that formation of a party was premature at this stage. Peking recognized the new party immediately.

The differences between the CPI-M and the CPI-ML cover the entire range of issues regarding revolution—its stage, strategy, and tactics. The CPI-M holds that the Indian state is a bourgeois-landlord state, led by a big bourgeoisie which pursues a capitalist path while both collaborating and bargaining with foreign monopoly capital. The CPI-ML, which generally follows the Chinese view, holds that India is a semifeudal and neocolonial country; that is to say, its obsolete semifeudal social system serves as a base for United States imperialism and Soviet social imperialism and facilitates exploitation by a class of big comprador-bureaucrat capitalists who are simply pawns of imperialism. The basic task of the revolution is seen as the elimination of feudalism, comprador-bureaucratic capitalism, and imperialism. Of the major contradictions, that between feudalism and the broad masses of the people is viewed as the principal one.[14] This determines the present stage of the revolution—the democratic stage, the essence of which is agrarian revolution. The peasantry is to be the main force of the revolution, led by the working class through the medium of the CPI-ML. The working class must rely on landless and poor peasants, firmly unite with middle peasants, and win a section of the rich peasants while neutralizing the rest. Most urban petty-bourgeois and revolutionary intellectuals will be reliable allies of the revolution, while the small and middle bourgeoisie, the independent businessmen, and the bourgeois intellectuals will be its vacillating and unstable allies.

The CPI-ML seeks to build a democratic front through worker-peasant unity, to be achieved in the process of armed struggle and after red power has been established in at least some parts of the country. The path to liberation is people's war, to be waged by creating bases of armed struggle and consolidating the political power of the people through guerrilla warfare. This will remain the basic form of struggle through the period of democratic revolution.

The CPI-ML assertion that the principal contradiction is between feudalism and the broad masses of the people leaves unclear the anti-imperialist task of the democratic revolution that the CPI-ML has in view. It lays lopsided emphasis on the antifeudal task. By contrast, Maoists of the Andhra Pradesh Revolutionary Communist Committee, who are outside the CPI-ML, hold that the main contradiction is between the Indian people and imperialism (including social imperialism) in alliance with feudalism. They see imperialism and comprador-bureaucrat capitalism as the props of feudalism. The CPI-ML does not regard the national bourgeoisie as an ally of the revolution, either firm or vacillating.[15] But the Andhra Maoists want the national bourgeoisie in the front along with the workers, the poor peasantry, and the middle classes. Further, the CPI-ML is silent on the need to fight British imperialism;[16] its references are limited to United States imperialism and Soviet social imperialism. The Andhra Maoists are more specific on this point.

The major differences between the CPI-ML and other Maoist groups, especially the Andhra Maoists, relate to the tactical line, the methodology of revolution.

The first Indian attempt at working out a Maoist tactical line dates from the Naxalbari peasant struggle in 1967.[17] A year later the Indian Maoists, who were then collectively functioning through the All-India Coordinating Committee of Communist Revolutionaries, reviewed the situation and renewed the call to build a "true" communist party through Naxalbari-type struggles.[18] The AICCCR leadership innovated an unorthodox (in the Maoist context) tactical line—that the primary condition for party-building was to organize armed struggle in the countryside. They held that a party so built would not only be a revolutionary party but would at the same time be the people's armed force and the people's state power. These were seen as features of an indivisible struggle. Here, armed struggle was meant in the rather narrow sense of guerrilla squad actions. There was no reference to mass organizations or to other forms of struggle besides armed struggle.[19] As an afterthought, the leadership recognized the need to mobilize peasants on economic demands as the first step toward drawing in those backward sections which were late in grasping the politics of armed struggle.[20] But the leadership remained generally vague on the question of land distribution or an agrarian program as part of its program of armed struggle.

When the AICCCR met in October 1968, it decided that Naxalbari-type movements in the countryside had already entered the stage of guerrilla warfare. It therefore called upon revolutionaries to plunge into work among the peasantry and to set up revolutionary bases in the countryside. (The leaders were not clear about what they meant by "revolutionary bases." They may have meant guerrilla zones.)

Meanwhile serious differences were developing between the national AICCCR and the Andhra Pradesh Coordinating Committee of Communist Revolutionaries, which was leading the movement among the Girijan tribal people in the Srikakulam district of Andhra Pradesh state.[21] Communists had been organizing the tribal people in an 800-square-mile area since 1959. The movement, which predated Naxalbari and was quite independent of it, gained strength in 1967; police reprisals followed in 1968. The CPI-M, which was leading the movement prior to the Maoist revolt by its Andhra Pradesh unit, was not organizationally prepared for defense against police raids. The Srikakulam district unit of the party disagreed with the state unit over the timing of armed struggle and the need for military training to resist the police. In October 1968 the state unit, which had already left the CPI-M and was functioning independently as the Andhra Pradesh Coordinating Committee of Communist Revolutionaries, joined the national AICCCR. The Srikakulam district unit was already dealing directly with the AICCCR. In December 1968 the Srikakulam unit decided to launch armed struggle in the district, following the methodology of struggle recommended by the AICCCR, but without the approval of the Andhra Pradesh state unit, which had serious reservations about the timing and mode of operation. Shortly thereafter, in February 1969, the AICCCR disowned the Andhra Pradesh state committee and decided to go ahead with the formation of a Maoist party that excluded them. As the armed struggle continued in Srikakulam, the new party (CPI-ML) claimed that the Girijan tribal people were "learning warfare through warfare" and were setting up their own revolutionary organization, the Ryotanga Sangrama Samiti, which was described as "in embryo, the organ of people's political power in the villages." [22] Significantly, the party claimed that the Ryotanga Sangrama Samiti was a mass organization whose formation *followed* the "liberation" of an area, rather than being formed in advance of the struggle. According to the party, the Samiti set up people's courts, people's militia, and village administrations which undertook land distribution programs. The party claimed that "red power" had emerged in over 300 Srikakulam villages.

About this time, the CPI-ML leadership developed a new tactical line: mass organizations were unnecessary, and guerrilla warfare should be the sole tactic of any peasant revolutionary struggle. The peasants as a whole need not participate in guerrilla warfare, which could be initiated by an advanced section of the peasantry. The accent was on secret politicization. The earlier line, which involved drawing in the backward among the peasantry by mobilizing them first on economic demands, was abandoned. [23]

The CPI-ML leadership further introduced the controversial tactic of "annihilating the class enemy" in the countryside. After the party unit had done some preliminary propaganda for seizure of political power, guerrilla squads were to be armed in secret and charged with annihilating the most hated class enemies. After the first action, political cadres were to whisper to the peasants about the benefits that would result when the oppressor landlords were forced to flee the village. Peasants would be aroused and drawn into the struggle. When a number of such squad actions had taken place and the annihilation line had been firmly established, political cadres would advance the slogan for the seizure of crops.[24] The sequence was guerrilla terror—political propaganda—guerrilla terror. Mass organizations and mass participation were not part of the annihilation campaign.

These tactics were first tried in Srikakulam district and, because there was already a well-rooted mass movement there, met with some success. Since 1959 the peasantry had been organized on class and general demands under the leadership of the Communists. The movement had been directed against the tyranny of the landlords, the village-level bureaucracy, and the forest administration. When the annihilation tactic was tried here, the effort was no mere stealthy guerrilla squad action to kill landlords. There was a high degree of mass participation. Thousands of peasants accompanied the guerrillas on raids of landlords' houses, to execute landlords, or to storm police stations. But after a point the tactic proved counterproductive even in Srikakulam. The actions provoked police reprisals and the guerrillas were forced to flee.

The same tactics were tried indiscriminately in other Andhra Pradesh districts where there was no tradition of mass movement. The results were disastrous: the guerrilla actions were unrelated to peasant demands. Squads belonging to one region would travel scores of miles to carry out an annihilation raid, and then flee to another region. In the absence of political follow-up work, the raids appeared to the local peasants no different from acts of banditry, devoid of political significance.

In Srikakulam it was claimed that "red political power" had emerged in 300 villages, from which terror-stricken landlords had fled following the annihilation campaign. The CPI-ML expected Srikakulam to develop into India's Yenan, where a people's liberation army could be formed. But the party did not explain how this could happen through mere terrorist tactics; and in less than eighteen months the red bases crumbled in the face of the government's counterinsurgency drive. The guerrillas abandoned the peasantry to police onslaughts.[25]

Meanwhile the Andhra Maoists who were functioning through the Andhra Pradesh Revolutionary Communist Committee were conducting limited actions in areas under their influence. Despite their reservations about the CPI-ML's tactical line in Srikakulam, they supported the movement there because it was a question of protecting the peasants against the government's armed raids.

The differences between the CPI-ML and the Andhra Pradesh Revolutionary Communist Committee (APRCC) involve not only organizational issues but the whole philosophy of armed struggle. To the APRCC, armed struggle should begin only as response to landlord attacks. It holds that people's war always begins as resistance and not as an offensive, and, further, that the CPI-ML's methodology of struggle, by rejecting mass participation, has been unrelated to the people's demands. This became even clearer in areas other than Srikakulam, where the CPI-ML's guerrilla squads killed individual landlords in the absence of a mass movement of any type.

While the CPI-ML regards every armed struggle as a "national liberation struggle," the APRCC maintains that only after a series of armed actions by the peasantry and their coordination into a people's army does a national liberation struggle truly emerge. To call every peasant struggle a struggle for state power is to divert the people's attention from their basic and immediate demands. Further, when people are not organized around their demands and given leadership to win them, guerrilla terror merely distracts them. According to the APRCC, people should be their own liberators under the party's leadership, which in turn means that the people must be part of all guerrilla actions. The CPI-ML's methodology, they say, makes the people feel that outsiders are their liberators. Indeed, in Srikakulam, as in other regions, CPI-ML guerrillas frequently included activists who did not belong to the region and had not lived among the local people.[26]

According to the APRCC, the beginning, development, consolidation, and extension of peasant struggles must all be based on an agrarian program. While complete liberation is possible only after setting up base areas, seizing power throughout the country, and establishing a new democratic state, "liberation begins with the starting of anti-landlord struggle, with the starting of [an] agrarian revolutionary program."

The CPI-ML's "annihilation" line, on the other hand, postpones the agrarian program to a later stage and regards destruction of the state machinery as its first task. Agrarian revolution has ceased to be part of the CPI-ML's immediate program, while the APRCC believes that agrarian revolution is the main content of people's war, in theory as well as in practice. Peasant struggles to implement agrarian programs will naturally develop into armed struggle if the masses are trained to resist the reprisals that peasant actions invite. A program of agrarian revolution should, according to the APRCC, be coordinated so that the masses understand the relationship between agrarian revolution and seizure of power. They should also be made to understand that the gains of their agrarian struggles can be protected only by seizing political power, which is possible only through people's war.

The CPI-ML seeks to create "base areas" by annihilating individual landlords, arguing that "when the guerrilla units begin to act in this manner in any area, the class enemies will be forced to flee the countryside and the villages will be liberated." [27] The APRCC counters that this is contrary to Mao Tse-tung's concept of liberated areas. Mao has laid down three conditions for developing a liberated area: (1) build the armed forces, (2) defeat the enemy, and (3) mobilize the broad masses of people. As the APRCC understands Mao, "build the armed forces" means building the people's armed forces; "defeat the class enemy" does not mean the annihilation of the class enemy but defeating the class enemy along with his armed forces, and "mobilize the masses" means mobilizing and arming them against the class enemy and its armed forces in complete coordination with the people's armed forces. [28]

The APRCC's line is summed up in a recent document:

> Armed struggle is the main form of struggle but mass struggles have to be coordinated with armed struggle and mass organizations should be coordinated with the organization of the red army. By coordinating class struggles in urban areas and in the countryside and by coordinating other forms of struggle with armed struggle, the majority of the people should be drawn into conscious participation in armed struggle. [29]

The failure of the CPI-ML's tactical line in the countryside is evident from the severe setbacks the party has received in Srikakulam and in Debra-Gopivallabpur and other rural areas of West Bengal. In May 1970, shortly after the party's first congress, its activity in West Bengal shifted from the countryside to the city of Calcutta. The urban movement, which has taken the form of low-level guerrilla squad actions based on the annihilation tactic, is not coordinated with any movement in the countryside.[30] The CPI-ML has become a truncated party, virtually limited to West Bengal. The Srikakulam unit has repudiated the central authority of the party, while the Bihar and Uttar Pradesh units, as well as part of the Orissa unit, have broken away. Thus the Indian Maoist movement, which showed signs of consolidation through the AICCCR, has begun fragmenting since the hasty formation of the party in 1969.

While the Srikakulam movement has collapsed under CPI-ML leadership, the APRCC's movement has recorded some progress. In April 1969 the Committee prepared the tribal people of Warangal and Khammam districts in Andhra Pradesh to reoccupy land which had been taken from them by neighboring landlords. Once the landlords had been made ineffective, a land program was begun in earnest. Thousands of acres of government wasteland, forest land, and landlords' farms were occupied. All forms of feudal exploitation were ended. It took almost a year to implement the first stage of the program. In retaliation, hundreds of tribal people who had occupied land were jailed, and repressive measures were launched by police and paramilitary forces. This raised guerrilla resistance to a new level and the movement spread. In late 1969 the APRCC claimed an area of 5,000–6,000 square miles, inhabited by 350,000–400,000 people, to be under its control. By mid-1970 it was claimed that this area had expanded to 7,000–8,000 square miles, with a population of 500,000–600,000.

Repression has since been greatly intensified. The government never felt called upon to deploy its regular army against the Srikakulam movement, but in the areas where the APRCC has tried to develop a guerrilla zone it has recently done so. On March 1, 1971, about 5,000 troops and 10,000 paramilitary forces carried out a major operation in Warangal, Khammam, and Karimnagar districts. On that day the civil administration helplessly handed over control to the army for a Vietnam-style clean-up operation. Something similar to the "strategic hamlet" plan is being attempted: many scattered villages are herded together into concentration camps so that all food supplies to the guerrillas are cut off. According to one report, camps have been set up at three-mile intervals all over the area. No civilian is allowed out after dusk.[31]

Despite its fragmentation, the Maoist movement has registered extensive growth in the country. A strong Maoist undercurrent is evident within the CPI-M, and its leadership is under heavy pressure to quit the parliamentary system. There is a growing conviction in CPI-M ranks that the party cannot achieve anything significant within the framework of the bourgeois constitution, which concentrates power in the federal government and leaves state governments powerless to implement any substantial part of the party's program. Those who hold this conviction believe that the taste of power via the ballot box, which the party has enjoyed in Kerala and West Bengal, has made it a victim of parliamentary cretinism. In the absence of a viable Maoist party on a national scale to serve as a rallying point, many dissenters in the CPI-M continue to work in the party. There is a possibility that these dissidents may force a split in the CPI-M or leave it in strength to launch a new Maoist party.

The emergence of a viable Maoist party in India depends on two factors: (1) the ability of the Indian Maoists to work out a unified tactical line to coordinate peasant movements with each other and with urban movements, and (2) the entrance of a large number of CPI-M cadres into the Maoist movement (the CPI-M has by far the largest number of militant cadres in both urban and rural areas).

Revolutionary potential has existed in India for quite some time. The serious economic crisis in the country, including a severe unemployment problem and growing tensions in the countryside, adds to this potential. The failure of the Indian Maoist movement to exploit it is a measure of the movement's weakness and of the need for a clearer Maoist perspective on the Indian revolution.

Notes

1. The Communist Party of India has been recognized by the Soviet bloc as the only communist party in the country. The independent Communist Party of India-Marxist, recognized neither by Moscow nor by Peking, has been trying to build a bridge to the international communist movement through the neutral or independent bloc of parties—Rumanian, North Korean, North Vietnamese, and Cuban. The Communist Party of India (Marxist-Leninist) is, in Peking's view, the only genuine communist party.
2. For a detailed analysis supporting this conclusion, see Mohan Ram, *Indian Communism: Split Within a Split* (Vikas Publications, Delhi, 1969).
3. Before the formation of the CPI-ML, most Indian Maoists were functioning through the All-India Coordinating Committee of Communist

Revolutionaries. The AICCCR expelled its Andhra unit before convert- ing itself into the CPI-ML. Its Maharashtra unit chose to keep out of the new party; it opposed the hasty formation of a party from above and the policy of exclusion of the Andhra Maoists.

4. A. Zhdanov, "The International Situation," in *For a Lasting Peace, For a People's Democracy*, November 10, 1947, quoted in Mohan Ram, op. cit., p. 12.

5. A four-class alliance refers to an alliance led by the proletariat, with the peasants as their main allies, the petty bourgeoisie as allies to be won over through careful organizational work, and the nonmonopoly bour- geoisie as potential but less reliable allies (Mao Tse-tung, "The Chinese Revolution and the Chinese Communist Party," *Selected Works*, Vol. 111, pp. 92–93).

6. See Ajoy Ghosh, "The United Front," *New Age* (CPI monthly, New Delhi), February 1956.

7. A brilliant analysis of the issues can be found in Victor M. Fic, *Peaceful Transition to Communism in India: Strategy of the Communist Party* (Nichiketa, Bombay, 1969).

8. Mohit Sen, a CPI theoretician, claimed in 1961 that although the "state of national democracy" was a new concept in the international commu- nist movement, his party had, since 1956, been putting forward a pro- gram and producing an analysis which was the same as the Moscow statement's. It was the culmination of a "very precise formulation of the CPI" (*Maral*, New Delhi, January 1961).

9. The Communist Party of China, supporting the Naxalbari uprising, called upon the CPI-M following to repudiate its leadership. The CPC's analysis was that India was a semifeudal, semicolonial, only nominally independent country and that the Indian bourgeoisie had turned com- prador. It held that the objective conditions for a revolution existed in India. For the CPI-M's views expressing disagreement with the CPC's analysis, see "Divergent Views Between Our Party and the CPC on Fundamental Issues," Resolution of the CPI-M Central Committee, August 1967.

10. In the pre-split CPI the right wing, which had Moscow's backing in its struggle against the left wing, succeeded in committing the party to So- viet positions in the ideological dispute without a proper party discus- sion. Since the split the CPI has been consistent in its support of Moscow on issues of ideology.

11. See Mohan Ram, *Indian Communism: Split Within a Split*, for a detailed analysis.

12. For these positions, see "A Proposal Concerning the General Line of the International Communist Movement," Letter from the Central Com-

mittee of the Chinese Communist Party, June 14, 1963, in reply to the Letter from the Central Committee of the Communist Party of the Soviet Union, March 30, 1963.

13. For a study of the evolution of the Maoist tactical line in India, see Mohan Ram, *Maoism in India* (Vikas Publications, Delhi, 1971).

14. The Chinese Party has never endorsed this position because it has never stated publicly what the principal contradiction in India is.

15. This analysis of the CPI-ML's program is based on unpublished documents.

16. Andhra Pradesh Revolutionary Communist Committee, *Immediate Program,* unpublished, mimeographed, April 1969. Also Andhra Pradesh Revolutionary Communist Committee, *Problems of People's War,* unpublished, mimeographed, early 1970.

17. An authoritative report on the lessons of the Naxalbari struggle by one of its leaders, Kanu Sanyal, "A Report on the Peasant Movement in the Terai Region," in *Liberation* (Calcutta) bears striking resemblance in its methodology to the famous Hunan Report of Mao Tse-tung.

18. "Declaration of the All-India Coordinating Committee of Communist Revolutionaries," *Liberation,* June 1968.

19. For an analysis of the AICCCR's, and later the CPI-ML's, tactical line, see Abhijnan Sen, "The Naxalite Tactical Line," *Frontier* (Calcutta), July 4, 1969.

20. Charu Mazumdar, "Develop Peasant Class Struggles Through Class Analysis, Investigation and Study," *Liberation,* November 1968.

21. Andhra Pradesh Revolutionary Communist Committee, *On Srikakulam Girijan Armed Struggle,* unpublished, mimeographed, April 1969.

22. "Srikakulam Marches On," *Liberation,* April 1969.

23. Charu Mazumdar, "Some Current Organizational and Political Problems," *Liberation,* July 1969.

24. Charu Mazumdar, "A Few Words on Guerrilla Actions," *Deshabrati* (Bengal weekly, Calcutta), January 15, 1970.

25. Another area where the tactic was tried without success was in Debra-Gopivallabpur in Midnapur district of West Bengal. See "Revolutionary Armed Struggle in Debra in West Bengal," report of the Debra Thana Organizing Committee (CPI-ML), *Liberation,* December 1969.

26. Narayanamurthi, "The Srikakulam Story—II," *Frontier,* September 20, 1969; also Andhra Pradesh Revolutionary Communist Committee, "On Armed Struggle in Andhra Pradesh," July 1969, mimeographed.

27. Charu Mazumdar, "Carry Forward the Peasant Struggle," *Liberation,* November 1969.

28. Andhra Pradesh Revolutionary Communist Committee, *Problems of People's War,* op. cit.

29. Andhra Pradesh Revolutionary Communist Committee, *Some Problems Concerning the Path of People's War in India*, clandestine publication, late 1970.
30. Abhijnan Sen, "Naxalite Tactics in the Cities," *Frontier*, October 3, 1970.
31. C. Chandrasekhara Rao, "What to Do?", *Frontier*, June 12, 1971.

4. The Red Sun Is Rising:
Revolutionary Struggle in India

Inquilab Zindabad

Peasant unrest is increasing throughout India at such a rate and in such a manner that the police and military forces, as well as hired thugs, are unable to suppress the people effectively. Support for the Communist Party of India (Marxist-Leninist) is growing rapidly precisely because India at last has a communist party which sincerely represents the interests of the majority of the population rather than those of opportunistic petty-bourgeois leaders. Deteriorating economic conditions and increased exploitation have brought semifeudal, semicolonial India to the threshold of people's war.

At the present time (January 1972), open armed conflict is commonplace in West Bengal. Since early 1971 the military build-up there has steadily increased. At first the buildup was attributed to "safeguarding" the state elections in March 1971. The subsequent genocide perpetrated by Yahya Khan on the unprepared people of East Pakistan meant that even greater numbers of Indian military forces were brought in, at first to guard the borders and later to invade and occupy East Pakistan. Now that East Pakistan has become Bangladesh and Sheikh Mujibur Rahman has been released by Zulfikar Ali Bhutto to become Bangladesh's Prime Minister, we can be sure that the national bourgeoisie of Bangladesh will continue its alliance with the Indian bourgeoisie, not merely because of economic dependence but with the mutual hope of containing people's war. This ruling class alliance will mean continued military occupation of both East and West Bengal, as well as further repression directed at members, supporters, and sympathizers of the CPI-ML and the Communist Party of East Pakistan (Marxist-Leninist) or CPEP-ML.

Inquilab Zindabad ("Long Live the Revolution") is the pseudonym of a partisan of the Communist Party of India (Marxist-Leninist).

It is also clear that every attempt will be made to use Bengali nationalism to foster anti-Chinese feeling. However, it is unlikely that such a ploy will succeed. At present the Bangladesh government is vainly attempting to recall weapons issued to Mukti Bahini fighters. In West Bengal weapons are being stockpiled by the CPI-ML for use by the People's Liberation Army which it is in process of forming. This gun-snatching campaign has reached such proportions that the police and military usually have their rifles *chained* to their belts. This forces the rifle-bearer to defend his weapon with his life—a policy which inhumanely values the weapon more than the man.

The Communist Party of India (CPI) and the Communist Party of India-Marxist (CPI-M) are now reactionary forces. In 1958 the CPI took the "peaceful road to socialism" and has been on it ever since. In 1964 the CPI-M was founded in response to rank-and-file dissatisfaction with CPI revisionist policies, as well as with the CPI's support of the reactionary Indian government at the time of the Indo-Sino border dispute in 1962. However, the new leadership stubbornly refused to set up secret operations and it put forth the program of forming united fronts with "leftist" parties in order to bring socialism and communism to India *peacefully!* Following this line, West Bengal's first united front government took power in February 1967. The CPI-M was the largest component, but did not enjoy a majority. There was much discontent when even the new united front government did not implement the land reform provisions that had been law for several years. *Benami* (holding land in several names to circumvent the laws fixing the maximum legal landownership) remained a common practice.

In May 1967, in Darjeeling district, West Bengal, peasants led by rebel ex-CPI-M cadres seized some land on a tea plantation whose acreage was in excess of the legal ceiling on landownership. Police parties arrived and a policeman was killed with a bow and arrow. In retaliation, seven peasant women and three children were shot. The CPI-M ministers in the United Front government helped to organize repression in the face of great popular support for the new revolutionaries, who were called "Naxalites" (the original incident took place at Naxalbari). This uprising covered an area of 256 square miles under the three *thanas* (police stations) of Naxalbari, Phansidewa, and Kharibari. A call went out from Charu Mazumdar, Jangal Santhal, Kanu Sanyal, and other leaders in north Bengal: organize an All-India Coordinating Committee of Communist Revolutionaries and create Naxalbaris all over India!

After Naxalbari, other areas began to organize, with poor and landless peasants taking a leading role. In the Srikakulam district of Andhra Pradesh, a hilly, heavily wooded area with a history of intense class exploitation, a renewed struggle was launched in the autumn of 1968. This struggle swiftly created the first liberated base area in India, which was able to withstand constant attack from large detachments of heavily armed state and federal troops and grew to cover 800 square miles, encompassing 300 villages. However, in less than two years continued police repression managed to put the movement down. A recent (mid-1971) party document of the CPI-ML contains critical self-analysis regarding Srikakulam. In the Srikakulam hills the party cadres were isolated both from the plains-people and from struggles going on elsewhere in Andhra Pradesh; also, functioning in a concentrated area, they were much too easily attacked. Even more crucial, before a liberated zone can be safely established, is the need for a People's Liberation Army as well as a politically conscious population under the leadership of a Marxist-Leninist party.

At the same time as the struggle in Srikakulam, armed struggle was developing throughout India, notably in West Bengal, Bihar, Assam, Orissa, Uttar Pradesh, and Punjab. In April 1969 a new communist party was formed: the Communist Party of India (Marxist-Leninist). In the words of an early political resolution of the CPI-ML:

> If the poor and landless peasants, who constitute the majority of the peasantry, the firm ally of the working class, unite with the middle peasants, then the vastest section of the Indian people will be united and the democratic revolution will inevitably win victory. It is the responsibility of the working class as the leader of the revolution to unite with the peasantry—the main force of the revolution—and to advance toward the seizure of power through armed struggle. It is on the basis of the worker-peasant alliance that a revolutionary united front of all revolutionary classes will be built up. The resistance of our people, both in the rural and in the urban areas, is fast developing and bringing about a new upsurge in the agrarian revolution—the main content of the democratic revolution.

The CPI-ML is a fighting force and a tool of the working class and the peasantry for waging class struggle. Because the party must remain a secret organization or be wiped out, secrecy is maintained regarding the activities of any given member. No comrade discusses with any other comrade the particular task he or she is working on unless they are working together. On the other hand, the party must develop and maintain firm links with the masses and become a *thing of* the masses. The party pays strict attention to Mao's concept of the mass line and continually recruits its cadres from the most exploited sectors of the population and places full reliance on them. By doing so, the level of competence of the entire working class and peasantry and the ability to direct their own affairs are swiftly raised. Experience shows that such cadres make the best fighters and are the most trustworthy leaders. The CPI-ML must act in accordance with the mass line to lead the Indian peoples to victory.

The programs undertaken by the party must be of such a nature that they will enhance political consciousness and bring revolutionary joy to the oppressed masses. Two good examples of such programs are the present campaigns of (1) annihilation of class enemies, and (2) seizure of weapons from police, military, and class enemies.

The annihilation of class enemies is the highest form of class struggle as well as the beginning of guerrilla warfare. Great care is taken to define the enemy with the utmost precision. It is found that middle peasants, and even some rich peasants who themselves still work, are capable of supporting the revolutionary movement. The class enemy in the countryside is most often a large landholder and/or usurer. Only these hard-core exploiters are singled out for attack and annihilation. Otherwise, the party would be creating enemies out of possible friends.

To carry out an action, a guerrilla band is formed in utmost secrecy. This band takes the annihilation of a well-known oppressor as its task. The news of such a person's death is always a great relief to the community and raises party prestige immensely. The news of the death also frightens his fellow exploiters, who then flee to the towns for safety. This eases the situation even further. The absence of class enemies in the countryside deprives the government of its information sources and the party becomes able to move and organize more freely.

The seizure of rifles, guns, and revolvers from the police, military, and class enemies started in early 1971. Previously, comrades relied on indigenous weapons, such as choppers and axes. These weapons are more familiar to peasant comrades and require combat at close quarters. Such initial experience is considered necessary to enable guerrilla fighters to understand the importance of relying on revolutionary spirit rather than on sophisticated weaponry. Unless a comrade has conquered his fear and accepts the idea of a revolutionary death, he will falter in a situation of close combat. By now guerrilla units are extending their field experience and are seizing weapons for use in the People's Liberation Army's military operations.

The need for guerrilla armed struggle to precede, rather than to follow, the creation of mass movements has recently been spelled out in an article in the CPI-ML's journal:

> Today armed struggle is being linked with mass movements in the countryside—mass movements for land and crops. Several areas have been freed of class enemies and their agents: the most hated ones were annihilated and the others have fled away. Revolutionary Committees backed by the PLA units led by the party have been formed as new organs of power. By confiscating and distributing the land and crops of the class enemies who have been annihilated or who have fled away, the Revolutionary Committees are unleashing powerful mass movements. The oppressed people in those areas are rallying around the Revolutionary Committees. It is on this issue that all revisionists, renegades, and scabs oppose Comrade Charu Mazumdar's [CPI-ML theoretician and Central Committee member] revolutionary line. They have even tried to put the cart before the horse: they always insist that mass movements for partial demands must precede armed struggle. That has been the revisionist practice in India for more than forty years—until Naxalbari. Objectively, this line amounts to the liquidation of armed struggle.[1]

The CPI-ML's ability to lead the Indian people forward to liberation is questioned by a wide spectrum of political groups, several of whom claim to be Marxist-Leninist. Academic debate will not, however, provide an answer. Class conflict is so far advanced in India today that no "objective" view is possible. Most written source material has a serious class bias which, coupled with the class interest of the researcher, presents the activities of the CPI-ML in a generally unfavorable light. One of the most unsubstantiated charges, which personal experience convinces me is totally false, is that the party appeals primarily to urban petty-bourgeois students and intellectuals.

If this is correct, how is it that the annihilation of class enemies and the gun-snatching campaign have been so successful in the countryside? Continually increased police and military repression is one good index of the threat that CPI-ML activity poses to the present power structure in the rural areas. Another index is the unchallenged fact that several hundred class enemies were annihilated in West Bengal by the end of 1971. Finally, it is well known that great care is taken that poor and landless peasants form the guerrilla squads. This fact eliminates confusion as to the motives and class interest of the guerrilla fighters.

The revolutionary interaction between guerrilla fighters and the masses of peasants under conditions of repression is well expressed in the following passage describing recent events in Naxalbari:

> In the Naxalbari area nine Revolutionary Committees have been formed. Since Magurjan, guerrilla comrades have launched 12 attacks, nine of which have been fully successful. The enemy is carrying on an "encirclement and suppression" campaign. The police camps have been strengthened and the army has set up camps within the area. But this campaign is meeting with failure after failure. Far from suppressing the fighting peasantry, it has raised their morale. Ready to leave their homes, more and more peasant men and women are coming forward every day to join the People's Army. The guerrilla comrades disperse for purposes of political propaganda but they concentrate while attacking the enemy. Every PLA unit has a commander and a political commissar. In those units where the peasants' level of political consciousness is high, the political commissar is elected from among the peasants. The regional commander and political commissar are peasants. The leadership of the poor and landless peasants over the Revolutionary Committees is being established. On this depends how successfully the Revolutionary Committees will be able to establish the peasants' power in the area.[2]

Although the main thrust of party activity is in the countryside among the peasantry, there is, however, a substantial following in urban areas among the proletariat and the petty bourgeoisie, as the following citation makes clear:

> Today, as Comrade Charu Mazumdar has said, the main task of the party units in urban areas is to carry the politics of seizure of political power by armed force to the workers, to propagate Mao Tse-tung Thought among them and to build party organizations with the advanced elements among them. This task is being fulfilled and party

units with the best elements of the proletariat are being formed. A major section of the workers in some industrial areas is rallying around these party units. It is also a feature today that in many areas the party units and comrades enjoy in an overwhelming measure the support, love, and affection of the urban poor. . . . Under the leadership of the party the masses of workers are rising in militant revolts. On June 1, the workers counterattacked the central industrial security force at Durgapur with whatever they could lay their hands on when a worker was beaten up. Led by our comrades, the revolutionary workers inflicted serious injuries on 21 officers and men of the so-called security force and annihilated a police spy. The struggle spread to different factories—AVB, Graphite, SCIRG, Damodar Iron and Steel, etc. It spread also to neighboring areas. The railway workers at Andal, an important railway center, went on protest strike. Even revisionist trade union leaders working in close collusion with the police and the administration failed to suppress this revolt. On April 29, a guerrilla squad of nine workers annihilated Bireswar Mondal, a despotic landlord and police informer, in Baktarnagar village in Andal area. Party units are being organized among the coal miners, one of the most oppressed sections of workers in India. Already their guerrilla squads have annihilated class enemies and snatched away guns. Workers, peasants, and revolutionary youths are fighting shoulder to shoulder to carry forward the agrarian revolution.[3]

The party encourages unemployed workers to leave the cities and take up revolution. An Indian worker is at most one generation away from the village where his extended family still lives. He is well suited for leading struggles because he is highly exploited and understands machines and industrial techniques. The party must develop working class leadership to avoid falling into revisionist practice. The party supports trade union struggles at certain times, but *never* leads them and is always careful to point out the dangers of economic demands as a basis for struggle. Workers' struggles can no longer develop peacefully, but must take different forms of armed struggle. These new forms of struggle are being created by the workers as their understanding of Marxism-Leninism increases. The CPI-ML is working to build workers' solidarity by stressing their political line rather than by denouncing the revisionism of traditional trade union activity. The leadership of the working class in the coming liberation struggles can be ensured only by raising class consciousness through revolutionary politics.

Students and teachers are encouraged to leave their schools and universities and to integrate themselves with the poor and landless peasants and with the workers. In order to do this they must engage in productive work and do manual labor. After this first step they should then engage in "Red Guard" action—agitational political propaganda—whose purpose it is to mobilize students and youth in support of the workers and peasants. This supportive role will at times result in armed struggle against the class enemy, for which the revolutionary youth must be prepared ideologically as well as practically.

The CPI-ML pays close attention to the works of Mao Tse-tung, as applied to the concrete conditions of India today. To quote Charu Mazumdar, leader of the CPI-ML:

> Today, the peasant armed struggle is being waged in India and guerrilla bases have already been established. This proves conclusively that it is irresistible and the Indian reactionaries are totally unable either to arrest its growth or to prevent it from developing. More and more people are becoming convinced of the immense power of Mao Tse-tung Thought, the peasant armed struggle is steadily expanding, and more guerrilla bases are being established. All this shows how deeply Mao Tse-tung Thought has stuck its root in the soil of India. It will grow deeper with every passing day, every passing hour, and will create a storm that will envelop the entire country; it will become a material force of tremendous power that will sweep away all kinds of reactionaries and revisionists of all hues, like so many dry and withered leaves from this great land of ours. A people's democratic India is no longer a distant objective.

Point 38 of the forty-point program adopted by the CPI-ML Party Congress of May 1970 gives some indication of what a people's democratic India might be like:

> The People's Democratic State will carry out the following major tasks:
> —Confiscation of all the banks and enterprises of foreign capital and liquidation of all imperialist debt.
> —Confiscation of all the enterprises of the comprador-bureaucrat capitalists.
> —Confiscation of all land belonging to the landlords and their redistribution among the landless and poor peasants on the principle of land to the tillers; cancellation of all debts of the peasantry and other toiling people. All facilities necessary for development of agriculture to be guaranteed.

—Enforce the eight-hour day, increase wages, institute unemployment relief and social insurance, remove all inequalities on the basis of equal pay for equal work.

—Improve the living conditions of soldiers and give land and jobs to the ex-servicemen.

—Enforce better living conditions of the people and remove unemployment.

—Develop a new democratic culture in place of the colonial and feudal culture.

—Abolish the present educational system and educational institutions and build up a new educational system and new educational institutions consistent with the needs of People's Democratic India.

—Abolish the caste system, remove all social inequalities and all discrimination on religious grounds, and guarantee equality of status of women.

—Unify India and recognize the right of self-determination.

—Give equal status to all national languages.

—Abolish all exorbitant taxes and miscellaneous assessments and adopt a consolidated progressive tax system.

—People's political power to be exercised through Revolutionary People's Councils at all levels.

—Alliance to be formed with the international proletariat and the oppressed nations of the world under the leadership of the CPC.

DARE TO STRUGGLE AND DARE TO WIN ! ! !

Notes

1. *Liberation* (Calcutta), April–June, 1971.
2. Ibid., pp. 91–92.
3. Ibid., pp. 100–102.

5. Revolutionary Movements in Ceylon

Jayasumana Obeysekara

Ceylon covers about 25,000 square miles and has a population of 12.5 million. The south-central part of the island, called the "up country," forms a massif rising to 8,000 feet. The contrasting "low country" comprises the northern part of the island together with a coastal belt of varying width.

The hill country has been a fortress against invasion. The Portuguese and the Dutch, who occupied the maritime provinces in 1505 and 1683, respectively, never wrested control of it from the Sinhala kings. The British, who finally annexed the Kandyan kingdom located in the uplands, did so by intrigue rather than military combat.

Ceylon's strategic position in the Indian Ocean invited its occupation; indeed, the British initially occupied it while fighting the French in the French revolutionary and Napoleonic wars. There were British air and naval bases in Ceylon until 1956. Recently, there has been renewed interest among imperialist powers in the "security" of the Indian Ocean. The Russian naval presence and the "communist threat" were among the reasons given for Britain's decision to sell arms to South Africa. Meanwhile revolutionary struggle has advanced in Southeast Asia and imperialism is internally threatened in Southern Asia as a whole. Ceylon's strategic location may invite yet another occupation. The American and British governments have already supplied arms and equipment to bolster up the government, but such indirect assistance may not suffice to prevent the collapse of capitalist rule.

Socioeconomy

During the 152 years of their rule (1796–1948), the British transformed the socioeconomic system. Their impact differed from that of

This article was written in January 1972.

the Portuguese and the Dutch, who barely tampered with indigenous social relations: the British destroyed the largely self-sufficient agricultural economy. They introduced systematic cultivation of commercial crops such as tea, rubber, and coffee, and created a predominantly export-import economy. They confiscated peasant land and sold it to British planters for as little as a shilling an acre.

The British who took away peasant lands expected the peasants to become wage workers on their tea and coffee plantations. The peasants, however, resisted, so that the British were obliged to bring in indentured laborers from South India. In non-plantation villages, the imposition of capitalist property relations meant that traditional services rendered by various birth status groups to the community at large could no longer be adequately fulfilled. No one, for example, remained responsible for maintaining the dams and canals which irrigated the dry zone of the country—the granary of Ceylon.

In such ways the British disrupted Ceylonese society. The changes they effected still dominate the country's economic and political life. Ceylon's commercial economy is today largely dependent on the export of tea, which accounts for almost two-thirds of its foreign exchange earnings.[1] A country which exported rice before the advent of the Europeans now imports more than half this staple food. In the last ten years, Ceylon's balance-of-payments situation has deteriorated precipitously because of the continual decline of world market tea prices.

Ceylon produces two other principal commercial crops. With the development of synthetic processes, rubber, now sold mainly to the People's Republic of China, has become less important. Coconut and its by-products form the third significant export crop.

In addition to export crops oriented to the needs of imperialism, the Ceylonese grow subsistence crops for internal consumption, using mainly traditional techniques. Few finished products are manufactured, although some service industries closely linked to the export of primary products have created a small urban working class. Local property owners have recently tried to establish light industries, e.g., biscuit manufacturing. The governments of the past eighteen years have also exploited differences between the imperialist countries and the workers' states to obtain long-term loans and "aid" to establish small assembly plants for cars and bicycles and factories for tires and textiles. These changes do not, however, alter the fundamental character of Ceylon's economy. The most important development in the last twenty-five years has been in rural areas, where the proportion of agricultural workers and, in general, of the landless poor has steadily increased.[2] One reason for this is that the native bourgeoisie has invested much of its profits in cultivable land and in building, which involved buying up the land of small and poor peasants. Growing rural indebtedness has also accelerated this process.

Culture, Religion, and Caste

Ceylon has two main ethnic groups, the Sinhala and the Tamils. The Sinhala people make up about 71 percent of the population; the Tamils, about 21 percent. The Tamils include the "Ceylon Tamils," who began to arrive at least 2,000 years ago, and the "Indian Tamils," who were brought from South India by the British to work on the tea plantations. There are few cultural differences between the Ceylon Tamils (about 1.5 million, who chiefly inhabit the northern and eastern regions) and the plantation workers (about 1 million). The latter are, however, not legal citizens of Ceylon and were disenfranchised in 1950. A large majority of these plantation workers are stateless persons who do not enjoy even basic civil rights. They are the most oppressed sector of the Ceylonese wage-working class.

Among other minorities we find the Muslims, who constitute about 5 percent of the people, and the Burghers, who number about 50,000. The Muslims descend from unions between Arab and Indian immigrants and native people. The Burghers descend from Dutch and Portuguese settlers and, together with a small proportion of the Sinhala and Tamil peoples, make up the Christian community.

Buddhism is the predominant religion. The great majority of the Sinhala people are Buddhists; most Tamils are Hindus.

The caste system differs from that of India. It is not rigidly observed except in the more conservative Tamil areas, and is declining in significance in Ceylon today.

The native bourgeoisie as well as the colonial masters have used ethnic and religious differences skillfully to divide and disorient the working class. Both the United National Party and the Sri Lanka Freedom Party governments have nurtured anti-Tamil ethnocentrism. These pseudo-racial prejudices have been primarily directed at the Tamil plantation workers. Not only have they been disenfranchised, but successive governments have played on the theme of "Ceylonization" of the economy. The notorious pact between Mrs. Bandaranaike and the late Indian Prime Minister Shastri, in which they agreed to deport 300,000 of these workers to India without consultation with any of them, is one example how the wrath of unemployed Sinhalese has been used against this most oppressed section of the people.

Dilemma of the Brown Sahebs

The British government, having "considered the well-being of the native people of Ceylon, and noting that they had reached a sufficient level of development to undertake responsibility for their internal affairs," granted independence in 1948. A parliamentary system on the British model was introduced. In fact, the British simply realized they could not hold back the colonial revolution throughout South Asia. They could only make the best of an unhappy situation.

A Marxist opposition (the Lanka Sama Samaja Party), which had emerged from World War II with mass support and nationwide popularity, was the only organized anti-imperialist force in the country. Unlike India, where the bourgeoisie, led by Nehru and Gandhi, spearheaded the nationalist movement, in Ceylon it was almost completely tied to its imperialist patrons. There were, here and there, individual Buddhist nationalists who opposed British imperialism, but the overwhelming majority of the propertied class worked within the system, petitioning the imperialists for the right to rule.

Therefore the problem for the British Raj was not whether political power should be transferred to their local junior partners, but whether these partners would be capable of safeguarding British interests. The British had to take the risk, but they retained air and naval bases on the island as a provision for direct intervention should the situation go out of control.

The average Ceylonese had a higher standard of living than most of his neighbors. Ceylon's bourgeoisie was thus initially in a stronger position than the Indian or Pakistani bourgeoisie.

The British had not succeeded in crushing the old ruling class completely; they had had to make certain compromises. The old ruling class, in turn, had been able to adapt itself to the new system of property relations and to prosper as capitalist junior partners of the

British. Although its failure to wage an anti-imperialist struggle compromised the Ceylonese bourgeoisie in the eyes of the people, its historical continuity made it stronger than, for example, the newly emerging Indian bourgeoisie. This explains why it has been able to maintain the façade of a two-party bourgeois "democracy" for a longer period than most other semicolonial countries, even though each successive government has been compelled to rule more and more through special powers and "emergency regulations."

Despite such initial advantages, the Ceylonese bourgeoisie's ability to grant concessions to the masses has greatly diminished. Living standards have been continuously eroded and the level of unemployment has increased year by year.

World market prices of tea have been falling rapidly and are now at their lowest point. The same British companies that own most of the plantations in Ceylon have ensured alternative sources of supply by opening up plantations in Kenya and India. The Ceylonese bourgeoisie has not been able to diversify the economy or to produce import substitutes. At the same time the highly literate population contains a large percentage of educated unemployed youth who have no prospect of obtaining even manual jobs. As the balance of payments and the general economic situation deteriorate, the local bourgeoisie depends increasingly on imperialism for survival. Ceylon owes a debt to the World Bank of about $50 million, and the present government has applied for further loans. These loans are required not to initiate new development projects but to pay for essential imports and repay overdue loans.[3]

The rural poor and the working class have been highly politicized over the past twenty-five years, notably through the spread of Marxist ideas and organizations. So strong are these institutions that no government has been able to destroy them. Nevertheless, the economic plight of Ceylon leaves no alternative to the bourgeoisie but to withdraw the concessions it has granted. This dilemma explains the varying tactics employed by the governments in power since "independence."

The "Uncle-Nephew Party"

The outcome of the parliamentary elections of 1948 was indecisive. The main bourgeois party, the United National Party (UNP), failed to gain a clear majority of seats. Had the Communist Party supported the other Marxist parties instead of the UNP, there could at least temporarily have been a Left united front government. Instead, the UNP formed a minority government with the aid of appointed members and Independents. After the government was formed, representatives of the Tamil bourgeoisie, in the form of the Ceylon Tamil Congress, joined it and the UNP was able to consolidate its position.

During the 1948 elections the UNP leaders were faced with two well-organized Marxist parties, the LSSP and the Bolshevik Leninist Party (BLP). The UNP based its campaign on the danger of communism, painting grim pictures of how Marxists would burn down Buddhist temples and destroy Buddhist civilization. To complement such scare stories, the UNP promised that, if elected, it would give "two measures of rice at 25 cents a measure." [4] This meant that the government, having imported rice at 60 cents a measure, had to sell it to the people at a net loss of 35 cents. In order to win rural voters, the UNP also guaranteed rice producers a subsidized price. Each subsequent government has found these two subsidies burdensome, but every attempt to discontinue them has aroused immediate opposition. Indeed, the first effort to remove them provoked a partial insurrection.

Once the UNP had consolidated its power, its government took steps to destroy the electoral base of the working class parties. In 1948 tea plantation workers had voted for the Ceylon Indian Congress and the LSSP. In 1949 the Ceylon (Parliamentary Elections) Amendment Act No. 48, one of the most reactionary pieces of legislation in the island's history, disenfranchised these workers. The new act ensured that seats in those regions would in future fall to the UNP.

The UNP's foreign policy was staunchly anticommunist. The government refused even diplomatic relations with the workers' states, and supported the imperialist bloc at every international conference. In the Korean War the UNP granted refueling and landing facilities to U.S. and allied troops.

Following the death of the first Prime Minister, D. S. Senanayeke, in March 1952, his son Dudley Senanayeke succeeded him. More senior UNP leaders resented this selection. In the election that followed, however, despite its internal dissensions, the UNP was returned to power with an increased majority, partly because of the disenfranchisement of the plantation workers. Within a year, Mr. Senanayeke and his colleagues had to face tensions and squabbles within the party, accusations of nepotism, and a serious economic crisis.

Ceylon's economy was greatly stimulated by the Korean War, which boosted the U.S. demand for natural rubber and provided handsome profits for Ceylonese rubber producers. At the same time, the price of rice skyrocketed because of the war, so that the government had to make substantial economies. Its leaders decided to withdraw the rice subsidy, since Ceylon was spending more than half its income on importing rice. The government also discontinued school meals and increased postal and rail charges.

Three Left parties were now in existence: the Communist Party; the LSSP, with which the BLP had reunified; and the United Front, a splinter from the LSSP. These groups organized a day of civil disobedience *(hartal)* on August 12, 1953. Trade unions under the leadership of these three parties called for a general strike. When the government alerted the army and deployed troops in several parts of the country, the peaceful protest turned into a three-day insurrection. The Left party leaders were unprepared for further struggle and could give no perspective to the militants in the streets.

The *hartal* led, however, to the Prime Minister's resignation and to partial restoration of the rice subsidy. UNP prestige suffered a heavy blow and many workers sensed their strength. The UNP tottered for three more years and was routed at the 1956 elections.

The UNP leaders had aped their British predecessors. They conducted their business in English in a country where 92 percent of the population did not read or write that language. They maintained the former economic patterns and traditions. Except for the fact that they now had brown- instead of white-skinned rulers, "independence" had brought little change for most people.

The Sri Lanka Freedom Party

Internal differences based largely on personal antagonisms resulted in a UNP split in 1951. The Oxford-educated leader of the House of Representatives, Solomon West Ridgeway Dias Bandaranaike, broke away to form the Sri Lanka (Ceylon) Freedom Party.

Until 1952 the main opposition party in parliament had been the LSSP, led by N. M. Perera. After the 1952 election, however, although the LSSP won the same number of seats as the SLFP, Bandaranaike became leader of the opposition. The three Communist Party members supported Bandaranaike.

Immediately after the war the CP had supported the UNP, but the rabid anticommunism of the latter, coupled with its growing unpopularity, eventually compelled the CP to change its line. The CP did not, of course, abandon its theory of a two-stage revolution or its attempt to distinguish between the "reactionary" and "progressive" bourgeoisie. But the SLFP was now seen as representing the "progressive" bourgeoisie; the demagogic nationalism of Bandaranaike lent credibility to these assertions.

The LSSP leaders expressed opposition to such a broad "anti-UNP" front and counterposed a united front of working class parties and organizations. At that date (1952) they recognized that the only forces capable of sustaining a consistent anti-UNP struggle were the urban working class and the rural proletariat. They argued that to mobilize these classes would challenge not only the UNP but its class interests, since these were expressed through capitalist property relations. Any front which included bourgeois and petty-bourgeois forces would, they argued, enter a blind alley the moment the bourgeoisie adopted another vehicle through which to represent its interests.

The SLFP filled precisely that role. It served as a safety valve for the ruling class. Bandaranaike skillfully exploited the frustrated aspirations of the Sinhala Buddhist petty bourgeoisie. He appeared as the champion of the Sinhala underdog, a crusader against the privileged, who could be interpreted at will as the rich, the Tamils, or the Christians. In his election manifesto he promised to replace English with Sinhala as the official language along with "reasonable use of Tamil," but did not explain what this meant. He demanded abrogation of the agreement by which the British were allowed naval and air bases in Ceylon. To give credibility to his socialist pretensions he even promised to nationalize the ports and the omnibus companies. Finally, in 1956, he launched his election campaign not as the SLFP leader but as the leader of the MEP (Mahajana Eksath Peramuna— People's Liberation Front), a popular front of "progressive forces" which included, in addition to the SLFP, a collection of ex-LSSP members such as Philip Goonewordene and Dahanayake. Bandaranaike realized that without posing as a socialist and a progressive he could not compete successfully with the LSSP, which had a consistent history of opposition to the UNP.

Decline of the LSSP

Not surprisingly, the Communist Party supported this electoral bloc. More unexpected, however, was the LSSP decision to agree to an electoral arrangement whereby the LSSP and the Bandaranaike-led popular front decided not to contest each other in certain constituencies. This was the first crack in the LSSP's resolute anticapitalist position.

It may be useful to examine why the LSSP, which in the past had politicized the working class, had led an uncompromising struggle against imperialism, and had correctly analyzed Bandaranaike's political role, now began to take the first steps away from revolutionary practice. Reference has been made to a split in the LSSP and to its reunification in the 1950s. The two groups, the Lanka Sama Samaja Party and the Bolshevist Leninist Party, contested the 1948 general elections as separate organizations and between them won 25 out of 95 seats.

These two political currents had existed from early days within the LSSP. One, a populist current, wished to launch a broadly based mass organization; this group was led by Perera, Goonewordene, Dahanayake, and others. The second group, the Bolshevist Leninists, wished to build a disciplined vanguard party. Although both groups called themselves "Trotskyists," there was a fundamental difference in the way they approached political problems. These differences were exploited by the Communist Party, and there was pressure within both groups to close ranks against the CP. This partly explains why the BLP was prepared to reunify with the populist group.

The BLP leaders were intellectually committed to Bolshevism, but never came to grips with the actuality of the Ceylon revolution. They did not, for example, have a serious attitude toward the rural poor. This was not accidental, for they did not understand the dynamics of capitalism in rural Ceylon. The Communist Party was completely off the mark, its members still speaking about "feudal relations" in the rural areas as late as the 1960s. The BLP, and even the LSSP, recognized that capitalist property relations had penetrated even the remotest villages in Ceylon—that is to say, the rural economy was a money economy: capitalist laws of value operated throughout the society. Nevertheless, these "Trotskyists" did not draw the logical conclusions of their analysis. They did not evaluate the increasing tendency of the local bourgeoisie to buy up land from the peasants, nor did they take note of the high level of rural indebtedness that accelerated this process. It is because of such factors that a majority of rural people today belong to the rural proletariat. Most of them are seasonal workers who exchange their labor power for a daily wage. It is in fact quite incorrect to call them "peasantry" in the European sense, for European peasants hold land. This was largely true even in prerevolutionary Russia.

Although most of the small and middle peasants of Ceylon can rightly be included within the petty bourgeoisie, to classify the landless laborers and rural seasonal workers with the petty bourgeoisie, as the BLP tended to do, was a quite mistaken application of Marxist concepts. This scholastic approach to theory contributed to the degeneration of the BLP.

If the BLP had remained independent, its members might have come to grips with the problem of mobilizing the rural masses. Lenin and the Russian Bolsheviks themselves made many mistakes; they were, however, able to swing the party back to a successful course because they had made a fundamental break with the Mensheviks in 1903 and did not backpedal later. By contrast, once the BLP had reunited with the LSSP in 1950, it forewent the opportunity of learning from its own mistakes.

The BLP—and later the LSSP—was affiliated with the Fourth International, but the leadership of the International lacked the authority to intervene in Ceylon. Most of the international working class owed allegiance to social-democratic or "Stalinist" parties. Only in a few places like Ceylon, indeed, had Trotskyists gained a foothold among the people; the International's leadership therefore had no power to do more than advise.

Leninist and populist currents coexisted for some time within the LSSP; hence the contradictory character of its policies. For example, the party contested a large number of parliamentary seats. At first this was seen as a tactic to educate people about the revolutionary program. Parliament was to be used as a platform from which its own futility could be exposed. Gradually, however, the LSSP made concessions to popular prejudices. Candidates were chosen for their ability to win, which often meant choosing a person of a particular caste or ethnic group.

The Samajists unionized and politicized a large number of workers. But in time the LSSP unions, like those of other parties, succumbed to economism.

The criticisms made by the Bolshevist current were, in fact, pertinent. In the 1930s, when a small group of leftists launched their anti-imperialist struggle against the British, they gained a large number of followers. The LSSP was not, however, a cadre organization, and it is doubtful whether most of its leaders ever intended it to become one. Marxist theory was monopolized by the English-educated elite, who failed to provide political education for rank-and-file members. In the thirty-odd years of its existence the party did not translate any Marxist classics into the vernacular. Such failures perpetuated a vast gap in political understanding between leaders and followers. Since the followers relied entirely on the leaders for theoretical interpretations, they were unable to call a halt to the leaders' degeneration.

In the decade that followed the party's reunification, the Sama Samaja leaders became ever more deeply involved in parliamentarism. Their formal adherence to Marxism and to the political positions they had previously adopted became burdensome. They were, for example, pledged to fight for the citizenship rights of plantation workers. But plantation workers had no votes and could do nothing to increase the LSSP's parliamentary representation. Moreover, demands in behalf of the plantation workers did not help the party to win the existing rural vote, for the bourgeois parties were able to exploit anti-Tamil prejudices.

Lacking the ability to mobilize the rural poor around concrete programs issuing from long-range theory, the LSSP gradually abandoned its Marxist heritage for parliamentary politics. The party recruited fewer workers and more electoral functionaries. The largest branches grew up in the electorates of Sama Samaja M.P.'s, not in plantations or rural centers with large concentrations of workers. Trade union militants of yesteryear became trade union bureaucrats. By 1960 the LSSP had transformed itself from a potentially revolutionary movement into a reformist party. In exploited countries there is no room for independent social-democratic groups; they rapidly become appendages of bourgeois political forces.

Bandaranaike's Triumph

Lacking a revolutionary leadership, the rural poor tended to follow one of the bourgeois parties: the UNP or the SLFP (which was leading the MEP). In 1956, Bandaranaike rallied them in a spectacular electoral victory for the MEP. The LSSP's no-contest pact in the election was the first open indication that it had in effect accepted the Communist Party view that whereas the UNP represented the "reactionary bourgeoisie," the SLFP was its more "progressive" wing.

Bandaranaike's government initially enjoyed great support. He gave an impression of following genuine socialist policies: he nationalized the port of Colombo and the bus companies, introduced the Paddy Lands Act as a start to agrarian reform, and for a short time allowed wages and salaries to rise. These moves did not, however, affect the lives of the majority. The nationalization measures were comparable in scope to those of Kenneth Kaunda, Alvarado Valesco, or Indira Gandhi: their primary aim was to strengthen the national bourgeoisie's ability to bargain more effectively with imperialism, although they offered hope to the common people and so alleviated mass pressures. Even these reforms could not be successfully implemented because of the obstinate opposition of the SLFP right wing. The Paddy Lands Act, for instance, was so amended that its purpose was defeated.

Meanwhile the MEP government's stand on the language issue alienated Tamil speakers. The "Sinhala Only" Act replaced English with Sinhala as the official language. Influenced by chauvinists in his own party, Bandaranaike withdrew even the limited provisions he had made for the use of Tamil. This retreat invited further demands for discriminatory laws against the Tamils. Resurgent Sinhala chauvinism culminated in an anti-Tamil pogrom and brought relations between the two peoples to their lowest point.

Bandaranaike's policies proved futile in the face of increasing unemployment, inflation, and deteriorating living standards. Enthusiasm turned to discontent. When strikes occurred, he used the police and the army to crush them, as in the widely reported public servants' strike of April 1958. The draconian Public Security Act which followed has since been used repeatedly to defeat or prevent strikes and other forms of industrial action.

Although the LSSP and the CP had entered a no-contest pact with Bandaranaike, they refrained from joining the government. The CP supported the government's "progressive" measures; the LSSP gave it "critical support." But the anti-working class legislation, the "Sinhala Only" Act, and the anti-Tamil pogrom compelled LSSP leaders to switch from critical support to total opposition. Moving briefly to the left, the LSSP trade unions called a one-day political strike against the Public Security Act on March 3, 1959. Despite its verbal opposition to the Act, the Communist Party failed to support and even tried to sabotage the strike.

LSSP Crossroads

Bandaranaike's party was rent by factional strife. The left wing, led by Goonewordene, resigned from the cabinet and joined the opposition in May 1959. The right wing conspired to get rid of the Prime Minister, and on September 26, 1959, he was assassinated. The fact and manner of his death aroused great sympathy, but there was confusion and dissatisfaction in the country, with the SLFP now leaderless and disorganized. When a general election was held in March 1960, after six months of caretaker government, no party obtained a majority. The UNP was returned with 50 seats, while the SLFP showing dropped to 45. LSSP leaders completely misjudged the situation: they campaigned for a "Sama Samaja government," fielded 100 candidates, but won only 10 seats. Instead of abandoning the parliamentary strategy after this shattering blow, they abandoned the political principles that appeared to have cost them votes.

The UNP formed a minority government. Within a month, parliament was again dissolved and another election was held in July. At this point the degeneration of the LSSP became widely apparent. At a special conference just before the July elections, a right-wing proposal not only to support the SLFP but, if possible, to accept office under its prime ministership was carried.

Sirimavo Bandaranaike, wife of the former Prime Minister, took over the leadership of the SLFP and won a decisive majority, so decisive that she did not need the LSSP to form a government. The UNP reemerged as the main opposition. On the surface, Ceylon had achieved a British parliamentary model with two main parties, both committed to private property and "free" enterprise. Their influence declining, the left-wing parties moved to the right. The CP continued its support of the "progressive" national bourgeoisie while the LSSP gave "responsive" cooperation to the government. With the help of the left-wing parties, Mrs. Bandaranaike's government was briefly able to create the illusion that the SLFP was more progressive than the UNP. But by the end of 1961 mass discontent had erupted in demonstrations and strikes.

The CP and the LSSP tried to avoid being identified with these extra-parliamentary struggles, fearing they might cost them votes. In late 1962 the dock workers struck against the wishes of both CP and LSSP trade union leaders. Immediately afterward, the transport workers launched a national strike. These strikes for the first time united workers of different trade unions and political parties in grass-roots actions. They embarrassed the left-wing party leaders and compelled a shift in their policies. But instead of mobilizing the workers, these leaders took advantage of their desire for unity in struggle in order to create a three-party electoral bloc.

Betrayal

This bloc, comprising the right wing of the CP, the LSSP, and the MEP, called itself the United Left Front. In order to join it, the Sama Samaja leaders had to abandon their policies on the Tamil language and the citizenship rights of plantation workers. The Front was a triumph for the Communist Party. Its program involved no great threat to the Ceylonese capitalist class. It called for the "Ceylonization" of foreign interests rather than for nationalization of the means of production, distribution, and exchange. "Ceylonization" artificially separated the anti-imperialist from the anticapitalist struggle. By accepting it the LSSP, in effect, accepted the Stalinist theory of a two-stage revolution.

In each of the three Left parties there were small but influential groups opposed to this front. These groups presented an alternative strategy of uniting the working class in struggle on transitional demands. The right-wing leaders could not oppose this proposal outright. Accordingly all trade unions, including those not affiliated to any political party (notably those of the plantation workers), formed a joint committee and hammered out a series of twenty-one demands. The enthusiasm with which these demands were greeted in April 1964 contrasted strongly with the workers' apathy over the formation of the United Left Front in August 1963. Indeed, the demands threatened the capitalist structure of Ceylon. They were presented to the government at a mass rally in April, held in direct violation of the emergency regulations then obtaining.

Never before had all the trade unions forged such unity. Mrs. Bandaranaike realized that the government could not afford a frontal attack on the workers, yet it could not grant the demands without endangering the capitalist system. Instead, it bought off a small number of influential working class leaders. Ceylon's harassed bourgeoisie consented to this gambit, and the Left parties' leaders jumped for the bait. They even competed in offering terms to the ruling class to obtain a few ministerial posts. The Prime Minister showed her astuteness. She refrained from offering jobs to the MEP leaders, who lacked any significant working class following. She could rely on the support of the Communists since it followed from their political analysis. The most important party on the Left was the LSSP: it had a mass following and a significant trade union base. Accordingly she co-opted the right-wing leaders of the LSSP.

The party's left wing had predicted this development in August 1963. It could not, however, prevent the disastrous regroupment, and in June 1964 a special conference of the LSSP voted to form a coalition government with the SLFP on terms similar to those proposed by the Prime Minister. Bargaining was limited to trivialities relating to the number of cabinet posts to be held by the LSSP. The party's left wing then split away to form the LSSP (Revolutionary). The Fourth International at once recognized it and expelled the majority party.

The coalition government precisely fulfilled the Prime Minister's aims. Some workers believed it would bring the changes they desired; the working class was thus split between supporters and opponents of the government. The three left-wing parties split into six different groups; soon, some of these began to disintegrate altogether. The threat of a mass general strike receded and the twenty-one demands were forgotten. The capitalists not only regained their confidence; they soon began to reconsider the advisability of hiring any Marxists. More conservative elements in the SLFP could not understand the importance of the Prime Minister's tactical maneuver; in any case, the defection of these elements from the SLFP caused the coalition to collapse in eight months.

Afraid to jeopardize their cabinet positions, the LSSP leaders betrayed the working class. The struggle at the Velona factory was a crass example. One thousand of its workers were dismissed by the owner, a traditional capitalist and a UNP supporter, because of their attempt to join a union of their choice. Mainly young and women, the Velona workers labored under medieval conditions. Yet the "progressive" government did nothing to help them; instead it sent the police to smash the heads of teen-agers who dared to organize a picket line. The government could have applied labor laws already on the statute books to discipline the Velona management, but this it dared not do lest other sections of the workers also strike. By persuading the workers to return to work and take the issue to the courts, the LSSP and its unions helped defeat the strike.

Despite such events, the sudden collapse of the government prevented many workers from learning through experience that popular front coalitions help class enemies. Eight months was, moreover, too short a time for the left wing, which had broken with the reformists, to build an alternative leadership. The early defeat of the coalition government left the working class confused.

Return of the UNP

In the new elections of January 1965, conservatives who had split from the SLFP joined the UNP. With their help, the UNP secured a narrow majority over the coalition parties. (The CP also joined the coalition soon after the defeat of the latter.) With the aid of the Federal Party, which represented the interests of the Tamil bourgeoisie, the UNP formed a "national government." The MEP also joined this hotch-potch. Thus, except for two small revolutionary nuclei—the LSSP (Revolutionary) and the CP (pro-Peking)—all the left-wing leaders and parties became appendages of one of the two bourgeois parties.

UNP members recognized that they could not pursue the same course as in 1948–1956. At that time they had preached the advantages of "free enterprise" unashamedly, but that was now impracticable. The UNP also recognized the advantages of Bandaranaike's foreign policy, which enabled the government to obtain aid from both power blocs. The UNP was, however, no better than the previous coalition in its attempts to salvage Ceylon's economy. It had to obtain loans from the World Bank on humiliating terms. In order to repress strikes in support of wage demands, it ruled the country under emergency regulations for three and a half of its five years in office. During this period the rice subsidy was withdrawn and expenditures on education drastically cut.

Although mass discontent reached a boiling point, there was no effective leadership to mobilize people in action. The CP and the LSSP had one strategy: to wait for the next elections. The Maoist party (CP, pro-Peking), which initially controlled a number of trade unions, lost them to the pro-Moscow CP. Although the Maoists retained a certain influence among the plantation workers, it was insignificant compared to that of the unions led by Thondaman and Aziz, which were organized on the basis of the religious affiliations and national origins of the workers.[5]

The LSSP-R split after a special conference in 1967. A section led by Edmund Samarakkody left it and formed the Revolutionary Sama Samaja Party (RSSP). The latter, as well as the LSSP-R, now led by the trade union leader Bala Tampoe, consisted of small groups which lacked the forces to organize mass actions against the UNP. Although the Ceylon mercantile union, led by Tampoe, did initiate a number of united front struggles where they had influence, almost all of them were sabotaged by the coalition trade unions, which each time pulled out as early as possible. The coalition leaders were marking time until the next general elections scheduled for April 1970.

By the time of the election campaign of March 1970, the UNP's defeat seemed certain. The party had a miserable record: it offered nothing to the unemployed, the workers, or the rural poor, whose conditions had deteriorated during UNP rule. True, the coalition parties offered little better. The only significant concession they were prepared to make was restoration of the rice subsidy, withdrawn by the UNP. The coalition program also included (a) recognition of North Vietnam, the Provisional Revolutionary Government of South Vietnam, North Korea, and East Germany; (b) the creation of People's Committees and Workers' Committees; and (c) control of the export-import trade and especially of the trade in tea.

The first of these was designed to improve the "socialist" image of the coalition, while the second and third were deceptive. Even before her election Mrs. Bandaranaike had made it clear that the People's and Workers' Committees would be strictly advisory, not soviets or centers of power. Control of exports and imports did not mean that the trade would be nationalized, but only that measures would be taken to improve the efficiency of the export-import sector and the production and marketing of tea.

Despite these vague promises, the large majority of workers and youth, who still had illusions about the reformist leaders, voted for the coalition. Their protest votes once again routed the UNP, and the coalition parties were swept into power in May 1970, winning 120 out of 150 seats. Of these 120, 95 were won by the SLFP.

Second Coalition Government

The coalition parties, especially their younger members, had campaigned against the UNP with much anticapitalist rhetoric. The young SLFP candidate Nanda Ellawala, for example, described to his rural voters how he would skin capitalists alive on the Galleface Green when he came to power. The coalition thus came to office on the promise to destroy capitalism, create a socialist society, and give everyone a job and a decent livelihood.

Soon after the election the more advanced sections of the people began to carry out what their leaders had promised. The day after the elections there was a spontaneous demonstration against the pro-UNP Lake House Press and the building was almost burned down. More important, in several areas where people lacked housing, they began to occupy the land of landlords. The government condemned these actions and sent the army and police to evict the squatters. Leslie Goonewordene, former secretary of the LSSP and a Member of Parliament, issued a statement attacking these irresponsible moves and stating that he would support legal action against them.

Similarly, the Velona workers and those of the Dasawa Publishing House learned through bitter experience that it was irresponsible to ask for such elementary rights as that of organizing in a union of their choice, and that it was perhaps even criminal to strike for such demands. These workers were not led by the "wreckers" of the LSSP-R but by "responsible" leaders of the LSSP.[6] Mrs. Bandaranaike sent her Finance Minister, Dr. N. M. Perera, to explain to the workers why they should go back to work without their comrades, who had been fired by the boss, and, further, that they should apologize to the boss for striking. At the Norwood estate, police under the control of the Bandaranaike government shot and killed two plantation workers. Yet the government had nothing to offer the thousands of unemployed youth or the urban and rural workers whose living standards were continually deteriorating. The much-publicized budget gave nothing to the people. Its sole purpose seemed to be to allay the fears of local and foreign capitalists about the coalition government and its "Marxist" ministers.

These developments began to radicalize the more politically aware among the people, especially the impatient youth. They looked for new leadership, and found that its framework already existed.

Birth of the JVP

The Ceylon public first heard of the Janata Vimukthi Peramuna, or People's Liberation Front, in the spring of 1970. They were referred to as the "Che Guevarists." The JVP had in fact organized clandestinely for over four years before anyone heard of them. Just before the general elections of May 1970, the UNP government announced the arrest of a few JVP members, charging them with a plot to attack polling booths and ballot boxes. Today it is known that there was no such plot. The "information" may have come from a section of the UNP, who were themselves toying with the idea of a coup d'état because they faced certain defeat in the elections. During the campaign the JVP supported "progressive" candidates of the coalition parties. In fact, only the LSSP-R opposed both the UNP and the Bandaranaike-led coalition composed of the SLFP, the pro-Moscow CP, and the LSSP. Even the Maoists tried to join the coalition bloc; it was only when they were rebuffed that they called for a boycott of the elections.

When the JVP militants were held in custody even after the elections, their movement organized a poster campaign to demand the release of their leader, Rohan Wijeweera. This campaign alarmed the government. The posters were hand-written and appeared everywhere at once, and no one knew who had put them up. Their timing suggested a widespread organization.

When Wijeweera was eventually released by the courts, he sought to answer some of the questions that puzzled the Left in general. Rohan Wijeweera had been a student at Lumumba University in Moscow. During the Sino-Soviet dispute he supported the Chinese position. Naturally displeased, the Russians refused to renew his visa when he returned to Ceylon on vacation. For a short time Wijeweera worked for the pro-Moscow CP, but soon left it with a small group to join the Maoist Communists. Not long after, he and his comrades became disillusioned with the Maoists too, and formed their own organization. Their disillusionment with existing parties sprang from a sense that the old generation of leftists had either fallen by the wayside into social democracy or, even if still revolutionary, could not come to grips with today's realities.

The political understanding of JVP members was limited. They initially held a "Debrayist" view of the urban working class, namely, that its members, having a higher standard of living than the rural poor, lacked the political consciousness of the latter. Similarly, one of their three main slogans was "Against Indian Expansionism," which in view of the presence of Indian plantation workers in Ceylon could be interpreted as chauvinism (their other two slogans were "Against Imperialism" and "Against Capitalism"). They opposed the Bandaranaike coalition because they concluded that coalitions between bourgeois and working class parties always lead to the defeat and disorientation of the working class. They cited the example of Indonesia, yet explained that the massacre of Indonesian Communists resulted from the failure of the Aidit leadership to follow the thoughts of Mao. This shows that they failed to make a complete theoretical assessment of Maoism.

The discipline and organization of these comrades were, however, remarkable. They stopped smoking and drinking alcohol and used the money thus saved for political work. They organized themselves clandestinely, realizing that the period of bourgeois democracy was coming to an end in Ceylon.

The first indications of this were evident in the summer of 1970, when the government strengthened the apparatus of repression. It increased the police force by 55 percent and formed an antirevolutionary committee in the army (among whose distinguished members was the pro-Moscow leader, Pieter Keuneman). In August the JVP held mass meetings throughout the country to explain their politics, attracting crowds of ten to fifteen thousand. The JVP explained that it was not a terrorist organization. Speakers attacked and exposed the coalition as a capitalist government and explained that they wished to build a Leninist revolutionary party. The pro-Moscow CP, and later the other coalition parties, slandered the JVP as a CIA-backed organization. The JVP ridiculed these charges and asked the CP why they had supported imperialism during World War II and why they had made a bloc with the UNP in 1948. They gathered a large following among the youth and their paper sold over 40,000 copies a few days after its publication, but because of police intimidation the movement could not find a printer to produce more copies. About this time the police began to arrest and intimidate JVP militants to obtain information on their strength and influence. When this harassment began, the JVP sought allies.

Revolutionary United Front

The JVP leaders now made contact with the revolutionary Trotskyists of the LSSP-R, led by Bala Tampoe. Tampoe was also the leader of the Ceylon Mercantile Union. The most militant union in Ceylon, it had a membership of 35,000 and a policy-making General Council of 400. JVP leaders were well-informed about CMU policies, and instructed their urban members to join the CMU.

A parallel development took place on the tea plantations. The estate workers, disillusioned by the coalition and recognizing the bankruptcy of communal leaders like Thondaman, were seeking new leadership. They therefore approached the CMU. The LSSP-R leaders' response was, however, that the plantation workers had no tradition of militancy, that their desire to join the CMU was merely an effort to replace one "savior" with another, and that the first lesson the plantation militants must drive home to their fellow workers was to rely on their own class strength. Tampoe agreed, however, to assist the tea workers. Their militants accepted this advice and formed their own political organization, the Young Socialist Front, whose policies were close to those of the LSSP-R and whose aim was to politicize and mobilize plantation workers and at a suitable moment to fuse their organization with the LSSP-R.

When the JVP learned about this organization, they requested discussions with the YSF. Out of these discussions a new front emerged, uniting the YSF, the LSSP-R, and the JVP. Their first meeting as a united front was held at the Norwood estate to protest the police shooting of two Indian workers. This was an important occasion for the JVP because they wanted to demonstrate that they were not opposed to Indian workers, and that, contrary to the slanders of the orthodox Communists, they were not a chauvinist movement.

The growing unity between the JVP, the LSSP-R, and the YSF frightened the coalition leaders. The government was facing a foreign-exchange crisis and was making appeals to the World Bank and to imperialist countries for aid and loans. The World Bank had, however, already granted $50 million and the Ceylon government had failed even to make regular interest payments. The World Bank was prepared to grant further loans only under certain conditions, and the government agreed. In an interview with the *Ceylon Times*, Finance Minister Dr. Perera admitted that "harsh measures" would have to be taken to set the economy right. The budget for 1971, to be announced in the spring, would undoubtedly impose more burdens on the people. Meanwhile the masses were becoming impatient. The tea and rubber workers had presented a wage demand six months previously and were still awaiting a reply. Disillusion among coalition supporters was worrying the government.

These three factors—the possible emergence of a permanent revolutionary united front, the growing dependence of the government on the imperialists, and the swelling mass discontent—account for the events that followed.

Repression and Resistance

Faced with rising opposition, the government struck first. Its object was (1) to isolate and destroy the political vanguard before the people were ready to come out in struggle, and (2) to use emergency regulations to ward off the threatened unrest. The imperialists decided to give the government their full cooperation if only because of their strategic and military interests in Ceylon.

The post-March 5, 1971, events resulted from a well-planned government operation. In the first week of March the police were put on "alert." On March 6 a group of "youth" attacked the U.S. embassy with petrol bombs and left some leaflets in the vicinity of the embassy. They claimed to be the Mao Youth Front and demanded that the U.S.A. get out of Vietnam and that it stop its aid to the "Anti-Che Guevara" movement. The government attributed this action to the JVP and invoked special powers, including the power to search, arrest, and detain without trial. The JVP disclaimed responsibility and stated that this was an act of provocateurs.

Ceylon has no Mao Youth Front, and the government provided no evidence to substantiate its charges. Shortly afterward, it began to arrest every known militant in the JVP, including Rohan Wijeweera. The government also arrested the pro-Chinese leader, N. Shanmugathasan, and even some LSSP militants. On March 13 the government "disclosed" a "plot" by the JVP to overthrow it, declared a state of emergency, and imposed a dusk-to-dawn curfew.

Mrs. Bandaranaike claimed that the security forces foiled an attempt by the JVP to seize power. Government communiqués in April stated that the army was engaged in mopping-up operations. At the same time, however, the government made frantic appeals to the British and U.S. governments, who provided military aid. On the request of Mrs. Bandaranaike, the Indian government also sent four frigates and a few helicopters, while Yahya Khan of Pakistan, even while engaged in the invasion of East Pakistan, added his own assistance, as did the UAR and Yugoslavia. The Soviet government enthusiastically joined this united front by providing MIGs and helicopters to the Ceylon government. The Chinese government also provided an interest-free loan of $30 million.

The main purpose of the government operation was, it seems, to destroy the infrastructure of the JVP. The government used extraordinary powers under the emergency laws to carry out an extensive search for every person suspected of revolutionary activity. A majority of JVP members, at least, were on the alert for this. They had not planned to initiate a struggle at that point; neither the plantation workers nor the urban sector was ready. Nevertheless, they decided that they would not passively allow their organization to be destroyed and that if the government decided to attack they would resist.

The government leaders underestimated both the organizational strength and the mass support of the JVP. They also overestimated the capacity of the army to fight in the countryside. Not only were they unaware of the combat strength of the JVP; they also forgot that most army privates come from rural areas and are likely to have more sympathy with the JVP than with the government. Repression was therefore effected only after fierce fighting and the bloody slaughter, by government forces, of several thousand militants and civilians.

Strict censorship was in force during the repression and it was difficult to obtain precise information about the struggle. It is clear, however, that the government has still not succeeded in gaining complete control. It has, for instance, admitted that the army has not been totally successful in its operation in the interior and that some "guerrillas" survive and are avoiding contact with security forces. Although the government slandered the JVP as a "right-wing" and "fascist" formation, the mass of people do not appear to be deceived. The brutality with which the army and police have dealt not only with JVP suspects but with innocent civilians has increased sympathy for the JVP in both the cities and the countryside. The fact that the armed resistance of the JVP was most successful in precisely those areas where the SLFP scored sweeping electoral victories last year is politically significant. It appears to have stricken the SLFP leaders with terror. The arrest and detention of at least two SLFP Members of Parliament suggest that the JVP may indeed have had sympathizers within the government ranks. The government's attempt to eliminate the JVP has been at least partly damaging to itself.

Some of the extreme savagery displayed by the Bandaranaike administration will undoubtedly have far-reaching effects: the same CP and LSSP government ministers who participated in and justified the crushing of the insurrection will soon find that they themselves are not immune and that the Ceylonese ruling class can do' without them. There is increasing evidence to suggest that rank-and-file members of these two parties are already in a state of turmoil. On a more general level some of the atrocities of the regime have been brought to light *inside* Ceylon itself: the two officers accused of raping and murdering 21-year-old Prema Manamperi (Ceylon's "Beauty Queen" and a JVP sympathizer) have been brought to trial. The two men claimed that they were merely acting on instructions from superior officers.[7] Meanwhile, even the Ceylonese government has so far been unable to kill all the JVP prisoners. There are still 16,000 political prisoners in concentration camps spread all over Ceylon. The bourgeois press in Europe and North America, which goes into ecstasies in describing persecution of militants in the U.S.S.R. and Eastern Europe, has so far ignored the plight of these prisoners and the indignities being inflicted on them. It is possible that many will be killed or tortured to death because at the moment they pose a permanent political threat. The very fact that the government has herded them into concentration camps has resulted in the JVP militants embarking on a whole series of political discussions and analyzing the reasons for their defeat. In other words, they have succeeded in preserving a collective identity and developing self-critical analyses even inside the concentration camps. Very few have been demoralized, and morale in the camps is reported to be fairly high.[8]

Prospects

Struggle was forced upon the oppressed people of Ceylon before they were politically prepared for it. Equally obviously, however, no capitalist government will be able to solve the island's deepest problems and every government from now on will be compelled to use brutal force to maintain the capitalist system.

Although the urban and plantation workers may be confused by recent developments, they too will now be confronted by "emergency regulations" whenever they seek to back up their demands with industrial action. And for that reason they too may begin to move. Today the urgent need is to overcome the uneven development of political consciousness among different sections of the working people and to build quickly an effective leadership to unite them. Comrades of the JVP, the LSSP(R), and the YSF realize that the struggle will be protracted and bitter: the acute crisis of the Ceylonese bourgeoisie and the growing impasse of imperialism can lead only to escalation of the struggle. There is little doubt that in this process the imperialist powers will go beyond material aid and send "advisers" or whatever else they deem necessary, for they are fully aware of the need to retain a foothold in Ceylon to police the Indian Ocean.

The Soviet bureaucracy, concerned with its own interests rather than with those of the world working class, has lined up with capitalism and imperialism against the suffering people of Ceylon. The politics of peaceful coexistence prove to be those of betrayal and counter-revolution. The People's Republic of China has also shamefully betrayed the revolutionary militants of Ceylon by giving aid and moral support to the Bandaranaike government.

Despite these events and despite the defection of its reformist "Left" leaders, the working class of Ceylon has not been tamed by its rulers; it has several times shown willingness to fight. The emergence of the JVP and the politicization of the rural proletariat are significant and welcome. Given the growing crisis of capitalism, Ceylonese workers and poor people must either accept greater oppression or prepare to overthrow capitalism with arms in hand.[9] This task cannot be accomplished by a disorganized and spontaneous rising of the masses. What is needed is not only a revolutionary leadership in Ceylon but also, as the experience of Indochina and Bangladesh demonstrates, a revolutionary international to ensure the final defeat of capitalism and imperialism.

Notes

1. The value of principal exports in 1968 was as follows:

	Rs. 1,000
Tea	1,160,910
Rubber	330,654
Dessicated coconut	163,820
Copra	33,703
Coconut oil	132,991
Plambago	7,848
Areca nut	245
Cocoa	7,339
Total	1,837,510

Tea thus accounted for 63 percent of principal export earnings.

2. *The Report of the Survey of Landless Laborers* (Ceylon Parliament, sessional papers XIII, 1952), published in July 1952, shows that in the rural sector of Ceylon 26.3 percent of all families dependent on subsistence agriculture owned no land at all; 42.3 percent owned less than half an acre;

and 54.1 percent owned less than one acre. The corresponding figures
for all families were 37.7 percent, 59.3 percent, and 70.6 percent. This
survey was made in 1948. Since then no comparable survey has been
made, but there is no doubt that in the past twenty-three years the proportion of landless rural poor has greatly increased. In Ceylon, moreover, the primitive methods of cultivation do not permit a person who
owns even one acre of land to produce enough food to sustain his family.

3. Terms of trade from 1964–1968 were as follows (in Rs. 1,000):

	1964	1965	1966	1967	1968
Exports	1,974,502	1,474,381	2,028,268	1,738,365	2,173,089
Imports	1,842,573	1,915,916	1,675,959	1,630,864	1,975,135

4. One measure equals two pounds of rice.

5. The two largest and most important unions on the plantations are organized on ethnic lines. The Ceylon Workers' Congress includes workers
who came from regions that are now in modern India. This union is led
by Mr. Thondaman, who has been made a distinguished citizen of Ceylon and is himself a plantation owner. The Democratic Workers' Congress has organized workers from regions that are now in Pakistan. It is
led by Mr. Aziz, a supporter of the pro-Moscow Communist Party.

6. To date there have been three strikes at Velona on the same issue, that
of organizing in a union of the workers' choice. The owner of the Velona
factory, a UNP member and an ex-MP, has a particularly brutal repu-
tation. In 1958 the Communist Party (at that time united and pro-Moscow) led a strike of workers in support of fellow workers who had been
fired for attempting to form a union. After a bitter struggle the dispute
was referred to the Arbitration Court. The lengthy court battle ended in
the owner being asked to make certain concessions, including reinstate-
ment of some of the dismissed employees. The owner, however, ignored
the court order without being penalized. In 1964 the workers were led
by the LSSP-R. Again the strike was lost and the owner recruited a new
batch of workers. A third strike in July 1970 was led by the LSSP, i.e.,
one of the parties in the coalition government. It was provoked by the
owner's intransigence rather than by the LSSP. LSSP leaders tried to
persuade the Labor Minister to refer the case to the Arbitration Court, a
procedure which in most cases aids the employer, who can afford long
and expensive legal battles. Meanwhile the factory owner made a deal
with leaders of the SLFP to form a rival union and affiliate it to the
SLFP trade union organization. The outcome of all these maneuvers
was the same: the strike was lost and the strike leaders were dismissed
from their jobs.

7. "Ceylon: The Rapists Defend Themselves," *The Red Mole*, No. 33, De-

cember 12, 1971, p. 9, provides details of the trial and the defense offered by the two men, Lieutenant Wijeysoora and Sergeant Ratnayaka. Both men claimed that their orders were: "Take no prisoners; bump them off; liquidate them."

8. For further details see Halliday, "The Ceylonese Insurrection," in *New Left Review*, No. 69. Readers who want further evidence on the concentration camps would be well advised to study the budget announced by LSSP Minister Perera on November 11, 1971. One of the items that was exempted from the new taxes was barbed wire, a hot item in Ceylon, and even the pro-Moscow CP newspaper allowed itself a sarcastic editorial comment entitled "Barbed Wire Is a Bargain."

9. The November 11, 1971, budget represented a vicious attack on the living standards of the working class. Perera informed the people that the price of rice would be raised, the sugar ration would be limited to two pounds a month per person, and free hospital care would be phased out. The workers responded to the budget with work stoppages, slowdowns, and street demonstrations, despite the official state of emergency. The pressure was so immense that the government was forced to retract and make some concessions. It was precisely the linking of the rural poor led by the JVP and the urban proletariat led by Tampoe that the Ceylonese bourgeoisie had been keen to prevent when they unleashed the repression against the JVP. A report in *Le Monde* on January 8, 1972, claimed that the Mercantile Union led by Tampoe "has not ceased to challenge the regime since the beginning of the repression." The options open to the Ceylonese coalition government are extremely limited: they will attempt to move in and smash completely the organizations of the working class, which would result in a massive response from the workers; if not, they will face the possibilities of being overthrown by a military coup d'état.

Part IV

Bangladesh and the South Asian Crisis

1. The Social Background of Bangladesh

Ramkrishna Mukherjee

Growth of the "Bengali" Ethnic Unit

Little is known about the people in "Bengal" before *aryanization* began with the consolidation of the Gupta empire in eastern India from about the fifth century A.D. It is known, however, that they were described as *koma* (tribal) and that many of them lived in rather undifferentiated societies. Sufficient division of labor had taken place among them to identify "merchants," but their social organization did not admit the supremacy of Brahmans or a caste structure of society.[1] Caste organization, an imported institution, developed when Brahmans were brought in as religious and legal authorities by rulers from western and southern India.[2] Eventually, all people (including the Brahmans) were categorized into castes according to their vocations, and the caste division of society became a hereditary phenomenon which carried with it all the familiar Hindu prohibitions against marriage, dining, and physical contact between people of different castes.[3] Even so, the caste structure of Bengal did not have the foundation or the stable growth found in the Indo-Gangetic plain proper.[4] Because of the existence of powerful social groups that were placed in ranks lower in the religious scale than that of the Brahmans, compromises had to be made between the Brahmanic and non-Brahmanic ways of life.

Beginning with the fifth century, the caste organization and the settlement of people on land cultivated with the plow developed

Earlier versions of this article were published by the Sociological Research Unit of the Indian Statistical Institute (Calcutta, 1971); in *The Economic and Political Weekly*, Bombay, Vol. VII, Nos. 5–7, 1972; and in S. P. Varma and Virendra Narain (eds.), *Pakistan Political System in Crisis—Emergence of Bangladesh* (Jaipur, 1972). I am indebted to my colleague Bhola Chatterji for his help in preparing this paper, particularly in connection with the statistical data.

399

simultaneously, and by the twelfth to thirteenth centuries both had become stabilized in Bengal society.[5] The indigenous people of Bengal accepted the Brahmanic way of life because of the accompanying economic privileges of a settled agricultural society, but they also contributed significantly to the social organization and the ideology that eventually emerged in Bengal from this process of culture-contact.[6] As a result, while Hinduism spread over Bengal, the Bengali Hindus were particularly distinguished from their coreligionists in the rest of the subcontinent. Even today, orthodox Brahmans in other parts of India will not dine with Bengali Brahmans who eat fish and are in other ways regarded as deviating from the vocation of the Brahmans. The Hindus of Bengal thus assumed a distinct "Bengali" character, as is currently reflected in the behavior of the Hindu refugees from East Pakistan who have been migrating to the Republic of India since 1947 but who, unlike their counterparts from Punjab and Sind, find it difficult to settle anywhere outside Bengal.

While the Hindus of Bengal were thus ethnically consolidated and correspondingly alienated from the Hindus in the rest of India, the course of Hinduization was not the same in the eastern and western regions of Bengal. The area east of the Padma River (a tributary of the Ganges), which comprised the bulk of East Bengal, was not easily accessible from the west. It was closely linked with Assam, where Buddhism and, later, a loose form of Hinduism prevailed.[7] Buddhism contented itself with superimposing a new religion upon the existing tribal societies, which it left largely unchanged with regard to the introduction of new economic activities and from which it did not even uproot animistic practices. Because of their remoteness from the seat of Hindu rule, the people of East Bengal were also relatively free from control by the Guptas and other Hindu rulers. As a result, there developed a combination of creeds and cults known as *sahajiya* (simplified religion), and the West Bengali Brahmans considered the area east of the Padma as defiling and detrimental to their status. Consequently, when in the wake of Muslim conquest the zeal of conversion to Islam was felt in Bengali society, the great majority of the people of East Bengal were converted. Some Muslims from the upper part of India no doubt settled in Bengal, and even some Brahmans were converted to Islam. But like the imported Brahmans among Bengali Hindus, they constituted a very small proportion of the Muslim population in both East and West Bengal.[8]

Regional distinction thus coincided with religious differentiation, and both played their role in Bengali society. The forces of consolidation of "Bengali" culture, however, were greater than these two forces of alienation. Muslim *sufism* (a branch of Islamic philosophy and religion) and Hindu "simplified religion" and worship of the deity Vishnu, as against orthodox religious systems, found a fertile soil in Bengal and helped in the development of Bengali culture and a Bengali language.[9] With the onset of the Bhakti or devotional movement in eastern India under Chaitanya's leadership, the Hindus and Muslims were brought closer to each other on the social and ideological planes.[10] The Bengali language was also raised to the status of a literary language and in course of time it was enriched with loan words and phrases from Persian and Arabic.[11] The Muslim rulers actively supported these trends. The most important of all Hindu epics—the *Ramayana*, the *Mahabharata*, and the *Bhagavata*—were translated from Sanskrit into Bengali under the patronage of Muslim rulers who also honored both Hindu and Muslim noblemen and men of letters, and employed both Hindus and Muslims as state officials, revenue farmers *(zamindars)*, etc.[12]

The economic structure of Bengal at that time facilitated and consolidated the unity achieved in the social and ideological life of the people, for it involved Hindus and Muslims who followed the same or similar vocations in East and West Bengal. The *jati-* or caste division of the people (which should not be confused with the *varna-*, or four-class distinction of the Hindus) [13] had become so deep-rooted in the society that many functional castes emerged among the Muslims. Cotton weaving had developed as an important industry in which both Hindu and Muslim castes were engaged. In riverine Bengal, fishing was also an important occupation of Hindu and Muslim castes. The castes of oil-pressers included both the Hindu *kolu* and the Muslim *khulu*.[14]

A Bengali ethnic unit had thus emerged irrespective of the regional and religious distinctions of the people, and it approached the point of attaining nationhood in the sixteenth to eighteenth centuries. The people of Bengal had a territorial identification, a common history, a community of culture and language, a common economic organization based on agriculture and industry (mainly the production of cotton and silk textiles demanded in the international market through the agencies of European East India Companies), and a distinct psychological identity that was asserted against superior or analogous powers. (Examples of the latter were the role of the *bar-bhuinyas*, the twelve feudatory lords of Bengal, who included both Hindus and Muslims and who sometimes combined, irrespective of religious faith, to overthrow the suzerainty of the Mughal rulers; the several attempts of the Nawabs of Bengal—who had both Hindu and Muslim generals and ministers—to declare the province of Bengal independent of the Mughal state power; and the sustained defense organized by the Bengalis against Maratha domination in the eighteenth century.) This Bengali unity, in the course of nation-building among its people and state-formation in its territory, has been particularly emphasized in recent years by the Muslim intelligentsia of Bangladesh:

> The whole thesis about the Bengali Muslims centred round two alternatives: either they were low caste Hindus converted to Islam, or they were immigrants, Mughal, Syeds, Pathans or at least Shaikhs. The third and possibly the more correct assessment, namely that they were essentially neither but a distinct cultural entity could never occur to any one. Bengali soil and Bengali blood are admittedly of innumerable origins but they are distinct identities in themselves. History of the growth and development also made the Bengali culture a distinct culture and the people a distinct people. . . . So long as the traces of peculiar origin are preserved the immigrants will remain alien residents in Bengal rather than become people of Bengal.[15]

Alienation of Bengali Muslims from Bengali Hindus

The economy of Bengal suffered serious reverses in the first phase of British rule, and this affected the Muslims more adversely than the Hindus. The Muslims were deliberately discriminated against in the field of administration and civic organization as well as in economic activities related to the interests of the British East India Company and its officials, who ruled the country in the late eighteenth and early nineteenth centuries. They were held in suspicion by the Company officials and were regarded as direct representatives of the previous rulers. The Muslim aristocracy also pursued a policy of aloofness from the Company's activities, and in general retreated to obscure stations or dispersed in the countryside, thereby losing the position of leadership in society which it had held previously along with its Hindu counterparts.[16]

The Hindus, on the other hand, were favored by the Company and its officials, although most of the previous Hindu revenue farmers, merchants, etc., were removed from the social scene.[17] There were, however, other Hindus who closely aligned themselves with the Company and its officials; as their agents (known as *baniyan* or *gomostha*), this group gained a strong footing in the economic organization of Bengal through dealings in its merchandise and other products.[18] But eventually, unlike their English counterparts, these agents were unable to thrive as merchants or to invest their gains in industrial production because the foreign ruler's policy was not conducive to such a course of development.[19] They could, however, turn themselves into a landed aristocracy, especially after the Permanent Settlement of Land in Bengal from 1793,[20] and in this pursuit East Bengal appeared to them as a virgin field because "Rajahs" were few and far between there. Consequently, by the middle of the nineteenth century the powerful landlords of East Bengal were Hindus, with a few exceptions—e.g., the Nawabs of Dacca, Bogra, and Jalpaiguri. Moreover, subinfeudation followed in the wake of the Permanent Settlement of Land,[21] and ever-increasing numbers of Hindus (who were in an advantageous position to accumulate some wealth) became subsidiary landlords. The process operated throughout Bengal, but in East Bengal it took the character of Hindu landlords versus Muslim peasantry (the latter constituted the bulk of the local population).

Because of their socioeconomic superiority, the Hindus could usurp almost all the facilities then available for education, which even wealthy Muslims kept away from for various reasons.[22] As a result the Bengali "baboos" (clerks) in the government and in mercantile firms were virtually all Hindus. At the same time, educated Hindus could employ their time in the pursuit of science, art, and literature while living on their rents from land. The socioeconomic structure of Bengal had changed so much in about a century that the 1871 census report recorded:

> Hindus, with exceptions of course, are the principal *zamindars, talukdars* [owners of large subinfeudatory estates], public officers, men of learning, moneylenders, traders, shopkeepers, and [are] engaging in most active pursuits of life and coming directly and frequently under the notice of the rulers of the country; while the Musalmans, with exceptions also, form a very large majority of the cultivators of the

ground and of the day labourers, and others engaged in the very humblest forms of mechanical skill and of buying and selling.[23]

The "middle class" that developed in Bengal by the end of the nineteenth century was thus composed almost entirely of Hindus, which affected the previously established harmony in Bengal's social structure and was felt more keenly in East Bengal because of its Muslim majority. Some Hindu intellectuals lamented the loss to Bengal because of the decay of Muslim literature and culture[24] but, in general, the Hindus remained oblivious to it. Moreover, their reaction to the situation was influenced by the resurgence, in the last quarter of the eighteenth century, of government supported religious orthodoxy in both communities; this tended to separate Hindus and Muslims who had previously been brought closer by the propagation of humanistic values.[25] The upshot was that the socioeconomically dominant group began to show indifference and even contempt toward the Muslim way of life, and the latter group reacted sharply. A conflict situation, which was perennial but not pervasive in earlier times, thus emerged and had a pernicious effect on the course of nation-building and state-formation in Bengal.

Yet the "Bengali" identity remained. In 1905, there was such a powerful movement against the British proposal to divide Bengal administratively into East and West that the proposal had to be hastily withdrawn. It may be that the intercommunity conflict, now in the open, failed to lead to a decisive rupture of Hindu-Muslim relations because anti-British stances (displayed mostly by Hindus) during the Sepoy Rebellion of 1857, as well as the growing national movement from the 1890s on, had led the rulers to shift their support to the Muslim community[26]—a support which the latter readily accepted in order to recover its social position and status. Muslim leaders persuaded the government to offer special facilities for education and jobs for the Muslims, and a Muslim middle class began to grow in Bengal, especially at the beginning of the present century.[27]

The concurrent shift in the agrarian economy of Bengal helped in the growth of the Muslim middle class. At the close of the nineteenth century, crops in Bengal were steadily acquiring a commodity value in the ever-growing external and home markets.[28] Accordingly, although they were a distinct minority in the total society, the peasants with substantial holdings which could not be cultivated solely by their own labor ceased to settle their surplus holdings on other peasants under the temporary tenures allowed under the rules of the Permanent Settlement of Land. Instead, they began to have these holdings cultivated by sharecroppers recruited from the ranks of impoverished peasants, since in this way they could acquire more land and employ their newly acquired holdings for the same mode of production. Thus a category known as *jotedar* (landholder) emerged in rural Bengal, distinct from the category of *zamindar* created by the Permanent Settlement of Land.[29] Naturally, in the Muslim majority area of East Bengal an appreciable number of *jotedars* were Muslims, and the number increased in course of time; some, like their Hindu counterparts, became petty *zamindars* in order to raise their social status. (See Table 1.)

Table 1

	% of total households	
Rural Bengal, 1946	*Hindu*	*Muslim*
Petty *zamindar*, *jotedar*, rich farmer	5	3
Self-sufficient owner-cultivator	37	44
Sharecropper, agricultural laborer	58	53
Total	100	100

Each category contains equivalent and corresponding rural occupations.
Source: Ramkrishna Mukherjee, *The Dynamics of a Rural Society* (Akademie-Verlag, Berlin; Popular Prakashan, Bombay, 1957), p. 88, Table 2.1.

Since most of the *jotedars* could afford the cost of higher education for their sons or provide them with capital to invest in businesses in neighboring towns, a large number of *jotedar* families forged links with the urban middle class, as one or more members of the family became a school or college teacher, a lawyer, doctor, businessman, government or civic official, clerk, etc. This process among both the Hindu and Muslim rural elites in the post-1920 period, and especially among the Muslims in the eastern region of Bengal, has been traced in intensive village and case studies.[30] They show how the Muslim middle class could grow at a rapid rate in the post-1920 period because Bengal, and particularly its eastern region, was over-whelmingly rural. (See Tables 2 and 3.)

Table 2

Highest social groups in Bengal, 1931	% literate to total population	% literate in English to total population
Brahman, Vaidya, Kayastha Hindu	36	40
Sayyad Muslim	22	28

Source: Ramkrishna Mukherjee, op. cit., p. 125, Table 2.7.

Table 3

Classes of economic structure in Bengal, 1931	% of total population			
	Brahman, Vaidya, Kayastha	Sayyad Muslim	All Hindus	All Muslims
I	61	31	20	14
II	22	47	44	67
III	17	22	36	19
Total	100	100	100	100

Source: Ramkrishna Mukherjee, op. cit., p. 96, Table 2.4.

It thus appeared that the emergence of a new economic structure in the first quarter of the present century would override the regional and religious distinctions of the "Bengali" people. It seemed likely that the growing propertied class of Hindus and Muslims would unite in relation to the impoverished but increasingly unified Hindu and Muslim peasantry and their like, and that further changes in Bengali society would be effected primarily on the economic plane, with repercussions in the social and ideological life of the people. There were indications to support this conjecture. Leaders of the Muslim middle class, such as Moulvi A. K. Fazlul Huq and Md. Az-izul Huq, organized the Krishak Praja Party (literally, Peasants and People's Party), which remained restricted to Bengal and served essentially as the mouthpiece of the *jotedar* interest in Bengal's economy and politics.[31] The party refrained from taking a religious or communal stand, and found members and allies among the Hindu middle class with substantial *jotedar* interest, as was evident from the Hindu members and supporters of the government formed by the party in Bengal. On the other hand, the peasant movement of Bengal, which flared up during the 1930s and the 1940s under the leadership of the Communist Party of India, was stronger in East Bengal and had a large following among the Muslim peasantry.

The Hindu middle class, however, was solidly entrenched in Bengal's economy. The corresponding Muslim interest could not compete with it even though it held political power from 1937. The urban population, the educated community, the landed interests, and the bureaucracy of Bengal were still predominantly Hindu. Regionally, moreover, West Bengal (with its Hindu stronghold) held East Bengal (with its Muslim stronghold) as its hinterland.

In the circumstances, the Bengali Muslim middle class envisaged a quicker and easier way to further its interests by responding to the call of the All-India Muslim League, which was steadily gaining strength with the demand for a Muslim homeland. In this way it expected to secure a territory and government of its own, as well as its own market in goods and services. Therefore, instead of pursuing only the Krishak Praja Party, Muslim leaders first aligned themselves with and later joined the Muslim League. They began to maneuver the Muslim peasantry (especially in East Bengal) through the influence they wielded in the countryside as *jotedars* and other variants of the rural elite.[32] The Congress Party, with its core leadership representing the Hindu landed and business interests, was regarded by the Muslims as a Hindu organization. The Communist Party and other left-wing parties were not strong enough to check the communal drift. As a result, influenced by the supra-Bengal course of religious separation in Indian society as a whole, the differing regional and religious identities of the "Bengali" people won out over their combined ethnic and national identity. Nation-building and state-formation in Bengal took an unprecedented turn: in 1947 the two regions of Bengal were awarded to two newly created state formations—West Bengal to the Indian Union and East Bengal to Pakistan.

Table 4

Bengal (before partition)		% of total	
		Hindu	Muslim
Urban population (1931 census)		12	4
Literate aged 5+ (1931 census)		16	7
	3–5	27	23
	5–10	51	58
	10–15	11	11
Yearly agricultural income (in	15–20	4	4
thousand rupees) of assessed	20–25	2	2
families of *jotedars*, large-scale	25–30	1	1
farmers, and owner-cultivators	30–40	1	
	40–50	1	1
	50–100	1	
	100+	1	
Government officers in executive, judicial, and police posts (1940)		59	37

Source: *Partition of Bengal* (H. Chatterjee and Co., Calcutta, 1947); *Bengal Ministry and the Hindus of Bengal* (Director of Public Information, Government of Bengal, Calcutta, 1940). Figures are computed by the writer.

Table 5

Perennial industries (with 20 or more workers in each factory) in Bengal, 1945	No. factories		No. workers (thousands)	
	West	East	West	East
Minerals and metals	30	—	25	—
Chemicals, paper, and printing	257	7	45	0.2
Raw materials processing (including food, drink, and tobacco) and service industries	593	29	94	4
Textiles (cotton, jute, silk)	155	18	326	11
Engineering, shipbuilding, power generation, manufacture and repair, transport and communication, government works	465	29	194	11
Total	1500	83	684	26

Source: *Large Industrial Establishments in India, 1946* (Government of India, Delhi, 1950). Figures are computed by the writer.

Alienation of Bengali Muslims from "Western" Muslims

It appeared that the Bengali Muslim interests would have free and full play in East Pakistan. The communal riots, which preceded the partition of India and recurred in East Pakistan several times afterward, led to the migration of 3.14 million Bengali Hindus from East Pakistan to West Bengal in 1947–1961.[33] This facilitated the growth of a Muslim market in goods and services, but Muslims indigenous to Bengal proved able only partially to utilize the opportunities thus created. Bengali Muslims were permitted rather easy access to the lower and middle ranges of economic activities, especially to the professions of lawyer, teacher, doctor, etc.; but the top governmental, commercial, and industrial positions became virtually the monopoly of West Pakistanis posted to Bengal from the center of gravity of Pakistan in Sind and West Punjab. Similarly, the big business interests, which flowered in East Pakistan, were controlled by West Pakistanis or by Urdu-speaking refugee Muslims from central and northern India who had migrated to Bengal with capital and/or business acumen and experience. As reported in an unpublished study made in the 1960s by an international research organization which must remain anonymous: "Of the largest factories in the East Wing, including the largest, all but one are owned by non-Bengalis." Again, in analyzing the factors in Bengali regionalism in Pakistan, Lambert noted that "many of the ways in which *paschimas* [people from West Pakistan] were supposed to be exploiting the East Bengalis were much the same as those formerly charged against the Hindus and the British."[34]

Regional, linguistic, and kinship ties strengthened the bonds between the East Pakistani top bureaucracy and big business, from which Bengali Muslims were virtually barred. Moreover, law and order, together with the security and defense of this wing of Pakistan, were almost entirely in the hands of West Pakistanis. The subservient position of the Bengali Muslims in the economic structure of East Pakistan was thus reinforced. (See Table 6.)

In the first few years, however, the discriminatory situation was not apparent to the Bengali Muslims. Their middle class elements had not yet emerged sufficiently for them to aspire to the top positions in the governmental, commercial, and industrial sectors. The

Table 6

| East Pakistan, 1955 | Number of: | |
	West Pakistanis	East Pakistanis
Civil servants		
Secretary	19	—
Joint Secretary	38	3
Deputy Secretary	123	10
Under Secretary	510	38
Total	690	51
Military officers		
Lt. General	3	—
Major General	20	—
Brigadier	34	1
Colonel	49	1
Lt. Colonel	198	2
Major	590	10
Air Force personnel	640	60
Naval officers	593	7
Total	2,127	81

Source: Richard D. Lambert, "Factors in Bengali Regionalism in Pakistan," *Far Eastern Survey*, April 1959, pp. 49–58.

Bengali Muslim elites, as well as the masses (with whom the former maintained live contact in rural and urban areas), were satisfied to fill the vacuum created by the emigration of Bengali Hindus from the middle stratum of economic activities, while the upper stratum was filled mainly by non-Bengali Muslims. Nevertheless, although truncated at the top, the market in goods and services which the Bengali Muslims obtained with the advent of Pakistan facilitated the spread of education among their children. According to census figures, from 1951 to 1961 the percentage of literates to the total population (excluding readers of the Holy Quran) rose from 13 to 18.[35] A sample survey of students in Dacca city in 1957 showed that 77 percent of the university and undergraduate students came from villages; the mother tongue of 93 percent of them was Bengali, and for 50 percent the father's education was under-matriculation or none.[36]

The Bengali Muslim middle class thus grew at a far more rapid rate than ever before, and within a few years the process began to provide an ever-increasing number of new aspirants for governmental, managerial, and executive jobs, while the vacuum created by the displacement of the Hindu population from East Pakistan was soon overfilled. In addition, those who had previously occupied the middle rungs of the economic ladder began to chafe at the lack of opportunity to further improve their positions.

The upshot was that the Bengali Muslims' orientation to social change became focused on regional disparities rather than on a comparison of their past and present conditions. They were no longer concerned with their position before and after the establishment of Pakistan in East Bengal, but with contrasting the opportunities available in the eastern and western wings of the republic. A social force thus began to gather momentum among the Bengali Muslims to throw off the lid that was obstructing the course of development they had aspired to when they subscribed to the ideology of Pakistan in the last phase of British rule in India, namely, to possess a territory and government of their own and to control their own market in goods and services. With this new perspective, they soon discovered that they were not only deprived of economic opportunities in their homeland but that the fruits of their capital and labor were being utilized more for the betterment of West than East Pakistan.

Table 7

Characteristics	West Pakistan	East Pakistan
Population in millions (1961 census)	43	51
Urban population as percentage of total (1961 census)	23	5
Percent share of total workers in large-scale manufacturing industries (1959–1960)	69	.31
Percent increase in civilian labor force (1951–1961)		
Agricultural	22	39
Nonagricultural	56	18
Percent increase in share of literate to total population aged 5 or more (1951–1961)	75	5
Percentage of population with 5+ years of schooling to the total aged 10+ (1961)		
Male	15	13
Female	4	2
Total	10	8

Table 7 (Continued)

Characteristics	West Pakistan	East Pakistan
Educational grants from central government (1947–1955, in Rs. billion)	1.5	0.2
Per capita yearly expenditure on education (Rs.)	9	6
Financial assistance and grants-in-aid from central government (1947–1955, in Rs. billion)	10.5	1.4
Number of hospital beds (1966, in thousands)	26	7
Road mileage (1953, in thousands)		
High-grade	8	0.8
Low-grade	24	25
Railway route-mileage (1961, in thousands)	5	2
Foreign aid allotted by central government (1947–1955, in Rs. billions)	0.7	0.2
Capital expenditure of central government (1947–1955, in Rs. billions)	2.1	0.6
Average yearly per capita consumption (1951–1960)		
Cereals (lbs.)	333	349
Sugar (lbs.)	54	19
Salt (lbs.)	17	12
Tea (lbs.)	1	0.1
Cigarettes (no.)	121	21
Cloth (yds.)	8	2
Paper (lbs.)	1	0.4
Matches (no.)	11	7
Coal (lbs.)	66	32
Petrol (gallons)	1	0.1
Electricity (kw)	19	1
Per capita gross regional product (GRP) in Rs. million factor cost of 1959/60		
Pre-Plan (1950/51–1954/55)	343	297
First Plan (1955/56–1959/60)	364	275
Second Plan (1960/61–1964/65)	393	301
East Pakistan GRP per capita as percentage of West Pakistan GRP per capita		
1950/51–1954/55	87	
1955/56–1959/60	76	
1960/61–1964/65	77	
Average annual compound rates of growth at 1959/60 factor (1949/50–1964/65)		
Agriculture	2.5	1.7
Nonagriculture	5.5	4.6
GRP	4.0	2.8
Population	2.5	2.5
GRP per capita	1.5	0.3
Average percent share of overseas trade at current prices (1950/51–1964/65)		
Imports	70	30
Exports	43	57

Table 7 (Continued)

Characteristics	West Pakistan	East Pakistan
Inter-wing (East to West or West to East Pakistan) imports of foreign merchandise on private account (in Rs. million, 1948/49–1956/57)	179	270
Percent increase in inter-wing balance of trade (exports minus imports), always adverse for East Pakistan (1950/51–1964/65)	162	
Average percent share of imports of capital goods and materials for capital goods (1951/52–1959/60)	70	30
Percent share of estimates of fixed investment (1959/60–1965/66)	68	32
Average percent of investment to GRP (1960/61–1964/65)	20	11
Average percent of saving to GRP (1960/61–1964/65)	12	8
Average percent of investment financed by own saving	60	80
Percent share of public sector investment or development expenditure (1950/51–1964/65)	61	39
Percent share of foreign private investments (including loans associated with equity investments) (1963–1964)	77	23
Percent share of loans from Pakistan Industrial Credit and Investment Corporation and Industrial Development Bank of Pakistan (1961/62–1966/67)	64	36
Defense expenditure of Central Government (1947–1955, in Rs. billions)	4.7	0.1

Source: Stephen R. Lewis, Jr., *Pakistan: Industrialization and Trade Policies* (Oxford University Press, London, 1970); Richard D. Lambert, op. cit.; G. S. Bhargava, *Pakistan in Crisis* (Vikas Publications, Delhi, 1969); F. B. Arnold, *Pakistan: Economic and Commercial Conditions* (Her Majesty's Stationary Office, London, 1955); *A Note on the Utilization of Agricultural Surpluses for Economic Development in Pakistan* (UN Economic Commission for Asia and the Far East, Bangkok, 1961); S. U. Khan, "A Measure of Economic Growth in East and West Pakistan," *Pakistan Development Review*, Vol. I, No. 2; Anwar Iqbal Qureshi, *Pakistan Economic Survey 1963–64* (Government of Pakistan, Rawalpindi, 1964); Akhlaqur M. Rahman, "The Role of the Public Sector in the Economic Development of Pakistan," in E. A. G. Robinson and Michael Kidron (eds.), *Economic Development of South Asia* (Macmillan and Co. Ltd., London, 1970). Figures are computed by the author.

Birth of Bangladesh

The germ of the East Pakistanis' alienation from the West Pakistanis was present from the time the Bengali Muslims responded to the call of Pakistan. Mr. Jinnah, the architect of Pakistan, had declared that "India is not a nation, nor a country" and that "the

Muslims are not a minority but a nation and self-determination is their birthright." But when the Bengali Moulvi A. K. Fazlul Huq moved the famous Lahore resolution of 1940, in which the Muslim League demanded explicitly, for the first time, the creation of Pakistan, the wording of the resolution made it clear that the demand was for two "Pakistans," one of which would be in Bengal: "The areas in which the Muslims are numerically in majority, as in the north-western and eastern zones of India, should be grouped to constitute 'Independent States' in which the constituent units shall be autonomous and sovereign." [37] During the last few years of British rule, however, the alienation of the Muslims from the Hindus overpowered the force of ethnic and national identity of the Bengalis. Correspondingly, the consolidation of the Muslims in the two wings of Pakistan was marked by the Bengalis in Pakistan identifying themselves primarily as Pakistanis. It thus appeared that the "two nation" theory of Mr. Jinnah was not merely a political maneuver: a nation was being built on the basis of the Muslim way of life.

Islamization of East Pakistan and Arabicization of the Bengali language and literature facilitated the course of religious consolidation. In addition to the fact that, from 1948 on, frequent declarations of Pakistan as an Islamic state were no less enthusiastically received in the east than in the west wing of Pakistan,[38] the 1951 census returned 8.9 million people in East Pakistan as "literates, including Holy Quran readers," [39] of which 3.3 million persons were exclusively of the latter category. A survey of undergraduate and postgraduate students in Dacca in 1957 showed that although Bengali was the mother tongue for 93 percent of them, 35 percent of these Bengali students could read, write, and speak in Urdu, and 34 percent could read and write Arabic; by contrast, only 2 percent of those whose mother tongue was not Bengali could read, write, and speak Bengali.[40] Also, the deliberate imposition of Arabic words upon the Bengali language and literature by the new enthusiasts was not resented at first. A possibility had thus opened up for the people of East Pakistan to drift further away from those of West Bengal and forge a stronger link with those of West Pakistan, the *paschimas*.

The honeymoon, however, was soon over. Economic and political discrimination against the East Pakistanis snapped the theocratic bond of all Pakistanis. Significantly, the 1961 census recorded that the number of Holy Quran readers in East Pakistan had dropped from 3.3 million in 1951 to 1.7 million.[41] Nation-building in East Pakistan again took a different turn. By 1948 the grumblings of discontent were heard in the Constituent Assembly of Pakistan: "A feeling is growing among the Eastern Pakistanis that Eastern Pakistan is being neglected and treated merely as a 'colony' of Western Pakistan." [42] A Bengali identity then began to reemerge, corresponding to the alienation of the East from the West Pakistanis. It first took shape in the demand for Bengali as a national language, and climaxed in the police firing on demonstrators on February 21, 1952. The floodgate of a new nationalism in East Pakistan opened up, and this day has since been observed as the "day of martyrs" *(Sahid Dibas)*.

In the new situation, the old leaders of the Bengali middle class became active again. Moulvi A. K. Fazlul Huq, mover of the 1940 Lahore resolution of the Muslim League, and erstwhile colleagues like Md. Azizul Huq formed the Krishak Sramik Party (Peasants' and Workers' Party) in the image of their previously established Krishak Praja Party. This party, like its predecessor noncommunal in character, demanded in its twelve-point program of July 29, 1953, recognition of Bengali as a state language and full regional autonomy for East Pakistan on the basis of the 1940 Lahore resolution. The initiative, however, passed from these older hands to such new leaders as Maulana Bhashani, as well as to Sheikh Mujibur Rahman who led the Awami League movement, launched a radical program for the future of East Pakistan, and found the broadest response from "radical Muslim intellectuals, members of the national bourgeoisie, peasants, workers, and owners of small and middle-size landholdings." [43]

In order to retain and consolidate its gains, the state retaliated with alternate measures of repression and concession, as had happened in the subcontinent of India during the last phase of British rule. And the results were also similar to those in British India: the adopted measures merely fed the ever-growing national upsurge of the East Pakistanis, who categorically ceased to identify themselves as Pakistanis. Sheikh Mujibur Rahman, the leader of the people, became henceforth Bangabandu (Friend of Bengal). On April 17, 1971, the territory of the eastern wing of Pakistan was renamed Bangladesh (the land of Bengal) and on December 16, 1971, Bangladesh became a free and sovereign country.

Notes

1. Niharranjan Ray, *Bangaleer Itihas* (in Bengali) (Book Emporium, Calcutta, 1951), chapters 4 and 7.

2. Ramkrishna Mukherjee, *The Rise and Fall of the East India Company* (Verlag der Wissenschaften, Berlin; Popular Prakashan, Bombay, 1958), p. 160.

3. Ramkrishna Mukherjee, *The Dynamics of a Rural Society* (Akademie-Verlag, Berlin; Popular Prakashan, Bombay, 1957), pp. 63–64.

4. Ramaprasad Chanda, *The Indo-Aryan Races* (Varendra Research Society, Rajshahi, Bengal, 1916), pp. 162–201.

5. Niharranjan Ray, op. cit., pp. 253, 278.

6. Bijoybhusan Ghosh-Chowdhury, *Asam o Bangadesher Bibaha Paddhati* (in Bengali) (published by author, 1938); A. Mitra, *The Tribes and Castes of West Bengal* (Government of West Bengal, Calcutta, 1953), p. 7; N. Ray, op. cit., pp. 266–267, 289, 310–311, 577–579, 592, 678.

7. Richard Fick, *Die Sociale Gliederung im Nordöstlichen Indien zu Buddha's Zeit* (Verlag für Orientalische Literatur, Kiel, 1897).

8. E. A. Gait, *Census of India, 1901*, Vol. VI (Government of India, Calcutta, 1902), pp. 165–181.

9. Shashibhusan Dasgupta, *Obscure Religious Cults as Background of Bengali Literature* (University of Calcutta, Calcutta, 1946).

10. Tara Chand, *Influence of Islam on Indian Culture* (Indian Press, Allahabad, 1954), pp. 213–220; R. Mukherjee, op. cit., pp. 185 ff.; Ishtisq Hussain Qureshi, *The Muslim Community of the Indo-Pakistan Subcontinent (610–1947)* (Mouton and Co., The Hague, 1962), pp. 70–75; Dinesh Chandra Sen, *The History of the Bengali Language and Literature* (University of Calcutta, Calcutta, 1911), pp. 234–235, 413–414.

11. R. C. Majumdar et al., *An Advanced History of India* (Macmillan, London, 1953), pp. 407, 582–583.

12. Ibid., pp. 402, 407–408, 417–418; Dinesh Chandra Sen, op. cit., pp. 10–14.

13. Ramkrishna Mukherjee, *The Dynamics of a Rural Society*, op. cit., pp. 61–80.

14. Azizur Rahman Mallick, *British Policy and the Muslims in Bengal: 1757–1856* (Asiatic Society of Pakistan, Dacca, 1961), pp. 3–26.

15. Abdul Majed Khan, "Research About Muslim Aristocracy in East Pakistan," in Pierre Bessaignet (ed.), *Social Research in East Pakistan* (Asiatic Society of Pakistan, Dacca, 1960), pp. 21–22.

16. Azizur Rahman Mallick, op. cit., pp. 27–65; Ishtisq Hussain Qureshi, op. cit., pp. 209–236.

17. R.C. Dutt, *The Economic History of India Under Early British Rule* (Routledge and Kegan Paul, London, 1950), chapters II–V; N. K. Sinha, *Economic History of Bengal*, Vol. I (Firma K. L. Mukhopadhyay, Calcutta, 1956), Chapter II.

18. N. K. Sinha, op. cit., chapters V–VI; R. Mukherjee, *The Rise and Fall of the East India Company*, op. cit., pp. 302–312.

19. Amiya Kumar Bagchi, "European and Indian Entrepreneurship in India, 1900–30," in Edmund Leach and S. N. Mukherjee (eds.), *Elites in South Asia* (Cambridge University Press, 1970), pp. 223–256.

20. R. Mukherjee, *The Dynamics of a Rural Society*, op. cit., pp. 32–34.

21. D. J. Mcniele, *Memorandum on the Revenue Administration of the Lower Provinces of Bengal* (Government of India, Calcutta, 1873), pp. 15–16.

22. Syed Mahmood, *A History of English Education in India* (M.A.–O. College, Aligarh, 1895), pp. 53–54, 75, 147–148.

23. Quoted in Abdul Majed Khan, op. cit., p. 19.

24. Haraprasad Sastri, "Musalmani Bangla," *Bibhu* (in Bengali), Calcutta, 1888.

25. J. N. Farquhar, *Modern Religious Movements in India* (The Macmillan Co., New York, 1919), pp. 1–28; Ahmad Khan Muin-Ud-Din, "Research in the Islamic Revivalism of the 19th Century and Its Effect on the Muslim Society of Bengal," in Pierre Bessaignet, op. cit., pp. 30–51; R. Mukherjee, *The Rise and Fall of the East India Company*, op. cit., pp. 313–328.

26. John Strachey, *India: Its Administration and Progress* (Macmillan, London, 1903), pp. 306–310.

27. Nazmul A. K. Karim, *Changing Society in India and Pakistan* (Oxford University Press, Dacca, 1956), pp. 138–143.

28. R. Mukherjee, *The Dynamics of a Rural Society*, op. cit., pp. 46–48.

29. Ibid., pp. 48–50.

30. Nazmul A. K. Karim, "Changing Patterns of an East Pakistan Family," in Barbara E. Ward (ed.), *Women in the New Asia* (UNESCO, Paris, 1963); R. Mukherjee, *Six Villages of Bengal* (Popular Prakashan, Bombay, 1971).

31. M. A. Huque, *The Man Behind the Plough* (The Book Company, Calcutta, 1939), p. vi; R. Mukherjee, *The Dynamics of a Rural Society*, op. cit., p. 57.

32. R. Mukherjee, *Six Villages of Bengal*, op. cit., pp. 13 ff.

33. R. Mukherjee, *The Sociologist and Social Change in India Today* (Prentice-Hall, New Delhi, 1965), p. 163; C. N. Vakil, *Economic Consequences of Divided India* (Vora and Co., Bombay, 1950), p. 131.

34. Richard D. Lambert, "Factors in Bengali Regionalism in Pakistan," *Far Eastern Survey*, April 1959, p. 52.

35. Sultan S. Hashmi, "Main Features of Demographic Conditions in Pakistan," background paper for Asian Population Conference, New Delhi, December 1963.

36. A. N. M. Muniruzzaman, *The Living and Working Conditions of Students of the University and College of Dacca, 1957* (University of Dacca, 1961), tables II-2, II-6, II-14.
37. Quoted in K. Callard, *Pakistan: A Political Study* (George Allen and Unwin, London, 1957), p. 158.
38. Khalid B. Sayeed, *The Political System of Pakistan* (Houghton Mifflin, Boston, 1967), pp. 160, 168.
39. Sultan S. Hashmi, op. cit.
40. A. N. M. Muniruzzaman, op. cit., tables II-6, II-7.
41. Sultan S. Hashmi, op. cit.
42. Quoted in Khalid B. Sayeed, op. cit., p. 64.
43. Y. V. Gankovsky and L. R. Gordon-Polonskaya, *A History of Pakistan* (U.S.S.R. Academy of Sciences, Moscow, 1964), p. 194.

2. The Structural Matrix of the Struggle in Bangladesh

Feroz Ahmed

Ever since its creation in 1947, Pakistan has been a geographical ab-
surdity, with its two parts separated by one thousand miles of un-
friendly Indian territory. Greater than the spatial distance is the difference in the social structure, economy, and culture. Adherence to
a common religion, Islam, was never sufficient to make these two dissimilar parts a single nation. But for almost twenty-four years Pakistan weathered all storms and maintained a precarious unity. That
unity was finally broken in March 1971 when the West Pakistani
military launched an all-out war to suppress the movement for regional autonomy in East Pakistan, forcing the region to declare itself
an independent People's Republic of Bangladesh. The genocidal attacks of the West Pakistani army against the Bengali people and the
agony of the millions of refugees who were forced to flee to India
have now become a familiar story.[1]

While focusing their attention on the massacre and the inhuman
conditions of the refugees, the Western media have by and large ignored the roots of the crisis. The most common explanation of the
conflict, the traditional hatred between the Bengalis and Punjabis,
misses the point entirely. In this brief article I shall attempt to show
that the conflict in Pakistan is a synergetic product of U.S. foreign
policy operating within Pakistan's social structure.

Social Structure

Basic to an understanding of political developments in any country is the analysis of its social structure. Here I shall not attempt to

This article was first published in the *Bulletin of Concerned Asian Scholars*, Vol. 4, No. 1,
Winter 1972. It was completed prior to outbreak of the Indo-Pakistan war of December 1971.

discuss the economic rationale for the creation of Pakistan,[2] but shall begin with the social structure inherited by Pakistan at the time of its creation.

The regions which came to constitute the state of Pakistan had traditionally been the suppliers of raw materials to the industries located in other parts of India and in England. East Bengal (or East Pakistan) grew jute, the so-called golden fiber, for West Bengal factories. It did not have a single jute mill of its own. West Pakistan produced wheat and cotton, which it exchanged for manufactured goods produced elsewhere. The emerging industrial capitalist class of India was almost totally non-Muslim, and the commercial life of the regions which later became Pakistan was dominated by Hindu and other non-Muslim businessmen. While landlords and peasants in West Pakistan were Muslims, rural life in the East was stratified along religious lines, with almost all landlords being Hindus and almost all rural Muslims being peasants.

The partition and the consequent emigration of Hindu landlords to India created an enormous power vacuum in East Bengal. The land left behind by the Hindus was redistributed among the peasants, 52 percent of whom thus came to own their own land, with family farms averaging 3.5 acres. In the urban areas, the Bengali elite consisted of the elements of the decaying Muslim aristocracy, represented by the regional Muslim League. In the absence of an urban bourgeois class and real economic power of the aristocracy, the emerging petty bourgeoisie, consisting of small traders, shopkeepers, professional people, teachers, and clerks, became potentially the most important class. Culturally, the influence of this class was predominant, but economically it was weak.

In West Pakistan, which also lacked a bourgeois class, the absentee landlords became the most powerful class. However, the landlords were not politically well organized and lacked the ability to run a state which had inherited many modern institutions from the British colonialists. The bureaucracy, which was trained by the British as an instrument of colonial rule, became the most effective political force in its own right. Although this bureaucracy had strong links with the landlord class, the needs of a modern state and the chaotic conditions of the partition enabled it to become a semi-autonomous social force and to fill the vacuum created by the departure of the British. The bureaucracy was drawn almost entirely from the Punjab province and from the Urdu-speaking refugees who had settled in Sind. Still another political force was the military, again British-trained and drawn mainly from the Punjab. But the political influence of the military was limited in the beginning.[3]

West Pakistan also received, among its immigrants, traders belonging to the Memon, Bohra, and Khoja communities of Gujarat and Bombay who settled in Karachi. They and other commercial elements later transformed themselves into an industrial capitalist class. Because of their small size, narrow community base, and lack of roots in Pakistan, these industrial entrepreneurs never asserted themselves as a political force. Their marriage of convenience with the bureaucrats simply ensured them policies to support their enterprises.

Because of the virtual absence of capitalists, feudal landlords, bureaucracy, and the military in East Pakistan, the West Pakistani power structure became the national power structure as well, ruling the eastern part with the collaboration of the dying Muslim aristocracy.

Colonization of East Bengal

At independence, the Gross Domestic Product (GDP) of East Pakistan exceeded the GDP of West Pakistan (see Table 1). Education was also more extensive in the East than in the West, as Table 2 in-

Table 1

Gross Domestic Product in 1959–60 Constant Prices
(million rupees)

	East	West
1949–50	13,130	11,830
1954–55	14,320	14,310
1959–60	15,550	16,790
1964–65	18,014	21,788
1968–69	20,670	27,744

Sources: Gustav Papanek, *Pakistan's Development*, Harvard University Press, Cambridge, 1967, p. 317; A. R. Khan, "A New Look at Disparity," *Forum*, January 3, 1970.

Table 2
Educational Disparities

	East Pakistan		West Pakistan	
	1947	1967	1947	1967
Primary level				
Institutions	29,633	28,225	8,413	33,271
Students	2,020,000	4,310,000	550,000	2,740,000
Secondary level				
Institutions	3,481	4,390	2,598	4,563
Students	53,000	107,000	51,000	153,000
General College				
Institutions	50	173	40	239
Enrollment	19,000	138,000	13,000	142,000
General University				
Institutions	1	2	2	4
Enrollment	1,600	8,000	700	10,000

Source: Ministry of Education, Government of Pakistan, *Education Statistics of Pakistan (1947–57)*; A. O. Huque, "Educational Disparities in Pakistan," *Forum*, December 20, 1969.

dicates. However, given the economic disruption of the partition and the difference in the social structures in East and West Pakistan, in addition to certain advantages of economic infrastructure in West Pakistan, inevitably the industrialization of Pakistan turned the eastern region into a colony of the West and created disparities in the economic and social development of both regions.

The process of industrialization in Pakistan began with the investment of capital in cotton textile industries in West Pakistan and jute mills in East Pakistan by the commercial bourgeoisie of West Pakistan. The development of industries in East Pakistan was carried out only to the extent that it benefited the West Pakistani capitalists. It was not simply a profit-making enterprise but an essential condition for the industrial development of West Pakistan itself. The availability of certain raw materials, such as cotton; the presence of an economic infrastructure, such as the seaport of Karachi, the railways, and roads; the location of the central government and of financial institutions; and the lesser militancy of the proletariat—all these factors offered a more suitable climate for investment in West Pakistan. But such industrialization required the importation of capital goods and some essential raw materials. Development of the jute industry in the East by West Pakistani capitalists therefore amounted to increasing the capacity of foreign exchange earning, since East Pakistan, which produced more than 80 percent of the world's jute, had ready-made world markets. In the early years, the export of raw and processed jute accounted for 70 percent of Pakistan's foreign exchange earnings, but this foreign exchange was used for the industrialization of West Pakistan. East Pakistan received only 25–30 percent of the total imports. Data on various economic indicators are given in Table 3.

Thus, the penetration of West Pakistan-based capital into East Pakistan not only established an antagonistic relationship between the Bengali worker and the West Pakistani capitalist, but also triggered a process of draining East Pakistan's resources for the industrial development of West Pakistan. Policies imposed in order to guarantee cheap raw materials for the factories resulted in the exploitation and increased impoverishment of the Bengali peasants. Such policies were adopted and enforced on behalf of the West Pakistani capitalists by the bureaucracy, which was also largely West Pakistani. Not trusting the Bengalis, the West Pakistani capitalists brought along with them West Pakistani managers for their factories, many of them trained in the University of Pennsylvania-initiated business school in Karachi. Members of the Bengali petty bourgeoisie who aspired to have a slice of the industrial cake or to obtain civil and military positions and managerial jobs in industry found the West Pakistani ruling structure and its local allies obstructing their development. Thus all the classes of East Pakistan—the proletariat, the peasantry, and the petty bourgeoisie—stood in an antagonistic relationship with the West Pakistani power structure and its local collaborators.

In addition to the exploitation of East Pakistan's raw materials and cheap labor, the third important ingredient of classical colonialism—use of the colony as a market for the mother country's manufactures—was also present from the inception of Pakistan. Table 4 shows the relative values of exports of one region to the other, with West Pakistan consistently having a favorable balance of trade. With the industrialization of West Pakistan, the need for the captive mar-

Table 3

Some Economic Indicators

	East Pakistan	West Pakistan
Area (square miles)	54,501	310,236
Population (1970 estimate)	70 million	60 million
Five-year plan allocations		
1st	32%	68%
2nd	32%	68%
3rd	36%	64%
4th (unlikely to be implemented)	52.5%	47.5%
Foreign aid allocation	20–30%	70–80%
Export earnings	50–70%	30–50%
Import expenditures	25–30%	70–75%
Industrial assets owned by Bengalis	11%	
Civil service jobs	16–20%	80–84%
Military jobs	10%	90%
Resources transferred from East to West between 1948–49 and 1968–69	Rs. 31,120 million*	
Per capita income, official		
1964–65	Rs. 285.5	Rs. 419.0
1968–69	Rs. 291.5	Rs. 473.4
Regional difference in per capita income, official		
1959–60	32%	
1964–65	47%	
1968–69	62%	
Real difference in per capita income, 1968–69	95%	
Real difference in average standard of living, 1968–69	126%	
Proportion of income spent on food by industrial workers (1955–56 survey)	69–75%	60–63%

* At the official rate, U.S. $1 = 4.76 rupees (Rs.); current market exchange rate, $1 = Rs. 11.

Sources: Pakistan *Statistical Yearbooks* and *Pakistan Economic Survey* for the various years, Government of East Pakistan (1963), Papanek (1967), A. R. Khan (1970), Interim Reports (May 1970), and *Forum* (Feb. 27, 1971).

Table 4
Interregional Trade (*Exports*)
(millions of rupees)

Year	East Pakistan	West Pakistan
1948–49	18.8	137.6
1950–51	46.0	210.8
1955–56	220.7	318.9
1960–61	355.9	800.5
1965–66	649.7	1,189.8
1969–70	915.7	1,656.2

Sources: *Pakistan Economic Survey* 1967–68; *Pakistan Times*, June 14, 1971.

ket in East Pakistan grew more acute and manufactured goods began to occupy a much larger share of the exports to East Pakistan. The pattern of industrial development was based on the assumption that the East Pakistani market would consume a significant part of West Pakistani manufactures, since these high-cost products could not compete in the world market; for instance, cotton textiles, which constituted the largest single item in West Pakistan's exports to East Pakistan, faced stiff competition in the world market. On the other hand, the largest item in East Pakistan's list of exports to the West was tea, which is a popular item of consumption in West Pakistan but could always find a place in the world market. In fact, in recent years Pakistan had drastically curtailed its international exports of tea, leaving the market largely to two neighboring countries, India and Ceylon.[4]

Thus, in the context of Pakistan's given social structure, economic progress amounted to strengthening West Pakistan's power structure and further perpetuating the exploitation of East Pakistan. The only way to break this vicious cycle was to redefine the social relationships and to organize production along socialist lines. That was the only guarantee of national unity. But such a program could not possibly be conceived by the exploiting classes. They chose a path which only aggravated the existing relationships between the two regions.

Imperialism from Without Promotes Colonialism from Within

The colonization of East Bengal was inherent in the power vac- uum created by the partition, especially in the absence of an indigenous bourgeois class and in the exigencies of capitalist development in West Pakistan. But capitalism itself could not have experienced such an unbridled growth had not an external element been introduced into Pakistan's political dynamics and into the relationship between its two parts.

The celebrated "robber barons" of West Pakistan would have faced competition from, and yielded some ground to, the emerging bourgeoisie in Bengal had the rules of "free enterprise" and competitive capitalism prevailed. After all, West Pakistani entrepreneurs were not so invincible in the beginning as to be able to impose monopoly control over East Pakistan, despite the support they received from the all-powerful bureaucracy. The emergence of A. K. Khan, who served as a minister in Ayub Khan's first cabinet, and of a few other industrialists in Bengal was an indication of the possibilities of entrepreneurship in East Pakistan. But West Pakistan's capitalists were not a "national bourgeoisie" whose growth and prosperity would depend entirely on the exploitation of national resources and domestic savings. They sought collaboration with foreign capital in order to increase their fortunes, and were willing to offer benefits to the imperialist powers at the expense of the people of Pakistan.

Fortunately for them, the United States, the leading moneylender since World War II, was actively seeking Cold War allies and was eager to provide economic and military "assistance" to Third World ruling groups willing to collaborate with it. The Pakistani rulers seized this opportunity and in 1951 began to receive economic aid—mainly grants in the beginning—from the U.S.A. By 1954, Pakistan was firmly in the orbit of the United States, having signed a mutual security treaty and joined the Southeast Asian Treaty Organization (SEATO). In 1955 it also became a member of another American pact, the Baghdad Pact (later renamed the Central Treaty Organization, or CENTO), with Iran, Turkey, and Iraq as its allies. American military aid began rolling into Pakistan, amounting to $1.5–2.0 billion in 1969.[5] As part of its obligation to the U.S.A., the Pakistan government allowed America to build a military base near Peshawar and to use its civilian airfields for espionage flights, including the ill-fated U-2 plane that was shot down in the Soviet Union and caused a major international crisis. Pakistan's leaders repeatedly assured the U.S.A. of their complete allegiance. In a 1961 address to the U.S. Congress, Pakistan's then-President Ayub Khan said, "If there is real trouble, there is no country in Asia where you will be able to put your foot in. The only people who will stand by you are the people of Pakistan." [6]

Although U.S. economic aid, like its military aid, was designed to maintain "a position of influence and control around the world," [7] the economic benefits to the U.S. were not unimportant. With its aid program as an entering wedge, the U.S. expanded its share of Pakistan's imports from 6 percent in 1952 to as much as 40 percent in the early 1960s.

What we are mainly concerned with here is the effect of foreign economic and military aid on political developments in Pakistan, especially the relationship between East and West Pakistan.

Economic Aid

By 1969 the United States had provided $3 billion in grants and loans—mainly loans in the later years—for Pakistan's economic development.[8] Among the many strings attached to U.S. aid was the explicit guideline to encourage "private enterprise." For this purpose American advisers, under the Harvard University Development Advisory Service (DAS), were sent to Pakistan to influence the policies of the Planning Commission and of other economic decision-making agencies.[9] The U.S. aid mission in Pakistan played no small role in initiating economic policies for Pakistan.[10] In the interest of Pakistan's robber barons, Pakistan's bureaucrats—and later its military officers as well—followed American advice. So faithfully did the Pakistani rulers do this that one of the top advisers to Pakistan had this to say about its development:

> Policies have been framed to assure that the government intervenes in the economy when such intervention is *in theory* desirable, while leaving in private hands decisions which, *according to theory,* should be left to private initiative.[11]

Pakistan's dependence on foreign economic aid was so colossal that 35 percent of its First Five-Year Plan, 50 percent of its second plan, and 26 percent of the third plan were supported by external loans and grants. The lower percentage in the last plan does not indicate relative self-sufficiency; it was caused by strains in the Pakistan-U.S. alliance as a result of Sino-Pakistan "friendship." Pakistan's economic success was heralded throughout the capitalist world, and Pakistan was often cited as the "showcase" of noncommunist development.[12] According to Professor Edward Mason, foreign aid was the single most important factor in Pakistan's economic growth.[13]

But a model of economic development which envisaged growth through the agency of a handful of robber barons was bound to lead to contradictions and to negate the limited gains already achieved. As a result of the capitalist model followed by Pakistan, twenty families came to control 80 percent of the banking, 70 percent of the insurance, and 66 percent of the industrial assets of Pakistan.[14] The gulf in income created by such accumulation of wealth, the disruption of traditional life, and the consequent alienation of the masses found their expression in the massive countrywide upsurge that lasted for five months in 1968–1969 and overthrew Ayub Khan's dictatorship. The volcano was tranquilized by the imposition of martial law and the promise of free elections. But the momentum of economic growth lost in 1968 has not been regained since.[15]

These developments not only intensified the class struggle but aggravated already existing regional strains. The robber barons were all West Pakistani; given their preference to invest in West Pakistan, the growth of this class amounted to increased disparity between the two regions. By the end of the notorious "decade of development" (1958–1968), West Pakistan's GDP exceeded that of East Pakistan by 34 percent, the official disparity in per capita income had become 62 percent, and the real difference in the average standard of living had widened to 126 percent.[16] Table 1 shows the widening economic gap between the two regions over a period of twenty years.

The manner in which foreign aid and foreign advice helped in widening this gulf may be stated simply: foreign advice emphasized private enterprise; private enterprise, being mainly West Pakistani, preferred to invest in the more "conducive" atmosphere of West Pakistan; the public sector followed suit by heavy allocations for the economic infrastructure centered in West Pakistan. At the same time, the growing power of the West Pakistani capitalists and the prevailing philosophy of economic development prevented higher taxes on the rich. Insufficient public resources meant insufficient allocation to East Pakistan—even if it had received its due share of public resources.[17]

Regional disparaties in allocation, and therefore in economic growth, have been given a great deal of attention by East Pakistani economists, most of whom supported the Awami League. But in view of the fact that the private sector was almost entirely West Pakistani[18] and the public sector existed merely to augment the private sector, removal of disparities would have led only to the equalization of the superficial economic indicators, such as GDP and per capita income. It would not have changed the colonial nature of the economy.

Military Aid

After 1954 Pakistan's status as an active ally of the United States in the Cold War necessitated altering the internal balance of forces. According to the U.S. Department of Defense:

> From a political viewpoint, U.S. military aid has strengthened Pakistan's armed services, the greatest stabilizing force in the country, and has encouraged Pakistan to participate in collective defense agreements.[19]

U.S. military assistance converted Pakistan's army into the paramount political force in the country—the great defender of the propertied classes and a deterrent to possible social revolution. In 1958 the army asserted its hegemony by staging a coup in order to prevent the scheduled general elections. The leader of the coup, General Ayub Khan, later revealed that he had consulted officials in Washington, including CIA chief Allen Dulles, before declaring martial law in Pakistan.[20]

In terms of the regional relations in Pakistan, the ascendancy of the military amounted to the greater enslavement of East Pakistan. Military rule not only precluded any possibility of East Pakistan asserting its demographic strength in parliamentary elections, but the army's growth also led to more brutal exploitation of East Pakistan. The overgrown military establishment consumed as much as 60 percent of the country's revenue budget. Not only did it consume resources of both regions, but East Pakistan's foreign exchange was vital to its survival, especially after 1965, when it had to buy spare parts and new weapons in the black market. Since military headquarters were located in West Pakistan and 90 percent of its ranks and almost 100 percent of its top positions were held by West Pakistanis, East Pakistan was denied a share in the local expenditure of the military and of the job opportunities it created. Above all, the military's role as the guardian of capitalism and the pulverizer of the popular will expedited the colonization of East Bengal and diminished the possibilities of peaceful change in the regional relationships.

It is evident from the above discussion that Pakistan's social structure was predisposed to creating colonial relationships between its two regions. Furthermore, the possibilities of altering such relations were greatly reduced by the imperialist interference in Pakistan. While the Pakistani approach to economic development based on foreign aid and advice exacerbated the existing contradictions between the mother country and the colony, the political power of the West Pakistani military—a power based on military alliances with the U.S.A.—made it impossible for East Pakistan to secure its rights through parliamentary processes.

Cultural Imperialism

No discussion of the conflict between East and West Pakistan would be complete without referring to East Bengal's national question. Although linked intimately with the colonial question, the cultural issue by itself was an important source of regional tensions.

Geographical and historical conditions produced enormous cultural differences between East and West Pakistan. Whereas the West was greatly influenced by the Middle East, with all of its written languages using modified Arabic scripts, East Pakistan was culturally homogeneous with West Bengal in India, with whom it shared a long common history, a rich cultural heritage, and a Sanskrit-like script. The centrifugal potential of this cultural gap was immediately recognized by the ruling classes of West Pakistan, who feared that religious unity alone might not be able to maintain "national unity."

True to colonial traditions, the West Pakistani rulers embarked upon a campaign of "assimilating" the Bengalis into Pakistan's "mainstream." As a result, Urdu, the language of 3.7 percent of all Pakistanis, was imposed as the sole national language, despite Bengali protests. Bengali legislators trying to speak in their own language in the assembly were warned that they could be tried for treason. The political and economic implications of this cultural imperialism were seen clearly by the Bengali masses, whose spontaneous uprisings in 1947–1948 and again in 1952 resulted in the acceptance of Bengali as the second national language of Pakistan. But this was not accomplished without a massacre of the Bengali protesters.[21]

With the emergence of the West Pakistani (more accurately, Punjabi) military as the paramount political force, and with the acceleration of capitalist development, the onslaught against Bengali culture and simultaneous attempts at "Islamization" and "Pakistanization" also intensified. Former President Ayub Khan remarked several times that the Bengalis should be freed from the "evil influence" of the Hindu culture. He even banned the playing of Tagore's songs on Radio Pakistan because Tagore was Hindu and, therefore, an evil influence. But the Nobel prize-winning Tagore was the national poet of Bengalis, loved and admired by Hindus and Muslims alike.[22] The Bengali masses considered this assault against their culture a weapon in West Pakistan's colonial domination over East Pakistan.

In order to set back East Pakistan's cultural development, not only were there official attempts at "national integration," but educational progress in the region was retarded, and Bengalis, who had previously been better educated than the West Pakistanis, were forced into a secondary position, as can be seen in Table 2. This educational disparity was then used to rationalize the lower participation of Bengalis in the civil service and the fewer scholarships awarded to Bengalis for advanced studies in foreign countries. In a survey I conducted in 1966–1967, I found that barely 20 percent of Pakistani students enrolled in U.S. universities came from East Pakistani institutions.[23]

Colonial ruling classes, in order to exact the support of their own oppressed masses, not only throw them a few crumbs but try to justify their conquest by inventing and perpetuating myths about the racial and cultural inferiority of the colonized people. The British had already left behind myths about the lethargy, cowardice, and untrustworthiness of the Bengalis; the West Pakistani rulers added the promiscuity and semi-Hinduism of the Bengali Muslims. These stereotypes were readily accepted by a large segment of the West Pakistani intelligentsia who benefited from such discrimination.[24] One of the favorite right-wing "scholars" of the ruling alliance, I. H.

Qureshi, went to the extent of stating that Bengalis were a different (implying inferior) race than the West Pakistanis.

The results of this indoctrination of West Pakistanis were reflected in the vengeance, pride, and venom with which West Pakistani military officers carried out the carnage in East Bengal after March 25, 1971. Particularly illuminating were the remarks of one Major Kamal, who told an American construction worker, interviewed on CBS television, that once the West Pakistanis had conquered East Bengal each of his soldiers would have a Bengali mistress and that neither dogs nor Bengalis would be allowed in the exclusive Chittagong Club. As a member of the West Pakistani "educated class," I can testify that this is by no means an isolated case. Anti-Bengali and anti-Hindu bigotry is rampant in West Pakistan and has now been adopted as the official doctrine of the regime.

Political Response

The colonial relationship between East and West Pakistan overshadowed the class struggle and united virtually all classes of Bengali society against West Pakistani domination. The urban petty bourgeoisie, because of its commercial, industrial, and bureaucratic aspirations, as well as its self-image as the preserver of Bengali culture, was in the forefront of the struggle.

The first manifestation of Bengali resistance appeared in the form of the language movements of 1947–1948 and 1952. But the growing political strength of the petty bourgeoisie was demonstrated most clearly in the 1954 regional elections: the petty-bourgeois United Front, with the Awami League as its major component, gave a crushing defeat to the Muslim League, the party of the West Pakistani landlords, commercial bourgeoisie, and the bureaucracy, represented in East Pakistan by the dying Muslim aristocracy. The United Front program essentially envisaged a bourgeois-democratic revolution in East Pakistan and reflected the hope of the petty bourgeoisie for a peaceful sharing of the cake with West Pakistani capitalism, which at that time had not yet exerted its monopolistic power. East Pakistan still had a slight edge in GDP over West Pakistan, Bengali nationalism had not grown as intense as it did afterward, and class issues were still very much alive. The Communist Party, campaigning on the basis of class issues, won four of the ten seats it contested. Twenty-two other members of the party and several sympathizers were elected to the assembly on the ticket of the Awami League or as independents.

But 1954 was the decisive year in which Pakistan's ruling classes threw in their lot unequivocally with the United States by joining Cold War pacts. The stage was set for the development of West Pakistani monopolies through the tripling of foreign economic aid and for the conversion of the military into the paramount political force through massive U.S. military assistance. The election results in East Pakistan provided a serious warning to the West Pakistani rulers, who quickly rendered the Bengali challenge ineffective by paralyzing the parliamentary process with the dismissal of ministries and dissolution of the parliament, and by the co-optation of selected leaders of the United Front into the central government. The Communist Party was declared illegal in 1954.

With the old aristocracy completely routed and the opportunism of the Bengali petty-bourgeois leadership exposed, there was a growing frustration among the masses and a serious split within the ranks of the petty bourgeoisie. Not only was the United Front dismembered; but a large faction of the Awami League, with its component of Communists, left the party to merge with several nationalist groups in West Pakistan and a tiny left-liberal organization, the Ganatantri Dal, in East Pakistan, forming the National Awami Party (NAP) in 1957. Besides advocating many bourgeois-democratic reforms in both parts of the country, the NAP became the only party to demand Pakistan's withdrawal from SEATO and the Baghdad Pact and its pursuance of a nonaligned foreign policy. The growing influence of the NAP threatened the interests of the United States and its West Pakistani collaborators. Before elections could be held in 1958, the military, led by General Ayub Khan, staged a coup, abrogated the constitution, and banned all political parties.

The subsequent "decade of development" was a period of unbridled growth of West Pakistani monopoly capitalists. The Bengalis not only faced more brutal exploitation, but were deprived of the forum for airing their grievances—the parliament. The Ayub regime did not even consider it necessary to co-opt members of the Bengali petty bourgeoisie to give an appearance of Bengali representation.

With the intensification of economic exploitation and political repression, Bengali nationalism also grew more virulent, clouding the class issues and leading toward a generalized hatred of West Pakistanis. The Bengali Left, represented by the NAP, partly because of its insistence on nationwide social justice and partly due to its cooperation with the regime on account of its "friendship" with China, alienated itself from the national movement. The NAP was a national party which was not only concerned with the regional grievances of East Pakistan but was also seeking an end to the imperialist grip over Pakistan as a whole. However, since political consciousness in East Bengal was essentially Bengali-nationalist, any support for the government was viewed by Bengalis as collaboration with the enemy. Under Chinese influence, the NAP went beyond according a principled support for the regime's "anti-imperialist" policies; it shied away from confronting the West Pakistani ruling structure on all substantive issues.

The Awami League (AL), with its six-point program of regional autonomy,[25] became the unchallenged standard-bearer of the Bengali movement. The AL program was essentially a bill of rights for the Bengali petty bourgeoisie; but by demanding the right to negotiate foreign aid and trade for the province, it threatened the vested interests of the West Pakistani military and bourgeoisie. Its program of abolishing the central civil service and replacing it with proportional representation from the provinces ran counter to the interests of the West Pakistani bureaucracy. The Ayub regime responded to that program by jailing several members of the AL and indicting its leader, Sheikh Mujibur Rahman, for treason.

But in 1968–1969, before a judgment against Mujib could be handed down, both parts of Pakistan were shaken by a massive popular upsurge against the regime. The charges against Mujib were dropped, most of the political prisoners were freed, Ayub Khan resigned, and the new military ruler, General Yahya Khan, declared martial law and promised future elections.[26]

General Yahya Khan fulfilled his promise by holding elections in December 1970—the first direct countrywide elections in Pakistan's history. The Awami League, campaigning on the platform of its six-point program of regional autonomy, was expected to emerge as the largest single party in the new assembly. But no one expected it to win a simple majority nationwide. A devastating cyclone and tidal wave—this century's worst natural disaster—hit the coastal areas of East Pakistan three weeks before the elections, leaving approximately half a million people dead and another three million ma-rooned. The military government's callous inefficiency in providing relief to the affected people inflamed Bengali passions and dashed the prospects of the political parties which did not support the de-mand for autonomy. Maulana Bhashani, the octogenerian peasant leader and the president of the NAP, demanded independence for East Pakistan and boycotted the elections. A combination of these factors gave the AL 160 out of 162 contested National Assembly seats in East Pakistan—a clear nationwide majority in a house of 300 members. The way was now open for the AL to frame a new consti-tution on the basis of its six-point program.

But, as the world knows today, the AL was never allowed to frame a constitution or to form a government. Instead, East Bengal has be-come a theater of the most gruesome drama of death and destruction since Auschwitz. This catastrophic end of Pakistan's honeymoon with democracy can only be explained in terms of the colonial rela-tions between East and West Pakistan and the semifascist character of the West Pakistani military.

On the basis of the analysis of the Awami League's class character and political program, I had asserted earlier that the AL sought the limited objective of controlling East Pakistan's resources, but in order to develop itself into an industrial capitalist class, the Bengali petty bourgeoisie needed the cooperation of West Pakistani and for-eign capital.[27] By implication I suggested that independence was not on the AL's agenda because, given the peculiar class structure of East Pakistan, independence could lead to a rapid collapse of the nascent bourgeois political power and pave the way for a possible po-pular revolution whose objective would be socialism.

There is evidence that the Awami League had contemplated a compromise with the West Pakistani power structure.[28] But the abso-lute majority won by the AL in the assembly, the increasingly un-compromising mood of the Bengali masses,[29] and the fear that Bhashani's demand for independence might destroy the credibility of the AL made it almost impossible for Sheikh Mujib to give in to the West Pakistani rulers during the constitutional talks. The West Paki-stani bourgeois politicians probably understood the dilemma of the AL and continued to support it despite its insistence on including all six points in the constitution.[30] It is not unusual in Pakistani politics to go back on election promises. The West Pakistani capitalists probably had reason to believe that partnership with the AL would be possible even if the constitution were drafted on the basis of the six points.

The military, however, believed it would be impossible to perpetuate West Pakistani dominance and win other concessions from the Awami League once the constitution incorporated all six points. Even if the Awami League compromised with the military after assuming governmental responsibilities, there was no guarantee that the NAP or a future leadership of the AL would not demand implementation of East Pakistan's constitutional rights. Clearly the Awami League's policy of seeking a détente with India, basically through provincial control of foreign trade, acted against the military's raison d'être.[31] The military had two possible ways to sabotage an unfavorable constitution: it could nullify the elections or it could refuse to validate the constitution after it had been passed by the AL-dominated assembly. In view of the popular sentiment for a return to parliamentary politics, both alternatives were somewhat risky.

The military refused to convene the assembly before the AL had yielded to it in the extra-parliamentary talks initiated by Yahya Khan between himself, Mujib, and the Pakistan People's Party chief, Zulfikar Ali Bhutto. But Yahya's blatant support for Bhutto's announced boycott of the session scheduled for March 3, his indefinite postponement of the assembly session without consultation with Mujib, and his highly provocative speech of March 6 made it evident that the military was not prepared for a "businesslike" deal. It wanted an outright surrender from the Awami League. The non-cooperation movement in East Bengal, begun in response to the military's arbitrary actions, convinced the semifascist hard core in the junta that brute force, which had previously been used in Baluchistan and the North West Frontier Province, was the only answer to Bengali nationalism. The dismissal of East Pakistan's moderate governor, Admiral Ahsan, the appointment of the notorious General Tikka Khan as the new governor, and the dissolution of the semi-civilian central cabinet were the warning signals of the impending military onslaught. Only the logistic problem of transporting troops from West Pakistan via the over-water route around Ceylon had to be solved. In a tactical move General Yahya flew to Dacca for talks with the AL leaders; he appeared very conciliatory. But as soon as the troop buildup was completed, with approximately 50,000 West

Pakistani soldiers in East Bengal, General Yahya left for West Pakistan and a reign of terror was unleashed on the people of East Bengal.

Interestingly enough, in his March 26 speech, the General made no mention of any Awami League *conspiracy* to separate East Pakistan from the union; instead, he used the AL's alleged proposal of calling separate sessions of East and West Pakistani legislators and the noncooperation movement as the *signs* of the AL's *intention* to "break away completely from the country." [32] The Prime Minister of the "Provisional Government of Bangladesh," Tajuddin Ahmed, later stated that the proposal for the separate sessions was Yahya's own and that "at no stage was there any breakdown of talks or any indication by General Yahya or his team that they had a final position which could not be abandoned." [33] Indeed, it took six weeks for the military to fabricate charges and to issue its "official exposé" of the Awami League's "secessionist plot."

> All evidence goes to show that the small hours of March 26 had been set as the zero hour for an armed uprising, and the formal launching of "the independent Republic of Bangladesh." The plan was to seize Dacca and Chittagong, lying astride the army's air/sea lifelines to West Pakistan . . . the armed forces made a series of preemptive strikes around midnight of March 25–26, seized the initiative and saved the country. [34]

If there was indeed a plot for secession, it is a very poor reflection on the American-trained Pakistani intelligence corps for discovering it six weeks after the fact, or on the celebrated "Information" Ministry for revealing it that late. But the "evidence" the military government is referring to has been presented nowhere.

Simultaneously with the crackdown against the Bengali autonomy movement, the army launched repression in West Pakistan, where a number of leftist politicians and working class leaders were thrown into jail. [35] The army then announced the decision to appoint "experts" to frame the constitution, to disallow regional political parties, and to continue martial law even after the formal transfer of government to civilians. [36] These developments were consistent with the army's role in 1958 and 1969 in sabotaging the possibilities of freeing Pakistan from the imperialist noose and of bringing radical social changes within the country.

The Struggle Ahead

The Pakistan army's decision to seek a "final solution" of the "Bengal problem" by a genocidal attack, besides resulting in the massacre of hundreds of thousands of innocent civilians, the burning and strafing of thousands of towns and villages, and the exodus of millions of refugees, has qualitatively changed the nature of the struggle in Bangladesh and has generated new possibilities and dangers throughout South Asia.

For the struggle in East Bengal itself, the military operation proved the futility of the parliamentary politics of the petty bourgeois Awami League and vindicated the Left groups which had demanded independence or resorted to guerrilla training instead of participating in the elections. The dream of achieving regional autonomy within the union of Pakistan died with the first blast of cannons on the night of March 25, 1971. Instead, an armed national liberation struggle was born. The military's offensive had already liquidated or put out of action a number of important Awami League leaders. Others, at the first sight of mortar fire, fled across the border to form the so-called "Provisional Government" in the safe haven of West Bengal. Based on published reports, on messages received from our colleagues on the scene, and on interviews with Bengalis who have returned from West Bengal, it appears that the "Provisional Government" is firmly in the grip of the Indian government, which has prevented the AL from including any leftists in it and has carefully scrutinized the guerrillas training on Indian soil. Besides having nominal ties with the Mukti Fouj or Mukti Bahini (liberation army), consisting of the Bengali elements of the former East Pakistan Rifles and Bengal Regiment, the Provisional Government is mainly occupied with obtaining international recognition, appealing to the humanitarianism of the people of the world, and co-sponsoring conferences on genocide with Western liberal organizations.

As the struggle intensifies, there is no doubt that the legitimacy of the Awami League will be progressively eroded. The legitimacy gained as a result of an election victory will no longer be relevant. The new legitimacy will have to be gained in the battlefield and it is here that the Awami League has been weakest.

The Left Groups

The inability of the petty-bourgeois Awami League to lead armed struggle for independence is readily recognized by most observers of the Pakistani scene. Given the class makeup of East Bengali society, a tradition of working class militancy, and the change in the nature of struggle since March 25, if the independence of Bangladesh does not come about quickly as a result of the economic collapse of West Pakistan, or an Indo-Pakistan war, or big-power pressure, it seems likely that the leadership of the movement will pass to the revolutionary Left.

Before considering the possibility of the transformation of the Bengali nationalist movement into a genuine revolutionary national liberation struggle, it is useful to examine the state of the Left in East Bengal. After the banning of the Communist Party in 1954, party workers either operated underground or inside the Awami League and the small left-liberal Ganatantri Dal. In 1957, the leftist faction of the Awami League, with its component of Communists, left the party in protest against its pro-Western foreign policy. It then merged with the Ganatantri Dal and various nationalist parties in West Pakistan to form the National Awami Party (NAP) under the leadership of Bengali peasant leader Maulana Bhashani. Little is known about the underground activities of the Communist Party. However, many Communists were active in the trade unions, the peasants' committees, the East Pakistan Students' Union, various cultural bodies, and other mass organizations.

Differences arose among the Communists over the Sino-Soviet ideological dispute, the Sino-Indian border clash of 1962, and the Indo-Pakistan war of 1965. By the beginning of 1968, both the underground party and the NAP had split into "pro-Moscow" and "pro-Peking" factions. On the national level, the "pro-Moscow" wing of the NAP was led by Wali Khan, a Pathan leader; in East Pakistan, by Professor Muzaffar Ahmed, a long-time Communist. Maulana Bhashani became the national leader of the "pro-Peking" wing of the NAP. The underground organization of the "pro-Moscow" Communists was headed by Moni Singh, a veteran of peasant revolts of the 1940s. Whereas the policies of the "pro-Moscow" Communists remained consistent with the declaration of the 1960 Moscow conference of eighty-one communist parties,[37] the so-called "pro-Peking" group, despite its revolutionary rhetoric, failed to offer a coherent alternative program.

The esteem and organization of the "pro-Peking" leftists were seriously damaged by their reluctance to oppose the dictatorial regime of Ayub Khan and to clearly support the demand for East Pakistan's autonomy. Maulana Bhashani's idiosyncracies had alienated many radical members of the NAP and the Krishik Samity. The countrywide mass spontaneous upsurge in 1968–1969 brought the conflicts among the pro-Peking leftists into the open. Those advocating the formation of a genuine working class party separated themselves from the NAP and split into at least three major factions in 1970. The Pabna-based Matin-Allaudin group called itself the Purbo Bangla Communist Party; the Toaha-Abdul Huq group, based mainly in Jessore and Noakhali, presented itself as the East Pakistani counterpart of the West Bengali Naxalites and assumed the name of East Pakistan Communist Party (Marxist-Leninist); and two former student leaders, Kazi Zafar Ahmed and Rashid Khan Menon, formed the East Bengal Coordinating Committee of Communist Revolutionaries. All of them opposed participation in the elections. The CPEP-ML even rejected mass and class organizations, concentrating instead on organizing guerrilla actions against class enemies in the countryside.[38] Those staying with Bhashani did so mainly because of their interest in the elections. Thus, when Bhashani withdrew his party from the elections and demanded independence for East Pakistan in the wake of the devastating cyclone of November 1970, a large number of party leaders, including Haji Danesh and Anwar Zahid, left the NAP.[39]

The "pro-Peking" Left was in a state of complete disarray when the military launched its offensive against the Bengali people in March 1971. As a result of the military action, tactical differences among leftists began to disappear, and it was expected that the Left would once again forge its unity on the basis of a program for armed national liberation. However, personal differences among the leaders led to further fragmentation of the existing factions. Bhashani, despite his age (89), managed to escape to India and urged the world leaders to recognize the Provisional Government set up by the

Awami League leaders.[40] He also met with the leaders of all "Maoist" factions, except the CPEP-ML, on April 25 to press for the formation of a National Liberation Front.[41] On June 1 these groups announced the formation of the "Bangladesh National Liberation Struggle Co-ordination Committee"; it urged the formation of a national liberation front of all parties, including the Awami League, and issued a declaration calling for the establishment of an "anti-imperialist, antifeudal, and antimonopoly" social system in Bangladesh.[42]

Pro-Moscow leaders Muzaffar Ahmed and Moni Singh—the latter having escaped from the Rajshahi prison—endorsed the Awami League's Provisional Government and extended their cooperation to the League and the Mukti Bahini (the Awami League-affiliated liberation army), without publicly calling for the formation of a national liberation front.

The CPEP-ML, unlike the other "Maoists" and the pro-Moscow Communists, termed the struggle in East Bengal a conflict between the West Pakistani monopoly capitalists and the East Pakistani nascent bourgeoisie. They remained inside East Bengal and refused to have any contact with the Awami League and the Indian government. Their attitude was interpreted by their critics as Peking-directed opposition to the independence movement. Many non-Communist reporters have carried stories concerning CPEP encounters with the Pakistan army and co-operation with Mukti Bahini at the local level.[43] But Professor Muzaffar Ahmed insists that the party does not support independence and that their actions consist only of killing landlords and distributing land to the peasants.[44]

The organizational strength of the CPEP-ML and the support it is capable of drawing from its Naxalite comrades across the border have worried the Indian government, the AL, and pro-Moscow Communists. The Indian government fears a radical Marxist—especially Maoist—Bangladesh on its borders. The Indian leaders have made it clear in their pronouncements that they want an Awami League-led government installed in Bangladesh. Such a government will be similar to their own in terms of its class character and ideology. The AL hopes for a quick victory—preferably the result of an Indo-Pakistan war—to establish its rule before it has lost its legitimacy. The pro-Moscow Communists, who are quite adept at forming united fronts with bourgeois parties, would prefer a route to independence which ensured increased Indian and Awami League dependence on the Soviet Union.

The signing of the twenty-year friendship treaty between India and the Soviet Union, which was necessitated, among other things, by the continued U.S. and Chinese support for Pakistan, represents a significant victory for Soviet strategy in the region. Soon after the signing of the treaty, the Awami League, under pressure from New Delhi, agreed to the formation of a five-party Consultative Committee of Bangladesh Struggle. This committee, which is expected to be the precursor of a united front, gives pro-Moscow Communists representation out of proportion to their strength. It includes one member each from the pro-Moscow Bangladesh Communist Party and its front organization, the NAP (Muzaffar). Maulana Bhashani has been included in it in an individual capacity because of his enormous popularity and in order to create a façade of all-party representation. The Hindu Bangladesh National Congress, which had submerged itself in the AL, also has one representative. The Awami League has four members. All members of the committee have accepted the all-Awami League Provisional Government as the sole legitimate authority in Bangladesh. All "Maoist" groups, which had originally called for the formation of a national liberation front, have been excluded from the Consultative Committee.

The strategy of the pro-Moscow Communists seems to be consistent with their policy of achieving "independent national democracy" as the first stage of the two-stage socialist revolution. The independence of Bangladesh is supposed to accomplish only the first stage in this process of transition. One of the two main ingredients of this line, as applied to the present situation, is the acceptance of the hegemony of the Awami League, as discussed earlier. The other important ingredient is the pursuance of a military strategy that does not entail radicalization of the masses. Both the Awami League and the pro-Moscow Left consider self-sustained and protracted guerrilla warfare inimical to their interests because such strategy will not only postpone the independence of Bangladesh but will require intense ideological education of the masses and create conditions favorable to the more radical "Maoist" groups. A slight prolongation of the struggle, however, will enable the pro-Moscow Left to take advantage of the inertia of the Awami League leadership, consolidate its influence in the Mukti Bahini and among the Awami League political cadres, and acquire greater leverage within the coalition. The gains thus made will presumably place the pro-Moscow Communists in a favorable position to take independent Bangladesh toward the path of independent national democracy and eventually toward socialism.

The military strategy employed by the Awami League and the pro-Moscow Left at this stage has consisted mainly in the Mukti Bahini commandos and leftist guerrillas disrupting the communications and power supply in the interior, and in the Mukti Bahini regulars, operating from sanctuaries in India, making incursions along the border and trying to hold a few liberated areas. It is quite obvious that the Bangladesh coalition does not envisage that the Mukti Bahini will alone defeat the Pakistani army. It will require lengthy training and costly equipment for the Mukti Bahini regulars to become a match for the 80,000-strong well-trained and well-equipped occupation army of Pakistan. The Bangladesh strategy, therefore, implies the involvement of Indian troops against the Pakistani army at some point. The chances of Indian intervention grow in direct proportion to the erosion of the Awami League's legitimacy and the radicalization of the liberation movement. Unless the Bangladesh crisis is solved quickly, the chances of having a friendly petty-bourgeois regime in East Bengal will be greatly reduced. International support for India's actions can come mainly from the Soviet-bloc countries. Acceptance of pro-Moscow Communists in the Bangladesh coalition is, therefore, a small price to pay for Soviet material and moral support in a venture designed to protect the class interests of the Indian rulers.

To ensure the success of Soviet strategy in South Asia—which includes domination of the Indian Ocean and containment of Chinese influence—it is more important to have friendly and dependent governments (preferably a petty-bourgeois and Communist coalition) than equality and freedom for the peoples of the region. Ceylon, where the pro-Moscow Communists have formed a coalition government with the petty-bourgeois Sri Lanka Freedom Party, is the archetype of the kinds of governments the Soviets would like to have in Bangladesh and India. Such a development would constitute a major breakthrough for the Soviet policy of establishing a regional security alliance against China, first propounded in June 1969.

The growing Soviet influence in South Asia makes it imperative for the United States not only to attempt a neutralization of India, Ceylon, and Bangladesh, but to strengthen its stranglehold in West Pakistan. This leaves China limited alternatives in the region. It is difficult for China to support the independence of Bangladesh, since such independence is likely to strengthen the Indo-Soviet front against it. On the other hand, despite friendly state relations between Pakistan and China, the West Pakistani ruling oligarchy is unmistakably fascist and pro-imperialist. China's denunciations of India notwithstanding, it is not expected to involve itself militarily on Pakistan's side. Unlike 1965, when the Chinese diverted India from launching a major assault against Pakistan, today China feels seriously threatened by possible Soviet moves against its territory and its nuclear installations.

The dilemma of China is reflected in the dilemma of Bangladesh "Maoists." The objective conditions in Bangladesh offer an opportunity of carrying out a protracted people's war that would radicalize the masses and allow the development of revolutionary infrastructures during the course of struggle. But such developments are contrary to the interests of the East Bengali petty bourgeoisie, the Indian ruling classes, and the Soviet Union. The "Maoists" know that if independence comes quickly as a result of Indo-Soviet pressure, it will substitute new exploiters for the old. Yet at the same time they cannot sit idly by and watch their country being ravaged, their people being slaughtered, and their women being raped by the fascist hordes from West Pakistan.

Whether or not the Chinese openly support the "Maoist" insurrectionists in Bangladesh, the CPEP-ML and other "Maoists" are likely to continue building bases, training guerrillas, forming administrative infrastructures in the villages, and eliminating class enemies. The Awami League and pro-Moscow Communist coalition, which has now excluded the "Maoists," will have to face the reality of their presence. If an accommodation is not brought about soon enough, an independent Bangladesh will most likely be ripe for its own civil war in which Soviet and Indian arms, supplied to the coalition, may be used against the "Maoist" peasants demanding radical restructuring of the society in place of the Awami League's parliamentary democracy and the pro-Moscow Communists' "independent national democracy."

Notes

1. The most authentic report of the genocide is to be found in the account of a West Pakistani journalist, Anthony Mascarenhas: "Genocide: Why the Refugees Fled," *Sunday Times* (London), June 13, 1971. For a reliable account of the conditions of the refugees, see Congressman Gallagher's testimony in the *Congressional Record*, June 11, 1971.

2. See Gunnar Myrdal, *Asian Drama* (Pantheon, New York, 1968), Vol. I, pp. 234–244; Tariq Ali, *Pakistan: Military Rule or People's Power?* (William Morrow & Co., New York, 1970), pp. 25–36.

3. For a discussion of the military and the bureaucracy as semi-autonomous social forces, see Hamza Alavi, "Army and Bureaucracy in Pakistan," *International Socialist Journal*, March–April 1966.

4. Since the launching of the military operation in East Bengal, the government of Pakistan has engaged in a wild propaganda war which attempts to disprove the widely accepted facts about the economic exploitation of East Bengal. As part of this propaganda, the government-controlled news agency, PPI, released an item that was printed in every Pakistani paper on June 14, 1971, and circulated by Pakistani missions abroad. It read in part as follows: "The latest figures of trade between East and West Pakistan disprove the myth West Pakistan has turned East Pakistan into a market for its industrial products." Even if the figures used for this story are taken at face value, the surplus of East Pakistan's export of manufactures over that of West Pakistan amounts to only Rs. 100,000 for the year 1969–70, whereas the overall surplus of West Pakistani exports comes to Rs. 740 million. Two additional facts regarding interregional trade should be taken into account: (1) East Pakistan's largest item of export to West Pakistan, tea, is counted as a manufactured good, and (2) most of the industry and plantations in East Pakistan are owned by West Pakistanis and foreigners anyway. No amount of statistical juggling can change the facts about colonialism.

5. Figures cited in Mason, Dorfman, and Marglin, "Conflict in East Pakistan: Background and Prospects," *Congressional Record*, April 7, 1971.

6. This well-known statement has been quoted widely, including in the U.S. government manual for military personnel, *Area Handbook for Pakistan*, DA Pam. No. 550-48 (Washington, D.C., Superintendent of Documents, October 1965), p. 339.

7. America's late President Kennedy, quoted by Harry Magdoff in *The Age of Imperialism* (Monthly Review Press, New York, 1969), p. 117.

8. M. A. Sattar, *United States Aid and Pakistan's Economic Development* (unpublished Ph.D. dissertation, Tufts University, 1969).

9. For a discussion of the role of Harvard's Development Advisory Service

446   *Feroz Ahmed*

in Pakistan, see "Underdeveloping the World," a pamphlet prepared by students and movement research people in Cambridge, Mass.; reprinted in *Forum* (Dacca), September 26, 1970.

10. Hamza Alavi, "Pakistan: the Burden of U.S. Aid," op. cit.

11. Gustav Papanek, *Pakistan's Development* (Harvard University Press, Cambridge, Mass., 1967), p. 226. (Emphasis added.)

12. Among the numerous favorable reports and commentaries about Pakistan's economic development, one warrants special mention: the World Bank-sponsored Pearson Report—Lester B. Pearson, *Partners in Development* (Praeger, New York, 1969).

13. Edward S. Mason, *Economic Development in India and Pakistan* (Center for International Affairs, Harvard University, No. 13, September 1966). M. A. Sattar's recent study showed that Pakistan's economic growth rate would have been much slower without U.S. aid.

14. This widely quoted revelation by Pakistan's chief economist, Mahbub-ul Haq, appears in a number of places, including "Underdeveloping the World," op. cit.

15. For a discussion of the consequences of Pakistan's model of economic development, see Arthur MacEwan, "Contradictions in Capitalist Development: The Case of Pakistan" (paper read at Conference on Economic Growth and Distributive Justice in Pakistan, University of Rochester, July 29–31, 1970), abstract published in *Pakistan Forum*, October–November 1970.

16. A. R. Khan, "A New Look at Disparity," *Forum*, January 3, 1970.

17. A confidential report on regional disparities singled out the policies of the central government as the most important cause of the widening gap between the two regions: Government of East Pakistan Planning Department, *Economic Disparities Between East and West Pakistan*, Officer on Special Duty, S. & G. A. Department, In-charge (East Pakistan Government Press, Dacca, 1963), p. 15. For more recent discussion of governmental policies, see several articles by Rahman Sobhan in *Forum*: "Fourth Plan Fiasco," February 14, 1970; "Doing Justice in the Fourth Plan," June 6, 1970; "Forced Five Year Plan," June 13, 1970; and "Budget from the Past," July 11, 1970; also, several unsigned articles in *Forum*: "Fourth Plan Maneuvers," November 29, 1969; "Finance Committee," May 23, 1970; "Budget Anti-Climax," July 4, 1970; and "Past Panels and Committees: An Appraisal," September 5, 1970.

18. Papanek, op. cit.

19. Department of State and Department of Defense, *The Mutual Security Program Fiscal Year 1958* (Washington D.C., 1962), Vol. I, p. 359.

20. M. Ayub Khan, *Friends, Not Masters* (Oxford University Press, New York, 1967), p. 59.

21. An authoritative account of the language movement appears in Badrud-

din Umar, *The Language Movement in East Bengal and Its Contemporary Politics* (in Bengali), published November 1970. English serialization of the book was terminated by the events of February–March 1971 in East Pakistan. The first installment appeared in *Forum*, February 20, 1971.

22. After declaring their independence, the people of East Bengal adopted one of Tagore's songs as their national anthem.

23. *Pakistan Student*, May–June 1967.

24. The recent massacre, flight, and purging of the Bengali intelligentsia have opened up many job opportunities for unemployed West Pakistanis and promotions for others. If the attitude of the West Pakistani employees of the Pakistan embassy in Washington is any indicator of the mood of the West Pakistani educated segment, the Bengal carnage has been greeted as a blessing in that region.

25. These points are: (1) a federal and parliamentary form of government, with supremacy of the legislature, based on direct adult franchise and proportional representation; (2) the federal government to have responsibilities of defense and foreign policy only; (3) separate currencies or other alternate means of preventing the transfer of resources from one region to the other; (4) fiscal policy and power of taxation to be in the hands of the regional governments; (5) regional governments to control their foreign exchange earnings and to have the power of negotiating foreign aid and trade; and (6) paramilitary forces to be provided to the regions. For details, see A. H. M. Kamruzzaman, *Manifesto of All Pakistan Awami League* (Dacca, June 1970).

26. For a graphic account of the events of 1968–1969, see Tariq Ali, op. cit., chapters V, VI, and VII.

27. Feroz Ahmed, "Veillée d'Armes Electorale au Pakistan," *Africasia*, November 9, 1970.

28. The Awami League could not have worked out an agreement with the West Pakistani right-wing Muslim League without assuring the latter of changes in its six-point formula after the election victory. In fact the ML chief, Mr. Daulatana, confirmed to Tariq Ali that such a deal was struck between him and Mujib (see Tariq Ali, op. cit., p. 215). Mujib himself was on the payroll of West Pakistan's leading pro-American capitalist, Yusuf Haroon, and the Awami League officially supported Yusuf's younger brother Saeed for a National Assembly seat from Karachi (*Dawn*, December 6, 1970). See also General Yahya Khan's statement of June 28, 1971 (*Pakistan Affairs*, June 30, 1971).

29. Rashed Akhtar, "From Non-cooperation to the People's Raj," *Forum*, March 13, 1971.

30. The West Pakistani right-wing parties not only insisted that the Awami League be allowed to frame a constitution on the basis of the six-points but supported the AL's four supplementary demands, including the

transfer of the interim government to the elected representatives (*Pakistan Times*, March 14, 1971).

31. Sheikh Mujibur Rahman's nationwide television speech (*Dawn*, October 29, 1970).

32. *Pakistan Affairs*, March 31, 1971.

33. Tajuddin Ahmed's statement of April 17, 1971, mimeographed; distributed by the Mission of Bangladesh in Calcutta.

34. *Pakistan Affairs*, May 11, 1971.

35. *Pakistan Forum*, June–July, 1971.

36. Yahya Khan's June 28 speech.

37. For the pro-Moscow position, see "Leninism Is Our Guide," *World Marxist Review*, May 1970.

38. For a critical analysis of the splits in the East Bengali Left, see the three-part article by A. H. Khan in *Forum* (Dacca), December 19 and 26, 1970, and January 2, 1971.

39. Most of these leaders have now refused to support independence and have joined hands with West Pakistan-based parties.

40. "Maulana Abdul Hamid Khan Bhashani's Appeal to World Leaders," published by the Provisional Government of Bangladesh.

41. *Far Eastern Economic Review*, May 15, 1971.

42. *Sphulinga* (bulletin of the Bangladesh Association of Quebec), Vol. I, No. 3.

43. *Far Eastern Economic Review*, April 4, 1971, and *Economist*, July 10, 1971.

44. Interview with the author, *Pakistan Forum*, October 1971.

3. Explosion in South Asia

Tariq Ali

The recent war between two bourgeois states on the subcontinent of India highlights the strategic military, political, and economic significance of South Asia today. This land mass has the greatest importance for American imperialism, which would like to retain South Asia as an area of capital investment and as part of the capitalist world market for as long as possible. The last three decades have seen the liberation of increasing parts of Asia from the sway of capitalism and imperialism, a process that started in 1949 with the national and social liberation of China, the largest country in the world. Since then the struggle has developed, particularly in Indochina, and has colored the development of the revolutionary movement throughout the world.

Today South Asia is strategically crucial for imperialism both because of its proximity to the Soviet Union and the People's Republic of China, and also because the loss of South Asia would create a completely new situation throughout the world. For if the Chinese and the Indochinese revolutions have had an impact on political consciousness in Western Europe and North America, a revolution in South Asia would have an even more fundamental impact, since it would coincide with an economic crisis in Western Europe and North America. This crisis is already tending to disrupt the normal functioning of capitalism in many parts of the world—particularly in Western Europe, where a working class upsurge has been taking place since 1968 and shows no sign of abating. Crisis is also evident in North America, where the very foundations of the civilization are being called into question and where the working class is beginning to become active again. This coincidence of revolution in colonial

This article is an edited version of a speech to the Vanguard Forum, Vancouver, B.C., January 24, 1972.

449

and semicolonial countries with the upsurge in the West is something that has not been seen since the 1920s. For these reasons, an understanding of the Indian revolution is fundamental for all radicals and revolutionists.

What happened in the subcontinent between March and December 1971? What is the likely evolution of class and national forces there? And what impact will this have, internally and externally?

We shall first discuss what the war between India and Pakistan in November and December 1971 represented for the people of the subcontinent. Basic to that war was the oppression of the Bengali nation, an oppression that stemmed from the establishment of Pakistan on the basis of religion in 1947. From the beginning, a contradiction developed between the two wings of Pakistan because of the political, economic, and national exploitation of the oppressed *majority* of the new state which resided in its eastern wing—not the oppressed minority, as is usually the case—by an oligarchy representing vested interests in West Pakistan, where a minority of the population resided.

Bengal is the key to the present and future development of the Indian subcontinent. The process of disintegration of South Asian society with which the ruling classes are now faced began in East Bengal. It started as a national struggle against the domination of East Bengal by the West Pakistani oligarchy. This struggle culminated in the mass resistance of the East Bengalis against the West Pakistani invasion and genocide of March–December 1971. Following this genuine nationalist struggle, however, the recent intervention by the Indian army in East Bengal was designed to create a new bourgeois state, the state of Bangladesh—indeed, literally to transplant a political regime from Calcutta to Dacca—and was aimed at retaining the political status quo indefinitely in the subcontinent as a whole. That is why congratulations are now being exchanged among the ruling groups of South Asia, for all the bourgeoisies in the South Asian countries now think that, having solved this problem, they can go back to business as usual. This means going back to the business of trying to hold down the developing mass movements in different parts of the subcontinent, as exemplified and symbolized by the heroic uprising of the Janata Vimukthi Peramuna in Ceylon and the uprising of the Bengali masses in March and April 1971.

Bengal is today the potential pivot in a strategy for liberating the whole subcontinent. This is not surprising in view of the political history and the development of class forces in Bengal. Bengal was the first area in the Indian subcontinent to be colonized by the British East India Company in the eighteenth century. The first wars between British colonialism and forces representing the native classes took place in the province of Bengal. Bengal was the first region in which the British systematically de-industrialized and depopulated the cities, plundered the countryside, and made it into a source of raw materials and a market for British industry. It was in Bengal that the British first introduced a form of colonial semifeudalism and established a new mode of production in the villages. It was in Bengal that the first signs of armed rebellion against British imperialism occurred in the so-called Indian Mutiny of 1857 and 1858. And it was in Bengal that there first developed the terrorist movement for revolutionary nationalism in the early part of the twentieth century. In the 1920s, the Communist movement arose in Bengal; and in the mid-1940s and late 1960s, peasant uprisings under Communist leadership led the way for similar uprisings elsewhere in India. Historically, therefore, Bengal has acted as an advance post of developing political class consciousness and has served as the conscience of the Indian subcontinent. The adage, "What Bengal thinks today, India thinks tomorrow," sums up this vanguard role.

It was because of this role that Bengalis were especially victimized by British imperialism. The British prevented the recruitment of Bengalis into the Indian army and civil service precisely because they were not to be trusted politically. To justify this discrimination, British imperialism constructed a barrage of myths. One of these was the myth of martial races, of races which had emerged in certain other parts of the subcontinent with one quality: the ability to fight. It was of course no coincidence that these so-called martial races were always confined to the most politically backward regions, where extreme forms of tenant slavery or feudalism existed. In such regions the peasants could be trusted to enter the army because their families were always left as hostages in the villages dominated by landlords, who had themselves been created by British imperialism as a class designed to buttress the conquerors. Such discrimination against the Bengalis was rationalized by another myth, namely, that being a small, short black people, they could not fight very well, unlike the tall, fair, sturdy Pathans of the North West Frontier Province, the Javans of Kamalpur and Jalim, or the Gurkhas of Nepal.

After the creation of modern India and Pakistan, these imperialist and racist arguments were retained by the Pakistani and Indian armies, themselves the direct descendants of the British Indian army. At the time of independence this army broke up into two units, but for some time British generals continued to command both, training them in the traditional manner.[1]

After the creation of Pakistan, one of the myths which the West Pakistani army particularly used in order to maintain its dominance in Eastern Bengal was that the Bengalis were an inferior race, incapable of fighting, and therefore unsuitable for recruitment into the Pakistani army. Today, however, that myth is exploded. Whoever believed it must have been disillusioned by the capacity of the Bengali national movement to develop its own guerrilla force and to start waging a struggle that prevented the Pakistani army from gaining the quick victory its generals had promised the rulers in Islamabad.

The invasion of East Bengal by the Pakistani army in March 1971 was consciously planned by the generals, who thought that they would be able to crush the Bengali resistance for certain definite reasons. First, they knew that the groups of the extreme Left, largely dominated by Maoist ideology, would be demoralized by the political position taken by the People's Republic of China. The military regime in Pakistan knew that from 1963 to 1968, because of President Ayub's friendship with China, the Pakistani Maoists had ceased the task of political opposition. They had created a political vacuum, which in turn had allowed such demagogic politicians as Sheikh Mujibur Rahman in East Pakistan and Zulfikar Ali Bhutto in West Pakistan to virtually monopolize popular political influence. The generals knew that the far-left groups were small, localized, and isolated from the mass movement. They were not afraid of a mass Communist insurgency.

The second fact of which they were aware was the ideological and practical limitations of the Awami League. This party had traditionally been a petty-bourgeois nationalist party, similar to the Indian National Congress before India gained independence. The generals knew that Mujibur Rahman's policy was a Gandhian policy of non-violent mass civil disobedience, for he had exhibited it many times. Six months before the invasion of East Pakistan, Mujib tried to use the mass movement as a pressure group to show the generals in Islamabad how strong he was. To do so is not reprehensible, but to restrict such a movement to nonviolent demonstrations is criminal because it leads to massacres. Long before the bulk of the army actually invaded East Bengal, the Awami League had displayed its prowess; it had brought thousands of unarmed workers, students, and peasants into the streets without any form of protection, and many of them had been killed by the Pakistani army.

For these reasons the generals understandably thought that the Bengali nationalist movement would be crushed in a matter of days or weeks. What they underestimated was the impact of the invasion on the infrastructure of Bengali society. As soon as the troops landed and began their massacres, the Bengali part of the state apparatus collapsed. Bengali soldiers and officers serving in the army left and went to form the nucleus of the Mukti Bahini (liberation army). Bengali policemen left the police stations with their weaponry and joined this new army. Many other elements then joined the liberation army and it became a sizable force. This indicates that it is dangerous to assume dogmatically that because there is no prior revolutionary organization, one cannot develop in the heat of the struggle itself. There were, of course, frightful losses: about three million people were killed. In the first two weeks of the massacre more people may have been killed in East Bengal than have died in Vietnam in the last ten years, even with the American bombing. That catastrophe, like the Indonesian catastrophe of 1965, occurred because of the lack of a viable organization to prepare and politically educate the masses by explaining to them the course that the struggle would have to take to be successful. This the Awami League failed to do. The struggle that followed took place despite the Awami League. The political leadership of the Awami League fled to Calcutta and sought shelter in the bosom of the Indian bourgeoisie. The military leadership stayed, but increasingly tensions developed between the political leadership in Calcutta and the military leadership in East Bengal. And then a new element entered the scene: the Indian ruling class in the shape of the Indian Prime Minister, who represented the leading bourgeois party in India, the Indian National Congress. Indira Gandhi, who had watched the situation carefully from the beginning, would have liked one of two easy solutions: a quick military victory by General Yahya Khan, which would have preserved the status quo, or a quick negotiated victory by Mujibur Rahman. Neither of these was forthcoming. Instead, the instinct of the Bengali people for self-preservation proved stronger than their lack of organization, and they began to fight. Within two to three months they had forced the West Pakistani army to restrict itself to the major garrisoned towns and cities, between which there was a sea of countryside. The communication lines of the Pakistani army had to be overextended, and the Bengali guerrillas were beginning to make small advances and even to attack strategic targets inside Dacca to show the people that the resistance was alive and functioning. But Mrs. Gandhi, an extremely able politician, understood the dynamics of liberation struggles in semicolonial countries. She knew that a protracted struggle against an occupation army requires the people's army to develop roots in the masses. The only way it can grow such roots is by beginning to transform the social relations of production in the countryside at the same time that it fights the occupying army. Thus, as it smashes the existing village structure, it creates new institutions and organs of popular power. Unless it does this, the revolution reaches an impasse. This is the lesson of all protracted wars of liberation—from the Chinese to the Indochinese revolutions—and this must be the course that most liberation wars in colonial and semicolonial countries will take.

Since revolutionary groups did exist and were growing in East Bengal, and since large sections of the Mukti Bahini were becoming radicalized, Indira Gandhi could not sit by quietly, for the impact of the Bangladesh war on West Bengal and on bourgeois power in the subcontinent would have been phenomenal. The military intervention of the Indian bourgeoisie therefore took place for two reasons. Its first goal was to place in power the Awami League's political leadership, which was rapidly being transcended as the resistance war unfolded. The second objective was to prevent the 10 million refugees from posing a political threat to the already unstable situation in West Bengal. Some of the refugees were highly political people, and an explosive situation would eventually have developed in the refugee camps. This might have forced Indira Gandhi to behave in the same way in which the Hashemite monarch in Jordan behaved when he attacked the Palestinian guerrillas and destroyed their main armed organizations because they posed a threat to the stability of the regime in Jordan. Mrs. Gandhi wished to avoid sending the Indian army to crush an uprising in the refugee camps, which had already attracted world attention.

At first Mrs. Gandhi tried to persuade imperialism to pressure its puppet, Yahya Khan, to pull back and negotiate. Nixon now tells us that he was trying to do this and might have succeeded if Mrs. Gandhi had given him a little more time. The Indian bourgeoisie, however, had very little time itself in West Bengal; it could not vacillate much longer. Therefore the second option was taken: the Indian army invaded and defeated the Pakistani army.

It is interesting that the Indian army did not inflict a severe military defeat on the Pakistani army, but only a rapid political defeat. I suggest that this strategy was both stressed and worked out by imperialist interests, for a little less than half the total strength of the Pakistani army was concentrated in East Bengal. To smash it militarily would have meant destroying a sizable chunk of the repressive forces which protect the bourgeois state apparatus in West Pakistan. This would not have helped American imperialism, nor would it have helped the Indian bourgeoisie in the long run. The Pakistani army also understood this. The Americans sent the Seventh Fleet into the Bay of Bengal, and little real fighting took place. What really occurred in that war was skirmishes between the two armies. At the end, even after the defeat had been signed by the Pakistani army, the generals shook hands as if after a football match and congratulated each other on the abilities of their troops. "Your chaps fought very well," said the Indian general. And the Pakistani general replied, "No, your chaps fought much better or else you wouldn't be here." So they patted each other on the back, exchanged reminiscences about when they were in Indian military academies together, recalled the time they used to play golf and bridge in Indian army messes, regaled each other with barrack-room jokes, and went back to business as usual. The generals were transported by plane to comfortable residences in India, and the troops by train to prisoner-of-war camps, whence no doubt they will be returned to the Pakistani bourgeoisie, courtesy of the Indian ruling class, for further use as the mass movement develops within the subcontinent.

What interested United States imperialism, therefore, was that the Pakistani army not be smashed. That is why Nixon chose to support Yahya Khan instead of Mujibur Rahman. However low the political level of the American bourgeoisie, it is realistic in choosing its friends. And when confronted with a party like the Awami League—with no army, a very weak bourgeoisie, and virtually no state apparatus, on the one hand, and a strong, ruthless military apparatus in West Pakistan on the other—it was natural for the Americans to choose the armed force of West Pakistan. This explains the peculiar position taken by the American imperialists, who were looking far-sightedly to their interests in South Asia as a whole.

What has the intervention of the Indian army in East Bengal accomplished? First, it has distorted the struggle for national self-determination which was taking place in East Bengal by installing a regime that would not otherwise have come to power. In addition, the Indian army, by its physical, political, and moral presence, is helping to construct a new state apparatus for Bangladesh. There are problems, of course. It is possible to construct a powerful state apparatus, but one has to have economic power on which to base it. And because the West Pakistani oligarchy did not allow a strong Bengali bourgeoisie to develop in East Bengal, one of the most important tasks confronting the Awami League, the Indian bourgeoisie, and the U.S. imperialists is to rapidly create a bourgeoisie in East Bengal in collaboration with the Indian ruling class. Here I would suggest that Japanese imperialism may also play a prominent role in providing investment aid for the new state of Bangladesh. The bourgeoisie of this state will from the beginning be a comprador bourgeoisie, tied to Indian monopolists. It may, however, become tied to Japanese imperialism as well. A struggle is occurring today in many parts of Asia between Japanese, American, and European capital, with the Japanese having the edge. Because their production costs are lower and their commodities cheaper, they are making gains in Southeast Asia. Bangladesh may become a new field for their expansion.

Will the struggle continue or is it over? To ask the question is partly to answer it. For what now exists is a new bourgeois regime which, because of its links with the international bourgeoisie and the world capitalist market, will be incapable of exorcising the specter that stalks Bengal: the social and economic crisis that has haunted the Bengali countryside since 1966–1967. Institutionalized famine has arisen in East Bengal, where scores of people die daily because there is not enough food, there is not enough care for newborn children, and there are not enough social services to attend to the vast numbers suffering from disease and malnutrition. The only way to begin to solve these problems is to change the mode of production, that is, to smash the existing social structure, break East Bengal's links with the capitalist world market, and establish close links with the noncapitalist countries of the world. That Sheikh Mujibur Rahman will not do. Since his return from West Pakistan he has announced that he wishes to reproduce the British parliamentary system in Bangladesh—a truly bizarre response to the needs of the Bengali people. Eventually, these needs will bring the downfall of Mujibur Rahman or of any other bourgeois leader who may succeed him.

The war in Bengal also exacerbated the instability within the subcontinent as a whole. This instability will remain until the now-raging class struggle has smashed bourgeois power in India, beginning in West Bengal.

While the Indian army was supposedly liberating East Bengal, a fierce repression was being unleashed in West Bengal. In Alipore central jail in Calcutta, over the last six months, 300 political prisoners have been killed, about fifty of them in late November. In other parts of West Bengal and Bihar, several thousand more revolutionaries, political prisoners, and civilians have been shot in jails, in homes, or in the streets. West Bengal remains extremely unstable for the Indian bourgeoisie.

Census experts predict that by 1975 Calcutta will have a population of 15 million; it may already have 10 million. The class divisions in that city between the bourgeoisie on the one hand and, on the other, the working class, the unemployed, the marginal population living on the edges of the cities, the slum dwellers, the beggars, the prostitutes, the people who die in the streets, the children who rummage for food in dustbins—these divisions create a chronically unstable situation. That is why in every sizable working class suburb in Calcutta, Indian troops with arms now wait in trucks. If, as I did, you ask a bourgeois, "What are they waiting for?", he will answer, "The explosion." The Indian bourgeoisie has become so cynical that it simply stations its troops in its trucks, waiting for the people to rise so that it can mow them down.

When Indira Gandhi proclaims the rights of the Bangladesh people to national self-determination, that is a contradiction in terms, for Bangladesh means "Bengali nation" and Bengal includes West

Bengal. Inevitably, there will be interaction between the class struggles that will now develop in East Bengal and those already taking place in West Bengal.

The tragedy in West Bengal is the weakness of revolutionary political organization. The largest political organization there is the Communist Party of India-Marxist, which has massive support in the trade unions and even in the countryside. Its political leadership is, however, addicted to electoralism and constitutionalism, and it participates in popular front governments. Some of the best militants are to be found in the rank and file of this party, but its leaders have imagined, as did Aidit's PKI in Indonesia, that their size and strength are enough to protect them against repression. They have in fact made the same mistake as the Awami League made, for size is no guarantee against repression by a powerful army unless the party warns and educates the people and develops the nucleus of a revolutionary army. In West Bengal the CPI-M has called general strike after general strike, but after a time general strikes become sterile unless they lead to a seizure of power. Meanwhile the Indian bourgeoisie has begun serious repression of everyone they have doubts about—Naxalites, other revolutionaries, young people, slum dwellers, and now, increasingly, militants of the CPI-M. The Left is undergoing a massive repression in Western Bengal, and this is part of the price which Indira Gandhi as well as the Indian people must pay. If Indira Gandhi is to survive and to maintain the Congress Party as the ruling party, she must show the Indian ruling class that she is capable of smashing the mass movement and eliminating the CPI-M as a political factor in West Bengal.

The struggle in East Bengal marks the end of a political phase in the Indian subcontinent, the phase of bourgeois democracy and of a measure of civil liberties and freedom of public activities. If Indira Gandhi succeeds with the repression in West Bengal, she may be able to retain the formal appearance of electoral democracy for a few more years. If she fails, we shall rapidly see the establishment of a dictatorship in India. This may come either as an open military dictatorship or as a party of the Right, backed by the army. Once that happens, the only remaining strategy for the Left is to root itself in the people, build a revolutionary army, and confront the bourgeois army with a people's liberation war. The development of strong bourgeois states in South Asia has, of course, already been exemplified in the dictatorship and genocide of Yahya Khan and in the severe repression and martial law in Ceylon. India is not immune from this process; it follows inevitably from the inability of the ruling party to control rebellion by normal or slightly abnormal methods. But the attempt to establish a strong state in India will, I am convinced, lead to a breakup of the Indian Union. In West Bengal, Kashmir, Assam, Kerala, Andhra, and perhaps other regions, we shall see the power of the Indian government disintegrating and the unfolding of the revolution which is already incipient in those regions.

The effect of the war in Bengal on the bourgeoisie of West Pakistan has also been catastrophic. After all, it is not every day that a military regime can boast that it has lost the bulk of its population, the bulk of its foreign exchange reserves, and a sizable part of its internal market. These things cannot occur without any effect. That is why a new regime has been established in West Pakistan. It is, to be sure, part of the old regime, for Bhutto was a member of the junta which ruled Pakistan from 1963 to 1968, and in March 1971 he supported Yahya Khan's invasion of East Bengal. Now that he has come to power he is, essentially, using gimmicks. At present, for example, he is announcing the nationalization of the largest West Pakistani firms' assets and the arrest of two of the twenty-two families of monopolists. What is not mentioned is that nationalization merely involves shuffles in the boards of directors of the big companies, and that the two families arrested are the families the bulk of whose capital assets were located in East Bengal. But the crisis in West Pakistan is too far advanced for such moves to deceive the people indefinitely. From the five-month upsurge of 1968 until the outbreak of the war in 1971, there occurred one of the most unprecedented strike waves ever seen in any colonial or semicolonial country. The chauvinism engendered by the war temporarily curbed this upsurge, but it is not over. Immediately after Bhutto came to power, the dock workers of Karachi paralyzed the economy. Since then militant strikes have occurred in all the major factories of Karachi. Today Lyallpur is threatened with another strike wave and workers' demonstrations are taking place in the streets. In the countryside, peasants have fought back against the police and the landlords who have tried to evict them. Even in West Pakistan, therefore, Bhutto cannot maintain the appearance of liberty for too long; there, too, it will be back to business as usual with army officers and bayonets. And this time the same-sized Pakistani army has a much smaller country to rule. It will act more repressively to try to maintain its grip over West Pakistan as long as possible.

Given the strategic importance of South Asia, American imperialism is now likely to bring pressure on the bourgeoisies in India, Pakistan, and Ceylon to come to terms with one another. In 1962 the Americans tried to persuade Nehru and Ayub to sign a joint defense agreement against China. Ayub was willing but Nehru refused. Today, the U.S. government would not try to persuade these countries to sign a joint defense pact against a mythical foreign aggressor, but rather against their own rising mass movements. U.S. imperialism has learned from its involvement in Indochina that it is unwise to commit land troops to a colonial country thousands of miles away unless that is absolutely vital: first, because it is militarily and politically disadvantageous in the country to be conquered; second, because it begins to erode bourgeois ideology at home. The magnificent and epic struggle of the Vietnamese against American imperialism has had a phenomenal impact not only in Asia but in Europe and North America, especially in the United States and in the U.S. army. The radicalization among American soldiers and ex-servicemen is unprecedented in the history of any imperialist army. Because of this the U.S. government will be reluctant to commit troops to South Asia. Instead it will try to create efficient indigenous units of repression that are capable of dealing with internal mass movements, possibly with a little air support and napalm, courtesy of the Seventh Fleet, but with its own personnel. To ensure this it will be necessary for Indira Gandhi, Mujibur Rahman, and Bhutto to reach a common understanding to aid each other if a mass movement threatens to topple any of their governments. I would go further and predict that these armies will never again fight a war against each other. The next time they fight a major war, it will be against a revolutionary struggle in any area of the subcontinent. Ceylon provides an image of the possible future. The massive counter-revolutionary intervention which took place in Ceylon in March and April 1971 did not symbolize the political, military, or economic significance of Ceylon. Rather, it symbolized the determination of imperialism and its client states, and also of both the Russian and the Chinese bureaucracies, to prevent a change in the status quo of

Ceylon. Ceylon might then, as the *New York Times* put it, have become a "Cuba in Asia," and its effect on South Asia would have been similar to that of Cuba on Latin America, creating a radicalization of India, Pakistan, and neighboring countries. The coalescence of all the major and many minor powers against the revolutionaries of Ceylon must serve as a lesson of what may happen when a serious mass struggle develops in the Indian subcontinent.

The task confronting the revolutionary movement, internationally and in India, is to aid in the development of an independent revolutionary Marxist organization which is capable of analyzing concrete political situations and acting on the basis of its analysis. Revolutionary organizations are needed in South Asia which are dependent neither on the state power of Moscow nor on the state power of Peking, but are capable of analyzing their own situations despite the political positions of these state powers. One of the tragedies of the Indian Left has been that the old Communist Party of India, which today tags behind the Indian National Congress, has been tied to the bureaucracy of the Soviet Union for five decades. By contrast, the Maoist movements in Asia today are of a different caliber. The majority who join South Asian Maoist organizations today are genuine militants who aid in the development of the socialist revolution. But what the recent turn taken by the Chinese state has done is to confuse and demoralize these people completely. They don't know what has hit them. This is all the more true in that they have not adequately analyzed the historical development of China and especially of the Cultural Revolution. They became too dependent for their political thought and analyses on what was published in *Peking Review* or in the *People's Daily*. This dependence, and the influence of China, have contributed to revolutionary weakness in Bangladesh and West Pakistan at the same time that they have contributed to adventurist revolutionary tactics in India. I shall try briefly to substantiate this statement.

In West Pakistan the Maoist groups supporting Peking supported Yahya Khan's invasion of East Bengal. They said it was necessary to invade East Bengal to maintain the unity of Pakistan. In East Bengal (formerly East Pakistan) the Maoist groups opposed the invaders who were trying to crush them, took up arms, and actually had to fight against the armies of Yahya Khan despite the political positions taken by the Chinese. So the Maoists in West Pakistan supported the Yahya army and rationalized its continuing repression in East Bengal, while their own comrades were fighting against this same army.

Similarly, the positions taken by the Chinese state created havoc in the Naxalite movement in India, the chief component of which is the Communist Party of India (Marxist-Leninist). Of the two leading factions of this party in West Bengal, one of them, the Ashim Chatterjee faction, adopted the position that Yahya Khan had to be supported because he represented the progressive wing of the Pakistani bourgeoisie. The mind boggles. If Yahya, who murdered three million East Bengalis for upholding parliamentary democracy, represented the progressive wing of the Pakistani bourgeoisie, one wonders what the reactionary wing of the Pakistani bourgeoisie comprises. This faction of the CPI-ML argued that Yahya Khan was the Prince Norodom Sihanouk of the Indian subcontinent. Even if this were true—which it is not, for Yahya was not struggling against Western imperialism—the entire role of Sihanouk in Cambodia is not something on which to model new regimes or revolutionary movements. The other faction of the CPI-ML, led by Charu Mazumdar, adopted a position which in its essentials was quite correct, saying that the class struggle must be developed at the same time as a struggle was carried on against Yahya Khan. But even this faction, like the Communist Party of East Pakistan (Marxist-Leninist), underestimated the importance of national oppression and the whole question of national self-determination raised by the struggle in Bengal.

The Maoists in Western Europe and North America have been totally befuddled. In the major Western European countries they have split down the middle. In the United States their largest group, the Progressive Labor Party, which was formerly recognized by Peking and whose literature was distributed there, has now adopted the same attitude that the Chinese earlier adopted toward the Soviet Union. After Khrushchev's Twentieth Party Congress speech, the Chinese concluded that somehow the mode of production in the Soviet Union had changed and suddenly capitalism had been restored. The economic base of the Soviet Union was believed to have changed, Russia became fascist and social imperialist, and new tsars had replaced the Tsar Nicholas. The Progressive Labor Party has now ironically applied the same un-Marxist methodology to China.

Immediately after the Chinese issued their statements on Bengal and Ceylon, PL announced that capitalism had been restored in China and that Chinese bosses were the same as Russian bosses, who were the same as American bosses, who were the same as bosses the world over. This means that nothing practical can be done in that field for the moment, so that all one's fire must be concentrated on kindling political consciousness within the United States of America. That is a retreat to political isolationism.

Now that the pictures of a beaming Nixon greeting a beaming Mao Tse-tung have been published in the press, many other people who adopt impressionistic images rather than carrying out political analyses will doubtless reach similar conclusions. Thus one of the tasks that will confront revolutionary Marxists will be to defend the Chinese Revolution against the ex-Maoists, and also to defend it against those who remain its supporters but adopt a semireligious attitude, reciting from the writings of Chinese political leaders as if they were Bible-thumpers. More such people will be disillusioned. Our task remains to defend the gains of the Chinese Revolution, to defend it against imperialism, and to understand the objective impact which it has had on Asia and which it will continue to have, because the Chinese Revolution is by no means over. Successful social revolutions in other parts of Asia will revive the Chinese Revolution in new forms, and extend the victories gained in 1949, and rekindle some of the sparks ignited during the Cultural Revolution. That is the best way to defend the Chinese Revolution—not by alliances with reactionary military regimes, not by praising bourgeois armies, the same bourgeois armies which will participate in attempts to set back the advance of the Chinese Revolution, but by placing one's trust in the masses and in the movements they develop.

For the Chinese to make a turn, to come to some sort of political understanding with Nixon, is of course tragic for the Asian revolution. In the past I have argued against the China-worshippers for whom the Chinese revolution held no evils. Now, amusingly enough, China-worship is no longer a monopoly of the Left; both the theoretical journals and the daily newspapers of the American bourgeoisie have begun to indulge in it. In these journals over the past twenty years there were famines in China; Mao Tse-tung died fifty times over; Chinese society was collapsing. Now suddenly all is well: the Chinese produce very good ping-pong bats and light consumer goods and have made phenomenal economic advances. Unfortunately, all this is not only a joke; it presages a serious, perhaps tragic, phase for the Asian revolution. My own view is that we are going to see a Yalta-type pact between China and the United States to divide Asia into spheres of influence. This would be similar to Stalin's agreement in Europe, which strangled the Greek revolution and the mass movements in France and Italy. This is what I am afraid the Chinese will attempt to do. I say "attempt to do" because the period in which Stalinism triumphed in Western Europe was a different period. The working class movement in Europe had stumbled from one defeat to another. The rise of Mussolini in Italy and of Nazism in Germany, and the triumph of Franco's fascism in Spain, had created a situation in which the entire working class of Europe was demoralized. Stemming from this demoralization, the midnight years could develop and Stalinism could triumph for a time.

Today we are in a different period in Asia. We have had some serious defeats like Indonesia, but already the picture begins to change, even in Indonesia. The Indochinese revolution continues despite stabs in the back—sometimes by the Russians, sometimes by the Chinese. To be sure, these stabs are serious. In 1967 Kosygin visited Glassboro to shake hands with Lyndon Johnson and exchange notes about their grandchildren, and the Chinese went berserk. Correctly, all of us went berserk, saying, "How dare the Russian Prime Minister visit the imperialist stronghold at a time when the Vietnamese are being bombarded day and night?" Today—history plays strange tricks on us—the chief imperialist bandit, as the Chinese have endearingly referred to American presidents in the past, has visited Peking, where he was welcomed, briefed, and toasted. The Chinese could not of course arrange diplomatic functions for him, for that would have meant inviting the North Vietnamese and the NLF delegations, against whom the United States is fighting. Nevertheless, the general picture appears to be one of détente and agreement. However, the Indochinese revolution will still succeed in liberating Vietnam, Laos, and Cambodia; it will succeed in liberating Thailand. All this paints a picture of Asia quite dissimilar to the Europe of Stalin's day. The continuing rise of the revolutionary movement in Asia will make Comrade Chou En-lai's task difficult.

We are therefore very confident that the social revolution will continue. There will be defeats. We are not cynical about this—we are realistic. There will be defeats—and you can have the strongest mass movement in the world, and it can lead one general strike after another, but unless you have a strong revolutionary party and an army capable of defeating the bourgeois army, creating dual power, and finally seizing state power, the mass movement will not succeed. We are very far from that stage in South Asia today, but that is the task to which we must dedicate ourselves.

Note

1. Earlier, the Indian army had of course played an extremely servile role under British imperialism. Under the command of General Gracey, for example, it had been responsible for holding Saigon and for crushing hundreds of Communists, until the French could find enough troops to come back and carry on the war against the Vietnamese resistance.

Notes on the Contributors

Saghir Ahmad was born in Bihar, India, and migrated to Lahore, Pakistan, at the age of eleven after half his kinsfolk had been killed in pogroms associated with the partition of India and Pakistan. He studied at the University of the Punjab, and obtained his doctorate from Michigan State University in sociology and anthropology. At the time of his accidental death in July 1971 he was employed at Simon Fraser University in British Columbia, and had published a number of articles on South Asian sociology. His book, *Class and Power in a Punjabi Village*, and his essays on South Asian decolonization are being edited for publication.

Feroz Ahmed, a Pakistani demographer and sociologist, holds a doctorate from Johns Hopkins University, teaches at Algoma College, Sault Ste. Marie, Ontario, and edits *Pakistan Forum*. He has published a number of articles on demography and on the politics and sociology of Pakistan.

Hamza Alavi is a Pakistani scholar well known for his numerous publications on South Asian capitalism and imperialism, U.S. aid to Pakistan, peasant revolutions, the nature of the state and class structure of post-colonial societies, and race relations in Britain. In 1953 he resigned an appointment as Principal Officer and Secretary to the Central Board of the State Bank of Pakistan and went to work on a farm in Tanzania (then Tanganyika). He later studied at the London School of Economics, edited and wrote much of *Pakistan Today* in the late 1950s and early 1960s, did research in Punjabi villages, and obtained a Ph.D. in anthropology. Until recently a Research Officer at the Institute of Development Studies at the University of Sussex, he now lectures in political studies at Leeds University, and is working on a book on the politics of Punjabi villages.

Tariq Ali is a Pakistani revolutionary writer and activist in the Fourth International, and a past president of the Oxford Union. The author of *Pakistan: Military Rule or People's Power* (London: Jonathan Cape, 1970) and *The Coming British Revolution* (Red Books, 182 Pentonville Street, London N. 1), Ali is an editor of *Red Mole* (London) and a frequent contributor to *Intercontinental Press* and *Le Monde diplomatique*. He served as a member of the investigating team of the International War Crimes Tribunal, helped organize the International Marxist Group in Britain, and has traveled in Bolivia, the Middle East, Greece, North Korea, China, India, Europe, and Canada in the course of revolutionary work.

Amiya Kumar Bagchi is an Indian economist and former Fellow and assistant lecturer of Jesus College, Cambridge. He is now Professor of Economics at Presidency College, Calcutta, and has published widely on Indian economic development and underdevelopment. His book, *Private Investment in India, 1900–1939*, was published by Cambridge University Press in 1972.

Paresh Chattopadhyay was born in East Bengal, now Bangladesh, and was educated at the University of Calcutta. Since obtaining his doctorate in Economic Sciences from the University of Paris, he has taught at North Bengal University, Delhi University, and the Indian Statistical Institute, and is now Professor of Economics at the Indian Institute of Management in Calcutta. He publishes on Indian economics in English and French in India and abroad.

Hassan N. Gardezi, a Pakistani sociologist, holds a doctorate from Washington State University. Chairman of the Department of Sociology at the University of the Punjab, Lahore, from 1962–1966, he is now an Associate Professor at Algoma College, Sault Ste. Marie, Ontario. He has edited a book, *Sociology in Pakistan* (Lahore: University of the Punjab Press), and has published numerous articles and research monographs.

Kathleen Gough is a British anthropologist who has lived and researched in South Indian villages for five years since 1947. She received her Ph.D. from Cambridge University, has researched or taught in eleven universities in Britain and North America, and is currently a visiting professor at the University of Toronto. She has published widely on Indian social institutions, comparative kinship, and the ethics of social science research, and is a co-author with David M. Schneider and others of *Matrilineal Kinship* (Berkeley: University of California Press, 1961).

David Ludden is a graduate student in history at the University of Pennsylvania. With Dr. M. Shanmugam Pillai he is translating the *Kuruntokai*, a classical Tamil anthology of love poetry, into English, and is deeply involved in antiwar work.

Ramkrishna Mukherjee is an Indian anthropologist well known for his work on human genetics, statistical methods in social research, Indian rural society, and comparative kinship, as well as his studies of colonialism and imperialism in India. He holds a Ph.D. from Cambridge University and has worked as a consultant to the Turkish Central Statistical Office, as director of field research methods for the Indian National Sample Survey, and as a Professor of Indian Studies at Humboldt University, Berlin. Since 1957 he has been Research Professor of Sociology at the Indian Statistical Institute in Calcutta, and since 1970, Additional Director of its Research and Training School. In addition to a large number of scholarly articles, his best known works include *The Dynamics of a Rural Society* (Berlin: Akademie Verlag, 1957, and Bombay: Popular Prakashan), *Six Villages of Bengal* (Calcutta: Asiatic Society of Bengal, 1958, and Bombay: Popular Prakashan), *The Rise and Fall of the East India Company* (Berlin: VEB Deutscher Verlag Der Wissenschaften, 1958, and Bombay: Popular Prakashan), and *The Sociologist and Social Change in India Today* (New Delhi: Prentice Hall, 1965). He is currently completing two books, one on the classification of family structures and the other on nation-building and state-formation in India, Uganda, and Bangladesh.

Jayasumana Obeysekara is the pen-name of a revolutionary writer and activist in the Fourth International. Born and educated in Ceylon, he joined the Lanka Sama Samaja Party in the late 1950s but left it when the LSSP capitulated and joined a bourgeois government in 1963. He is now a member of the Lanka Sama Samaja Party (Revolutionary), the Ceylonese affiliate of the Fourth International. While in Britain in 1968–1969 he helped found the Ceylon Solidarity Campaign and mobilized support for the LSSP-R and the revolutionary Janata Vimukthi Peramuna of Ceylon. He has since returned to

Ceylon and is active in revolutionary circles there. His book, *Ceylon: A Cuba in Asia?*, will shortly be published in England.

Mohan Ram was a university teacher until 1960 and is a political commentator and journalist in New Delhi, writing for several Indian and foreign journals and news agencies. His books include two controversial studies of the contemporary Indian Communist movement: *Indian Communism: Split Within a Split* (1969) and *Maoism in India* (1971), both published by Vikas, Delhi. His *Politics of the Sino-Indian Confrontation* is to be published shortly.

Hari P. Sharma, an Indian sociologist, holds a doctorate from Cornell University, has taught at Delhi University and the University of California in Los Angeles, and now teaches at Simon Fraser University. He has traveled throughout the states of India studying incipient revolutionary movements, has made field studies in a Delhi village, and has published many short stories in Hindi, as well as a book, *Hamare Adivasi* (Indian Aborigines) (Delhi: Bansal and Co., 1961). He has written a number of articles on sociology and politics for Indian and U.S. journals.

Mythily Shivaraman is a freelance journalist in Madras and a frequent contributor to *The Radical Review* (8 Madnavalli Street, Madras 28).

Inquilab Zindabad is the pseudonym of a revolutionary partisan who recently spent five years in rural Bengal, and who is presently engaged in Marxist-Leninist activity in the United States.